God and Evolution

A Reader

Edited by

Mary Kathleen Cunningham

Routledge
Taylor & Francis Group

LONDON AND NEW YORK

First published 2007
by Routledge
2 Park Square, Milton Park, Abingdon, Oxon OX14 4RN

Simultaneously published in the USA and Canada
by Routledge
270 Madison Ave, New York, NY 10016

Routledge is an imprint of the Taylor & Francis Group, an informa business

© 2007 Mary Kathleen Cunningham for selection and editorial matter.
Individual contributions © the original copyright holders.

Typeset in Joanna and Bell Gothic by
RefineCatch Limited, Bungay, Suffolk
Printed and bound in Great Britain by
The Cromwell Press Ltd, Trowbridge, Wiltshire

British Library Cataloguing in Publication Data
A catalogue record for this book is available from the British Library

Library of Congress Cataloging in Publication Data
A catalog record for this book has been requested

ISBN10: 0–415–38013–8 (hbk)
ISBN10: 0–415–38014–6 (pbk)

ISBN-13: 978–0–415–38013–3 (hbk)
ISBN-13: 978–0–415–38014–0 (pbk)

God and Evolution

Can we reconcile belief in God and Darwinism, divine action and an evolutionary world? The first book of its kind, *God and Evolution: A Reader* represents the diversity of views that surrounds the interaction of evolutionary theory and the Christian tradition.

Ideal for students with no previous knowledge of the field, the book introduces the methodologies of the study of science and religion and the fundamental principles of evolutionary biology and presents the views of influential thinkers from a variety of disciplines, including the natural sciences, history, theology and philosophy. Editorial introductions frame the selections and explain their significance to the debates.

From scientific developments to philosophical and theological perspectives, Darwin to Dawkins, Dennett to Midgley, Creationism to Intelligent Design and Evolutionary Theism, *God and Evolution: A Reader* gives voice to neglected but significant views, such as those of feminist scholars and contemporary revisionist theologians, while also featuring the ideas of some of the best-known writers in the field. It is the essential resource for everyone wishing to understand more about this important and fascinating topic.

Mary Kathleen Cunningham is Associate Professor of Religious Studies at North Carolina State University.

Dedication

In memory of Kathleen W. Cunningham

Contents

Notes on contributors   xi
Preface   xiv
Acknowledgements   xvii

PART ONE
Methodology   1

1 Charles Hodge   7
   THE PROTESTANT RULE OF FAITH

2 Sallie McFague   15
   METAPHOR

3 Mary Midgley   28
   HOW MYTHS WORK

4 Ian G. Barbour   34
   THE STRUCTURES OF SCIENCE AND RELIGION

PART TWO
Evolutionary theory   49

5   Charles Darwin   54
    ON THE ORIGIN OF SPECIES

6   Francisco J. Ayala   58
    THE EVOLUTION OF LIFE: AN OVERVIEW

7   Michael Ruse   68
    IS THERE A LIMIT TO OUR KNOWLEDGE OF EVOLUTION?

PART THREE
Creationism   81

8   Genesis 1–2   86

9   Ronald L. Numbers   90
    THE CREATIONISTS

PART FOUR
Intelligent design   123

10 William Paley   129
    NATURAL THEOLOGY

11 Michael J. Behe   138
    IRREDUCIBLE COMPLEXITY: OBSTACLE
    TO DARWINIAN EVOLUTION

12 Kenneth R. Miller   159
    ANSWERING THE BIOCHEMICAL ARGUMENT FROM DESIGN

PART FIVE
Naturalism   175

13 Richard Dawkins   181
    THE BLIND WATCHMAKER

14 Richard Dawkins   186
   GOD'S UTILITY FUNCTION

15 Daniel C. Dennett   192
   DARWIN'S DANGEROUS IDEA

16 Mary Midgley   216
   THE QUEST FOR A UNIVERSAL ACID

17 Michael Ruse   219
   METHODOLOGICAL NATURALISM UNDER ATTACK

PART SIX
Evolutionary theism   221

18 Howard J. Van Till   227
   THE CREATION: INTELLIGENTLY DESIGNED OR
   OPTIMALLY EQUIPPED?

19 Arthur Peacocke   251
   BIOLOGICAL EVOLUTION — A POSITIVE
   THEOLOGICAL APPRAISAL

20 Jürgen Moltmann   273
   GOD'S KENOSIS IN THE CREATION AND CONSUMMATION OF
   THE WORLD

21 Elizabeth A. Johnson   286
   DOES GOD PLAY DICE? DIVINE PROVIDENCE AND CHANCE

PART SEVEN
Reformulations of tradition   305

22 John F. Haught   310
   EVOLUTION, TRAGEDY, AND COSMIC PURPOSE

23 Sallie McFague   325
   GOD AND THE WORLD

24   Ruth Page   349
     PANENTHEISM AND PANSYNTHEISM: GOD IN RELATION

25   Gordon D. Kaufman   360
     ON THINKING OF GOD AS SERENDIPITOUS CREATIVITY

     Index   377

Contributors

Francisco J. Ayala, Donald Bren Professor of Biological Sciences, Department of Ecology and Evolutionary Biology, University of California-Irvine. He is the author of *Darwin and Intelligent Design*, numerous articles published in scientific journals, and several textbooks on genetics and molecular biology. He has also coedited anthologies including *Evolutionary and Molecular Biology: Scientific Perspectives on Divine Action* (with Robert John Russell and William R. Stoeger) and *Studies in the Philosophy of Biology: Reduction and Related Problems* (with Theodosius Dobzhansky).

Michael J. Behe, Professor, Department of Biological Sciences, Lehigh University. He is the author of *Darwin's Black Box: The Biochemical Challenge to Evolution*.

Ian G. Barbour, Bean Professor Emeritus of Science, Technology, and Society, Carleton College. His publications include *Religion in an Age of Science*, *Religion and Science: Historical and Contemporary Issues*, *When Science Meets Religion*, and *Nature, Human Nature, and God*.

Charles Darwin (1809–1882), British naturalist and author of *On The Origin of Species by Means of Natural Selection* and *The Descent of Man*.

Richard Dawkins, Charles Simonyi Professor of Public Understanding of Science at Oxford University. Among his publications are *The Selfish Gene*, *The Extended Phenotype*, *The Blind Watchmaker: Why the evidence of evolution reveals a universe without design*, *River Out of Eden: A Darwinian View of Life*, *Climbing Mount Improbable*, *Unweaving the Rainbow: Science, Delusion, and the Appetite for Wonder*, *The Ancestor's Tale: A Pilgrimage to the Dawn of Evolution*, and *The God Delusion*.

Daniel C. Dennett, University Professor and Director of the Center for Cognitive Studies at Tufts University. Among his publications are *Brainstorms: Philosophical Essays on Mind and Psychology*, *Elbow Room: The Varieties of Free Will Worth Wanting*, *Consciousness Explained*, *Freedom Evolves*, *Darwin's Dangerous Idea: Evolution and the Meanings of Life*, and *Breaking the Spell: Religion as a Natural Phenomenon*.

John F. Haught, Professor, Department of Theology, Georgetown University and Director of the Georgetown Center for the Study of Science and Religion. His publications include

The Promise of Nature: Ecology and Cosmic Purpose, Mystery and Promise: A Theology of Revelation, Science and Religion: From Conflict to Conversation, God after Darwin: A Theology of Evolution, Deeper Than Darwin: The Prospect for Religion in the Age of Evolution, and *Is Nature Enough? Meaning and Truth in the Age of Science.*

Charles Hodge (1797–1878), Professor at Princeton Theological Seminary and author of *Systematic Theology* and *What Is Darwinism?*

Elizabeth A. Johnson, C. S. J., Professor, Department of Theology, Fordham University. Her publications include *She Who Is: The Mystery of God in Feminist Theological Discourse, Friends of Gods and Prophets: A Feminist Theological Reading of the Communion of Saints, The Church Women Want: Catholic Women in Dialogue,* and *Truly Our Sister: A Theology of Mary in the Communion of Saints.*

Gordon D. Kaufman, Edward Mallinckrodt, Jr., Professor of Divinity Emeritus, Harvard Divinity School. Among his publications are *God the Problem, An Essay on Theological Method, The Theological Imagination: Constructing the Concept of God, Theology for a Nuclear Age, In Face of Mystery: A Constructive Theology, God-Mystery-Diversity: Christian Theology in a Pluralistic World,* and *In the Beginning . . . Creativity.*

Sallie McFague, Carpenter Professor Emeritus of Theology at Vanderbilt Divinity School. Among her publications are *Metaphorical Theology: Models of God in Religious Language, Models of God: Theology for an Ecological, Nuclear Age, The Body of God: An Ecological Theology, Super, Natural Christians: How we should love nature,* and *Life Abundant: Rethinking Theology and Economy for a Planet in Peril.*

Mary Midgley is a moral philosopher. Her publications include *Beast and Man: The Roots of Human Nature, Wickedness: A Philosophical Essay, Evolution as a Religion: Strange Hopes and Stranger Fears, The Ethical Primate: Humans, Freedom, and Morality, Science as Salvation: A Modern Myth and its Meaning, Utopias, Dolphins and Computers: Problems of Philosophical Plumbing, Science and Poetry* and *The Myths We Live By.*

Kenneth R. Miller, Professor of Biology, Department of Molecular Biology, Cell Biology, and Biochemistry, Brown University. He is the author of *Finding Darwin's God: A Scientist's Search for Common Ground between God and Evolution,* coauthor of widely used high school and college biology textbooks, and his articles have appeared in numerous scientific journals and magazines, including *Nature, Scientific American, Cell,* and *Discover.*

Jürgen Moltmann, Professor Emeritus of Systematic Theology at the University of Tübingen, Germany. Among his publications are *The Crucified God: The Cross of Christ as the Foundation and Criticism of Christian Theology, God in Creation: A New Theology of Creation and the Spirit of God, Theology of Hope: On the Ground and the Implications of a Christian Eschatology, The Way of Jesus Christ: Christology in Messianic Dimensions, The Spirit of Life: A Universal Affirmation, Jesus Christ for Today's World, Experiences in Theology: Ways and Forms of Christian Theology,* and *The Coming of God: Christian Eschatology.*

Ronald L. Numbers, Hilldale and William Coleman Professor of the History of Science and Medicine, Department of Medical History and Bioethics, University of Wisconsin-Madison. He is the author of *The Creationists* and *Darwinism Comes to America,* coeditor with John Stenhouse of *Disseminating Darwinism: The Role of Place, Race, Religion and Gender,* coeditor with David C. Lindberg of *God and Nature: Historical Essays on the Encounter between Christianity and Science* and *When Science and Christianity Meet* and is editing the eight-volume *Cambridge History of Science.*

Ruth Page, Retired Senior Lecturer in Divinity at the University of Edinburgh. She is the author of *God and the Web of Creation*, and *God with Us: Synergy in the Church*.

William Paley (1743–1805), Anglican Archdeacon of Carlisle, England, and author of *Natural Theology, or Evidences of the Existence and Attributes of the Deity collected from the Appearances of Nature*.

Arthur Peacocke (1924–2006), Senior Lecturer in Biophysics and Chemistry at the University of Birmingham and later at Oxford and Cambridge Universities, Director of the Ian Ramsey Centre in Oxford. Among his publications are *God and the New Biology*, *Theology for a Scientific Age: Being and Becoming—Natural, Divine, and Human*, *God and Science: The Quest for Christian Credibility*, and *Paths from Science towards God: The End of All Our Exploring*, and he is coeditor with Robert J. Russell of *Chaos and Complexity: Scientific Perspectives on Divine Action* and coeditor with Philip Clayton of *In Whom We Live and Move and Have Our Being: Panentheistic Reflections on God's Presence in a Scientific World*.

Michael Ruse, Lucyle T. Werkmeister Professor of Philosophy at Florida State University. His publications include *The Philosophy of Biology*, *Sociobiology: Sense or Nonsense?*, *The Darwinian Revolution: Science Red in Tooth and Claw*, *Darwinism Defended: A Guide to the Evolution Controversies*, *Taking Darwin Seriously: A Naturalistic Approach to Philosophy*, *But Is It Science? The Philosophical Question in the Evolution/Creation Controversy*, *Monad to Man: The Concept of Progress in Evolutionary Biology*, *Mystery of Mysteries: Is Evolution a Social Construction?*, *Can a Darwinian Be a Christian? The Relationship between Science and Religion*, *Darwin and Design: Does Evolution Have a Purpose?*, and *The Evolution-Creation Struggle*.

Howard J. Van Till, Professor Emeritus of Physics and Astronomy at Calvin College. He is the author of *The Fourth Day: What the Bible and the Heavens Are Telling Us about Creation*, the coauthor with Robert E. Snow and John H. Stek of *Portraits of Creation: Biblical and Scientific Perspectives on the World's Formation*, and the coauthor with Davis A. Young and Clarence Menninga of *Science Held Hostage: What's Wrong with Creation Science and Evolutionism*.

Preface

The publication in 1859 of Charles Darwin's book *On the Origin of Species* ignited a debate about the compatibility of God and evolution that continues to erupt today. In the US in particular the issue has been caught up in the broader societal discussion of values and has attracted much media attention. The "sound bite" journalism that prevails favors conflict and does not foster nuanced and complex exchanges of ideas. The issues are thus usually framed starkly as a matter of "evolution vs. creationism."

Casualties of this desire to simplify and polarize are not only clarity and accuracy in characterizing various positions but also the omission of many viewpoints along the spectrum of opinion about God and evolution that do not fit the warfare model. The goal of this anthology is to provide readings from influential thinkers from a variety of disciplines that taken together represent a greater diversity of views on the topic of God and evolution than is ordinarily found in either journalistic or classroom settings.

This volume is based on my "Darwinism and Christianity" course, which I teach at North Carolina State University, and for which I received a Center for Theology and the Natural Sciences award, sponsored by the John Templeton Foundation. Selections come from the fields of the natural sciences, history, theology, and philosophy and have been previously published in a variety of sources, including academic journals such as *BioScience, Theology Today*, and *Theological Studies* as well as monographs and books.

Like my course, this anthology focuses on the interaction of evolutionary theory and the Christian tradition. There is tremendous societal interest in these issues today, most notably in the US, where courts have addressed whether creationism or intelligent design should be taught along with Darwinian evolution in public school science classes. The discussion of God and evolution in the US thus involves a complicated mix of religion, science, law, and politics that has practical implications for public school curricula. Providing a selection of resources that captures the many dimensions of the debate necessitates limiting the focus to the interaction of evolutionary theory and Christianity. This decision is therefore pragmatic and is not intended to minimize the engagement of other religious traditions in considering the implications of contemporary science for their own deeply held commitments.

This anthology is designed in the first place to serve as a multidisciplinary academic text for college, university and divinity school or seminary courses on science and religion. As such it should be useful to natural and social scientists, philosophers, theologians and historians engaged in research and teaching in this field. However, given the intense societal attention to these issues today, the book should also be of interest to a more general audience, including educators and public policymakers.

The volume is divided into seven parts, each of which begins with an introduction that provides background information about the issues to be discussed and briefly characterizes the selections. The first two sections deal with theoretical matters that serve as a foundation for understanding the material in the remaining units. Part One offers readings on various methodological issues: how language functions in science and religion, including treatments of literalism, myth, metaphor, and symbol; the role of model and paradigm in the two disciplines; parallels and differences in the structures of scientific and religious thought and in the criteria used to assess scientific theories and theological proposals. Part Two examines evolutionary theory, including attention to Darwinism, the neo-Darwinian modern synthesis that added the insights of genetics and molecular biology to Darwin's theory, and the current scientific debates about evolutionary pathways and mechanisms.

The volume then turns to the issue of God and evolution, with the next three sections examining those who challenge the compatibility of Darwinian evolutionary theory and divine action. Part Three offers a historical examination of old-earth and young-earth creationism and explores the objections of these groups to Darwinism. The section further surveys the legal battles that have been fought in the US over the attempts by creationists to oppose the teaching of evolution or to introduce so-called "creation-science" alongside evolution in public school classrooms. Part Four turns to the contemporary intelligent design movement, which dates in the US from the mid-1980s. Proponents of ID insist that the complexity of life goes beyond what the theory of evolution through natural selection can explain and that therefore a scientific account of the history of life should include the actions of a supernatural agent. Their efforts to introduce the teaching of ID into public school science classes have also resulted in legal action in the US. Part Five examines thinkers from the other end of the spectrum, atheistic naturalists who claim that Darwin's theory of natural selection rules out any talk of God, purpose, or design.

The last two sections examine the work of Christian theologians and scientists from a variety of denominational identities who argue for the compatibility of God and evolution. Part Six deals with evolutionary theists who modify traditional models of the God-world relationship in light of views of reality coming to us from contemporary science. Part Seven surveys revisionists who offer dramatic new models for conceiving of God's presence in an evolutionary world. The dividing line between these groups is not, however, firm, and one might picture them positioned along a theological spectrum ranging from more traditional to revisionist perspectives rather than in sharply drawn categories. Although these authors differ in many respects, they are united in opposing what they view as the inadequate theology of creationism and intelligent design on the one hand and the unwarranted claim of atheistic naturalism that evolution excludes God on the other.

While the parts of this anthology can be read separately, the volume as a whole is highly interactive. The sections juxtapose authors with contrasting perspectives on the issues being discussed. Links between units are established by the fact that creationists, intelligent design proponents, atheistic naturalists, and evolutionary theists define their views in relation to one another. These exchanges involve both disagreements and some intriguing convergences.

The goal of this volume is thus to provide a representative selection of a broad range of views on the topic of God and evolution along with the methodological tools necessary to understand and evaluate these various arguments. It is not my intention to advocate any particular viewpoint in my introductions, which are designed to be descriptive rather than prescriptive. Criticisms of the various positions being promoted by the authors emerge from their interactions. Such an approach should enable this book to be useful as a text in a variety of academic settings as well as to serve as a valuable resource for general readers interested in exploring the very challenging topic of God and evolution.

Notes on the text

The selections are printed as in the original text, with the same spelling, punctuation, etc. Notes within the readings are included. Short deletions are indicated by three full stops, while more substantial deletions are indicated by square-bracketed omission dots. Occasional editorial modifications of the text for the sake of clarity are also enclosed in square brackets.

Acknowledgements

I thank the authors who allowed me permission to reprint their work. I owe a personal and intellectual debt to Ian Barbour, Greg Gibson, Sara Harding, Jeffrey Pugh, Christine Pierce, and Kathryn Johnson. I appreciate the helpful advice of the five anonymous readers of my initial proposal and the constructive responses of my students to my "Darwinism and Christianity" course on which this anthology is based. I thank Routledge Senior Editor Lesley Riddle and Editorial Assistant Gemma Dunn for their enthusiastic, cordial, and efficient shepherding of my work into publication and Ann Rives for her invaluable assistance with preparing the manuscript and seeking permissions. I am very grateful to the John Templeton Foundation for the generous financial support of the production costs of this volume. Finally, I would like to acknowledge a tremendous personal debt to my mother, Kathleen W. Cunningham, for her support and encouragement throughout my career. Sadly she is not alive to see this project come to fruition. It is to her memory that I dedicate this book.

I would also like to thank the following publishers and copyright holders for permission to reprint previously published material:

"The Protestant Rule of Faith" is a reprint with some omissions of Chapter VI, "The Protestant Rule of Faith," from Vol. I of *Systematic Theology*, by Charles Hodge (New York: Charles Scribner's Sons, 1872; reprint 1960 by Eerdmans).

"Metaphor" is taken from *Metaphorical Theology: Models of God in Religious Language*, by Sallie McFague (Minneapolis, MN: Fortress Press, 1982), © 1982 Fortress Press. Used by permission of Augsburg Fortress.

"How Myths Work" is reprinted with some omissions from *The Myths We Live By*, by Mary Midgley (London and New York: Routledge, 2003).

"The Structures of Science and Religion" consists of excerpts from pp. 106–21, 157–59 [6875 words in total] from *Religion and Science: Historical and Contemporary Issues*, by Ian G. Barbour. Copyright 1968 by Ian G. Barbour. Reprinted by permission of HarperCollins Publishers and SCM-Canterbury Press.

"On the Origin of Species" consists of extracts from *On the Origin of Species by Means of Natural Selection*, by Charles Darwin, originally published in 1859 (London: John Murray).

"The Evolution of Life: An Overview" is a reprint with some omissions of an article by the same title by Francisco J. Ayala that was originally published in *Evolutionary and Molecular Biology: Scientific Perspectives on Divine Action*, ed. by Robert John Russell, William R. Stoeger, S.J., and Francisco J. Ayala (Berkeley and Rome: Center for Theology and the Natural Sciences and the Vatican Observatory, 1998). Reprinted by permission.

"Is There a Limit to Our Knowledge of Evolution?," by Michael Ruse, is republished with permission of the American Institute of Biological Sciences (AIBS), from *Bioscience* Vol. 34, No. 2, 1984, pp. 100–104; permission conveyed through Copyright Clearance Center, Inc.

"Genesis 1–2." The Scripture quotations contained herein are from the New Revised Standard Version Bible, copyright © 1989 by the Division of Christian Education of the National Council of the Churches of Christ in the U.S.A. Used by permission. All rights reserved.

"The Creationists," by Ronald L. Numbers, is republished with the permission of the University of California Press from *God and Nature: Historical Essays on the Encounter between Christianity and Science*, eds. David C. Lindberg and Ronald L. Numbers, 1986; permission conveyed through Copyright Clearance Center, Inc.

"Natural Theology" is an excerpt from *Natural Theology*, by William Paley, originally published in 1802. *Natural Theology (Collected Works, IV)* (London: Rivington, 1819).

"Irreducible Complexity: Obstacle to Darwinian Evolution," by Michael J. Behe, was first published in *Debating Design: From Darwin to DNA*, ed. by William A. Dembski and Michael Ruse (Cambridge University Press, 2004), pp. 352–70. Reprinted with the permission of Cambridge University Press.

Figure 11.1 was previously published as "Figure 34–84: The bacterial flagellum," *Biochemistry*, by Donald Voet, 2nd edition. Copyright © 1995, John Wiley & Sons. Reprinted with permission of John Wiley & Sons, Inc.

Figure 11.3 is taken from the website of John H. McDonald <http://udel.edu/~mcdonald/mousetrap.html> and is reprinted with his permission.

"Answering the Biochemical Argument from Design" was originally published in *God and Design: The Teleological Argument and Modern Science*, ed. Neil A. Manson, Routledge, 2003, pp. 292–307 © Kenneth R. Miller. Reprinted with permission.

Figure 12.3, a cross-section of an eel sperm flagellum, is from "Studies on the eel sperm flagellum. I. The structure of the inner dynein arm complex," by D. M. Woolley, *Journal of Cell Science* 1997 (110: 85–94). Reprinted with permission from The Company of Biologists Ltd.

Figure 12.6 is adapted by Miller from the website of John H. McDonald <http://udel.edu/~mcdonald/mousetrap.html> and is reprinted here with McDonald's permission.

"The Blind Watchmaker" is an excerpt from *The Blind Watchmaker: Why the Evidence of Evolution Reveals a Universe Without Design*, by Richard Dawkins. Copyright © 1996, 1987, 1986 by Richard Dawkins. Used by permission of W. W. Norton & Company, Inc. Also reprinted by permission of Sll/sterling Lord Literistic, Inc. Copyright by Richard Dawkins.

"God's Utility Function" is an excerpt from *River Out of Eden*, by Richard Dawkins. Copyright © 1995 by Richard Dawkins. Reprinted by permission of Basic Books, a member of Perseus Books, L.L.C. Also reprinted by permission of Weidenfeld & Nicolson, an imprint of The Orion Publishing Group.

"Darwin's Dangerous Idea" is reprinted from *Darwin's Dangerous Idea: Evolution and the Meanings of Life*, by Daniel C. Dennett (Penguin Press, 1995), pp. 17–22, 48–51, 59–67, 73–76, 80–83, 526–49. Copyright © Daniel C. Dennett, 1995. Reproduced by permission of Penguin Books Ltd. Also reprinted with the permission of Simon & Schuster Adult Publishing Group from *Darwin's Dangerous Idea* by Daniel C. Dennett. Copyright © 1995 by Daniel C. Dennett.

"The Quest for a Universal Acid" was originally published in *Alas, Poor Darwin: Arguments Against Evolutionary Psychology*, eds. Hilary and Steven Rose (New York: Harmony Books, 2000), and was reprinted in *The Myths We Live By*, by Mary Midgley (London and New York: Routledge, 2003).

"Methodological Naturalism under Attack" is an extract from an article by the same title by Michael Ruse that was originally published in *Intelligent Design Creation and Its Critics: Philosophical, Theological, and Scientific Perspectives*, ed. by Robert T. Pennock, a Bradford Book © 2001 The MIT Press. Reprinted by permission.

"The Creation: Intelligently Designed or Optimally Equipped?," by Howard J. Van Till, was originally published in *Theology Today* Vol. 55, No. 3 (October 1998), pp. 344–64. Reprinted by permission.

"Biological Evolution—A Positive Theological Appraisal," by Arthur Peacocke, is reprinted with some omissions from *Evolutionary and Molecular Biology: Scientific Perspectives on Divine Action*, ed. by Robert John Russell, William R. Stoeger, S.J., and Francisco J. Ayala (Berkeley and Rome: Center for Theology and the Natural Sciences and the Vatican Observatory, 1998). Reprinted by permission.

"God's Kenosis in the Creation and Consummation of the World," by Jürgen Moltmann, was originally published in *The Work of Love: Creation as Kenosis*, ed. by John Polkinghorne © 1992 Wm. B. Eerdmans Publishing Company, Grand Rapids, Michigan. Reprinted by permission of the publisher; all rights reserved. Also reprinted by permission of SPCK Publishing.

"Does God Play Dice? Divine Providence and Chance," by Elizabeth A. Johnson, C.S.J, was originally published in *Theological Studies*, Vol. 57, No. 1 (March 1996), pp. 3–18. Reprinted by permission.

"Evolution, Tragedy, and Cosmic Purpose," is taken from *God After Darwin*, by John Haught. Copyright © 2000 by Westview Press. Reprinted by permission of Westview Press, a member of Perseus Books, L.L.C.

"God and the World" is a selection from *The Body of God: An Ecological Theology*, by Sallie McFague (Minneapolis, MN: Fortress Press, 1993), © 1993 Augsburg Fortress. Used by permission of Augsburg Fortress.

"Panentheism and Pansyntheism: God in Relation," by Ruth Page, was originally published in *In Whom We Live and Move and Have Our Being: Panentheistic Reflections on God's Presence in a Scientific World*, ed. by Philip Clayton and Arthur Peacocke © 1992 Wm. Eerdmans Publishing Company, Grand Rapids, Michigan. Reprinted by permission of the publisher; all rights reserved.

"On Thinking of God as Serendipitous Creativity" was originally published in the *Journal of the American Academy of Religion*, June 2001, Vol. 69, No. 2, pp. 409–25 (Oxford: Oxford University Press), and a slightly different version was published in *In the beginning . . . Creativity*, by Gordon D. Kaufman (Minneapolis, MN: Fortress Press, 2004), © 2004 Augsburg Fortress. Used by permission of Augsburg Fortress.

PART ONE

Methodology

INTRODUCTION TO PART ONE

THIS OPENING SECTION DEALS with methodological issues that are foundational to understanding and evaluating the selections in the following units. The first three pieces consider differing views of how language functions in science and religion, including literalism, myth, metaphor, and symbol. Disputes about this issue lie at the core of the debate about God and evolution. Creationists espousing a literal interpretation of Genesis believe that the theory of evolution conflicts with their religious faith, while advocates of metaphorical or symbolic interpretation of biblical texts are more apt to find God and evolution compatible.

The issue of the function of myth, metaphor, and symbol as conveyors of meaning is not, however, confined to the domain of religion. Several of the thinkers included in this section maintain that these categories are also central to the sciences and that those who fail to recognize this dependence manifest a kind of scientific literalism.

In the first selection in this part, "The Protestant Rule of Faith," nineteenth century American Presbyterian Charles Hodge presents a classic version of biblical literalism. The piece is taken from the first volume of his *Systematic Theology*, which was originally published in 1872. Hodge declares that scripture is the inspired Word of God and as such is both infallible and authoritative. Rejecting the so-called mechanical theory of inspiration, he insists that the Spirit used the writers not as machines or unconscious instruments but as "living, thinking, willing minds." He argues for a doctrine of plenary, as opposed to partial, inspiration, claiming that inspiration "is not confined to moral and religious truths, but extends to the statements of facts, whether scientific, historical, or geographical." He acknowledges, however, that while the writers were fully inspired as to all that they teach, concerning matters of science, philosophy, and history, "they stood on the same level with their contemporaries." Finally, he declares scripture "perspicuous," in that knowledge needed for salvation is clear from an examination of scripture "by the use of ordinary means and by the aid of the Holy Spirit."

In the last section of this piece Hodge confronts possible objections to the plenary inspiration of scripture, namely that there are contradictions in the sacred text and that the Bible teaches what is inconsistent with historical and scientific truth. His concluding "Rules of Interpretation" urge "spiritually minded" individuals to take the words of scripture "in their plain historical sense" under the guidance of the Holy Spirit.

In contrast to Hodge, theologian Sallie McFague argues that religious language should be interpreted metaphorically rather than literally. In the second selection in this part, which is taken from her book *Metaphorical Theology*, McFague characterizes a metaphor as "an assertion or judgment of similarity and difference between two thoughts in permanent tension with one another, which redescribes reality in an open-ended way but has structural as well as affective power." She argues that metaphorical thinking is not confined to the arts or religion but is in fact also central to the sciences. She insists that metaphorical thinking is not "illustrative, ornamental, or merely heuristic," but essential and unsubstitutable, functioning at the most basic level of understanding and conceptuality.

Examining the question of the reference and truth of a metaphor, McFague comments that a metaphor is not considered true because it corresponds to some uninterpreted reality but because it gives us an apt, fitting way of interpreting reality. She expresses concerns about what she sees as the dangers of losing the tension in a metaphor and lapsing into literalism. Religious metaphors, because of their familiarity, are in her view particularly prone to becoming idols.

Philosopher Mary Midgley explores the concept of myth in the third piece in this section, which comes from her book *The Myths We Live By*. Myths, she maintains, are "imaginative patterns, networks of powerful symbols that suggest particular ways of interpreting the world." Not lies, or detached stories, they shape meaning. In the same way that McFague finds metaphor to be an essential component of human understanding, Midgley argues that myths are not merely "surface dressing" or a kind of "optional" decorative paint but are instead integral to our thought-structure.

According to Midgley, myth and symbol do crucial work in science as well as religion. They are not "passive pieces of apparatus" but instead have their own influence. Recognizing that such general concepts, myths, and metaphors play a crucial role in our thinking in turn challenges the impression that science is just an "immense store-cupboard of objective facts." Instead, it involves a much more interesting imaginative structure of ideas by which scientists connect, understand, and interpret facts. While myths, metaphors and symbols are quite properly used by scientists, Midgley maintains, their function as conveyors of meaning should be recognized and not hidden behind false claims of scientific objectivity and neutrality.

The last selection in this unit, Ian Barbour's comparative analysis of the structures of science and religion, explores methodological parallels and differences between science and religion and examines the role of model and paradigm in the two disciplines. The extract is taken from his book *Religion and Science: Historical and Contemporary Issues*. Barbour dissects arguments in science and religion, diagramming the relationship between theory and data in science and belief and experience in religion. He surveys different views of truth and suggests that criteria for assessing theories in scientific research, namely agreement with data, coherence, scope, and fertility, can also be applied to evaluating beliefs within a religious community. Of course, given that science involves a research program and religion a way of life, application of the various criteria will differ. Yet by suggesting that there is a structural similarity between science and religion, Barbour challenges common stereotypes that are often promoted by antagonists from both sides. In their opposition to Darwinism, many creationists declare that "evolution is only a theory, not a fact," implying that a scientific theory is no more than a hunch or a guess. Many atheistic naturalists for their part consider religion a matter of "blind faith" rather than reason. By exploring the nature and limits of certainty of scientific theories and religious beliefs and suggesting that rational criteria for evaluating proposals can be applicable to both, Barbour challenges these very common stereotypes.

Barbour then examines the role of model in science and religion. Affirming a position of critical realism, he maintains that conceptual models, which often play a part in the fashioning of scientific theories and religious beliefs, are imaginative human constructs that are to be taken "seriously, but not literally." As he states, "they are neither literal pictures nor useful fictions but limited and inadequate ways of imagining what is not observable." His views are thus in line with those expressed by McFague on metaphor and Midgley on myth. Barbour further explores the role of paradigms, clusters of methodological presuppositions defined by particular historical communities that set the context for the use of metaphor, model, and theory in science and religion. In his concluding remarks, Barbour summarizes what he sees as similarities and differences between the structures of science and religion.

Chapter 1

Charles Hodge

THE PROTESTANT RULE OF FAITH

ALL PROTESTANTS AGREE in teaching that "the word of God, as contained in the Scriptures of the Old and New Testaments, is the only infallible rule of faith and practice." [. . .]

Protestants hold, (1.) That the Scriptures of the Old and New Testaments are the Word of God, written under the inspiration of the Holy Spirit, and are therefore infallible, and of divine authority in all things pertaining to faith and practice, and consequently free from all error whether of doctrine, fact, or precept. (2.) That they contain all the extant supernatural revelations of God designed to be a rule of faith and practice to his Church. (3.) That they are sufficiently perspicuous to be understood by the people, in the use of ordinary means and by the aid of the Holy Spirit, in all things necessary to faith or practice, without the need of any infallible interpreter. [. . .]

The infallibility and divine authority of the Scriptures are due to the fact that they are the word of God; and they are the word of God because they were given by the inspiration of the Holy Ghost.

The nature of inspiration is to be learnt from the Scriptures; from their didactic statements, and from their phenomena. There are certain general facts or principles which underlie the Bible, which are assumed in all its teachings, and which therefore must be assumed in its interpretation. We must, for example, assume, (1.) That God is not the unconscious ground of all things; nor an unintelligent force; nor a name for the moral order of the universe; nor mere causality; but a Spirit, – a self-conscious, intelligent, voluntary agent, possessing all the attributes of our spirits without limitation, and to an infinite degree. (2.) That He is the creator of the world, and extra-mundane, existing before, and independently of it; not its soul, life, or animating principle; but its maker, preserver, and ruler. (3.) That as a spirit He is everywhere present, and everywhere active, preserving and governing all his creatures and all their actions. (4.) That while both in the external world and in the world of mind He generally acts according to fixed laws and through secondary causes, He is free to act, and often does act immediately, or without the intervention of such causes, as in creation, regeneration, and miracles. (5.) That the Bible contains a divine, or supernatural revelation. The present question is not, Whether the Bible is what it claims to be; but, What does it teach as to the nature and effects of the influence under which it was written?

On this subject the common doctrine of the Church is, and ever has been, that inspiration was an influence of the Holy Spirit on the minds of certain select men, which rendered them the organs of God for the infallible communication of his mind and will. They were in such a sense the organs of God, that what they said God said.

This definition includes several distinct points. First. Inspiration is a supernatural influence. It is thus distinguished, on the one hand, from the providential agency of God, which is everywhere and always in operation; and on the other hand, from the gracious operations of the Spirit on the hearts of his people. According to the Scriptures, and the common views of men, a marked distinction is to be made between those effects which are due to the efficiency of God operating regularly through second causes, and those which are produced by his immediate efficiency without the intervention of such causes. The one class of effects is natural; the other, supernatural. Inspiration belongs to the latter class. It is not a natural effect due to the inward state of its subject, or to the influence of external circumstances.

No less obvious is the distinction which the Bible makes between the gracious operations of the Spirit and those by which extraordinary gifts are bestowed upon particular persons. Inspiration, therefore, is not to be confounded with spiritual illumination. They differ, first, as to their subjects. The subjects of inspiration are a few selected persons; the subjects of spiritual illumination are all true believers. And, secondly, they differ as to their design. The design of the former is to render certain men infallible as teachers; the design of the latter is to render men holy. . . .

Second. The above definition assumes a difference between revelation and inspiration. They differ, first, as to their object. The object of revelation is the communication of knowledge. The object or design of inspiration is to secure infallibility in teaching. Consequently they differ, secondly, in their effects. The effect of revelation was to render its recipient wiser. The effect of inspiration was to preserve him from error in teaching. These two gifts were often enjoyed by the same person at the same time. That is, the Spirit often imparted knowledge, and controlled [it] in its communication orally or in writing to others. This was no doubt the case with the Psalmists, and often with the Prophets and Apostles. Often, however, the revelations were made at one time, and were subsequently, under the guidance of the Spirit, committed to writing. Thus the Apostle Paul tells us that he received his knowledge of the gospel not from man, but by revelation from Jesus Christ; and this knowledge he communicated from time to time in his discourses and epistles. In many cases these gifts were separated. Many of the sacred writers, although inspired, received no revelations. This was probably the fact with the authors of the historical books of the Old Testament. The evangelist Luke does not refer his knowledge of the events which he records to revelation, but says he derived it from those "which from the beginning were eyewitnesses, and ministers of the Word." (Luke i. 2.) It is immaterial to us where Moses obtained his knowledge of the events recorded in the book of Genesis; whether from early documents, from tradition, or from direct revelation. No more causes are to be assumed for any effect than are necessary. If the sacred writers had sufficient sources of knowledge in themselves, or in those about them, there is no need to assume any direct revelation. It is enough for us that they were rendered infallible as teachers. [. . .] Often, however, the distinction [between revelation and inspiration] is overlooked. In popular language, inspiration is made to include both the supernatural communication of truth to the mind, and a supernatural control in making known that truth to others. The two gifts, however, differ in their nature, and should therefore be distinguished. Confounding them has sometimes led to serious error. When no revelation was necessary, no inspiration is admitted. [. . .] It is an illogical conclusion, however, to infer that because a historian did not need to have the facts dictated to him, that therefore he needed no control to preserve him from error.

A third point included in the Church doctrine of inspiration is, that the sacred writers were the organs of God, so that what they taught, God taught. It is to be remembered, however, that when God uses any of his creatures as his instruments, He uses them according to their nature. He uses angels as angels, men as men, the elements as elements. Men are intelligent voluntary agents; and as such were made the organs of God. The sacred writers were not made unconscious or irrational. The spirits of the prophets were subject to the prophets. (1 Cor. xiv. 32.) They were not like calculating machines which grind out logarithms with infallible correctness. The ancients, indeed, were accustomed to say, as some theologians have also said, that the sacred writers were as pens in the hand of the Spirit; or as harps, from which He drew what sounds

He pleased. These representations were, however, intended simply to illustrate one point, namely, that the words uttered or recorded by inspired men were the words of God. The Church has never held what has been stigmatized as the mechanical theory of inspiration. The sacred writers were not machines. Their self-consciousness was not suspended; nor were their intellectual powers superseded. Holy men spake as they were moved by the Holy Ghost. It was men, not machines; not unconscious instruments, but living, thinking, willing minds, whom the Spirit used as his organs. Moreover, as inspiration did not involve the suspension or suppression of the human faculties, so neither did it interfere with the free exercise of the distinctive mental characteristics of the individual. If a Hebrew was inspired, he spake Hebrew; if a Greek, he spake Greek; if an educated man, he spoke as a man of culture; if uneducated, he spoke as such a man is wont to speak. If his mind was logical, he reasoned, as Paul did; if emotional and contemplative, he wrote as John wrote. All this is involved in the fact that God uses his instruments according to their nature. The sacred writers impressed their peculiarities on their several productions as plainly as though they were the subjects of no extraordinary influence. This is one of the phenomena of the Bible patent to the most cursory reader. It lies in the very nature of inspiration that God spake in the language of men; that He uses men as his organs, each according to his peculiar gifts and endowments. When He ordains praise out of the mouth of babes, they must speak as babes, or the whole power and beauty of the tribute will be lost. There is no reason to believe that the operation of the Spirit in inspiration revealed itself any more in the consciousness of the sacred writers, than his operations in sanctification reveal themselves in the consciousness of the Christian. As the believer seems to himself to act, and in fact does act out of his own nature; so the inspired penmen wrote out of the fulness of their own thoughts and feelings, and employed the language and modes of expression which to them were the most natural and appropriate. Nevertheless, and none the less, they spoke as they were moved by the Holy Ghost, and their words were his words. [. . .]

[T]he fourth element of the Church doctrine on this subject [is that inspiration extends equally to all parts of Scripture]. It means, first, that all the books of Scripture are equally inspired. All alike are infallible in what they teach. And secondly, that inspiration extends to all the contents of these several books. It is not confined to moral and religious truths, but extends to the statements of facts, whether scientific, historical, or geographical. It is not confined to those facts the importance of which is obvious, or which are involved in matters of doctrine. It extends to everything which any sacred writer asserts to be true. [. . .]

The view presented above is known as the doctrine of plenary inspiration. Plenary is opposed to partial. The Church doctrine denies that inspiration is confined to parts of the Bible; and affirms that it applies to all the books of the sacred canon. It denies that the sacred writers were merely partially inspired; it asserts that they were fully inspired as to all that they teach, whether of doctrine or fact. This of course does not imply that the sacred writers were infallible except for the special purpose for which they were employed. They were not imbued with plenary knowledge. As to all matters of science, philosophy, and history, they stood on the same level with their contemporaries. They were infallible only as teachers, and when acting as the spokesmen of God. Their inspiration no more made them astronomers than it made them agriculturists. Isaiah was infallible in his predictions, although he shared with his countrymen the views then prevalent as to the mechanism of the universe. Paul could not err in anything he taught, although he could not recollect how many persons he had baptized in Corinth. [. . .] Nor does the Scriptural doctrine on this subject imply that the sacred writers were free from errors in conduct. Their infallibility did not arise from their holiness, nor did inspiration render them holy. Balaam was inspired, and Saul was among the prophets. David committed many crimes, although inspired to write psalms. Peter erred in conduct at Antioch; but this does not prove that he erred in teaching. The influence which preserved him from mistakes in teaching was not designed to preserve him from mistakes in conduct. [. . .]

[Objections]

The objection under consideration, namely, that the Bible contains errors, divides itself into two. The first, that the sacred writers contradict themselves, or one the other. The second, that the Bible teaches what is inconsistent with the facts of history or science.

As to the former of these objections, it would require, not a volume, but volumes to discuss all the cases of alleged discrepancies. All that can be expected here is a few general remarks: (1.) These apparent discrepancies, although numerous, are for the most part trivial; relating in most cases to numbers or dates. (2.) The great majority of them are only apparent, and yield to careful examination. (3.) Many of them may fairly be ascribed to errors of transcribers. (4.) The marvel and the miracle is that there are so few of any real importance. Considering that the different books of the Bible were written not only by different authors, but by men of all degrees of culture, living in the course of fifteen hundred or two thousand years, it is altogether unaccountable that they should agree perfectly, on any other hypothesis than that the writers were under the guidance of the Spirit of God. In this respect, as in all others, the Bible stands alone. It is enough to impress any mind with awe, when it contemplates the Sacred Scriptures filled with the highest truths, speaking with authority in the name of God, and so miraculously free from the soiling touch of human fingers. The errors in matters of fact which skeptics search out bear no proportion to the whole. No sane man would deny that the Parthenon was built of marble, even if here and there a speck of sandstone should be detected in its structure. Not less unreasonable is it to deny the inspiration of such a book as the Bible, because one sacred writer says that on a given occasion twenty-four thousand, and another says that twenty-three thousand, men were slain. Surely a Christian may be allowed to tread such objections under his feet.

Admitting that the Scriptures do contain, in a few instances, discrepancies which with our present means of knowledge, we are unable satisfactorily to explain, they furnish no rational ground for denying their infallibility. "The Scripture cannot be broken." (John x. 35.) This is the whole doctrine of plenary inspiration, taught by the lips of Christ himself. The universe teems with evidences of design, so manifold, so diverse, so wonderful, as to overwhelm the mind with the conviction that it has had an intelligent author. Yet here and there isolated cases of monstrosity appear. It is irrational, because we cannot account for such cases, to deny that the universe is the product of intelligence. So the Christian need not renounce his faith in the plenary inspiration of the Bible, although there may be some things about it in its present state which he cannot account for.

The second great objection to the plenary inspiration of the Scripture is that it teaches what is inconsistent with historical and scientific truth.

Here again it is to be remarked, (1.) That we must distinguish between what the sacred writers themselves thought or believed, and what they teach. They may have believed that the sun moves round the earth, but they do not so teach. (2.) The language of the Bible is the language of common life; and the language of common life is founded on apparent, and not upon scientific truth. It would be ridiculous to refuse to speak of the sun rising and setting, because we know that it is not a satellite of our planet. (3.) There is a great distinction between theories and facts. Theories are of men. Facts are of God. The Bible often contradicts the former, never the latter. (4.) There is also a distinction to be made between the Bible and our interpretation. The latter may come into competition with settled facts; and then it must yield. Science has in many things taught the Church how to understand the Scriptures. The Bible was for ages understood and explained according to the Ptolemaic system of the universe; it is now explained without doing the least violence to its language, according to the Copernican system. Christians have commonly believed that the earth has existed only a few thousands of years. If geologists finally prove that it has existed for myriads of ages, it will be found that the first chapter of Genesis is in full accord with the facts, and that the last results of science are embodied on the first page of the Bible. It may cost the Church a severe struggle to give up one interpretation and adopt another, as it did in the seventeenth century, but no real evil need be apprehended. The Bible has stood, and still stands in the presence of the whole scientific world with its claims unshaken. Men hostile or indifferent to its truths may, on insufficient grounds, or because of their personal opinions, reject its authority; but, even in the judgment of the greatest authorities in science, its teachings cannot fairly be impeached. [. . .]

Rules of interpretation

If every man has the right, and is bound to read the Scriptures, and to judge for himself what they teach, he must have certain rules to guide him in the exercise of this privilege and duty. These rules are not arbitrary. They are not imposed by human authority. They have no binding force which does not flow from their own intrinsic truth and propriety. They are few and simple.

1. The words of Scripture are to be taken in their plain historical sense. That is, they must be taken in the sense attached to them in the age and by the people to whom they were addressed. This only assumes that the sacred writers were honest, and meant to be understood.

2. If the Scriptures be what they claim to be, the word of God, they are the work of one mind, and that mind divine. From this it follows that Scripture cannot contradict Scripture. God cannot teach in one place anything which is inconsistent with what He teaches in another. Hence Scripture must explain Scripture. If a passage admits of different interpretations, that only can be the true one which agrees with what the Bible teaches elsewhere on the same subject. . . . This rule of interpretation is sometimes called the analogy of Scripture, and sometimes the analogy of faith. There is no material difference in the meaning of the two expressions.

3. The Scriptures are to be interpreted under the guidance of the Holy Spirit, which guidance is to be humbly and earnestly sought. The ground of this rule is twofold: First, the Spirit is promised as a guide and teacher. He was to come to lead the people of God into the knowledge of the truth. And secondly, the Scriptures teach, that "the natural man receiveth not the things of the Spirit of God: for they are foolishness unto him; neither can he know them, because they are spiritually discerned." (1 Cor. ii. 14.) The unrenewed mind is naturally blind to spiritual truth. His heart is in opposition to the things of God. Congeniality of mind is necessary to the proper apprehension of divine things. As only those who have a moral nature can discern moral truth, so those only who are spiritually minded can truly receive the things of the Spirit.

The fact that all the true people of God in every age and in every part of the Church, in the exercise of their private judgment, in accordance with the simple rules above stated, agree as to the meaning of Scripture in all things necessary either in faith or practice, is a decisive proof of the perspicuity of the Bible, and of the safety of allowing the people the enjoyment of the divine right of private judgment.

Chapter 2

Sallie McFague

METAPHOR

[. . .]

Metaphor

> Metaphor is as ultimate as speech itself, and speech as ultimate as
> thought. . . . Metaphor appears as the instinctive and necessary act
> of the mind exploring reality and ordering experience.[1]

IF **THIS COMMENT** by literary critic John Middleton Murry were
an isolated one, it could be dismissed as the prejudice of a humanist who
would like to see the process of thought in his field of poetry be the model for
all human thought. But this is not the case. The voices insisting on the primacy
of metaphor are legion, coming from philosophy, the sciences, religion, the
arts, and the social sciences.[2] It is as if, after centuries of dormancy, the world
has finally woken up to the significance of Aristotle's adage that the greatest
thing by far is to be a master of metaphor. But the level at which metaphor is
appreciated in all fields of human inquiry today is a more basic one than
suggested by Aristotle. For it is not geniuses who are being congratulated for
their ability to use metaphor; rather, it is being asserted that metaphor is
indigenous to all human learning from the simplest to the most complex.

In the animal world, and in our own beginnings, all that is known is bodily sensations. But unlike the other animals for whom the meanings of things are largely instinctive and adhere to the things signified, the essence of our uniqueness is that we use our bodily sensations as signs to stand for something else. Signs become symbols: the thing stands for and represents something else. Thus, "water" is not merely something that feels good on a dry throat, a bodily sensation, but also a symbol of refreshment and renewal (as well, paradoxically, of drowning and death). The animal world is there; our worlds are constructed. And they are constructed in a phenomenally economical way, by an infinite number of borrowings, cross-sortings, and associations. We start with very little—our bodily sensations as all that we are aware of directly—and we build from them. An analogy of how the process works is seen very clearly in the alphabet of the Indo-European languages: from its twenty-six letters, millions of words are created—a vast inverted pyramid of words with an infinite number of subtle shades of similarity and dissimilarity with one another. An unabridged dictionary is an outward and visible sign of the inward workings of the human mind in its incredible metaphorical capacity. The most outstanding feature of the human mind is its mobility, its constant, instantaneous power of association, its ability to be forever connecting this with that. It is as if everything in the world were similar to everything else, in at least one respect, and the task were to locate the similarities, especially the significant ones. When we learn a new thing, we invariably say, "I see it now," meaning that I connect the new thing in some way with what I already know. We cannot learn or understand except through connection, through association.

What is largely an unconscious process in a child's metaphorical construction of its world through acquiring an expanded vocabulary, becomes more conscious and manifest as we turn to examples in philosophy and science—two fields which, unlike the arts, have not usually been seen as dependent on metaphor. David Burrell points out that Plato's dialectic, in its constant movement from question to provisional answer to further question, is a form of the metaphorical process evident in ordinary language. In both instances, movement towards the truth is achieved by stretching language, by analogies with the familiar through borrowings, by judgments of aptness and appropriateness.[3] In logic of this sort, "truth" is never reached; rather, approximations are achieved to which persons commit themselves, but the process continues. A metaphorical pattern for rational human understanding is essentially a dramatic pattern for human knowing and becoming, a pattern which focuses on mobility, open-endedness, and tentativeness in its commitments.

Similarly strong cases for the centrality of metaphor could be made were we to look at the writings of philosophers such as Whitehead, Wittgenstein,

Heidegger, or Ricoeur. Any philosophy which understands language as the essence of human being, which sees the distinction of the human animal to be its image-making capacity, is bound to perceive philosophy's attempts to know and express reality on a continuum with the indirection of language, in other words, as relying on metaphor. If language always stands between us and reality, if it is the medium through which we are aware of both our relationship to "what is" and our distance from it, then metaphor is both our burden and our glory, from the first words of children to the most complex forays on reality by philosophers.

But if we take philosophy in the more general sense, not as philosophy of language or philosophy which gives priority to language, but simply as conceptual or abstract thought, an understanding of philosophy that would include Descartes, Kant, and Spinoza, can we still say that metaphor is central? Kenneth Burke points out that "abstraction" means "drawing from," the drawing out of similar strains and motifs from dissimilar situations.[4] The principal tasks of conceptual thought—analysis, classification, and synthesis—all depend on this process of "drawing out" similarities within dissimilars. As Burke notes, "the business of interpretation is accomplished by the two processes of oversimplification and analogical extension."[5] When we interpret, that is, when we analyze, classify, and synthesize a series of events, structures, objects, or whatever, we suppress the ways in which they are dissimilar because we have discovered significant similarities among them. It goes without saying that what we find to be significant is so from our own limited perspective: metaphorical thinking, which is to say, all thinking, is intrinsically perspectival. We say "this" is like "that," but we realize that it is also *not* like "that" and that other ways of linking up the similarities and dissimilarities are possible.

When we turn to the sciences, whether mathematics or the natural or social sciences, we also find metaphor to be central. Perhaps it is most surprising to those who suppose that metaphor belongs only in the arts and religion to discover it at the most basic level in mathematics: the numerical analogue. Seeing the similar number among otherwise disparate entities is a metaphorical act, as in six apples, six moons, six ideas, six generous acts.[6] In the social sciences the ubiquity of metaphor is obvious: the human being has been seen as a child of God, as half-angel and half-beast, as a machine; the state has been viewed as an organism and a mechanism; the brain has been understood through the metaphor of the computer and vice versa. When one turns to physics, the evidence for the importance of metaphor in the form of models is extensive. The critical nature of models in atomic physics, the inability of this area of study to do without models, is vividly captured by physicist Mary Hesse remarking on the use of models when entities such as protons and neutrons are observable only in virtue of their remote effects:

> It is as if the properties of cricket balls were known to us, not by seeing and handling them, but only by hearing a sharp impact as a batsman hits out and observing shattered windows. To speak of *atomic particles* at all is to employ a model based on dynamics and electrostatics.[7]

In a situation such as this in which the entity in question cannot be observed, it must be imagined in terms of something else with which we are more familiar. In this case, metaphorical thinking in terms of the use of models is not illustrative, ornamental, or merely heuristic, but essential if one is to talk about the entities at all. Jacob Bronowski speaks for many philosophers of science when he insists that ideas in science, as in any other field, are derived from images:

> We cannot form any theory to explain, say, the workings of nature without forming in our mind some pattern of movement, some arrangement and rearrangement of the units, which derives from our experience. (That is why, for example, the reasoning of physics is always arguing about waves and particles, which derive directly from our physical experience.) In this sense, the whole of science is shot through and through with metaphors, which transfer and link one part of our experience to another, and find likenesses between the parts. All our ideas derive from and embody such metaphorical likenesses.[8]

These several witnesses to the importance of metaphor in philosophy and the sciences are mentioned here only to make the point that metaphor is not the possession of poetry or the burden of religion as has often been supposed, but is evident in all fields and at the most basic level of their understanding and conceptuality. As we shall see, it is, in fact, the constructive thinkers in various fields who regard metaphor most highly. They recognize with Coleridge that the creative act, whether it be the solution to a mathematical puzzle, the writing of a poem, or a new and fruitful way to view the dynamics of world economics, is a selection, combination, and synthesis of the already familiar into new wholes. We never create—as the tradition says God did—out of nothing, but use what we have, seeing it in a new way. The new way is not simply a reshuffling of the old, for metaphorical thinking recognizes the unlike as well as the like, but it uses the similar to move beyond it into the unknown. The process of creation can be compared to a Rorschach test where one sees a pattern similar to something which is vaguely familiar and the mind jumps to fill in the unknown gaps in order to see it whole.[9] The whole that one sees is not identical with anything with which we are familiar, but the similarity has enabled us to see a new thing. Arthur Koestler's monumental study, *The Act of Creation*, gives hundreds of examples of breakthroughs in various fields, especially in science, through the "bisociative" ability of the human mind which, if freed from conventional matrices, "sees" new similarities formerly blocked.[10] The most famous example is undoubtedly Archimedes in his bathtub, but Koestler mentions many others: Lord Kelvin came to the idea of the mirror galvanometer after noticing a reflection of light on his monocle; Newton saw that the moon behaved like an apple; Pasteur recognized the analogy between a spoiled culture and a cowpox vaccine.[11] As Koestler notes, seeing the similarity that has not been seen before in two previously unrelated matrices of thought is the essence of discovery—and this is metaphor in its most obvious and brilliant form.

These remarks on metaphor, its ubiquity and importance, are not meant to suggest that "everything is metaphor." I am not suggesting that "metaphor" is the ultimate metaphor for interpreting human beings or even for describing the nature of language. While in many ways we are the "metaphorical creature" and language is profoundly metaphorical, if we are not to absolutize metaphor we must view it as *one* way—albeit a highly suggestive and fruitful way—by which to understand particular aspects of human being, especially those pertaining to expression and interpretation, creation and discovery, change and transformation. I do not believe, however, that it is an adequate perspective from which to view our sensuous, affectional, and active lives at their base level. Of course, this level of human existence, when expressed and interpreted, comes under the metaphorical, but it also lies beneath it, is its funding, and is more basic than it. In a sense, we feel more than we can express, we know more than we can interpret. Metaphor deals with expression and interpretation, not with the depths of human existence that lie even beyond words. This is a difficult distinction to maintain, because in a sense everything human beings feel and know is already interpreted and hence metaphorical; but just as it makes little sense to talk of metaphorical language unless there is a non-metaphorical language (dead metaphors, dictionary meanings), so it makes little sense to talk of "seeing this as that" unless there is a non-metaphorical base. This base, difficult as it is to stipulate, deals, it seems to me, with our sensuous, affectional, and active lives at the most primordial level. There are some things that lie too deep for words, among them, for instance, the touch of another human being, what occurs in human silence, the terror that can grip us in the night, or an act of human compassion. These are not metaphors, but the stuff from which metaphor is made.[12]

Having looked at the centrality of metaphor, we need to define it as precisely as we can. The history of efforts to understand the nature of metaphor begins with Aristotle whose view constitutes one of the two major perspectives on it. In spite of his appreciation for its importance, his relegation of it to the mark of genius indicates he saw it principally as a rhetorical device rather than as central to language as such. His view can be called "substitutable" while the other major view sees metaphor as "unsubstitutable." That is, Aristotle's understanding of metaphor, and the opinion that prevailed until the nineteenth century (except for Vico in the Renaissance who suspected that metaphor was considerably more important than his predecessors or anyone else until Coleridge), was that what metaphor said could be said some other way. But, increasingly, over the last two centuries, that opinion has been reversed and metaphor has been seen not as a trope but as the way language and, more basically, thought works.

The principal contemporary theorists on metaphor as unsubstitutable are I. A. Richards and Max Black. Richards says, "we all live, and speak, only through an eye for resemblances" and Black agrees.[13] The ways in which their understandings of metaphor differ are subtle and not crucial for our argument. What follows is an amalgam of their views as well as of other theorists, notably Douglas Berggren, Walter Ong, Nelson Goodman, and Paul Ricoeur. Richard's definition is a good beginning: "In the simplest formulation, when we use a metaphor we have two thoughts of different things active together and supported by a single word, or phrase, whose meaning is a resultant of their interaction."[14] The most important element in this definition is its insistence on *two active thoughts which remain in permanent tension or interaction with each other*. Thus, in the example from Black mentioned earlier, "war is a chess game," the vitality of the metaphor depends upon keeping both thoughts and what Black calls their "systems of associated commonplaces" active in the mind. The meaning of the phrase, "war is a chess game," is not the same as "war is *like* a chess game" which implies a simple comparison, describing war as similar to chess. As Black says, "looking at a scene through blue spectacles is different from *comparing* that scene with something else."[15] The difference is that the *tension* is lost, what Ricoeur calls the "is and is not" quality of metaphor. By retaining the inter-action of *two* thoughts active in the mind, one recalls, as one does not with a simile, that the two are dissimilar as well as similar. One difficulty with simile in contrast to metaphor is that simile softens the shock of the linkage through its "like," reducing an awareness of the dissimilarity, and hence allowing us to slip into literalistic thinking. A metaphor that works is sufficiently unconventional and shocking so that we instinctively say no as well as yes to it, thus avoiding absolutism. The difficulty with dead metaphors, of course, is that the shock and thus the tension is lost and literalism follows. Religious metaphors, because of their preservation in a tradition and repetition in ritual, are especially prone to becoming idols.

The tensive or interactive view of metaphor also reveals the fact that both fields or subjects are influenced or changed by being brought into relationship with the other. The names of these fields vary among theorists: Richards calls them "vehicle" and "tenor"; Black, "subsidiary" and "principal" subject; but, whatever the name, in our example of "war is a chess game," both war (as tenor or principal subject) and chess (as vehicle or subsidiary subject) undergo change by being thought of in relationship to the other. Thus, although chess is the filter or screen through which war is seen and hence influences our view of war, chess is also seen differently—in the present case as "warlike." This is a very important point for religious models because the human images that are chosen as metaphors for God gain in stature and take on divine qualities by being placed in an interactive relationship with the divine.

A third point which is only implicit in Richard's definition but one which he as well as Black, Ong, and Ricoeur all stress is that metaphor belongs to the semantics, not the syntax, of language. That is, it is concerned with meaning: it is in the form of assertions, of judgments. Metaphor of this sort, and at the level at which we are dealing with it, is not words but sentences with a subject and a predicate. The rhetorical, ornamental view of metaphor which sees it as a literary trope tends to concentrate on metaphorical words or phrases—for instance, Shakespeare's metaphor of "salad days" for Cleopatra's youth—rather than on two matrices of thought which are brought into conjunction with each other through a judgment of significant similarity.

Two points are crucial here: the indirection and tentativeness of all judgments and the structural, organizational power of metaphor. As Walter Ong points out, judgment is always binary; we can grasp nothing in itself but only as related to and set apart from something else.[16] Metaphor, because of its explicitly binary nature, is a reminder that we never apprehend simply and in a unitary fashion as idealism would have it. The "bifocal" or "twinned" vision of metaphor—what we have called the tension of metaphor which actively entertains the similarity and dissimilarity of both subjects—is a reminder, says Ong, of the duality which is always at the heart of human truth and judgment. Moreover, in the semantical view of metaphor, the judgment of similarity (and difference) has structural and organizing possibilities because we are dealing here with two matrices of thought, two systems of associated commonplaces. The most fruitful metaphors are the ones with sufficiently complex grids to allow for extension of thought, structural expansion, suggestions beyond immediate linkages. Thus, in this sense, "liberator" is a good metaphor for God because it entails a complex structure for thought which can be elaborated. Similarly, chess is a complex game which teases the mind into new connections with war the longer one reflects on it. It is because some metaphors have structural possibilities that, as we shall see, models can develop from them, for models are dominant metaphors with comprehensive, organizational potential.

There is, however, a deeper level to the semantics of metaphor: it is not just that a judgment is being made that one subject is both like and unlike another, but the tension of duality in such a judgment is, as Ricoeur insists, between a literal or conventional interpretation which self-destructs and an extended, new interpretation which is recognized as plausible or possible.[17] Thus, war is not literally seen as a game of chess (as Ricoeur points out, such an assertion is literally absurd), but because both subjects and their systems of associated commonplaces are actively entertained together, one can see a kind of sense, a nonliteral sense, to the assertion. The response to a metaphor is similar to the response to a riddle: one "gets" it or one does not, and what one "gets" is the new, extended meaning which is a result of the interaction of the subjects. Nelson Goodman expresses it colorfully when he says that "metaphor, it seems, is a matter of teaching an old word new tricks—of applying an old label in a new way."[18] Or as he says elsewhere, "a metaphor might be regarded . . . as a happy and revitalizing, even if bigamous, second marriage."[19] In more prosaic terms, metaphorical meaning depends upon a literal, conventional base as our point of contact, but through being applied to a new field, new meaning is created. As Ricoeur puts it, reality is redescribed through metaphor. This is a weighty assertion, resting on the capacity of metaphor both to rely on a literal meaning and to subvert and extend it through transformation. As we shall see, the parables of Jesus and Jesus as a parable are metaphorical in this sense. While we shall often be dealing with questions of the reference and truth of metaphor, a few initial remarks may be helpful. When Ricoeur says that metaphor redescribes reality, at one level he is only saying that in metaphor old views of reality are traded for new ones. As Goodman says in his characteristically colorful way, "a metaphor is simply a juvenile fact, and a fact a senile metaphor."[20] While metaphor does not refer to the conventional or literal view of the aspect of reality in question, neither does it refer to "another world" or to no reality outside itself. As an assertion, it has not only meaning but reference, not only internal sense but outward directionality. And the reality to which it refers is the ordinary world to which every interpretation refers.[21] The theory of gravitation refers to that world in one way; a poem in another; a philosophy of organism and process in a third way; the parables of Jesus in yet another way. Each models reality in a different way; none has direct or literal access to it. Metaphor is basically a new or unconventional interpretation of reality, whether that interpretation refers to a limited aspect of reality or to the totality of it. John Donne's line of poetry, "I am a little world made cunningly," is a redescription of reality as is Heraclitus's root-metaphor of change as the nature of reality.

The centrality of metaphor in all constructive fields—our world as modeled and we as the modelers—means that the question of the truth of metaphor cannot be dealt with in a direct, literalistic, positivistic way. What we consider realistic or literal is, as Goodman points out, what we are used to; traditional labels are old metaphors.[22] Even in science, which has a more settled context or set of conventions for its "facts" than do other fields, unrelated empirical truths are not significant. What matters in science as in other fields is whether individual "facts" fit into some whole, raise or answer significant questions, are related to other facts. The criteria of truth for a hypothesis in science are not unlike criteria applied to metaphors in poetry and religion: "Truth of a hypothesis . . . is a matter of fit—fit with a body of theory, and fit of hypothesis and theory to the data at hand and the facts to be encountered."[23] One speaks of a metaphor as apt or appropriate because it fits into the assumptions of a poem or into a system of doctrines or to life as lived. The hypothesis or metaphor may well transform or even revolutionize the conventional theory or set of expectations, but in either case it is not considered true because it corresponds with some uninterpreted reality but because it gives us a more apt, fitting way of interpreting reality than did the traditional view.

Finally, some comments on the abuse and dangers of metaphor are now appropriate. The greatest danger is assimilation—the shocking, powerful metaphor becomes trite and accepted. A parable by Franz Kafka makes the point with eerie power:

> Leopards break into the temple and drink up the sacrificial wine; this is repeated over and over again; eventually it becomes predictable, and is incorporated into the ceremony.[24]

Habit will always, it seems, triumph over novelty, no matter how shocking the novelty. Jesus said, "This is my body," and instead of surprise, joy, or disbelief, we do not even hear the metaphor. Colin Turbayne has listed three stages of metaphor.[25] Initially, when newly coined, it seems inappropriate or unconventional; the response is often rejection. At a second stage, when it is a living metaphor, it has dual meaning—the literal and metaphorical—and is insightful. Finally, the metaphor becomes commonplace, either dead and/or literalized. At this stage, says Turbayne, we are no longer like the Wizard of Oz who knew green glasses made Oz green, but, like all the other inhabitants of Oz, we believe that Oz *is* green.

What has occurred, of course, is that similarity has become identity; the *tension* that is so critical in metaphor has been lost. This is an ever present danger in religious metaphors, though also in scientific ones, for in both cases models of reality, especially ones with long-term and widespread backing, are identified with reality. "It is," says Douglas Berggren, "the familiar, or inherited or submerged metaphor which is the most dangerous."[26] Religion is obviously a prime candidate for housing familiar and submerged metaphors, since religious images—through tradition and ritual—seldom change and become accepted as ordinary language. But scientific models are equally susceptible, in part because science is not usually perceived as even trafficking in models.

Moreover, a metaphor used frequently, a metaphor that is believed in as the "thing itself," affects attitudes at profound levels. All metaphors, at least in poetry and religion (but also in advertising), have a strong attitudinal component, for we respond at an affectional level to metaphors which have significant associations for us. Thus, at an amusing level we can see Turbayne's point when he says, "a Dry-Martini health drink loses its flavor";[27] at a more serious level, when we see God as "suffering companion," we have a different attitude toward the deity than when we see God as "hunter." But metaphors that are literalized affect our attitudes at subconscious levels. If one believes that the death of Jesus is (literally) a substitutionary sacrifice to free all others from sin and guilt, that belief will have a more pervasive influence on one's attitudes than if one sees it as one interpretation among other possible ones. To sum up, one must be careful of metaphors; they are not to be taken lightly.

In conclusion, we recall that human thought and language grow and change by seeing one thing in terms of another: they are intrinsically metaphorical. Explicit or alive metaphors make us aware of this mobile, tensive characteristic of our way of being in the world. The distinctive features of alive metaphors can be summed up in the following way: a metaphor is an assertion or judgment of similarity and difference between two thoughts in permanent tension with one another, which redescribes reality in an open-ended way but has structural as well as affective power.

[. . .]

Notes

1   John Middleton Murry, *Countries of the Mind: Essays in Literary Criticism*, 2d series (London: Oxford Univ. Press, 1931), pp. 1–2.

2   The literature supporting this point is vast; to date, the most comprehensive bibliography on metaphor is by Warren A. Shibles, *Metaphor: An Annotated Bibliography and History* (Whitewater, Wis.: Language Press, 1971). It consists of 400 pages of entries; however, it is less comprehensive on models in science than on metaphor in other fields. A sprinkling of quotations from its frontispiece will give, in brief, both the passion with which the centrality of metaphor is supported and the breadth of fields from which such support comes. "Both philosophers and poets live by metaphor," S. Pepper; "All thinking is metaphorical," R. Frost; "The history of philosophy should be written as that of seven or eight metaphors," T. Hulme; "The most profound social creativity consists in the invention and imposition of new,

radical metaphors," R. Kaufman; "Something like a paradigm is prerequisite to perception itself. . . . Paradigms prove to be constitutive of the research activity," T. Kuhn; "All our truth, or all but a few fragments, is won by metaphor," C. S. Lewis; "To know is merely to work with one's favorite metaphors," F. Nietzsche; "The conduct of even the plainest, most 'direct' untechnical prose is a ceaseless exercise in metaphor," I. A. Richards.

3   David Burrell's argument stretches throughout his book, *Analogy and Philosophical Language* (New Haven, Conn.: Yale Univ. Press, 1973). He contrasts the metaphorical pattern for human knowing with another perspective which sees metaphor as merely decorative and rhetorical. Such a perspective, he says, implies that we can know the world directly and can describe it adequately, given time and effort. The paragraph is worth quoting:

The more we are led to recognize the ubiquity of metaphor in ordinary speech, the less plausible is the Renaissance account of its role as decorating a skeleton of expository prose or rational argument. In fact, the contrary seems to be the case: metaphor plays a unique and irreplaceable part in human discourse, from poetry to ordinary conversation to scientific models. Nor is this merely a thesis about language. For as the decorative theory reflected a world view—that of the Age of Reason—so does the contrary inherent theory. And the implications of the contrasting world view are extraordinarily far-reaching. The nub of the Renaissance theory about metaphor was an assumption about the nature of the universe, and one shared in many ways by latter-day positivism. Counting metaphor as a replaceable rhetorical device presumes that we must always be able, sooner or later, to hit upon a proper and unambiguous description. But this presumption reaches to the very structure of the world. It assumes that the world is of such a piece with our language that (in principle) nothing prohibits our giving a complete description of it. The uncertainties of our ordinary language may have to be corrected, and much ingenuity shown in constructing a language equal to the task, but an unambiguous picture of the world is renderable in principle. Hence it is but a matter of time and effort (pp. 258–59).

4   Kenneth Burke, *Permanence and Change: An Anatomy of Purpose* (New York: New Republic, 1935), pp. 137ff.

5   Ibid., p. 141.

6   W. H. Leatherdale, *The Role of Analogy, Model and Metaphor in Science* (Amsterdam: North-Holland Publishing Co., 1974), pp. 28–29.

7   Mary B. Hesse, "Models in Physics," *British Journal for the Philosophy of Science* 4 (1953): 203.

8   Jacob Bronowski, *The Visionary Eye: Essays in the Arts, Literature and Science*, ed. Piero E. Ariotti (Cambridge, Mass.: M. I. T. Press, 1978), p. 28.

9   Roy Dreistadt, "An Analysis of the Use of Analogies and Metaphors in Science," *Journal of Psychology* 68 (1968): 112–13.

10   Arthur Koestler, *The Act of Creation* (New York: Macmillan Co., 1964), pp. 119–121.

11   Ibid., pp. 199–200.

12   Paul Ricoeur suggests, similarly, a nonmetaphorical base for metaphor in his distinction between symbol and metaphor. Symbols are rooted in reality at a cosmic, prelinguistic level, while metaphors are the linguistic innovation of symbols, interpreting and reinterpreting them. Symbol is at "the dividing line between *bios* and *logos*," while metaphor is at the level of articulation. However, they are in a symbiotic relationship, for symbols give roots in the cosmos and lived world to metaphor, while metaphors bring symbols to language, clarify symbols, and display the endless associations and connections of symbols. Thus, "stain" is a symbol; metaphors of guilt and evil build upon and interpret stain. Ricoeur's fullest discussion of this relationship is in the essay, "Metaphor and Symbol," in his *Interpretation Theory: Discourse and the Surplus of Meaning* (Fort Worth, Tex.: Texas Christian Univ. Press, 1976), pp. 45–69.

13   I. A. Richards, *The Philosophy of Rhetoric* (New York and London: Oxford Univ. Press, 1965), p. 89.

14   Ibid., p. 93.

15   Max Black, "More About Metaphor," in *Metaphor and Thought*, ed. Andrew Ortony (New York and Cambridge: Cambridge Univ. Press, 1979), p. 31.

16   Walter J. Ong, "Metaphor and the Twinned Vision," in his *The Barbarian Within and Other Fugitive Essays and Studies* (New York: Macmillan Co., 1962), pp. 42–43.

17   Ricoeur, *Interpretation Theory*, p. 50.

18   Nelson Goodman, *Languages of Art: An Approach to a Theory of Symbols* (Indianapolis: Bobbs-Merrill, 1968), p. 69.

19   Ibid., p. 73.

20   Goodman, *Languages of Art*, p. 68.

21   Metaphor is not a different way of perceiving reality, but only a heightening of the ordinary way. As John Hick points out, perception involves "seeing-as"; things do not simply register on the retina but an act of perception involves recognition, seeing something *as* something. This basic process is repeated at different levels in all our interpreting; hence, Hick calls faith "experiencing-as," the interpretation of experience *as* living in the presence of God. The point is that metaphor raises the "seeing-as" which occurs at *all* levels in an explicit way and makes us aware that we are always interpreting. See Hick, "Religious Faith as Experiencing-As," in *Talk of God*, Royal Institute of Philosophy Lectures, vol. 2, 1967–68 (New York: St. Martin's Press, 1969), pp. 20–35.

22   Goodman, *Languages of Art*, pp. 79, 80.

23   Ibid., p. 264.

24   Franz Kafka, "Leopard in the Temple," in *Parables and Paradoxes* (New York: Schocken Books, 1962), p. 93.

25   Colin M. Turbayne, *The Myth of Metaphor* (New Haven, Conn.: Yale Univ. Press, 1962), pp. 24–25.

26   Douglas Berggren, "The Use and Abuse of Metaphor," *Review of Metaphysics* 16 (1963): 456.

27   C. S. Lewis makes a somewhat similar point in a most engaging way when he insists that in order to avoid fossilized metaphors, one must use several metaphors as well as new ones. "If a man has seen ships and the sea, he may abandon the metaphor of a *sea-stallion* and call a boat a boat. But suppose a man has never seen the sea, or ships, yet who knows of them just as much as he can glean, say from the following list of Kenningar—sea-stallions, winged logs, wave riders, ocean trains. If he keeps all these together in his mind, and knows them for the metaphors they are, he will be able to think of ships, very imperfectly indeed, and under strict limits, but not wholly in vain. But if instead of this he pins his faith on the particular kenning, *ocean trains*, because that kenning with its comfortable air of machinery, seems to him somehow more safely prosaic, less flighty and dangerous than its fellows, and if, contracting that to the form *oshtrans*, he proceeds to forget that it was a metaphor, then, while he talks grammatically, he has ceased to think of anything. It will not avail him to stamp his feet and swear that he is literal; to say 'An oshtran is an oshtran and there's an end!' " See "Bluspels and Flalansferes," in *The Importance of Language*, ed. Max Black (Englewood Cliffs, N.J.: Prentice-Hall, 1962), p. 47.

Chapter 3

Mary Midgley

HOW MYTHS WORK

Symbolism and significance

WE ARE ACCUSTOMED to think of myths as the opposite of science. But in fact they are a central part of it: the part that decides its significance in our lives. So we very much need to understand them.

Myths are not lies. Nor are they detached stories. They are imaginative patterns, networks of powerful symbols that suggest particular ways of interpreting the world. They shape its meaning. For instance, machine imagery, which began to pervade our thought in the seventeenth century, is still potent today. We still often tend to see ourselves, and the living things around us, as pieces of clockwork: items of a kind that we ourselves could make, and might decide to remake if it suits us better. Hence the confident language of 'genetic engineering' and 'the building-blocks of life'.

Again, the reductive, atomistic picture of explanation, which suggests that the right way to understand complex wholes is always to break them down into their smallest parts, leads us to think that truth is always revealed at the end of that other seventeenth-century invention, the microscope. Where microscopes dominate our imagination, we feel that the large wholes we deal with in everyday experience are mere appearances. Only the particles revealed at the bottom of the microscope are real. Thus, to an extent unknown in earlier times, our dominant technology shapes our symbolism and thereby our metaphysics, our view about what is real. The heathen in his blindness bows down to wood and stone – steel and glass, plastic and rubber and silicon – of his own devising and sees them as the final truth.

Of course this mechanistic imagery does not rule alone. Older myths survive and are still potent, but they are often given a reductive and techno-logical form. Thus, for instance, we are still using the familiar social-contract image of citizens as essentially separate and autonomous individuals. But we are less likely now to defend it on humanistic or religious grounds than by appealing to a neo-Darwinist vision of universal competition between separate entities in an atomised world, which are easily seen as machinery – distinct cogs or bytes put together within a larger mechanism. Social atomism strikes us as scientific.

This same reductive and atomistic picture now leads many enquirers to propose biochemical solutions to today's social and psychological problems, offering each citizen more and better Prozac rather than asking what made them unhappy in the first place. Society appears as split into organisms and organisms into their constituent cogs. The only wider context easily seen as containing all these parts is evolution, understood (in a way that would have surprised Darwin) as a cosmic projection of nineteenth-century economics, a competitive arena pervading the development, not just of life but of our thought and of the whole physical universe.

At present, when people become aware of this imagery, they tend to think of it as merely a surface dressing of isolated metaphors – as a kind of optional decorative paint that is sometimes added to ideas after they are formed, so as to make them clear to outsiders. But really such symbolism is an integral part of our thought-structure. It does crucial work on all topics, not just in a few supposedly marginal areas such as religion and emotion, where symbols are known to be at home, but throughout our thinking. The way in which we imagine the world determines what we think important in it, what we select for our attention among the welter of facts that constantly flood in upon us. Only after we have made that selection can we start to form our official, literal, thoughts and descriptions. That is why we need to become aware of these symbols.

How neutral is science?

What, then, is the right place of such imaginative visions in our serious thinking? In particular, how do they relate to science? This question occurred to me forcibly some six years back when Amnesty International asked me to contribute to their lecture series entitled 'The Values of Science'. It struck me as remarkable that people answer questions about the values of science in two quite opposite ways today.

On the one hand, they often praise science for being value-free: objective, unbiased, neutral, a pure source of facts. Just as often, however, they speak of it as being itself a source of values, perhaps indeed the only true source of them. For example, the great evolutionist Conrad Waddington wrote in 1941 that 'Science by itself is able to provide mankind with a way of life which is . . . self-consistent and harmonious. . . . So far as I can see, the scientific attitude of mind is the only one which is, at the present day, adequate to do this'.[1] As we shall see, too, many serious theorists have claimed that science is 'omnicompetent', that is, able to answer every kind of question. And that must naturally include questions about value.

The eminent molecular biologist Jacques Monod noticed this difficulty and suggested heroically that science should take over this apparently alien realm of thought altogether:

> Science attacks values. Not directly, since science is no judge of them and must ignore them; but it subverts every one of the mythical ontogenies upon which the animist tradition, from the Australian aborigines to the dialectical materialists, has based morality: values, duties, rights, prohibitions . . . True knowledge is ignorant of values, but it has to be grounded on a value judgment, or rather on an axiomatic value . . . In order to establish the norm for knowledge, the objectivity principle defines a value; that value is objective knowledge itself . . . The ethic of knowledge that created the modern world is the only ethic compatible with it, the only one capable, once understood and accepted, of guiding its evolution.[2]

Not surprisingly, Monod was for a time the favourite author of many scientists. Since what he meant by 'knowledge' was exclusively scientific knowledge, his ruling implied that the only value judgements that remained would be ones about whether a proposition in science was true or not.

This, however, would not have been a very convenient arrangement for the rest of life. The clash remained, and, as usual, the truth about it was more complicated than it looked. The word 'science' surely has a different meaning in these two claims. We do indeed sometimes think of science just as an immense store-cupboard of objective facts, unquestionable data about such things as measurements, temperatures and chemical composition. But a store-cupboard is not, in itself, very exciting.

What makes science into something much grander and more interesting than this is the huge, ever-changing imaginative structure of ideas by which scientists contrive to connect, understand and interpret these facts. The general concepts, metaphors and images that make up this structure cannot possibly be objective and antiseptic in this same way. They grow out of images drawn from everyday experience, because that is the only place to get them. They relate theory to everyday life and are meant to influence it. These concepts and images change constantly as the way of life around them changes. And after they have been used in science they are often reflected back into everyday life in altered forms, seemingly charged with a new scientific authority.

[W]e will consider several very potent ideas that have moved in this way from ordinary thought to affect the course of science and have then returned to outside usage reshaped by scientific use. Right away, one might name the concept of a *machine*, of a *self-interested individual*, and of *competition* between such individuals. Metaphorical concepts like these are quite properly used by scientists, but they are not just passive pieces of apparatus like thermostats. They have their own influence. They are living parts of powerful myths – imaginative patterns that we all take for granted – ongoing dramas inside which we live our lives. These patterns shape the mental maps that we refer to when we want to place something. Such ideas are not just a distraction from real thought, as positivists have suggested. Nor are they a disease. They are the matrix of thought, the background that shapes our mental habits. They decide what we think important and what we ignore. They provide the tools with which we organise the mass of incoming data. When they are bad they can do a great deal of harm by distorting our selection and slanting our thinking. That is why we need to watch them so carefully.

How do ideas change?

This question is specially urgent in times of rapid change, because patterns of thought that are really useful in one age can make serious trouble in the next one. They don't then necessarily have to be dropped. But they do often have to be reshaped or balanced by other thought-patterns in order to correct their faults.

In this process, myths do not alter in the rather brisk, wholesale way that much contemporary imagery suggests. The belief in instant ideological change is itself a favourite myth of the recent epoch that we are now beginning to abuse as 'modern'. Descartes may have started it when he launched his still-popular town-planning metaphor, comparing the whole of current thought to an unsatisfactory city which should be knocked down and replaced by a better one:

> Those ancient cities which were originally mere boroughs, and
> have become large towns in process of time, are as a rule badly laid
> out, as compared with those towns of regular pattern that are laid
> out by a designer on an open plain to suit his fancy . . . one would
> say that it was chance that placed them so, not the will of men who
> had the use of reason.[3]

Today, too, another influential image, drawn from Nietzsche, works on the model of the *Deaths* column in a newspaper. Here you just report the death of something: Art, or Poetry, or History, or the Author, or God, or Nature, or Metaphysics or whatever, publish its obituary and then forget about it.

The trouble about this is that such large-scale items don't suddenly vanish. Prominent ideas cannot die until the problems that arise within them have been resolved. They are not just a kind of external parasite. They are not alien organisms, viruses: 'memes' that happen to have infested us and can be cleared away with the right insecticide. . . .They are organic parts of our lives, cognitive and emotional habits, structures that shape our thinking. So they follow conservation laws within it. Instead of dying, they transform themselves gradually into something different, something that is often hard to recognise and to understand. The Marxist pattern of complete final revolution is not at all appropriate here. We do better to talk organically of our thought as an ecosystem trying painfully to adapt itself to changes in the world around it.

The downside of drama

[C]ertain particular myths which have come down to us from the Enlightenment . . . are now giving trouble . . . . Enlightenment concepts need our attention because they tend to be particularly simple and sweeping. Dramatic simplicity has been one of their chief attractions and is also their chronic weakness, a serious one when they need to be applied in detail. . . .

In the case of the physical sciences, we already know that Enlightenment ideas have been much too naive and dramatic. They suggested that physics could expect to reveal a far simpler kind of order in the world than has turned out to be available. Of course this simplification played a great part in making possible the astonishing success of the physical sciences. It gave western civilisation an understanding of natural 'mechanisms' (as we still call them) far beyond that of any other culture, and a wealth of technology that other cultures have never dreamed of. And it is right to celebrate this tremendous achievement. But we, the heirs of this great intellectual empire, don't actually need to come together simply to praise it.

We don't now need to tell each other that science is good any more than we need to say that freedom is good or democracy is good. As ideals, these things are established in our society. But when particular ideals are established and are supposed to be working, we have to deal with the institutions that are invented to express them. Today, some people plainly do *not* think that science is altogether good. At times there are similar doubts about democracy and freedom. In such cases, those of us who care about the ideals need to ask what is going wrong with the way they are being incorporated in the world. We have to consider how best to understand the present condition of science, how best to live with its difficulties and responsibilities, and how to shape its further development so as to avoid these distortions. . . .

Exaggerated and distorted ideas about what physical science can do for us led, during the nineteenth and twentieth centuries, to the rise of powerful, supposedly scientific ideologies such as Marxism and behaviourism. These systems are obviously not actually part of physical science but, by claiming its authority, they have injured its image. People who want to defend science today need to take outgrowths of this kind seriously and go to some trouble to understand its relation to them. It is equally urgent to get rid of the absurd and embarrassing claim to 'omnicompetence'. Science, which has its own magnificent work to do, does not need to rush in and take over extraneous kinds of question (historical, logical, ethical, linguistic or the like) as well. Lovers of physical science can be happy to see it as it is, as one great department of human thought among others which all cooperate in our efforts at understanding the world. This is a far more honourable status than that of a nineteenth-century political power trying to enlarge its empire by universal conquest.

Notes

1   C. H. Waddington, *The Scientific Attitude* (Harmondsworth: Penguin, 1941), p. 170, emphases mine.
2   Jacques Monod, *Chance and Necessity*, trans. Austryn Wainhouse (Glasgow: Collins, 1972), pp. 160–4, author's emphases.
3   René Descartes, *Discourse on Method*, part 2, opening section.

Chapter 4

Ian G. Barbour

THE STRUCTURES OF SCIENCE AND RELIGION

WE LOOK FIRST at the relation between the two basic components of science: data and theory. It is then suggested that in religion the data are religious experience, story, and ritual and that religious beliefs have some functions similar to those of scientific theories.[1] . . .

1 Theory and data in science

In describing the work of Galileo, Newton, and Darwin I suggested that the fundamental components of modern science are (1) particular observations and experimental data, and (2) general concepts and theories. How are theories related to data? Since Bacon and Mill, the *inductive view* has held that the scientist starts with observations and formulates theories by generalizing the patterns in the data (this would be represented by an arrow *upward* from data to theories in figure 4.1). But this view is inadequate because theories involve novel concepts and hypotheses not found in the data, and they often refer to entities and relationships that are not directly observable.

There is, then, no direct upward line of logical reasoning from data to theories in the diagram, but only the indirect line at the left, representing acts of *creative imagination* for which no rules can be given. Often a new concept or relationship is first thought of by analogy with a more familiar concept or

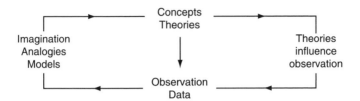

Figure 4.1 The Structure of Science

relationship, but with a novel modification or adaptation. Frequently the analogy is systematically developed as a *conceptual model* of a postulated entity that cannot be directly observed. The model leads to the formulation of a generalized and abstract theory. For example, the billiard ball model of a gas postulated invisible gas particles that were imagined to collide and bounce off each other like billiard balls. From the model, the kinetic theory of gases was developed.

To be scientifically useful, a theory must be tested experimentally. A theory leads us to expect some observations and not others. This is the *hypothetico-deductive* view of science, represented by the *downward arrow* from theory to observation. The context of discovery (left-hand loop) differs from the context of justification (downward arrow). If a theory or hypothesis is valid, then particular observational patterns are expected, though the reasoning process always involves a variety of background assumptions, auxiliary hypotheses, and rules of correspondence linking theoretical and observational terms. In the case of the kinetic theory of gases, we can calculate the change in the momentum of the hypothetical particles when they strike the walls of the containing vessel. If we assume perfectly elastic collisions and particles of negligible size, we can derive Boyle's Law relating the observed pressure and volume of a gas sample. The corroboration of such deductions leads us at least tentatively to accept a theory.[2]

This hypothetico-deductive view dominated philosophy of science in the 1950s and early 1960s. It assumed that data are describable in a theory-free observation language and that alternative theories are tested against these fixed, objective data. Even though *agreement* with data does not verify a theory (since there may be other theories that would also agree), it was claimed by Karl Popper and others that *disagreement* with data will conclusively *falsify* a theory. But studies in the history of science cast doubt on this claim.

In some cases, discordant data were brought into harmony with a theoretical prediction by the introduction of *ad hoc auxiliary hypotheses*. Early opponents of Copernican astronomy said the hypothesis that the earth moves around the sun must be false because there is no visible annual change in the apparent position of near stars relative to distant stars. But Copernicus dismissed this discrepancy by introducing the hypothesis (for which there was then no independent evidence) that all the stars are very distant compared to the size of the solar system. In other historical cases a theory was retained without modification and the discordant data were simply set to one side as an *unexplained anomaly*. Newton in his *Principia* admitted that the observed motion of the apogee (the most distant point) of the moon's elliptical orbit in successive revolutions was twice that predicted by his theory. For sixty years the disagreement, which far exceeded the limits of experimental error, could not be accounted for, yet it was never taken to disprove the theory.

We can never test a theory alone, but only as part of *a network of theories*. If a theory fits poorly with the data at one point, other parts of the network can usually be adjusted to improve the fit. Theories with terms far from the observational boundaries are not uniquely determined by the data.[3] Normally, a group of background theories is simply assumed and treated as unproblematic while attention is directed to a new or controversial theory. In many scientific disputes, the contending parties agree on most of these background assumptions, and so they can agree on the kinds of experimental data that both sides will accept as a crucial test for adjudicating between rival theories. But in some cases two theories of broad scope involve differing ways of interpreting the data, or they are correlated with differing bodies of data or differing types of explanation, and no simple experimental adjudication is possible.

Moreover, *all data are theory-laden*. There simply is no theory-free observational language. Theories influence observations in many ways (as shown in the right-hand loop in the diagram). The selection of phenomena to study and the choice of variables considered significant to measure are theory-dependent. The form of the questions we ask determines the kind of answers we receive. Theories are reflected in our assumptions about the operation of our equipment and in the language in which observations are reported.[4] This account differs sharply from the empiricist account, in which the edifice of knowledge is built on the secure foundation of unchanging facts.

In addition, the object observed may be altered by *the process of observation* itself. We will see that this is particularly problematic in the microworld of quantum physics and in the complex networks of ecosystems. We are not detached observers separate from observed objects; we are participant observers who are part of an interactive system.

Thomas Kuhn has argued that scientific data are strongly dependent on dominant *paradigms*. A paradigm ... is a cluster of conceptual and methodological presuppositions embodied in an exemplary body of scientific work, such as Newtonian mechanics in the eighteenth century or relativity and quantum physics in the twentieth century. A paradigm implicitly defines for a given scientific community the kinds of questions that may fruitfully be asked and the types of explanations to be sought. Through standard examples, students learn what kinds of entities exist in the world and what methods are suitable for studying them. A paradigm shift is "a scientific revolution," "a radical transformation of the scientific imagination," which is not unequivocally determined by experimental data or by the normal criteria of research. Accepted paradigms are thus more resistant to change and more difficult to overthrow than are particular theories. Paradigms are the products of particular historical communities.[5] Here we see a contextualism, a historicism, and a relativism contrasting with the formalism and the empiricism of Popper's account.

There are four criteria for assessing theories in normal scientific research:

1. *Agreement with Data*. This is the most important criterion, though it never provides proof that a theory is true. For other theories not yet developed may fit the data as well or better. Theories are always underdetermined by data. Nor does disagreement with data prove a theory false, since *ad hoc* modifications or unexplained anomalies can be tolerated for an indefinite period. However, agreement with data and predictive success—especially the prediction of novel phenomena not previously anticipated—constitute impressive support for a theory.

2. *Coherence*. A theory should be consistent with other accepted theories and, if possible, conceptually interconnected with them. Scientists also value the internal coherence and simplicity of a theory (simplicity of formal structure, smallest number of independent or *ad hoc* assumptions, aesthetic elegance, transformational symmetry, and so forth).

3. *Scope*. Theories can be judged by their comprehensiveness or generality. A theory is valued if it unifies previously disparate domains, if it is supported by a variety of kinds of evidence, or if it is applicable to wide ranges of the relevant variables.

4. *Fertility*. A theory is evaluated not just by its past accomplishments but by its current ability and future promise in providing the framework for an ongoing research program. Is the theory fruitful in encouraging further theoretical elaboration, in generating new hypotheses, and in suggesting new experiments? Attention is directed here to the continuing research activity of a scientific community rather than to the finished product of their work.

Western thought has included three main *views of truth*, and each emphasizes particular criteria from the list above. The *correspondence* view says that a proposition is true if it corresponds to reality. This is the common-sense understanding of truth. The statement "it is raining" is true if in fact it is raining. This is the position adopted by classical realism, and it seems to fit the empirical side of science as specified by the first criterion: theories must agree with data. But we have said that there are no theory-free data with which a theory can be compared. Many theories postulate unobservable entities only indirectly related to observable data. We have no direct access to reality to compare it with our theories.

The *coherence* view says that a set of propositions is true if it is comprehensive and internally coherent. This view has been adopted by rationalists and philosophical idealists, and it seems to fit the theoretical side of science. We have said that a single theory can never be evaluated in isolation, but only as part of a network of theories, so scope should be considered along with coherence. But this position is also problematic, since there may be more than one internally coherent set of theories in a given domain. Moreover, judgments of agreement with data differ in character from judgments of internal coherence and cannot be assimilated to the latter. In addition, reality seems to be more paradoxical and less logical than the rationalists assume.

The *pragmatic* view says that a proposition is true if it works in practice. We should judge by the consequences. Is an idea fruitful and suggestive? Is it useful in satisfying individual and social needs and interests? Ideas and theories are guides to action in particular contexts. Instrumentalists and linguistic analysts usually dismiss questions of truth, and they talk only about the diverse functions of language. But they often adopt a pragmatic view of scientific language. There is a pragmatic element in Kuhn's thesis that scientific inquiry is problem-solving in a particular historical context and within a particular paradigm community. This side of science is reflected in our last criterion: fertility. But taken alone this criterion is inadequate; whether an idea "works" or is "useful" remains vague unless these concepts are further specified by other criteria.

My own conclusion is that the *meaning* of truth is correspondence with reality. But because reality is inaccessible to us, the *criteria* of truth must include all four of the criteria mentioned above. The criteria taken together include the valid insights in all these views of truth. One or another of the criteria may be more important than the others at a particular stage of scientific inquiry. Because correspondence is taken as the definition of truth, this is a form of realism, but it is a *critical realism* because a combination of criteria is used. . . .

In sum, science does not lead to certainty. Its conclusions are always incomplete, tentative, and subject to revision. Theories change in time, and we should expect current theories to be modified or overthrown, as previous ones have been. But science does offer reliable procedures for testing and evaluating theories by a complex set of criteria. . . .

2 Belief and experience in religion

The basic structure of religion is similar to that of science in some respects, though it differs at several crucial points. The data for a religious community consist of the distinctive experiences of individuals and the stories and rituals of a religious tradition. Let us start by considering *religious experience*, which is always interpreted by a set of concepts and beliefs. These concepts and beliefs are not the product of logical reasoning from the data; they result from acts of creative imagination in which, as in the scientific case, analogies and models are prominent (figure 4.2). Models are also drawn from the stories of a tradition and express the structural elements that recur in dynamic form in narratives. Models, in turn, lead to abstract concepts and articulated beliefs that are systematically formalized as theological doctrines.

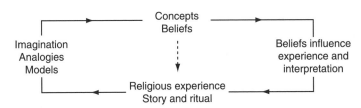

Figure 4.2 The Structure of Religion

The experiential testing of *religious beliefs* is problematic (so the downward arrow is shown as a dashed line), though we will find that there are criteria for judging the adequacy of beliefs. Moreover, there are no uninterpreted experiences, as there are no theory-free data in science. Religious beliefs influence experience and the interpretation of traditional stories and rituals (the loop on the right of the diagram)—an even stronger influence than that of scientific theories on data. Here, too, paradigms are extraordinarily resistant to change, and when paradigm shifts do occur a whole network of conceptual and methodological assumptions is altered. [. . .]

If the task of the theologian is systematic reflection on the life and thought of the religious community, this will include critical assessment according to particular criteria. I suggest that assessment of beliefs *within a paradigm community* can be undertaken with the same criteria listed above for scientific theories, though the criteria will have to be applied somewhat differently. . . .

1. *Agreement with Data.* Religious beliefs must provide a faithful rendition of the areas of experience that are taken by the community to be especially significant. I have argued that the primary data are individual religious experience and

communal story and ritual. Here the data are much more theory-laden than in the case of science. . . .

2. *Coherence*. Consistency with other accepted beliefs ensures the continuity of a paradigm tradition. The intersubjective judgment of the community provides protection against individualism and arbitrariness. But there is room for reformulation and reinterpretation, and the ideas of religious communities have indeed undergone considerable change throughout history. There are also close internal relationships among a set of religious beliefs.

3. *Scope*. Religious beliefs can be extended to interpret other kinds of human experience beyond the primary data, particularly other aspects of our personal and social lives. In a scientific age, they must also at least be consistent with the findings of science. Religious beliefs can contribute to a coherent world view and a comprehensive metaphysics.

4. *Fertility*. In the case of science, theories are judged partly by their promise for encouraging an ongoing research program, which is the central activity of science. Because religion involves a greater diversity of activities and serves some functions quite different from those of science, fertility here has many dimensions. At the personal level, religious beliefs can be judged by their power to effect personal transformation and the integration of personality. What are their effects on human character? Do they have the capacity to inspire and sustain compassion and create love? Are they relevant to urgent issues of our age, for example, environmental destruction and nuclear war? Judgments on such questions will of course be paradigm-dependent, but they are an important part of the evaluation of religion as a way of life. [. . .]

The role of models

[T]he role of models is particularly interesting both in science and in religion.

1 Models in science

We have seen that in science there is no direct route by logical reasoning from data to theory. Theories arise in acts of creative imagination in which models often play a role. Here we are talking about conceptual or theoretical models, not experimental or scale models constructed in the laboratory, nor logical or mathematical models, which are abstract and purely formal relationships. Theoretical models usually take the form of imagined mechanisms or processes postulated in a new domain by analogy with familiar mechanisms or processes.

Three general characteristics may be noted in theoretical models:[6]

1. *Models are analogical.* A scientist working in a new domain may posit entities having some of the properties of a familiar entity (the positive analogy) and some properties unlike those of the familiar entity (the negative analogy). The Bohr model of the atom, in which "planetary" electrons revolve in orbits around a central nucleus, resembled the familiar solar system in some of its dynamic properties, but the key assumption that only certain orbits are allowed (quantization) had no classical analogue at all. The model aided the formulation of the mathematical equations for the theory (for example, the equations for the energy levels of the electrons). It also suggested how theoretical terms characterizing entities not directly observable might be related to observable variables (for example, how the transition of an electron between two orbits might be related to the frequency of the light emitted).

2. *Models contribute to the extension of theories.* Some claim that a model is a temporarily useful psychological aid that can be discarded once the equations of the theory are formulated. But this ignores the fact that it is often the model rather than the theory that suggests its application to new phenomena or new domains. It was the billiard ball model that suggested how the kinetic theory of gases might be applied to gas diffusion, viscosity, and heat conduction. Moreover, the model was crucial to the modification of the theory. Gases under high pressure depart significantly from Boyle's Law. This could be accounted for with a revised model (elastic spheres with finite volume and attractive forces), which departs from the simple billiard ball model, but which would not have occurred to anyone without the earlier model. The suggestiveness and openendedness of models provide a continuing source of possible applications, extensions, and modifications of theories.

3. *Models are intelligible as units.* Models provide a mental picture whose unity can be more readily understood than that of a set of abstract equations. A model can be grasped as a whole, giving a vivid summary of complex relationships, which is useful in extending and applying the theory as well as in teaching it. Images are creative expressions of imagination in the sciences as well as in the humanities. The intuitive intelligibility of a model is, of course, no guarantee of its validity. Deductions from the theory to which the model leads must be tested carefully against the data, and more often than not the proposed model must be amended or discarded. Models are used to generate promising theories to test by the diverse criteria outlined earlier.

In the quantum theory that has replaced the Bohr model, mechanical models are given up and there are severe limitations on the use of visualizable models. Nevertheless, two basic models, the *wave model* and the *particle model*, underlie the formalisms of quantum theory and suggest ways of correlating theory and experiment. These two basic models cannot be satisfactorily unified (the wave/particle paradox), even though a unified set of equations can be provided in the abstract theory. From the theory we can predict only the probability that a measurement in the atomic or subatomic world will have a particular value; we cannot predict exact values for a measurement. The models are more than a temporary expedient, for they continue to contribute to the interpretation of the mathematical formalism and to the modification of the theory and its extension to new domains.

. . . [C]omplementary models are used despite their problematic status. Bohr formulated the Complementarity Principle, recognizing that "a complete elucidation of one and the same object may require diverse points of view which defy a unique description."[7] He acknowledged the interaction between subject and object and the importance of the particular experimental arrangement. But he also stressed the conceptual limitations of human understanding. We must choose between causal or spatiotemporal descriptions, between wave and particle models, between accurate knowledge of momentum or of position. We have successive and incomplete perspectives that cannot be neatly unified.

Such models and theories clearly cannot be taken as literal descriptions of entities in the world, as classical realism assumed. At the opposite extreme, instrumentalism holds that models and theories are calculating devices whose only function is to allow the correlation and prediction of observations. Instrumentalism sees them as useful intellectual instruments for organizing research and for controlling the world. According to instrumentalists, models and theories do not describe or refer to real entities in the world.

I have elsewhere defended the intermediate position of critical realism.[8] On this view, models and theories are abstract symbol systems, which inadequately and selectively represent particular aspects of the world for specific purposes. This view preserves the scientist's realistic intent while recognizing that models and theories are imaginative human constructs. Models, on this reading, are to be taken seriously but not literally; they are neither literal pictures nor useful fictions but limited and inadequate ways of imagining what is not observable. They make tentative ontological claims that there are entities in the world something like those postulated in the models.

Opponents of realism argue that successive scientific theories are not convergent, cumulative, or progressive. New theories often exhibit radical changes in conceptual framework rather than refinements that preserve and add to earlier concepts. The history of science is said to be littered with theories that were successful and fruitful in their day, but that were later totally rejected rather than being modified—including Ptolemaic astronomy, phlogiston chemistry, catastrophic geology, Lamarckian evolution, caloric heat theory, and ether theories in physics.[9]

But recent years have seen a revival of interest in realism. Many books and articles on the subject have appeared in the last few years.[10] For example, some have pointed out that new theories exhibit *continuity* as well as discontinuity in relation to the theories they replace. Usually some of the concepts in the old theory and much of the data accumulated under its guidance are carried over into the new context. Sometimes the laws of the old theory are actually included in the new theory as limiting cases. Thus the laws of classical mechanics are limiting cases of relativistic laws at low velocities, though the fundamental concepts have been radically redefined. Later theories typically provide a better empirical fit and extend to wider domains, so that one can indeed speak of progress according to the criteria listed earlier.

We have greater confidence in *the existence of a theoretical entity*, such as the electron, if it is linked to many different kinds of phenomena explored in diverse types of experiment. With a new theory, scientists believe they have a better understanding of the structure of the world, not just a more accurate formula for correlating observations. Theoretical concepts are tentative and revisable, but they are taken to characterize and refer to the world. Unless a theory is at least partially true, how can we account for its success in predicting entirely new phenomena with types of observation radically different from those that led to the theory? Science, in short, is at the same time a process of discovery and a venture in human imagination.

The basic assumption of realism is that *existence* is prior to *theorizing*. Constraints on our theorizing arise from structures and relationships already existing in nature. Scientific discoveries are often quite unexpected. Humility before the given is appropriate; we learn from nature in order to set limits on our imagination. While the history of science exhibits no simple convergence or "successive approximation," it does include a body of well-attested theory and data, most of which can be considered trustworthy, even though any part of it is revisable. Can anyone doubt, for example, that we know more about the human body than we did five hundred years ago, even though there is still much to be known, and some of our current ideas may be rejected?

Ernan McMullin defends *a critical realist view of models*, especially those postulating hidden structures. He holds that "a good model gives us insight into real structures, and that the long term success of a theory, in most cases, gives reason to believe that something like the theoretical entities of that theory actually exist."[11] A good model, he says, is not a dispensable temporary expedient but a fruitful and open-ended source of continuing ideas for possible extensions and modifications. Like a poetic metaphor, it offers tentative suggestions for exploring a new domain. A structural model may change as research progresses, McMullin observes, but it also exhibits substantial continuity as the original model is extended. One of his examples is the model of continental drift, which proved inconsistent with geological data but which itself suggested the tectonic plate model—a model supported by more recent evidence concerning midocean rifts and earthquake zones.

Most scientists are incurably realist, but their confidence in the *status of models and theoretical entities* varies among fields and in different historical periods. Models of larger scale and more familiar types of structure tend to be viewed more realistically. A geologist is not likely to doubt the existence of tectonic plates or prehistoric dinosaurs, though neither can be directly observed. In 1866, Mendel postulated hypothetical "units of hereditary transmission," which were later identified as genes in chromosomes and more recently as long segments of DNA. As we move further from familiar objects, instruments greatly extend our powers of direct or indirect observation.

When we get to the strange *subatomic world*, common sense fails us and we cannot visualize what is going on. Quarks behave like nothing familiar to us, and their quantum numbers (arbitrarily named strangeness, charm, top, bottom, and color) specify abstract rules for the ways they combine and interact. Even here . . . our theories are an attempt to represent reality, though microreality is not like the everyday world and ordinary language is inadequate to describe it.

2 Models in religion

Religious models, we have said, lead to beliefs that correlate patterns in human experience. In particular, models of the divine are crucial in the interpretation of religious experience. They represent in images the characteristics and relationships portrayed in narrative form in stories. But models are less conceptually articulated and less systematically developed than beliefs and doctrines, which take the form of propositional statements rather than narratives or images.

Like scientific models, religious models are *analogical*. Religious language often uses imaginative metaphors, symbols, and parables, all of which express analogies. The most frequently used and systematically developed analogies are incorporated in models, such as the model of God as Father. Religious models, too, are *extensible*. A model originating in religious experience and key historical events is extended to interpret other areas of individual and communal experience, and it may be modified in the process. Religious models are also *unitary*; they are grasped as a whole with vividness and immediacy.[12]

As in the scientific case, I defend a *critical realism* that takes religious models seriously but not literally. They are neither literal descriptions of reality nor useful fictions, but human constructs that help us interpret experience by imagining what cannot be observed. The biblical prohibition of graven images or "any likeness" (Exodus 20:4) is both a rejection of idolatry and an acknow-ledgment that God cannot be adequately represented in visual imagery. The sense of awe and mystery associated with numinous experience is an additional safeguard against literalism. But we do not have to go to the opposite extreme and take religious models as psychologically useful fictions whose only function is to express and evoke distinctive ethical attitudes, as some instrumentalists hold.[13] [. . .]

Religious models have additional functions without parallel in science, especially in expressing and evoking distinctive attitudes. We have said that religion is a way of life with practical as well as theoretical goals. The life-orienting and emotional power of religious models and their ability to affect value com-mitments should not be ignored. Models are crucial in the personal transformation and reorientation sought in most religious traditions. Some linguistic analysts and instrumentalists hold that religious language has only these noncognitive functions. I argue, in reply, that such noncognitive functions cannot stand alone because they presuppose cognitive beliefs. Religious traditions do endorse particular attitudes and ways of life, but they also make claims about reality.[14]

In science, models are always ancillary to theories. In religion, however, the models themselves are as important as conceptual beliefs, partly because of their close association with the stories prominent in religious life. Christian worship is based on those stories of creation, the covenant, and especially the life of Christ. The individual participates in communal ritual and liturgy that reenact and refer to portions of these stories. Narratives in dramatic form are more personally involving and evocative than models, which are relatively static, though models are less abstract than concepts. Moreover, biblical stories can often be correlated with our own life stories, which are also narrative in form. Nevertheless, the movement from stories to models to concepts and beliefs is a necessary part of the theological task of critical reflection.

[. . .]

Conclusions

Religion is indeed a way of life. Religious language serves diverse functions, many of which have no parallel in science. It encourages ethical attitudes and behavior. It evokes feelings and emotions. Its typical forms are worship and meditation. Above all, its goal is to effect personal transformation and reorienta-tion (salvation, fulfillment, liberation, or enlightenment). All of these aspects of religion require more total personal involvement than does scientific activity, affecting more diverse aspects of personality. Religion also fills psychological needs, including integration of personality and the envisioning of a larger framework of meaning and purpose. Many of these goals are fulfilled primarily through religious experience, story, and ritual.

In all these functions, the use of language is *noncognitive* and no explicit propositional assertions about reality are made. Yet each function presupposes *cognitive beliefs* and assertions. The appropriateness of a way of life, an ethical norm, a pattern of worship, a particular understanding of salvation, or a framework of meaning depends in each case on beliefs about the character of ultimate reality.

Let us look again at the four criteria [for assessing theories]. . . .

1. *Agreement with Data*. It is sometimes said that the distinctive feature of science is that from theories one can make *predictions*, which can be tested in *controlled experiments*. But not all sciences are predictive and experimental. Geology and astronomy are based on observations rather than experiments; in geology there are no predictions (though aspects of present or past states could have been predicted from earlier states). We have said that evolutionary history could not have been predicted in detail, and only certain portions of evolutionary theory can be tested experimentally. In science, then, we should talk about the *intersubjective testing* of theories against various kinds of data, with all the qualifications suggested earlier about theory-laden data, paradigm-laden theories, and culture-laden paradigms. Moreover, we have seen that because auxiliary hypotheses can usually be adjusted, we must reject any simple notion of verification and falsification.

In religion, the *intersubjective testing* of beliefs does occur within religious communities, and it provides some protection against arbitrariness and individual subjectivity. The interpretation of initiating events, formative experiences, and subsequent individual and communal experiences goes through a long process of testing, filtering, and public validation in the history of the community. Some experiences recur and are accepted as normative, others are reinterpreted, ignored, or discounted. But clearly the testing process is far less rigorous than in science, and religious communities are not as inter-cultural as scientific communities.

2. *Coherence*. Consistency with accepted theories and internal coherence are sought in science. We have learned from Lakatos that the continuity of a research program is maintained by commitment to its central core, which is protected by making modifications in auxiliary hypotheses. Religious beliefs, too, are judged by their consistency with the central core of a tradition, but here the core is correlated with story and ritual. The interpretation of story and ritual involves auxiliary hypotheses that are subject to modification. Anomalies can be tolerated for considerable periods, but the capacity to respond to them creatively without undermining the central core is a sign of the vitality of a

program. Theological formulations are corrigible and have changed substantially in the course of history. New principles of scriptural interpretation and new concepts of God are characteristic of the modern period. More recently, feminist and Third World writers have helped us see some of the biases in the classical tradition. Theology as critical reflection is also concerned about the coherence and systematic interconnection of beliefs.

3. *Scope*. A scientific theory is more secure if it is broad in scope and extensible, correlating diverse types of phenomena in domains different from those in which the theory was first developed. Religious beliefs, too, can be judged by their comprehensiveness in offering a coherent account of diverse kinds of experience, beyond the primary experiences from which they arose. Religious beliefs must be consistent with the well-supported findings of science, and this may sometimes require the reformulation of theological auxiliary hypotheses. . . . Religious beliefs can also contribute to a comprehensive metaphysics, though they are not the only source of such wider integrative frameworks that are broader than either science or religion. Metaphysical assumptions in turn feed back to affect paradigms in religion, as they do in science.

4. *Fertility*. Theories in science are judged by their achievement and promise in contributing to the vitality of an ongoing program over a period of time. In line with the goals of science, scientific fertility refers to the ability to stimulate theoretical development and experimental research. Religion has more diverse goals, so fertility here has many facets. It includes the capacity to stimulate creative theological reflection. But it also includes evidence of power to nourish religious experience and to effect personal transformation. Beyond this, fertility includes evidence of desirable influence on human character and the motivation to sustain ethical action. . . . Criteria for evaluating . . . individual and social consequences are of course strongly paradigm-dependent.

In short, religion cannot claim to be scientific or to be able to conform to the standards of science. But it can exemplify some of the same spirit of inquiry found in science. If theology is critical reflection on the life and thought of the religious community, it is always revisable and corrigible. There are no controlled experiments, but there is a process of testing in the life of the community, and there should be a continual demand that our concepts and beliefs be closely related to what we have experienced. There is no proof, but there is a cumulative case from converging lines of argument. Rational argument in theology is not a single sequence of ideas, like a chain that is as weak as its weakest link. Instead, it is woven of many strands, like a cable many times stronger than its strongest strand. Or, to use an analogy introduced earlier, religious beliefs are like an interlocking network that is not floating freely but is connected at many points to the experience of the community. [. . .]

Notes

1   Several sections of this [essay] are revisions or summaries of portions of two earlier books: Ian G. Barbour, *Issues in Science and Religion* (Englewood Cliffs, NJ: Prentice-Hall, 1966) and *Myths, Models, and Paradigms* (New York: Harper & Row, 1974).

2   Carl G. Hempel, *Philosophy of Natural Science* (Englewood Cliffs, NJ: Prentice-Hall, 1966); Karl R. Popper, *The Logic of Scientific Discovery* (London: Hutchinson's Univ. Library, 1956).

3   W. V. Quine, "Two Dogmas of Empiricism," in his *From a Logical Point of View*, 2d ed. (New York: Harper Torchbooks, 1963).

4   N. R. Hanson, *Patterns of Discovery* (Cambridge: Cambridge Univ. Press, 1958); Michael Polanyi, *Personal Knowledge* (Chicago: Univ. of Chicago Press, 1958).

5   Thomas S. Kuhn, *The Structure of Scientific Revolutions*, 2d ed. (Chicago: Univ. of Chicago Press, 1970).

6   In *Myths, Models, and Paradigms*, chap. 3, I discuss writings on scientific models by Mary Hesse, Max Black, Richard Braithwaite, Peter Achinstein, and others. See also W. H. Leatherdale, *The Role of Analogy, Model and Metaphor in Science* (New York: American Elsevier, 1974).

7   Niels Bohr, *Atomic Theory and the Description of Nature* (Cambridge: Cambridge Univ. Press, 1934), p. 96.

8   See Barbour, *Issues in Science and Religion*, pp. 162–74; also *Myths, Models, and Paradigms*, pp. 34–38.

9   Larry Laudan, "A Confutation of Convergent Realism," in *Scientific Realism*, ed. Jarret Leplin (Berkeley and Los Angeles: Univ. of California Press, 1984).

10   Ian Hacking, *Representing and Intervening* (Cambridge: Cambridge Univ. Press, 1983); Michael Devitt, *Realism and Truth* (Princeton: Princeton Univ. Press, 1984); James T. Cushing, C. F. Delaney, and Gary Gutting, eds., *Science and Reality* (Notre Dame: Univ. of Notre Dame Press, 1984); Ron Harré, *Varieties of Realism* (Oxford: Basil Blackwell, 1986); and Hilary Putnam, *The Many Faces of Realism* (LaSalle, IL: Open Court, 1987).

11   Ernan McMullin, "A Case for Scientific Realism," in *Scientific Realism*, ed. Leplin, p. 39.

12   In *Myths, Models, and Paradigms*, chap. 4, I discuss the writings of Ian Ramsey and Frederick Ferré on models in religion, and I develop a theory of religious models. There is some discussion of models in Earl MacCormac, *Metaphor and Myth in Science and Religion* (Durham, NC: Duke Univ. Press, 1976). [See also Janet Soskice, *Metaphor and Religious Language* (Oxford: Clarendon Press, 1985).]

13   Richard Braithwaite, *An Empiricist's View of the Nature of Religious Belief* (Cambridge: Cambridge Univ. Press, 1955); see William H. Austin, *The Relevance of Natural Science to Theology* (London: Macmillan, 1976), chap. 3.

14   Barbour, *Myths, Models, and Paradigms*, pp. 56–60.

PART TWO

Evolutionary theory

INTRODUCTION TO PART TWO

THE SELECTIONS IN THIS SECTION examine Darwin's theory of evolution, beginning with extracts from Chapter IV, "Natural Selection," and Chapter XIV, "Recapitulation and Conclusion" from Darwin's *On the Origins of Species by Means of Natural Selection*, first published in 1859. After exploring at the outset of his book variation brought about by domestic breeding and observing the variability of species in nature, Darwin introduces the idea of the struggle for existence and proposes natural selection as the mechanism of evolution. In the extracts included here he assembles these elements into a unified theory. As he maintains, variations among species exist; these variations can be inherited; some variations confer an advantage in the struggle for existence; those individuals with such an advantage will survive, while others will be destroyed. This "principle of preservation" he labels "natural selection." Instead of the independent creation of each species, he posits a long history of descent with modification from a common ancestor. To illustrate this theory, Darwin draws on the image of a branching tree and asks us, in what has become a famous passage, to contemplate the "grandeur in this view of life."

The second piece in this unit is taken from biologist Francisco J. Ayala's article "The Evolution of Life: An Overview," which appeared in *Evolutionary and Molecular Biology: Scientific Perspectives on Divine Action,* edited by Ayala, Robert John Russell, and William R. Stoeger. Ayala opens his study with an examination of historical precedents to Darwin's theory of evolution. He then briefly surveys Darwin's life and thought, focusing on how Darwin proposed natural selection to account for the adaptive organization of living beings. According to Ayala, Darwin was thus supplying an alternative explanation for the "appearance of purpose or design" in the universe, which had generally been attributed to the plan of an intelligent creator. As an example of the latter perspective, Ayala cites the watchmaker argument of theologian William Paley in his *Natural Theology*, first published in 1802. A selection from Paley's work is included in Part Four of this anthology.

Ayala examines the reception of Darwin's ideas in his day as well as the eventual modifications of Darwin's views brought about by discoveries in the disciplines of genetics and molecular biology, a fusion that has come to be known as the "neo-Darwinian synthesis." He points out that the theory of evolution is at the core of a variety of contemporary scientific disciplines, including genetics, biochemistry, neurobiology, physiology, and ecology. The selection concludes with Ayala's identification of three distinct though related issues: the fact of evolution; the details of evolutionary history; and the mechanisms by which evolution occurs. He claims that while the first is established with utmost certainty, the second and third are still matters of active scientific investigation. In particular, challenges to an over-emphasis on natural selection have come from nonselectionist and nonadaptationist data from the disciplines of population genetics, developmental biology, and paleontology.

In his article "Is There a Limit to Our Knowledge of Evolution?" which was published in the journal *BioScience*, Michael Ruse brings the insights of a philosopher to this final issue raised by Ayala. Acknowledging that evolution stands under a threat from biblical fundamentalists and that the mechanism of evolution posited by Darwin, natural selection, is attacked from many scientific quarters, Ruse offers his assessment of what we do and do not know about evolution today. Similar to Ayala, Ruse suggests a threefold division of the fact of evolution, the paths taken in the process, and the mechanisms of evolution, and he explores the limits of our knowledge in each area.

To the query, "is the fact of evolution securely known?" Ruse replies with a resounding "yes." He responds to those who insist "evolution is only a theory, not a fact" with observations about the nature of scientific method. Mirroring Ian Barbour's observations in "The Structures of Science and Religion" in Part One of this collection, Ruse states that ultimate certainty can never be achieved in science, which remains tentative. Nevertheless, in science "one can achieve as much certainty as any reasonable person could demand." Arguing on the grounds of a "consilience of inductions," Ruse maintains that the evidence supplied by many scientific disciplines in support of evolution leads one to conclude confidently that evolution, descent with modification, is a fact established "beyond reasonable doubt."

Concerning the paths taken in evolution, Ruse affirms that while the overall pattern of evolution seems fairly well established, much is not known about these "phylogenies." After detailing what he considers to be items of evolution that "seem now to have been established, as firmly as any reasonably minded person could demand or wish," he explores various gaps in our knowledge of specific pathways. Because of these uncertainties he foresees that new discoveries in a variety of scientific fields will fuel continuing debates about these evolutionary pathways.

Ruse finds the question of evolutionary mechanisms the most controversial issue among the three that he examines. Given the foundational role of selection in Darwin's theory, contemporary debate often focuses on how far selection extends, how it operates, and the nature of the alternatives. Ruse surveys differing views on these issues and addresses as well the theory of "punctuated equilibria," which sees evolution going in fits and starts, that some have proposed as a challenge to the gradualism of Darwinian evolution. He concludes that while there is much evidence for the power of selection, the scientific debates about just how effective a component selection is will continue.

Chapter 5

Charles Darwin

ON THE ORIGIN OF SPECIES

Natural selection

IF **DURING THE LONG** course of ages and under varying conditions of life, organic beings vary at all in the several parts of their organisation, and I think this cannot be disputed; if there be, owing to the high geometrical powers of increase of each species, at some age, season, or year, a severe struggle for life, and this certainly cannot be disputed; then, considering the infinite complexity of the relations of all organic beings to each other and to their conditions of existence, causing an infinite diversity in structure, constitution, and habits, to be advantageous to them, I think it would be a most extraordinary fact if no variation ever had occurred useful to each being's own welfare, in the same way as so many variations have occurred useful to man. But if variations useful to any organic being do occur, assuredly individuals thus characterised will have the best chance of being preserved in the struggle for life; and from the strong principle of inheritance they will tend to produce offspring similarly characterised. This principle of preservation, I have called, for the sake of brevity, Natural Selection. Natural selection, on the principle of qualities being inherited at corresponding ages, can modify the egg, seed, or young, as easily as the adult. Amongst many animals, sexual selection will give its aid to ordinary selection, by assuring to the most vigorous and best adapted males the greatest number of offspring.

Sexual selection will also give characters useful to the males alone, in their struggles with other males.

Whether natural selection has really thus acted in nature, in modifying and adapting the various forms of life to their several conditions and stations, must be judged of by the general tenour and balance of evidence given in the following chapters. But we already see how it entails extinction; and how largely extinction has acted in the world's history, geology plainly declares. Natural selection, also, leads to divergence of character; for more living beings can be supported on the same area the more they diverge in structure, habits, and constitution, of which we see proof by looking at the inhabitants of any small spot or at naturalised productions. Therefore during the modification of the descendants of any one species, and during the incessant struggle of all species to increase in numbers, the more diversified these descendants become, the better will be their chance of succeeding in the battle of life. Thus the small differences distinguishing varieties of the same species, will steadily tend to increase till they come to equal the greater differences between species of the same genus, or even of distinct genera.

We have seen that it is the common, the widely-diffused, and widely-ranging species, belonging to the larger genera, which vary most; and these will tend to transmit to their modified offspring that superiority which now makes them dominant in their own countries. Natural selection, as has just been remarked, leads to divergence of character and to much extinction of the less improved and intermediate forms of life. On these principles, I believe, the nature of the affinities of all organic beings may be explained. It is a truly wonderful fact – the wonder of which we are apt to overlook from familiarity – that all animals and all plants throughout all time and space should be related to each other in group subordinate to group, in the manner which we everywhere behold – namely, varieties of the same species most closely related together, species of the same genus less closely and unequally related together, forming sections and sub-genera, species of distinct genera much less closely related, and genera related in different degrees, forming sub-families, families, orders, sub-classes, and classes. The several subordinate groups in any class cannot be ranked in a single file, but seem rather to be clustered round points, and these round other points, and so on in almost endless cycles. On the view that each species has been independently created, I can see no explanation of this great fact in the classification of all organic beings; but, to the best of my judgment, it is explained through inheritance and the complex action of natural selection, entailing extinction and divergence of character, as we have seen illustrated in the diagram.

The affinities of all the beings of the same class have sometimes been represented by a great tree. I believe this simile largely speaks the truth. The green and budding twigs may represent existing species; and those produced during each former year may represent the long succession of extinct species. At each period of growth all the growing twigs have tried to branch out on all sides, and to overtop and kill the surrounding twigs and branches, in the same manner as species and groups of species have tried to overmaster other species in the great battle for life. The limbs divided into great branches, and these into lesser and lesser branches, were themselves once, when the tree was small, budding twigs; and this connexion of the former and present buds by ramifying branches may well represent the classification of all extinct and living species in groups subordinate to groups. Of the many twigs which flourished when the tree was a mere bush, only two or three, now grown into great branches, yet survive and bear all the other branches; so with the species which lived during long-past geological periods, very few now have living and modified descendants. From the first growth of the tree, many a limb and branch has decayed and dropped off; and these lost branches of various sizes may represent those whole orders, families, and genera which have now no living representatives, and which are known to us only from having been found in a fossil state. As we here and there see a thin straggling branch springing from a fork low down in a tree, and which by some chance has been favoured and is still alive on its summit, so we occasionally see an animal like the Ornithorhynchus or Lepidosiren, which in some small degree connects by its affinities two large branches of life, and which has apparently been saved from fatal competition by having inhabited a protected station. As buds give rise by growth to fresh buds, and these, if vigorous, branch out and overtop on all sides many a feebler branch, so by generation I believe it has been with the great Tree of Life, which fills with its dead and broken branches the crust of the earth, and covers the surface with its ever branching and beautiful ramifications.

[. . .]

Recapitulation and conclusion

It is interesting to contemplate an entangled bank, clothed with many plants of many kinds, with birds singing on the bushes, with various insects flitting about, and with worms crawling through the damp earth, and to reflect that these elaborately constructed forms, so different from each other, and dependent on each other in so complex a manner, have all been produced by laws acting around us. These laws, taken in the largest sense, being Growth with Reproduction; Inheritance which is almost implied by reproduction; Variability from the indirect and direct action of the external conditions of life, and from use and disuse; a Ratio of Increase so high as to lead to a Struggle for Life, and as a consequence to Natural Selection, entailing Divergence of Character and the Extinction of less-improved forms. Thus, from the war of nature, from famine and death, the most exalted object which we are capable of conceiving, namely, the production of the higher animals, directly follows. There is grandeur in this view of life, with its several powers, having been originally breathed into a few forms or into one; and that, whilst this planet has gone cycling on according to the fixed law of gravity, from so simple a beginning endless forms most beautiful and most wonderful have been, and are being, evolved.

Chapter 6

Francisco J. Ayala

THE EVOLUTION OF LIFE: AN OVERVIEW

1 Introduction

THE GREAT RUSSIAN-AMERICAN geneticist and evolutionist Theodosius Dobzhansky wrote in 1973 that "Nothing in biology makes sense except in the light of evolution." The evolution of organisms, that is, their common descent with modification from simple ancestors that lived many million years ago, is at the core of genetics, biochemistry, neurobiology, physiology, ecology, and other biological disciplines, and makes sense of the emergence of new infectious diseases and other matters of public health. The evolution of organisms is universally accepted by biological scientists, while the mechanisms of evolution are still actively investigated and are the subject of debate among scientists.

The nineteenth-century English naturalist, Charles Darwin, argued that organisms come about by evolution, and he provided a scientific explanation, essentially correct but incomplete, of how evolution occurs and why it is that organisms have features—such as wings, eyes, and kidneys—clearly structured to serve specific functions. Natural selection was the fundamental concept in his explanation. Genetics, a science born in the twentieth century, revealed in detail how natural selection works and led to the development of the modern theory of evolution. Since the 1960s a related scientific discipline, molecular biology, has advanced enormously our knowledge of biological evolution and has made it possible to investigate detailed problems that seemed completely out of reach a few years earlier—for example, how similar the genes of humans, chimpanzees, and gorillas are (they differ in about 1 or 2 percent of the units that make up the genes.)

The diversity of living species is staggering. More than two million existing species of plants and animals have been named and described: many more remain to be discovered, at least ten million according to most estimates. What is impressive is not just the numbers but also the incredible heterogeneity in size, shape, and ways of life: from lowly bacteria, less than one thousandth of a millimeter in diameter, to the stately sequoias of California, rising 300 feet (100 meters) above the ground and weighing several thousand tons; from microorganisms living in the hot springs of Yellowstone National Park at temperatures near the boiling point of water—some like *Pyrolobus fumarii* are able to grow at more than 100° C (212° F)—to fungi and algae thriving on the ice masses of Antarctica and in saline pools at −23° C (−73° F); from the strange worm-like creatures discovered in dark ocean depths at thousands of feet below the surface to spiders and larkspur plants existing on Mt. Everest nearly 20,000 feet above sea level.

These variations on life are the outcome of the evolutionary process. All organisms are related by descent from common ancestors. Humans and other mammals are descended from shrew-like creatures that lived more than 150 million years ago; mammals, birds, reptiles, amphibians, and fishes share as ancestors small worm-like creatures that lived in the world's oceans 600 million years ago; plants and animals are derived from bacteria-like micro-organisms that originated more than three billion years ago. Because of biological evolution, lineages of organisms change through time; diversity arises because lineages that descend from common ancestors diverge through the generations as they become adapted to different ways of life. . . .

Contrary to popular opinion, neither the term nor the idea of biological evolution began with Charles Darwin and his foremost work *On the Origin of Species by Means of Natural Selection* (1859). The *Oxford English Dictionary* (1933) tells us that the word *evolution*, to unfold or open out, derives from the Latin *evolvere*, which applied to the "unrolling of a book." It first appeared in the English language in 1647 in a non-biological connection, and it became widely used in English for all sorts of progressions from simpler beginnings. Evolution was first used as a biological term in 1670 to describe the changes observed in the maturation of insects. However, it was not until the 1873 edition of *The Origin of Species* that Darwin first used the term. He had earlier used the expression "descent with modification," which is still a good brief definition of biological evolution.

A distinction must be drawn at the outset between the questions 1) *whether* and 2) *how* biological evolution happened. The first refers to the finding, now supported by an overwhelming body of evidence, that descent with modification has occurred during some 3.5 billion years of the Earth's history. The second refers to the theory explaining how those changes came about. The mechanisms accounting for these changes are still undergoing investigation; the currently favored theory is an extensively modified version of Darwinian natural selection.

2 Early ideas about evolution

Explanations for the origin of the world, humans, and other creatures are found in all human cultures. Traditional Judaism, Christianity, and Islam explain the origin of living beings and their adaptations to their environments—wings, gills, hands, flowers—as the handiwork of an omniscient God. The philosophers of ancient Greece had their own creation accounts. Anaximander proposed that animals could be transformed from one kind into another, and Empedocles speculated that they could be made of various combinations of preexisting parts. Closer to modern evolutionary ideas were the proposals of early Church Fathers like Gregory of Nazianzus and Augustine, who maintained that not all species of plants and animals were created as such by God; rather some had developed in historical times from creatures created earlier by God. Their motivation was not biological but religious. Some species must have come into existence only after the Noachian Flood because it would have been impossible to hold representatives of all species in a single vessel such as Noah's Ark.

Christian theologians of the Middle Ages did not directly explore the notion that organisms may change by natural processes, but the matter was, usually incidentally, considered as a possibility by many, including Albertus Magnus and his student Thomas Aquinas. Aquinas concluded, after detailed discussion, that the development of living creatures like maggots and flies from non-living matter like decaying meat was not incompatible with Christian faith or philosophy. But he left it to scientists to decide whether this actually happened.

In the eighteenth century, Pierre-Louis Moreau de Maupertuis proposed the spontaneous generation and extinction of organisms as part of his theory of origins, but he advanced no theory about the possible transformation of one species into another through knowable, natural causes. One of the greatest naturalists of the time, Georges-Louis Leclerc (Buffon) explicitly considered—and rejected—the possible descent of several distinct kinds of organisms from a common ancestor. However, he made the claim that organisms arise from organic molecules by spontaneous generation, so that there could be as many kinds of animals and plants as there are viable combinations of organic molecules.

Erasmus Darwin, grandfather of Charles Darwin, offered in his *Zoonomia or the Laws of Organic Life* some evolutionary speculations, but they were not systematically developed and had no real influence on subsequent theories. The Swedish botanist Carolus Linnaeus devised the hierarchical system of plant and animal classification that is still in use in a modernized form. Although he insisted on the fixity of species, his classification system eventually contributed much to the acceptance of the concept of common descent.

The great French naturalist Jean-Baptiste Lamarck held the view that living organisms represent a progression, with humans as the highest form. In his *Philosophical Zoology*, published in 1809, the year in which Charles Darwin was born, he proposed the first broad theory of evolution. Organisms evolve through eons of time from lower to higher forms, a process still going on and always culminating in human beings. As organisms become adapted to their environments through their habits, modifications occur. Use of an organ or structure reinforces it; disuse leads to obliteration. The characteristics acquired by use and disuse, according to this theory, would be inherited. This assumption, later called the inheritance of acquired characteristics, was thoroughly disproved in the twentieth century. The notion that the same organisms repeatedly evolve in a fixed sequence of transitions has also been disproved.

3 Darwin's theory

Charles Darwin is appropriately considered the founder of the modern theory of evolution. The son and grandson of physicians, he enrolled as a medical student at the University of Edinburgh. After two years, however, he left to study at Cambridge University and prepare to become a clergyman. He was not an exceptional student, but he was deeply interested in natural history. On December 27, 1831, a few months after his graduation from Cambridge, he sailed as a naturalist aboard the HMS Beagle on a round-the-world trip that lasted until October 1836. Darwin was often able to disembark for extended trips ashore to collect specimens.

In Argentina he studied fossil bones from large extinct mammals. In the Galápagos Islands he observed numerous species of finches. These are among the events credited with stimulating Darwin's interest in how different species arise and become extinct. In 1859 he published *The Origin of Species*, a treatise providing extensive evidence for the evolution of organisms and proposing natural selection as the key process determining its course. He published many other books as well, notably *The Descent of Man and Selection in Relation to Sex* (1871), which provides an evolutionary account of human origins.

The origin of the Earth's living things, with their marvelous contrivances for adaptation, were generally attributed to the design of an omniscient God. In the nineteenth century, Christian theologians had argued that the presence of design, so evident in living beings, demonstrates the existence of a supreme Creator. The British theologian William Paley in his *Natural Theology* (1802) used natural history, physiology, and other contemporary knowledge to elaborate this argument from design. If a person should find a watch, even in an uninhabited desert, Paley contended, the intricate design and harmony of its many parts would force him to conclude that it had been created by a skilled watchmaker. How much more intricate and perfect in design is the human eye, Paley went on, with its transparent lens, its retina placed at the precise distance for forming a distinct image, and its large nerve transmitting signals to the brain.

Natural selection was proposed by Darwin primarily to account for the adaptive organizations of living beings: it is a process that promotes or maintains adaptation and, thus, gives the appearance of purpose or design.[1] Evolutionary change through time and evolutionary diversification (multiplication of species) are not directly promoted by natural selection, but they often ensue as by-products of natural selection as it fosters adaptation to different environments. Darwin's theory of natural selection is summarized in the *Origin of Species* as follows:

> As more individuals are produced than can possibly survive, there must in every case be a struggle for existence, either one individual with another of the same species, or with the individuals of distinct species, or with the physical conditions of life . . . Can it, then, be thought improbable, seeing that variations useful to man have undoubtedly occurred, that other variations useful in some way to each being in the great and complex battle of life, should sometimes occur in the course of thousands of generations? If such do occur, can we doubt (remembering that many more individuals are born than can possibly survive) that individuals having any advantage, however slight, over others, would have the best chance of surviving and of procreating their kind? On the other hand, we may feel sure that any variation in the least degree injurious would be rigidly destroyed. This preservation of favorable variations and the rejection of injurious variations, I call Natural Selection.[2]

The publication of the *Origin of Species* produced considerable public excitement. Scientists, politicians, clergymen, and notables of all kinds read and discussed the book, defending or deriding Darwin's ideas. The most visible actor in the controversies immediately following publication was T. H. Huxley, knows as "Darwin's bulldog," who defended the theory of evolution with articulate and sometimes mordant words on public occasions as well as in numerous writings. Serious scientific controversies also arose, first in Britain and then on the Continent and in the United States.

One occasional participant in the discussion was the naturalist Alfred Russel Wallace, who had independently discovered natural selection and had sent a short manuscript to Darwin from the Malay archipelago. A contemporary of Darwin with considerable influence during the latter part of the nineteenth and early twentieth centuries was Herbert Spencer. He was a philosopher rather than a biologist, but he became an energetic proponent of evolutionary ideas, popularized a number of slogans, like "survival of the fittest" (which was taken up by Darwin in later editions of the Origin), and engaged in social and metaphysical speculations. His ideas considerably damaged proper understanding and acceptance of the theory of evolution by natural selection. Most pernicious was Spencer's crude extension of the notion of "struggle for existence" to human economic and social life that became known as social Darwinism.

The most serious difficulty facing Darwin's evolutionary theory was the lack of an adequate theory of inheritance that would account for the preservation through the generations of the variations on which natural selection was supposed to act. Current theories of "blending inheritance" proposed that the characteristics of parents became averaged in the offspring. As Darwin became aware, "blending inheritance" could not account for the conservation of variations, because halving the differences among variant offspring would rapidly reduce the original variation to the average of the preexisting characteristics.

Mendelian genetics provided the missing link in Darwin's argument. About the time the Origin of Species was published, the Augustinian monk Gregor Mendel was performing a long series of experiments with peas in the garden of his monastery in Brünn (now Brno, Czech Republic). These experiments and the analysis of their results are an example of masterly scientific method. Mendel's theory accounts for biological inheritance through particulate factors (genes) inherited one from each parent, which do not mix or blend but segregate in the formation of the sex cells, or gametes. Mendel's discoveries, however, remained unknown to Darwin and, indeed, did not become generally known until 1900, when they were simultaneously rediscovered by a number of scientists on the Continent.

Darwinism, in the latter part of the nineteenth century, faced an alternative evolutionary theory known as neo-Lamarckism. This hypothesis shared with Lamarck's the importance of use and disuse in the development and obliteration of organs, and it added the notion that the environment acts directly on organic structures, which would explain their adaptation to their environments and ways of life. Adherents of this theory discarded natural selection as an explanation for adaptation to the environment. Prominent among the defenders of natural selection was the German biologist August Weismann, who in the 1880s published his germ-plasm theory. He distinguished two components in the make up an organism: the soma, which comprises most body parts and organs, and the germ-plasm, which contains the cells that give rise to the gametes and hence to progeny. The radical separation between germ and soma prompted Weismann to assert that inheritance of acquired characteristics was impossible, and it opened the way for his championship of natural selection as the only major process that would account for biological evolution. The formulation of the evolutionary theory championed by Weismann and his followers toward the end of the nineteenth century became known as "neo-Darwinism."

4 The modern theory of evolution

The rediscovery in 1900 of Mendel's theory of heredity ushered in an emphasis on the role of heredity in evolution. Hugo de Vries in the Netherlands proposed a new theory of evolution known as mutationism, which essentially did away with natural selection as a major evolutionary process. According to de Vries (joined by other geneticists such as William Bateson in England), there are two kinds of variation that take place in organisms. One is the "ordinary" variability observed among individuals of a species, which is of no lasting consequence in evolution because, according to de Vries, it could not "lead to a transgression of the species border even under conditions of the most stringent and continued selection." The other consists of the changes brought about by mutations, spontaneous alterations of genes that yield large modifications of the organism and gave rise to new species. Mutationism was opposed by many naturalists, and in particular by the so-called biometricians, led by Karl Pearson, who defended Darwinian natural selection as the major cause of evolution through the cumulative effects of small, continuous, individual variations.

Arguments between mutationists (also referred to at the time as Mendelians) and biometricians approached a resolution in the 1920s and '30s through the theoretical work of geneticists. They used mathematical arguments to show, first, that continuous variation (in such characteristics as size, number of eggs laid, and the like) could be explained by Mendel's laws; and second, that natural selection acting cumulatively on small variations could yield major evolutionary changes in form and function. Distinguished members of this group of theoretical geneticists were R. A. Fisher and J. B. S. Haldane in Britain and Sewall Wright in the United States. Their work provided a theoretical framework for the integration of genetics into Darwin's theory of natural selection. Yet their work had a limited impact on contemporary biologists because it was almost exclusively theoretical, formulated in mathematical language and with little empirical corroboration. A major breakthrough came in 1937 with the publication of *Genetics and the Origin of Species* by Theodosius Dobzhansky, a Russian-born American naturalist and experimental geneticist.

Dobzhansky advanced a reasonably comprehensive account of the evolutionary process in genetic terms, laced with experimental evidence supporting the theoretical argument. *Genetics and the Origin of Species* may be considered the most important landmark in the formulation of what came to be known as the synthetic theory of evolution, effectively combining Darwinian natural selection and Mendelian genetics. It had an enormous impact on naturalists and experimental biologists, who rapidly embraced the new understanding of the evolutionary process as one of genetic change in populations. Interest in evolutionary studies was greatly stimulated, and contributions to the theory soon began to follow, extending the synthesis of genetics and natural selection to a variety of biological fields. Other writers who importantly contributed to the formulation of the synthetic theory were the zoologists Ernst Mayr and Sir Julian Huxley, the paleontologist George G. Simpson, and the botanist George Ledyard Stebbins. By 1950 acceptance of Darwin's theory of evolution by natural selection was universal among biologists, and the synthetic theory had become widely adopted.

Since 1950, the most important line of investigation has been the application of molecular biology to evolutionary studies. In 1953 James Watson and Francis Crick discovered the structure of DNA (deoxyribonucleic acid), the hereditary material contained in the chromosomes of every cell's nucleus. The genetic information is contained within the sequence of components (nucleotides) that make up the long chainlike DNA molecules, very much in the same manner as semantic information is contained in the sequence of letters in an English text. This information determines the sequence of amino acids in the proteins, including the enzymes that carry out the organism's life processes. Comparisons of the amino-acid sequences of proteins in different species provides quantitatively precise measures of species divergence, a considerable improvement over the typically qualitative evaluations obtained by comparative anatomy and other evolutionary subdisciplines.

In 1968 the Japanese geneticist Motoo Kimura proposed the neutrality theory of molecular evolution, which assumes that at the level of DNA and protein sequence many changes are adaptively neutral and have little or no effect on the molecule's function. If the neutrality theory is correct, there should be a "molecular clock" of evolution; that is, the degree of divergence between species in amino acid or nucleotide sequence would provide a reliable estimate of the time since their divergence. This would make possible a reconstruction of evolutionary history that would reveal the order of branching of different lineages, such as those leading to humans, chimpanzees, and orang-utans, as well as the time in the past when the lineages split from one another. During the 1970s and '80s it gradually became clear that the molecular clock is not exact; nevertheless, it has become a reliable source of evidence for reconstructing a history of evolution. In the 1990s, the techniques of DNA cloning and sequencing have provided new and more powerful means of investigating evolution at the molecular level.

Important discoveries in the earth sciences and ecology during the second half of the twentieth century have also greatly advanced our understanding of the theory of evolution. The science of plate tectonics has shown that the configuration and position of the continents and oceans are dynamic, rather than static, features of the Earth. Oceans grow and shrink, while continents break into fragments or coalesce into larger masses. The continents move across the Earth's surface at rates of a few centimeters a year, and over millions of years of geological history this profoundly alters the face of the Earth, causing major climatic changes along the way. These previously unsuspected massive modifi-cations of the planet's environments have of necessity been reflected in the evolutionary history of life. Biogeography, the evolutionary study of plant and animal distribution, has been revolutionized by the knowledge, for example, that Africa and South America were part of a single landmass some 200 million years ago and that the Indian subcontinent was not connected with Asia until recent geologic times. The study of the interactions of organisms with their environments, known as the discipline of ecology, has evolved from descriptive studies—"natural history"—into a vigorous biological discipline with a strong mathematical component, both in the development of theoretical models and in the collection and analysis of quantitative data. Another active field of research in evolutionary biology is evolutionary ethology, the study of animal behavior. Sociobiology, the evolutionary study of social behavior, is perhaps the most active subfield of ethology and, because of its extension to human societies, the most controversial.

5 The impact of evolutionary theory

Three different, though related, issues have been the main subjects of evolutionary investigations: 1) the fact of evolution; that is, that organisms are related by common descent with modification; 2) evolutionary history; that is, the details of when lineages split from one another and of the changes that occurred in each lineage; and 3) the mechanisms or processes by which evolutionary change occurs.

The fact of evolution is the most fundamental issue and the one established with utmost certainty. Darwin gathered much evidence in its support, but the evidence has accumulated continuously ever since, derived from all biological disciplines. As Pope John Paul II has noted, "It is indeed remarkable that this theory [of evolution] has been progressively accepted by researchers, following a series of discoveries in various fields of knowledge. The convergence, neither sought nor fabricated, of the results of work that was conducted independently is in itself a significant argument in favor of this theory."[3] Indeed, the evolutionary origin of organisms is today a scientific conclusion established with the kind of certainty attributable to such scientific concepts as the roundness of the Earth, the heliocentric motions of the planets, and the molecular composition of matter. This degree of certainty beyond reasonable doubt is what is implied when biologists say that evolution is a "fact"; the evolutionary origin of organisms is accepted by virtually every biologist.

The second and third issues go much beyond the general affirmation that organisms evolve. The theory of evolution seeks to ascertain the evolutionary relationships between particular organisms and the events of evolutionary history, as well as to explain how and why evolution takes place. These are matters of active scientific investigation. Many conclusions are well established; for example, that the chimpanzee and gorilla are more closely related to humans than is any of those three species to the baboon or other monkeys; or that natural selection explains the adaptive configuration of such features as the human eye and the wings of birds. Some other matters are less certain, others are conjectural, and still others—such as precisely when life originated on earth and the characteristics of the first living things—remain largely unresolved. [. . .]

Notes

1   See my "Darwin's Devolution: Design Without Designer," [in *Evolutionary and Molecular Biology*, eds. Robert John Russell, et al., (Vatican Observatory Foundation, 1998), pp. 101–116.]

2   Charles Darwin, *Origin of Species* (New York: Avenel Books, 1979), 117, 130–31.

3   Message to the Pontifical Academy of Sciences on 22 October 1996. . . .

Chapter 7

Michael Ruse

IS THERE A LIMIT TO OUR KNOWLEDGE OF EVOLUTION?

CHARLES DARWIN DIED just over 100 years ago, in 1882, 23 years after he published his major evolutionary work, *On the Origin of Species by Means of Natural Selection* (1859). Darwin was not the first to argue for evolution—gradual descent of all organisms from "one or a few forms"—but it was he more than anyone who made the doctrine respectable and plausible (Ruse 1979).

Today, however, evolution stands under great threat from Biblical fundamentalists (Eldredge 1982, Futuyma 1983, Kitcher 1982, Newell 1982). And, in a different way, the adequacy of the mechanism that Darwin himself proposed for evolution, natural selection, has been strongly attacked from many different quarters (Gould 1980, Popper 1974, and in virtually every issue of *Systematic Zoology*). It seems, therefore, peculiarly appropriate to stand back for a moment and assess the extent of our knowledge of evolution and the extent to which we can hope for further knowledge.

In thinking of evolution, it is convenient to make a three-fold division. First, there is what we might call the putative fact or happening of evolution, the claim that organisms did not arrive here on earth miraculously, but by a process of descent. Second, there is the question of the paths taken in the process, what evolutionists call phylogenies. Did birds evolve via the dinosaurs, or directly from more primitive organisms? Third, there is the matter of the mechanism of evolution: the causes behind the process. Given

Darwin's seminal contributions, this question often becomes one of deciding just how far selection extends, how it operates, and the nature of the alternatives.

Fact. Paths. Mechanisms. These are not three entirely separate issues. Paths and mechanisms presuppose the fact of evolution. But, for the purposes of exposition, it is convenient to separate out the three issues.

Is the fact of evolution securely known?

In the development of scientific theories, there seems always to be the prospect of more work and more discoveries. For instance, in physics one deals with ever-smaller entities, and further discoveries seem constrained only by the rising costs (Rescher 1978). But, as far as historical facts are concerned this infinite prospect does not seem to apply to evolution. Either it occurred, or it did not. Therefore, in at least one sense, one could surely establish the fact, once and for all.

However, one does encounter difficulty at another level, because of the temporal dimension to evolution. No one was around to see the evolution of organisms from the beginnings to the sophisticated forms we see about us today. There are those, particularly the so-called scientific creationists, who argue that this is the end of the matter. Without eyewitnesses, they claim, any talk of origins is but a matter of faith. Scientific knowledge is impossible. Claims about evolution are no less religious than claims about Genesis (Gish 1973, Morris 1974).

Outside the creationist movement, few would go so far. Nevertheless, many people feel that there is something a bit "iffy" about evolution. A common complaint is that "evolution is only a theory, not a fact." It is felt that claims about evolution are somewhat on a par with speculations about John F. Kennedy's assassination. Indeed, even some professional biologists feel a little this way. For instance, Colin Patterson, a deservedly well-known ichthyologist at the British Museum, allows only that evolution is "neither fully scientific, like physics, for example, nor unscientific, like history" (Patterson 1978, p. 146). And this is a sentiment shared by others (Ruse 1982).

In response, two things need to be said. First, in some ultimate sense it is true that logical certainty can never be achieved in science. There is always the possibility, at some level, that one might be mistaken. In this sense, if you like, all science is tentative. If you doubt this, remember how certain the early Victorians were about the essential truth of Newtonian physics. Some even went so far as to "prove" that Newton's laws are *a priori* necessary.

But, second, let it also be noted that in science one can achieve as much certainty as any reasonable person could demand. By this, I mean as much certainty as any of us ask in everyday life. The metaphor I like is one borrowed from the law. A jury is told to convict, if the guilt seems established "beyond reasonable doubt." There is no demand that the guilt be put beyond all logical possibility. Similar standards do (and should) apply in science. It is "beyond reasonable doubt" that the earth goes round the sun and that water is H_2O (Ruse 1973). In a very strong sense of "know," we know that these are facts. (Note that this sense of knowledge is compatible with tentativeness, of the kind mentioned above. Even though we find a person guilty "beyond reasonable doubt," it could still be that new evidence would force a reopening of the case.)

Now, pushing the metaphor a little further, why would one find someone guilty "beyond reasonable doubt"? Obviously eyewitness testimony would count very heavily. But, suppose there was none. Then one would have to work by circumstantial evidence: Lord Rake was found dead in his library with a dagger through his heart. He was stabbed by a left-handed man, and the butler is left-handed. He was stabbed with an oriental knife, and the butler's parents spent years in China as missionaries. He was a notorious libertine, and the butler's daughter is pregnant. And so forth, and so forth. The evidence taken as a whole points overwhelmingly to the butler's guilt.

To philosophers, this form of argumentation is very familiar. It is what the 19th century man of science William Whewell (1840) called a "consilience of inductions." And, possibly the best consilience one can find in science is that pointing to evolution. Biological phenomenon after biological phenomenon converges on evolution: Why are homologies so common? Why do we have such similar bone structures between the functionally different arm of man, forelimb of horse, wing of bird, flipper of whale? Because of evolution! Why are embryos (e.g., man and dog) so similar, when adults are so different? Because of evolution! Why are the facts of biogeographical distribution so distinctive? Why would a group of islands like the Galapagos archipelago have no less than fourteen different species of Darwin's finch? Because of evolution! These and many other phenomena put the actual fact or happening of evolution "beyond reasonable doubt" (Futuyma 1983 and Kitcher 1982).

I should add that Darwin's consilience in the Origin did not come by chance. Darwin learned methodology from Whewell, even though later Whewell refused to allow the Origin into the library of the Cambridge College of which he was by then Master (Ruse 1979).

Can one know phylogenies?

The overall pattern of evolution seems fairly well established. It shows the transition from relatively simple early life-forms to the overwhelming organic diversity of today's world. Moreover, it shows fully the incredibly branching nature of the evolutionary process. Indeed, the main outlines of the history of life were discovered by antievolutionists, before Darwin and the Origin. In recent years, much progress has been made in uncovering the early history of life, and we can now trace it back about 3.5 billion years, that is for about three-fourths of the earth's 4.6 billion-year span (for details see Ayala and Valentine 1979, Eldredge 1982, Luria et al. 1981, Schopf 1978).

Again, certain specific items of evolution seem now to have been established, as firmly as any reasonably minded person could demand or wish. The evolution of birds and mammals from reptiles springs to mind. The fossil record showing the transitions is rock solid. Archaeopteryx, for instance, is a fossil organism that is, quite literally, a reptile with feathers. Indeed, just before the Origin, Archaeopteryx feathers had been discovered, which were thought simply to be rather humdrum bird feathers. It was only when the complete organism was discovered, just after the Origin, that the full significance of the earlier discoveries was appreciated (Feduccia 1980).

Coming closer to home, the fossil evidence of our own simian ancestry is overwhelming. Nineteenth-century critics of Darwin demanded the "missing link." In Australopithecus we have it. These organisms, which lived up to 4 million years ago, had brains the size of apes, but walked upright like humans. It is no longer reasonable to pretend that humans stand apart from chimps and gorillas (Futuyma 1983, Johanson and White 1979).

But one must acknowledge that there are many, many gaps in the fossil record. Moreover, given the high improbability of fossilization, there is no reason to think that all or most of these gaps will be bridged. In short, we will probably reach a limit of fossil evidence for phylogenies, with many things still unknown. Pertinent information will simply have been lost, irretrievably. Also, it would be disingenuous not to recognize that even with good fossil evidence, additional theorizing is needed to establish exactly what did happen in the past (Schaeffer et al. 1972).

Learning more about phylogenies

Nevertheless, I must not end this discussion on a negative note, suggesting that evolutionists can extract only a finite amount of information from their fossils, and then that is it. There are ever-developing techniques of getting more information from what we have already got. For instance, in the human sphere, much new information is being gathered from examining, not simply the size of the brain, but also the shape and marks that the brain left behind. This is a most valuable new tool for tracing phylogenies. The same holds also of techniques for examining microscopic scratches on teeth. One can discover all sorts of things about diet, thus tracing lineages and gleaning new information about the evolving animals (Johanson and Edey 1981).

Also, although fossils perform most visibly and crucially in the quest for phylogenies, they are far from providing the only source of pertinent information. Comparative studies on today's organisms tell a great deal. Long before any fossil evidence was discovered, it was obvious that humans are most closely related to apes. Similarities of every kind—anatomical, embryological, behavioural—cried out about common ancestry.

Moreover, powerful new techniques are also being developed in this direction. For instance, systematists now use the computer in their quest for the understanding of phylogenetic affinities. And molecular biology has been brought into play, most directly with the concept of a "molecular clock." If there is a molecular dimension to organisms, one that lies below the level at which most evolutionary processes operate, then change would be random and reasonably constant. In other words, comparison of molecular similarities and differences between organisms would tell of relationships, and of how long ago it was that different organisms took different evolutionary paths (Fitch 1976, Goodman 1982a).

This notion of a clock is already yielding much new information. Interest now centers on the human case. Molecular biology shows phenomenal similarities between men and apes. But when did the break come? Conventional paleoanthropology claims that we broke from the apes more than 10 million years ago. The clock suggests that the break occurred less than 5 million years ago. (We are closer to the apes than dogs are to foxes.) Which position is right? The answers, I hope, will come fairly soon, as more is learned about the record and about the accuracy of the clock.

I must emphasize that the clock is still a controversial notion. One should not assume automatically that, when molecules (physics) and fossils (biology) fall out, it is the former that has to be correct. A hundred years ago, relying on thermodynamical calculations about the Earth's rate of cooling, Lord Kelvin criticized Darwin for demanding too much time for evolution. But it was Darwin who was right. Perhaps history repeats itself, and again the fossils are a surer guide to the past than physics. Nevertheless, whatever the final judgment on the molecular clock, no one doubts that it is stimulating a successful drive to learn more about the course of human prehistory. (For a fascinating discussion of this whole topic, see Gribbin and

Cherfas 1982. See also Goodman 1982b, King and Wilson 1975, Templeton 1983.)

I conclude, therefore, that some (many/most?) phylogenies will never be known, certainly not in full detail. But, heuristically, there is no reason to stop the quest. Much is being learned, and will be learned, about phylogenies. Where fossils fail, comparative studies often succeed.

What can be known of mechanisms?

What do we know of evolutionary mechanisms and what can we hope to know are the most difficult questions of all. As noted earlier, for historical reasons, if for no other, these questions usually begin with Darwin's mechanism of natural selection. In the *Origin*, Darwin argued first to a universal struggle for existence and reproduction. Then he took this fact, that not all organisms do indeed survive and reproduce, and argued that the differential success is a function of distinctive "helpful" characteristics ("adaptations"). This process Darwin labeled "natural selection," because of the analogy with the artificial selection practiced by animal and plant breeders. Since the time of Darwin we have had the coming of Mendelian and of molecular genetics. Hence, selection today is usually thought of as a process involving gene ratios in populations. Ultimately, however, as with Darwin, the link is made to those organic features that help in the battle for life (Ayala and Valentine 1979, Ruse 1982).

That natural selection can be effective, and that it has been effective, is very solidly established. Many selection experiments have been performed, showing how selection can mold organisms, as theory predicts. Whole new species (reproductively isolated breeding groups) have been formed through the power of selection (Jones 1981). Moreover, selection operating in the wild has been documented, again and again. The best-known (although far from unique) case is that of the industrial melanism of moths in Britain. As trees got dirtier, because of pollution from the industrial revolution, many moth species got darker, thus remaining camouflaged against their main predators: robins. That this occurred through selection is granted by all (Kettlewell 1973). Indeed, even creationists agree that selection is at work here (Gish 1973).

Additionally, there is much indirect evidence for the power of selection. Certainly, no one has a convincing alternative for the many sophisticated adaptations that we find in nature. Why, for example, is the trilobite eye exactly of the form predicted by Descartes and Huygens, as that needed to avoid distortion due to different colors of light (Clarkson and Levi-Setti 1975)? Why the eye at all, indeed, if natural selection is not at work? Alternative explanations are occasionally suggested, like Lamarckism (the inheritance of acquired characteristics). Invariably, they have come tumbling down, despite the initial enthusiasm of proponents (Ruse 1982).

It is true that adaptations are indirect evidence of selection; but, invoking the legal analogy again, do not think the worse of them for that. Fingerprints are indirect evidence that the culprit held the murder weapon. Are they inferior even to eye-witness reports? I suggest that adaptations are natural selection's fingerprints.

How important is natural selection?

Allow, then, that natural selection is an effective component in the evolutionary process. The question now becomes one of just how effective a component selection is. There are three important matters of fact that bear on this most difficult question.

First, all agree that natural selection could not have been responsible for absolutely everything. Even the most enthusiastic of Darwinians (like myself) accept this much. As we saw in the last section, if there is any merit to the idea of a molecular clock, then there is at least nonselection-powered evolution at the molecular level (King and Jukes 1969). But, even at more "organic" levels, selection is not all-powerful. For instance, we know from studies of heredity that many genes are "pleiotropic," that is, they affect more than one character-istic at once. Both theory and experiment therefore suggest that, if one feature is very adaptive (and thus strongly selected), another feature, which may have no selective advantage, could thus "piggy-back" in. Because the second was pleiotropically linked to the first, such an unuseful feature could evolve right along with useful features.

Second, notwithstanding that all agree that selection does not do absolutely everything, evolutionists today are split down the middle on the full extent of the operation of nonselective forces and processes. There are strong neo-Darwinians, like Ernst Mayr (1982), Edward O. Wilson (1975), and John Maynard Smith (1981), who think selection very, very important. And, there are critics, like Stephen Jay Gould (1980), Niles Eldredge and Joel Cracraft (1980), and Steven M. Stanley (1979), who think there are many other processes at work.

These latter evolutionists endorse the theory of "punctuated equilibria," arguing that evolution goes in fits and starts, as opposed to the gradual change supposed by orthodox Darwinians. It has been suggested that the "engineering constraints" involved in putting a functioning organism together may dictate many features, which are not therefore themselves produced directly by selec-tion. For instance, strong Darwinians think the four-limbedness of vertebrates to have been the result of selection. Some punctuated equilibria supporters think it may simply be a condition on getting vertebrates to work at all. Because of constraints like this on organisms, one gets rapid switches in evolution, from one well-integrated functioning form to another (see Lewontin and Gould 1979 for some thoughts in this direction, and Maynard Smith 1981 for a Darwinian response).

Yet other critics of conventional Darwinism favor yet other causal factors. Some think randomness, at the nonmolecular level, has been very important (e.g., Kirmura and Ohta 1971). Recently, others have argued that thermo-dynamics offers insights into the evolutionary process (Wiley and Brooks 1982).

The third point about the effectiveness of natural selection is crucial to the quest for the limits to our knowledge of selection. There seems little hope of some sort of algorithm (as it were) that would decide effectively and defini-tively between Darwinians (selectionists) and critics. If there were such a decision procedure, we could all start working together! Unfortunately, rows about the effectiveness of selection have existed since the day of the Origin's publication, and I see no end to them. However often the Darwinian shows some feature to be controlled by selection, there will always be yet more features for the critic who would deny that selection applies generally.

Overall, therefore, I am somewhat pessimistic about the possibility of our ever knowing fully the causes of evolutionary change. Like Kafka's castle, it is a goal we shall never achieve.

Should we give up?

But, although this is a somewhat negative note that I have just struck, I do not intend it as a dismal one. I conclude by making three more points, qualifying and amplifying my claim about the unlikelihood of ever finding the full story to evolutionary mechanisms.

First, even though we may never know every causal detail behind evolutionary change, we can certainly anticipate learning a lot more about them. Indeed, in the past two decades we have learned more about the causes of evolution than at any previous time, at least since the coming of Mendelism, if not since the coming of Darwinism itself. There is no reason why this rapid advance should not continue.

To justify such a feeling, consider the recent advances made in sociobiol-ogy, particularly those pertaining to the Hymenoptera (ants, bees, wasps). Two questions about this group have puzzled evolutionists since Darwin. Why are there sterile workers in this group? Why are the workers always female and never male? At one stroke, William Hamilton (1964) solved these problems through the concept of "kin selection." The Hymenoptera are haplodiploid. Females have mother and father, and hence have a full (diploid) chromosome set. Males have only mothers, and have a half (haploid) chromosome set. This means that the sister-sister relationship is closer than the mother-daughter relationship. Hence, sterile workers better their evolutionary prospects when they raise fertile sisters rather than when they raise daughters. Evolution by proxy, as it were! Sons have no such close relationships, and hence for them there is no advantage to such sterile altruism. Thus, we get sterile females, but not sterile males (Maynard Smith 1978, Oster and Wilson 1978).

Although details of this explanation are still queried, the outline is now generally accepted. A major advance in our understanding of the evolutionary process has occurred. I see no reason why similar such advances should not occur, at least in the foreseeable future.

Second, despite the prospect of lack of complete success, I deny that evolutionists today are necessarily on the wrong track in what they are doing. Sometimes, it is suggested that we need a whole new "paradigm," as it were. A model that would cut through all our present difficulties and insecurities, throwing dazzling new light on evolution and its processes (Lewontin 1974, Rose 1982). Of course, part of the trouble with paradigms is that you do not know that you need them until you are right in the middle of them. However, given the continuing success of evolutionists in discovering mechanisms, I very much doubt that a totally new approach is needed. Certainly, there is no reason to think that a new approach would speed up discoveries or open the prospect of total knowledge.

I am not saying that no new breakthroughs will occur or are needed. I suspect, in fact, that we will learn more and more as we discover and apply molecular biology. (Already the molecular world has paid great dividends, showing the wide-spread nature of genetic variation.) But, there is no reason to conclude that evolutionary studies today are radically misdirected. And, given the very great recent advances in evolutionary work, there are good reasons to think the contrary: that such studies are well directed indeed.

A plea for time

Third, I end with a warning. A virtual axiom of research in the physical world is that, as one delves ever deeper and deeper and smaller and smaller, research costs escalate until they become prohibitive. We face a similar problem in evolutionary studies, although (as hinted before) the limits here are temporal, not spatial. Once one has gotten down to molecules (or, at most, to atoms), I doubt that going much smaller pays many evolutionary dividends. However, evolutionary studies, both in experiment and in nature, do demand lots of time. Even with relatively fast-breeding organisms, like fruitflies, one usually needs years to complete experiments. And, once-a-year breeders (or slower) require very long-term commitments.

This all does lead to problems, particularly given the way research is structured today. Evolutionists want ready results, particularly if they are up for tenure. And funding bodies want reassurance that their largess is not wasted. Hence, there is a natural tendency to go for quick answers, irrespective of their theoretical and practical significance and centrality. Consequently, important questions about the long-term effects of selection, particularly those operating in the wild, go unanswered (A. J. Cain 1979).

We need to think about this matter carefully. At the very least, the National Science Foundation needs to break from its short-term funding policies and to earmark some funds for long-term studies. Perhaps this is a vain hope, given the present fiscal climate. But, those of us who care about evolutionary studies must push for more enlightened research policies and attitudes. Evolution is one of the most glorious ideas of all time. Even though we may never achieve absolute knowledge, at least let us make sure that the limits are not self-imposed, for reasons of academic expediency.

Acknowledgement

Douglas Futuyma gave a typically thoughtful reading of the first draft of this essay.

References cited

Ayala, F. J., and J. W. Valentine. 1979. *Evolving: The Theory and Processes of Organic Evolution.* Benjamin Cummings, Menlo Park, CA.

Cain, A. J. 1979. Reply to Gould and Lewontin, *Proc. R. Soc. Lond. B. Biol. Sci.* 205: 599–604.

Clarkson, E. N. K., and R. Levi-Setti. 1975. Trilobite eyes and the optics of Descartes and Huygens. *Nature* 254: 663–667.

Darwin, C. 1859. *On the Origin of Species.* John Murray, London.

Eldredge, N. 1982. *The Monkey Business: A Scientist Looks at Creationism.* Washington Square Press, New York.

Eldredge, N., and J. Cracraft. 1980. *Phylogenetic Patterns and the Evolutionary Process.* Columbia University Press, New York.

Feduccia, A. 1980. *The Age of Birds.* Harvard University Press, Cambridge, MA.

Fitch, W. M. 1976. Molecular evolutionary clocks. Pages 160–178 in F. J. Ayala, ed., *Molecular Evolution*. Sinauer, Sunderland, MA.

Futuyma, D. 1983. *Science on Trial: The Case for Evolution*. Pantheon, New York.

Gish, D. T. 1973. *Evolution: The Fossils Say No!* Creation-Life Publ. San Diego, CA.

Goodman, M. 1982a. Decoding the pattern of protein evolution. *Prog. Biophys. Mol. Biol.* 38: 105.

———. 1982b. Biomolecular evidence on human origins from the standpoint of Darwinian theory. *Hum. Biol.* 54: 247–264.

———. 1979. The spandrels of San Marco and the Panglossian paradigm: a critique of the adaptationist programme. *Proc. R. Soc. Lond. B. Biol. Sci.* 205: 581–598.

Gould, S. J. 1980. Is a new and general theory of evolution emerging? *Paleobiology* 6: 119–130.

Gribbin, J., and J. Cherfas. 1982. *The Monkey Puzzle*. Bodley Head, London.

Hamilton, W. D. 1964. The genetic evolution of social behaviour. *J. Theor. Biol.* 7: 1–16, 17–32.

Johanson, D., and T. D. White. 1979. A systematic assessment of early African hominids. *Science* 203: 321–330.

Johanson, D., and M. Edey. 1981. *Lucy: The Beginnings of Humankind*. Simon and Schuster, New York.

Jones, J. S. 1981. Models of speciation—the evidence from *Drosophila*. *Nature* 289: 743–744.

Kettlewell, H. B. D. 1973. *The Evolution of Melanism*. Clarendon, Oxford, England.

Kimura, M., and T. Ohta. 1971. *Theoretical Aspects of Population Genetics*. Princeton University Press, Princeton, NJ.

King, J. L., and T. H. Jukes. 1969. Non-Darwinian evolution. *Science* 164: 788–798.

King, M. C., and A. C. Wilson. 1975. Evolution at two levels: molecular similarities and biological differences between humans and chimpanzees. *Science* 188: 107–116.

Kitcher, P. 1982. *Abusing Science*. Massachusetts Institute of Technology Press, Boston, MA.

Lewontin, R. 1974. *The Genetic Basis of Evolutionary Change*. Columbia University Press, New York.

Luria, S. E., S. J. Gould, and S. Singer. 1981. *A View of Life*. Benjamin Cummings, Menlo Park, CA.

Maynard Smith, J. 1978. The evolution of behavior. *Sci. Am.* 239: 176–193.

Maynard Smith, J. 1981. Did Darwin get it right? *London Review of Books*. 3(11): 10–11.

Mayr, E. 1982. *The Growth of Biological Thought*. Harvard University Press, Cambridge, MA.

Morris, H. M., ed. 1974. *Scientific Creationism*. Creation-Life Publishers, San Diego, CA.

Newell, N. 1982. *Creation and Evolution*. Columbia University Press, New York.

Oster, G., and E. O. Wilson. 1978. *Caste and Ecology in the Social Insects.* Princeton University Press, Princeton, NJ.

Patterson, C. 1978. *Evolution.* British Museum (Natural History), London.

Popper, K. 1974. Darwinism as a metaphysical research programme. Pages 133–143 in P. A. Schilpp, ed. *The Philosophy of Karl Popper.* Open Court, LaSalle, IL.

Rescher, N. 1978. *Scientific Progress.* University of Pittsburgh Press, Pittsburgh, PA.

Rose, S. 1982. *Towards a Liberatory Biology.* Allison and Busby, London.

Ruse, M. 1973. *The Philosophy of Biology.* Hutchinson, London.

———. 1979. *The Darwinian Revolution: Science Red in Tooth and Claw.* University of Chicago Press, Chicago, IL.

———. 1982. *Darwinism Defended: A Guide to the Evolution Controversies.* Addison-Wesley, Reading, MA.

Schaeffer, B., M. Hecht, and N. Eldredge. 1972. Phylogeny and paleontology. Pages 31–46 in T. Dobzhansky et al., eds., *Evolutionary Biology.* Appleton-Century-Crofts, NY.

Schopf, J. W. 1978. The evolution of the earliest cells. *Sci. Am.* 239 (Sept.): 110–138.

Stanley, S. M. 1979. *Macroevolution: Pattern and Process.* W. H. Freeman, San Francisco.

Templeton, A. R. 1983. Phylogenetic inference from restriction endonuclease clearage site maps with particular reference to the evolution of human and apes. *Evolution* 37: 221–244.

Whewell, W. 1840. *The Philosophy of the Inductive Sciences.* Parker, London.

Wiley, E. O., and D. R. Brooks. 1982. Victims of history—a non-equilibrium approach to evolution. *Syst. Zool.* 31: 1–24.

Wilson, E. O. 1975. *Sociobiology: The New Synthesis.* Harvard University Press, Cambridge, MA.

PART THREE

Creationism

INTRODUCTION TO PART THREE

DARWIN'S THEORY OF EVOLUTION, enhanced by insights from genetics and molecular biology, is at the core of a variety of modern scientific disciplines and is overwhelmingly accepted by the scientific community. Biologist Francisco Ayala and philosopher Michael Ruse acknowledge in their articles included in Part Two of this anthology that there are continuing debates among scientists about the pathways and mechanisms of evolution. They both insist, however, that there is no credible scientific opposition to what they call the "fact" of evolution, a long history of descent with modification from simpler life forms.

Yet from the first appearance of Darwin's *Origin of Species* in 1859 until today, the theory of evolution has been the target of religiously motivated attacks. In particular, the theory has drawn criticism from fundamentalist and evangelical Christians who see it as a threat to a literal interpretation of the Genesis creation story. It is these opponents of Darwinian evolution, known as the "creationists," who are the focus of this section of the anthology.

The first selection in this unit is the New Revised Standard Version of Genesis 1–2. Part One of this collection examined various approaches to scriptural interpretation, including literalism and metaphorical or symbolic interpretation. For strict creationists, the notion of a long evolutionary history is to be rejected because it conflicts with a literal interpretation of the days of creation described in Genesis 1.

Historian of science Ronald L. Numbers reveals in his article "The Creationists," the second selection in this part, that popular stereotypes have obscured the fact that there is actually a great diversity of opinion among those professing to be creationists. In this seminal essay, taken from *God and Nature: Historical Essays on the Encounter between Christianity and Science*, which he edited with David C. Lindberg, Numbers provides a historical survey of the varieties of creationism. He distinguishes between "progressive" creationists, who accept the antiquity of life on earth by appealing to either the so-called "day-age" or "gap" theories, and "strict" creationists, who insist on a recent creation in six literal days. Numbers focuses on these young-earth creationists and traces their rise as a social and political movement from the crusade to outlaw the teaching of evolution in public schools in the 1920s to the battle beginning in the 1970s to give creation equal time. He chronicles the strategic shift in the arguments of strict creationists from openly biblical defenses of their views to an effort to avoid scriptural references and to promote their ideas instead as "creation science."

Numbers points out that practical legal considerations played a part in this change in creationist tactics. The hallmark of the 1920s antievolution crusade was the 1925 guilty verdict of John Scopes, who had been accused of violating the state of Tennessee's law banning the teaching of human evolution in public schools. In contrast, in 1968 the US Supreme Court declared an Arkansas antievolution law unconstitutional, leading creationists to promote laws in Arkansas and Louisiana requiring not the outlawing of evolution but rather a "balanced treatment" in public schools of evolution and what they called "creation science." In 1982, however, a federal judge declared that the Arkansas law was an unconstitutional breach of the wall separating church and state. In 1987 the US Supreme Court reached a similar decision about the Louisiana law. These judgments reflected the decision of the courts that "creation science" was religion and not science in that it failed to meet the essential characteristics of science as based on naturalistic causes that are testable against the empirical world. A new chapter in these legal battles, the struggle over intelligent design, is examined in Part Four of this collection.

The decision in the Arkansas trial has been sharply criticized by philosopher Larry Laudan in his article "Commentary: Science at the Bar— Causes for Concern" that appeared in the Fall 1982 edition of *Science, Technology, and Human Values*. While commending the verdict itself, Laudan maintains that it was reached for all the wrong reasons. He insists that creationism makes empirical claims that are testable and that instead of debating whether or not what creationists do is "scientific," one should examine their arguments and the evidence they provide to support their views. The real question should thus be whether the existing evidence provides stronger arguments for evolutionary theory or for creationism. According to Laudan, in such a contest, evolutionary theory clearly triumphs.

Numbers maintains that creationist opposition to evolution is fueled by the assumption that Darwinism leads to moral decay. From identifying a link between Darwinian evolution and German militarism in World War I to perceiving that Darwinism inevitably leads to atheism, lawlessness, and immorality, creationists from the time of Darwin to today have considered acceptance of evolution as contributing to a variety of social ills. Fear of a threat to meaning and morality is a powerful motivator, Numbers insists, and he suggests that the enduring vigor of creationist opposition to evolution is inextricably linked to the perception of Darwinism as challenging traditional values.

Chapter 8

GENESIS 1–2

1 **IN THE BEGINNING** when God created the heavens and the earth, [2]the earth was a formless void and darkness covered the face of the deep, while a wind from God swept over the face of the waters. [3]Then God said, "Let there be light"; and there was light. [4]And God saw that the light was good; and God separated the light from the darkness. [5]God called the light Day, and the darkness he called Night. And there was evening and there was morning, the first day.

6 And God said, "Let there be a dome in the midst of the waters, and let it separate the waters from the waters." [7]So God made the dome and separated the waters that were under the dome from the waters that were above the dome. And it was so. [8]God called the dome Sky. And there was evening and there was morning, the second day.

9 And God said, "Let the waters under the sky be gathered together into one place, and let the dry land appear." And it was so. [10]God called the dry land Earth, and the waters that were gathered together he called Seas. And God saw that it was good. [11]Then God said, "Let the earth put forth vegetation: plants yielding seed, and fruit trees of every kind on earth that bear fruit with the seed in it." And it was so. [12]The earth brought forth vegetation: plants yielding seed of every kind, and trees of every kind bearing fruit with the seed in it. And God saw that it was good. [13]And there was evening and there was morning, the third day.

14 And God said, "Let there be lights in the dome of the sky to separate the day from the night; and let them be for signs and for seasons and for days and years, [15]and let them be lights in the dome of the sky to give light upon the earth." And it was so. [16]God made the two great lights – the greater light to rule the day and the lesser light to rule the night – and the stars. [17]God set them in the dome of the sky to give light upon the earth, [18]to rule over the day and over the night, and to separate the light from the darkness. And God saw that it was good. [19]And there was evening and there was morning, the fourth day.

20 And God said, "Let the waters bring forth swarms of living creatures, and let birds fly above the earth across the dome of the sky." [21]So God created the great sea monsters and every living creature that moves, of every kind, with which the waters swarm, and every winged bird of every kind. And God saw that it was good. [22]God blessed them, saying, "Be fruitful and multiply and fill the waters in the seas, and let birds multiply on the earth." [23]And there was evening and there was morning, the fifth day.

24 And God said, "Let the earth bring forth living creatures of every kind: cattle and creeping things and wild animals of the earth of every kind." And it was so. [25]God made the wild animals of the earth of every kind, and the cattle of every kind, and everything that creeps upon the ground of every kind. And God saw that it was good.

26 Then God said, "Let us make humankind in our image, according to our likeness; and let them have dominion over the fish of the sea, and over the birds of the air, and over the cattle, and over all the wild animals of the earth, and over every creeping thing that creeps upon the earth."

27 So God created humankind in his image,
    in the image of God he created them;
    male and female he created them.

28 God blessed them, and God said to them, "Be fruitful and multiply, and fill the earth and subdue it; and have dominion over the fish of the sea and over the birds of the air and over every living thing that moves upon the earth." [29]God said, "See, I have given you every plant yielding seed that is upon the face of all the earth, and every tree with seed in its fruit; you shall have them for food. [30]And to every beast of the earth, and to every bird of the air, and to everything that creeps on the earth, everything that has the breath of life, I have given every green plant for food." And it was so. [31]God saw everything that he had made, and indeed, it was very good. And there was evening and there was morning, the sixth day.

2 **THUS THE HEAVENS** and the earth were finished, and all their multitude. [2]And on the seventh day God finished the work that he had done, and he rested on the seventh day from all the work that he had done. [3]So God blessed the seventh day and hallowed it, because on it God rested from all the work that he had done in creation.

4 These are the generations of the heavens and the earth when they were created.

In the day that the LORD God made the earth and the heavens, [5]when no plant of the field was yet in the earth and no herb of the field had yet sprung up – for the LORD God had not caused it to rain upon the earth, and there was no one to till the ground; [6]but a stream would rise from the earth, and water the whole face of the ground – [7]then the LORD God formed man from the dust of the ground, and breathed into his nostrils the breath of life; and the man became a living being. [8]And the LORD God planted a garden in Eden, in the east; and there he put the man whom he had formed. [9]Out of the ground the LORD God made to grow every tree that is pleasant to the sight and good for food, the tree of life also in the midst of the garden, and the tree of the knowledge of good and evil.

10 A river flows out of Eden to water the garden, and from there it divides and becomes four branches. [11]The name of the first is Pishon; it is the one that flows around the whole land of Havilah, where there is gold; [12]and the gold of that land is good; bdellium and onyx stone are there. [13]The name of the second river is Gihon; it is the one that flows around the whole land of Cush. [14]The name of the third river is Tigris, which flows east of Assyria. And the fourth river is the Euphrates.

15 The LORD God took the man and put him in the garden of Eden to till it and keep it. [16]And the LORD God commanded the man, "You may freely eat of every tree of the garden; [17]but of the tree of the knowledge of good and evil you shall not eat, for in the day that you eat of it you shall die."

18 Then the LORD God said, "It is not good that the man should be alone; I will make him a helper as his partner." [19]So out of the ground the LORD God formed every animal of the field and every bird of the air, and brought them to the man to see what he would call them; and whatever the man called every living creature, that was its name. [20]The man gave names to all cattle, and to the birds of the air, and to every animal of the field; but for the man there was not found a helper as his partner. [21]So the LORD God caused a deep sleep to fall upon the man, and he slept; then he took one of his ribs and closed up its place with flesh. [22]And the rib that the LORD God had taken from the man he made into a woman and brought her to the man. [23]Then the man said,

"This at last is bone of my bones
 and flesh of my flesh;
this one shall be called Woman,
 for out of Man this one was taken."

24 Therefore a man leaves his father and his mother and clings to his wife, and they become one flesh. ²⁵And the man and his wife were both naked, and were not ashamed.

Chapter 9

Ronald L. Numbers

THE CREATIONISTS

SCARCELY TWENTY YEARS AFTER the publication of Charles Darwin's *Origin of Species* in 1859 special creationists could name only two working naturalists in North America, John William Dawson (1820–1899) of Montreal and Arnold Guyot (1806–1884) of Princeton, who had not succumbed to some theory of organic evolution. The situation in Great Britain looked equally bleak for creationists, and on both sides of the Atlantic liberal churchmen were beginning to follow their scientific colleagues into the evolutionist camp. By the closing years of the nineteenth century evolution was infiltrating even the ranks of the evangelicals, and, in the opinion of many observers, belief in special creation seemed destined to go the way of the dinosaur. But contrary to the hopes of liberals and the fears of conservatives, creationism did not become extinct. The majority of late-nineteenth-century Americans remained true to a traditional reading of Genesis, and as late as 1982 a public-opinion poll revealed that 44 percent of Americans, nearly a fourth of whom were college graduates, continued to believe that "God created man pretty much in his present form at one time within the last 10,000 years."[1]

Such surveys failed, however, to disclose the great diversity of opinion among those professing to be creationists. Risking oversimplification, we can divide creationists into two main camps: "strict creationists," who interpret the days of Genesis literally, and "progressive creationists," who construe the

Mosaic days to be immense periods of time. But even within these camps substantial differences exist. Among strict creationists, for example, some believe that God created all terrestrial life—past and present—less than ten thousand years ago, while others postulate one or more creations prior to the seven days of Genesis. Similarly, some progressive creationists believe in numerous creative acts, while others limit God's intervention to the creation of life and perhaps the human soul. Since this last species of creationism is practically indistinguishable from theistic evolutionism, this essay focuses on the strict creationists and the more conservative of the progressive creationists, particularly on the small number who claimed scientific expertise. Drawing on their writings, it traces the ideological development of creationism from the crusade to outlaw the teaching of evolution in the 1920s to the current battle for equal time. During this period the leading apologists for special creation shifted from an openly biblical defense of their views to one based largely on science. At the same time they grew less tolerant of notions of an old earth and symbolic days of creation, common among creationists early in the century, and more doctrinaire in their insistence on a recent creation in six literal days and on a universal flood.

The loyal majority

The general acceptance of organic evolution by the intellectual elite of the late Victorian era has often obscured the fact that the majority of Americans remained loyal to the doctrine of special creation. In addition to the masses who said nothing, there were many people who vocally rejected kinship with the apes and other, more reflective, persons who concurred with the Princeton theologian Charles Hodge (1797–1878) that Darwinism was atheism. Among the most intransigent foes of organic evolution were the premillennialists, whose predictions of Christ's imminent return depended on a literal reading of the Scriptures. Because of their conviction that one error in the Bible invalidated the entire book, they had little patience with scientists who, as described by the evangelist Dwight L. Moody (1837–1899), "dug up old carcasses . . . to make them testify against God."[2]

Such an attitude did not, however, prevent many biblical literalists from agreeing with geologists that the earth was far older than six thousand years. They did so by identifying two separate creations in the first chapter of Genesis: the first, "in the beginning," perhaps millions of years ago, and the second, in six actual days, approximately four thousand years before the birth of Christ. According to this so-called gap theory, most fossils were relics of the first creation, destroyed by God prior to the Adamic restoration. In 1909 the *Scofield*

Reference Bible, the most authoritative biblical guide in fundamentalist circles, sanctioned this view.[3]

Scientists like Guyot and Dawson, the last of the reputable nineteenth-century creationists, went still further to accommodate science by interpreting the days of Genesis as ages and by correlating them with successive epochs in the natural history of the world. Although they believed in special creative acts, especially of the first humans, they tended to minimize the number of super-natural interventions and to maximize the operation of natural law. During the late nineteenth century their theory of progressive creation circulated widely in the colleges and seminaries of America.[4]

The early Darwinian debate focused largely on the implications of evolution for natural theology; and so long as these discussions remained confined to scholarly circles, those who objected to evolution on biblical grounds saw little reason to participate. But when the debate spilled over into the public arena during the 1880s and 1890s, creationists grew alarmed. "When these vague speculations, scattered to the four winds by the million-tongued press, are caught up by ignorant and untrained men," declared one premillennialist in 1889, "it is time for earnest Christian men to call a halt."[5]

The questionable scientific status of Darwinism undoubtedly encouraged such critics to speak up. Although the overwhelming majority of scientists after 1880 accepted a long earth history and some form of organic evolution, many in the late nineteenth century were expressing serious reservations about the ability of Darwin's particular theory of natural selection to account for the origin of species. Their published criticisms of Darwinism led creationists mistakenly to conclude that scientists were in the midst of discarding evolution. The appearance of books with such titles as *The Collapse of Evolution* and *At the Death Bed of Darwinism* bolstered this belief and convinced antievolutionists that liberal Christians had capitulated to evolution too quickly. In view of this turn of events it seemed likely that those who had "abandoned the stronghold of faith out of sheer fright will soon be found scurrying back to the old and impregnable citadel, when they learn that 'the enemy is in full retreat.' "[6]

For the time being, however, those conservative Christians who would soon call themselves fundamentalists perceived a greater threat to orthodox faith than evolution—higher criticism, which treated the Bible more as a historical document than as God's inspired word. Their relative apathy toward evolution is evident in *The Fundamentals*, a mass-produced series of twelve booklets published between 1910 and 1915 to revitalize and reform Christianity around the world. Although one contributor identified evolution as the principal cause of disbelief in the Scriptures and another traced the roots of higher criticism to Darwin, the collection as a whole lacked the strident antievolutionism that would characterize the fundamentalist movement of the 1920s.[7]

This is particularly true of the writings of George Frederick Wright (1838–1921), a Congregational minister and amateur geologist of international repute. At first glance his selection to represent the fundamentalist point of view seems anomalous. As a prominent Christian Darwinist in the 1870s he had argued that the intended purpose of Genesis was to protest polytheism, not teach science. By the 1890s, however, he had come to espouse the progressive creationism of Guyot and Dawson, partly, it seems, in reaction to the claims of higher critics regarding the accuracy of the Pentateuch. Because of his standing as a scientific authority and his conservative view of the Scriptures, the editors of The Fundamentals selected him to address the question of the relationship between evolution and the Christian faith.[8]

In an essay misleadingly titled "The Passing of Evolution" Wright attempted to steer a middle course between the theistic evolution of his early days and the traditional views of some special creationists. On the one hand, he argued that the Bible itself taught evolution, "an orderly progress from lower to higher forms of matter and life." On the other hand, he limited evolution to the origin of species, pointing out that even Darwin had postulated the supernatural creation of several forms of plants and animals, endowed by the Creator with a "marvelous capacity for variation." Furthermore, he argued that, despite the physical similarity between human beings and the higher animals, the former "came into existence as the Bible represents, by the special creation of a single pair, from whom all the varieties of the race have sprung."[9]

Although Wright represented the left wing of fundamentalism, his moderate views on evolution contributed to the conciliatory tone that prevailed during the years leading up to World War I. Fundamentalists may not have liked evolution, but few, if any, at this time saw the necessity or desirability of launching a crusade to eradicate it from the schools and churches in America.

The antievolution crusade

Early in 1922 William Jennings Bryan (1860–1925), Presbyterian layman and thrice-defeated Democratic candidate for the presidency of the United States, heard of an effort in Kentucky to ban the teaching of evolution in public schools. "The movement will sweep the country," he predicted hopefully, "and we will drive Darwinism from our schools."[10] His prophecy proved overly optimistic, but before the end of the decade more than twenty state legislatures did debate antievolution laws, and four—Oklahoma, Tennessee, Mississippi, and Arkansas—banned the teaching of evolution in public schools. At times the controversy became so tumultuous that it looked to some as though "America might go mad." Many persons shared responsibility for these events, but none more than Bryan. His entry into the fray had a catalytic effect and gave antievolutionists what they needed most: "a spokesman with a national reputation, immense prestige, and a loyal following."[11]

The development of Bryan's own attitude toward evolution closely paralleled that of the fundamentalist movement. Since early in the century he had occasionally alluded to the silliness of believing in monkey ancestors and to the ethical dangers of thinking that might makes right, but until the outbreak of World War I he saw little reason to quarrel with those who disagreed. The war, however, exposed the darkest side of human nature and shattered his illusions about the future of Christian society. Obviously something had gone awry, and Bryan soon traced the source of the trouble to the paralyzing influence of Darwinism on the human conscience. By substituting the law of the jungle for the teaching of Christ, it threatened the principles he valued most: democracy and Christianity. Two books in particular confirmed his suspicion. The first, Vernon Kellogg's *Headquarters Nights* (1917), recounted firsthand conversations with German officers that revealed the role Darwin's biology had played in persuading the Germans to declare war. The second, Benjamin Kidd's *Science of Power* (1918), purported to demonstrate the historical and philosophical links between Darwinism and German militarism.[12]

About the time that Bryan discovered the Darwinian origins of the war, he also became aware, to his great distress, of unsettling effects the theory of evolution was having on America's own young people. From frequent visits to college campuses and from talks with parents, pastors, and Sunday-school teachers, he heard about an epidemic of unbelief that was sweeping the country. Upon investigating the cause, his wife reported, "he became convinced that the teaching of Evolution as a fact instead of a theory caused the students to lose faith in the Bible, first, in the story of creation, and later in other doctrines, which underlie the Christian religion." Again Bryan found confirming evidence in a recently published book, *Belief in God and Immortality* (1916), by the Bryn Mawr psychologist James H. Leuba, who demonstrated statistically that college attendance endangered traditional religious beliefs.[13]

Armed with this information about the cause of the world's and the nation's moral decay, Bryan launched a nationwide crusade against the offending doctrine. In one of his most popular and influential lectures, "The Menace of Darwinism," he summed up his case against evolution, arguing that it was both un-Christian and unscientific. Darwinism, he declared, was nothing but "guesses strung together," and poor guesses at that. Borrowing from a turn-of-the-century tract, he illustrated how the evolutionist explained the origin of the eye:

The evolutionist guesses that there was a time when eyes were unknown—that is a necessary part of the hypothesis. . . . a piece of pigment, or, as some say, a freckle appeared upon the skin of an animal that had no eyes. This piece of pigment or freckle converged the rays of the sun upon that spot and when the little animal felt the heat on that spot it turned the spot to the sun to get more heat. The increased heat irritated the skin—so the evolutionists guess, and a nerve came there and out of the nerve came the eye!

"Can you beat it?" he asked incredulously—and that it happened not once but twice? As for himself, he would take one verse in Genesis over all that Darwin wrote.[14]

Throughout his political career Bryan had placed his faith in the common people, and he resented the attempt of a few thousand scientists "to establish an oligarchy over the forty million American Christians," to dictate what should be taught in the schools.[15] To a democrat like Bryan it seemed preposterous that this "scientific soviet" would not only demand to teach its insidious philosophy but impudently insist that society pay its salaries. Confident that nine-tenths of the Christian citizens agreed with him, he decided to appeal directly to them, as he had done so successfully in fighting the liquor interests. "Commit your case to the people," he advised creationists. "Forget, if need be, the high-brows both in the political and college world, and carry this cause to the people. They are the final and efficiently corrective power."[16]

And who were the people who joined Bryan's crusade? As recent studies have shown, they came from all walks of life and from every region of the country. They lived in New York, Chicago, and Los Angeles as well as in small towns and in the country. Few possessed advanced degrees, but many were not without education. Nevertheless, Bryan undeniably found his staunchest supporters and won his greatest victories in the conservative and still largely rural South, described hyperbolically by one fundamentalist journal as "the last stronghold of orthodoxy on the North American continent," a region where the "masses of the people in all denominations 'believe the Bible from lid to lid.' "[17]

The strength of Bryan's following within the churches is perhaps more difficult to determine, because not all fundamentalists were creationists and many creationists refused to participate in the crusade against evolution. However, a 1929 survey of the theological beliefs of seven hundred Protestant ministers provides some valuable clues. The question "Do you believe that the creation of the world occurred in the manner and time recorded in Genesis?" elicited the following positive responses:

Lutheran	89%
Baptist	63%
Evangelical	62%
Presbyterian	35%
Methodist	24%
Congregational	12%
Episcopalian	11%
Other	60%

Unfortunately, these statistics tell us nothing about the various ways respondents may have interpreted the phrase "in the manner and time recorded in Genesis," nor do they reveal anything about the level of political involvement in the campaign against evolution. Lutherans, for example, despite their overwhelming rejection of evolution, generally preferred education to legislation and tended to view legal action against evolution as "a dangerous mingling of church and state." Similarly, premillennialists, who saw the spread of evolution as one more sign of the world's impending end, sometimes lacked incentive to correct the evils around them.[18]

Baptists and Presbyterians, who dominated the fundamentalist movement, participated actively in the campaign against evolution. The Southern Baptist Convention, spiritual home of some of the most outspoken foes of evolution, lent encouragement to the creationist crusaders by voting unanimously in 1926 that "this Convention accepts Genesis as teaching that man was the special creation of God, and rejects every theory, evolution or other, which teaches that man originated in, or came by way of, a lower animal ancestry." The Presbyterian Church contributed Bryan and other leaders to the creationist cause but, as the above survey indicates, also harbored many evolutionists. In 1923 the General Assembly turned back an attempt by Bryan and his fundamentalist cohorts to cut off funds to any church school found teaching human evolution, approving instead a compromise measure that condemned only materialistic evolution. The other major Protestant bodies paid relatively little attention to the debate over evolution; and Catholics, though divided on the question of evolution, seldom favored restrictive legislation.[19]

Leadership of the antievolution movement came not from the organized churches of America but from individuals like Bryan and interdenominational organizations such as the World's Christian Fundamentals Association, a predominantly premillennialist body founded in 1919 by William Bell Riley (1861–1947), pastor of the First Baptist Church in Minneapolis. Riley became active as an antievolutionist after discovering, to his apparent surprise, that evolutionists were teaching their views at the University of Minnesota. The early twentieth century witnessed an unprecedented expansion of public education—enrollment in public high schools nearly doubled between 1920 and 1930—and fundamentalists like Riley and Bryan wanted to make sure that students attending these institutions would not lose their faith. Thus they resolved to drive every evolutionist from the public-school payroll. Those who lost their jobs as a result deserved little sympathy, for, as one rabble-rousing creationist put it, the German soldiers who killed Belgian and French children with poisoned candy were angels compared with the teachers and textbook writers who corrupted the souls of children and thereby sentenced them to eternal death.[20]

The creationists, we should remember, did not always act without provocation. In many instances their opponents displayed equal intolerance and insensitivity. In fact, one contemporary observer blamed the creation-evolution controversy in part on the "intellectual flapperism" of irresponsible and poorly informed teachers who delighted in shocking naive students with unsupportable statements about evolution. It was understandable, wrote an Englishman, that American parents would resent sending their sons and daughters to public institutions that exposed them to "a multiple assault upon traditional faiths."[21]

Creationist science and scientists

In 1922 William Bell Riley outlined the reasons why fundamentalists opposed the teaching of evolution. "The first and most important reason for its elimination," he explained, "is the unquestioned fact that evolution is not a science; it is a hypothesis only, a speculation." Bryan often made the same point, defining true science as "classified knowledge . . . the explanation of facts."[22] Although creationists had far more compelling reasons for rejecting evolution than its alleged unscientific status, their insistence on this point was not merely an obscurantist ploy. Rather it stemmed from their commitment to a once-respected tradition, associated with the English philosopher Sir Francis Bacon (1561–1626), that emphasized the factual, nontheoretical nature of science. By identifying with the Baconian tradition, creationists could label evolution as false science, could claim equality with scientific authorities in comprehending facts, and could deny the charge of being antiscience. "It is not 'science' that orthodox Christians oppose," a fundamentalist editor insisted defensively. "No! no! a thousand times, No! They are opposed only to the theory of evolution, which has not yet been proved, and therefore is not to be called by the sacred name of *science*."[23]

Because of their conviction that evolution was unscientific, creationists assured themselves that the world's best scientists agreed with them. They received an important boost at the beginning of their campaign from an address by the distinguished British biologist William Bateson (1861–1926) in 1921, in which he declared that scientists had not discovered "the actual mode and process of evolution." Although he warned creationists against misinterpreting his statement as a rejection of evolution, they paid no more attention to that caveat than they did to the numerous proevolution resolutions passed by scientific societies.[24]

Unfortunately for the creationists, they could claim few legitimate scientists of their own: a couple of self-made men of science, one or two physicians, and a handful of teachers who, as one evolutionist described them, were "trying to hold down, not a chair, but a whole settee, of 'Natural Science' in some little institution."[25] Of this group the most influential were Harry Rimmer (1890–1952) and George McCready Price (1870–1963).

Rimmer, Presbyterian minister and self-styled "research scientist," obtained his limited exposure to science during a term or two at San Francisco's Hahnemann Medical College, a small homeopathic institution that required no more than a high-school diploma for admission. As a medical student he picked up a vocabulary of "double-jointed, twelve cylinder, knee-action words" that later served to impress the uninitiated. After his brief stint in medical school he attended Whittier College and the Bible Institute of Los Angeles for a year each before entering full-time evangelistic work. About 1919 he settled in Los Angeles, where he set up a small laboratory at the rear of his house to conduct experiments in embryology and related sciences. Within a year or two he established the Research Science Bureau "to prove through findings in biology, paleontology, and anthropology that science and the literal Bible were not contradictory." The bureau staff—that is, Rimmer—apparently used income from the sale of memberships to finance anthropological field trips in the western United States, but Rimmer's dream of visiting Africa to prove the dissimilarity of gorillas and humans failed to materialize. By the late 1920s the bureau lay dormant, and Rimmer signed on with Riley's World's Christian Fundamentals Association as a field secretary.[26]

Besides engaging in research, Rimmer delivered thousands of lectures, primarily to student groups, on the scientific accuracy of the Bible. Posing as a scientist, he attacked Darwinism and poked fun at the credulity of evolutionists. To attract attention, he repeatedly offered one hundred dollars to anyone who could discover a scientific error in the Scriptures; not surprisingly, the offer never cost him a dollar. He also, by his own reckoning, never lost a public debate. Following one encounter with an evolutionist in Philadelphia, he wrote home gleefully that "the debate was a simple walkover, a massacre—murder pure and simple. The eminent professor was simply scared stiff to advance any of the common arguments of the evolutionists, and he fizzled like a wet fire-cracker."[27]

George McCready Price, a Seventh-day Adventist geologist, was less skilled at debating than Rimmer but more influential scientifically. As a young man Price attended an Adventist college in Michigan for two years and later completed a teacher-training course at the provincial normal school in his native New Brunswick. The turn of the century found him serving as principal of a small high school in an isolated part of eastern Canada, where one of his few companions was a local physician. During their many conversations, the doctor almost converted his fundamentalist friend to evolution, but each time Price wavered, he was saved by prayer and by reading the works of the Seventh-day Adventist prophetess Ellen G. White (1827–1915), who claimed divine inspiration for her view that Noah's flood accounted for the fossil record on which evolutionists based their theory. As a result of these experiences, Price vowed to devote his life to promoting creationism of the strictest kind.[28]

By 1906 he was working as a handyman at an Adventist sanitarium in southern California. That year he published a slim volume entitled *Illogical Geology: The Weakest Point in the Evolution Theory*, in which he brashly offered one thousand dollars "to any one who will, in the face of the facts here presented, show me how to prove that one kind of fossil is older than another." (Like Rimmer, he never had to pay.) According to Price's argument, Darwinism rested "logically and historically on the succession of life idea as taught by geology" and "if this succession of life is not an actual scientific fact, then Darwinism . . . is a most gigantic hoax."[29]

Although a few fundamentalists praised Price's polemic, David Starr Jordan (1851–1931), president of Stanford University and an authority on fossil fishes, warned him that he should not expect "any geologist to take [his work] seriously." Jordan conceded that the unknown author had written "a very clever book" but described it as

> a sort of lawyer's plea, based on scattering mistakes, omissions and exceptions against general truths that anybody familiar with the facts in a general way cannot possibly dispute. It would be just as easy and just as plausible and just as convincing if one should take the facts of European history and attempt to show that all the various events were simultaneous.[30]

As Jordan recognized, Price lacked any formal training or field experience in geology. He was, however, a voracious reader of geological literature, an armchair scientist who self-consciously minimized the importance of field experience.

During the next fifteen years Price occupied scientific settees in several Seventh-day Adventist schools and authored six more books attacking evolution, particularly its geological foundation. Although not unknown outside his own church before the early 1920s, he did not attract national attention until then. Shortly after Bryan declared war on evolution, Price published *The New Geology* (1923), the most systematic and comprehensive of his many books. Uninhibited by false modesty, he presented his "great law of conformable stratigraphic sequences . . . by all odds the most important law ever formulated with reference to the order in which the strata occur." This law stated that "*any kind of fossiliferous beds whatever, 'young' or 'old,' may be found occurring conformably on any other fossiliferous beds, 'older' or 'younger.'*"[31] To Price, so-called deceptive conformities (where strata seem to be missing) and thrust faults (where the strata are apparently in the wrong order) proved that there was no natural order to the fossil-bearing rocks, all of which he attributed to the Genesis flood.

A Yale geologist reviewing the book for *Science* accused Price of "harboring a geological nightmare." But despite such criticism from the scientific establishment—and the fact that his theory contradicted both the day-age and gap interpretations of Genesis—Price's reputation among fundamentalists rose dramatically. Rimmer, for example, hailed *The New Geology* as "a masterpiece of REAL science [that] explodes in a convincing manner some of the ancient fallacies of science 'falsely so called.' "[32] By the mid–1920s Price's byline was appearing with increasing frequency in a broad spectrum of conservative religious periodicals, and the editor of *Science* could accurately describe him as "the principal scientific authority of the Fundamentalists."[33]

The Scopes trial and beyond

In the spring of 1925 John Thomas Scopes, a high-school teacher in the small town of Dayton, Tennessee, confessed to having violated the state's recently passed law banning the teaching of human evolution in public schools. His subsequent trial focused international attention on the antievolution crusade and brought William Jennings Bryan to Dayton to assist the prosecution. In anticipation of arguing the scientific merits of evolution, Bryan sought out the best scientific minds in the creationist camp to serve as expert witnesses. The response to his inquiries could only have disappointed the aging crusader. Price, then teaching in England, sent his regrets—along with advice for Bryan to stay away from scientific topics. Howard A. Kelly, a prominent Johns Hopkins physician who had contributed to *The Fundamentals*, confessed that, except for Adam and Eve, he believed in evolution. Louis T. More, a physicist who had just written a book on *The Dogma of Evolution* (1925), replied that he accepted evolution as a working hypothesis. Alfred W. McCann, author of *God—or Gorilla* (1922), took the opportunity to chide Bryan for supporting prohibition in the past and for now trying "to bottle-up the tendencies of men to think for themselves."[34]

At the trial itself things scarcely went better. When Bryan could name only Price and the deceased George Frederick Wright as scientists for whom he had respect, the caustic Clarence Darrow (1857–1938), attorney for the defense, scoffed: "You mentioned Price because he is the only human being in the world so far as you know that signs his name as a geologist that believes like you do. . . . every scientist in this country knows [he] is a mountebank and a pretender and not a geologist at all." Eventually Bryan conceded that the world was indeed far more than six thousand years old and that the six days of creation had probably been longer than twenty-four hours each—concessions that may have harmonized with the progressive creationism of Wright but hardly with the strict creationism of Price.[35]

Though one could scarcely have guessed it from some of his public pronouncements, Bryan had long been a progressive creationist. In fact, his beliefs regarding evolution diverged considerably from those of his more conservative supporters. Shortly before his trial he had confided to Dr. Kelly that he, too, had no objection to "evolution before man but for the fact that a concession as to the truth of evolution up to man furnishes our opponents with an argument which they are quick to use, namely, if evolution accounts for all the species up to man, does it not raise a presumption in behalf of evolution to include man?" Until biologists could actually demonstrate the evolution of one species into another, he thought it best to keep them on the defensive.[36]

Bryan's admission at Dayton spotlighted a serious and long-standing problem among antievolutionists: their failure to agree on a theory of creation. Even the most visible leaders could not reach a consensus. Riley, for example, followed Guyot and Dawson (and Bryan) in viewing the days of Genesis as ages, believing that the testimony of geology necessitated this interpretation. Rimmer favored the gap theory, which involved two separate creations, in part because his scientific mind could not fathom how, given Riley's scheme, plants created on the third day could have survived thousands of years without sunshine, until the sun appeared on the fourth. According to the testimony of acquaintances, he also believed that the Bible taught a local rather than a universal flood. Price, who cared not a whit about the opinion of geologists, insisted on nothing less than a recent creation in six literal days and a worldwide deluge. He regarded the day-age theory as "the devil's counterfeit" and the gap theory as only slightly more acceptable. Rimmer and Riley, who preferred to minimize the differences among creationists, attempted the logically impossible, if ecumenically desirable, task of incorporating Price's "new geology" into their own schemes.[37]

Although the court in Dayton found Scopes guilty as charged, creationists had little cause for rejoicing. The press had not treated them kindly, and the taxing ordeal no doubt contributed to Bryan's death a few days after the end of the trial. Nevertheless, the anti-evolutionists continued their crusade, winning victories in Mississippi in 1926 and in Arkansas two years later. By the end of the decade, however, their legislative campaign had lost its steam. The presidential election of 1928, pitting a Protestant against a Catholic, offered fundamentalists a new cause, and the onset of the depression in 1929 further diverted their attention.[38]

Contrary to appearances, the creationists were simply changing tactics, not giving up. Instead of lobbying state legislatures, they shifted their attack to local communities, where they engaged in what one critic described as "the emasculation of textbooks, the 'purging' of libraries, and above all the continued hounding of teachers." Their new approach attracted less attention but paid off handsomely, as school boards, textbook publishers, and teachers in both urban and rural areas, North and South, bowed to their pressure. Darwinism virtually disappeared from high-school texts, and for years many American teachers feared being identified as evolutionists.[39]

Creationism underground

During the heady days of the 1920s, when their activities made front-page headlines, creationists dreamed of converting the world; a decade later, forgotten and rejected by the establishment, they turned their energies inward and began creating an institutional base of their own. Deprived of the popular press and frustrated by their inability to publish their views in organs controlled by orthodox scientists, they determined to organize their own societies and edit their own journals.[40] Their early efforts, however, encountered two problems: the absence of a critical mass of scientifically trained creationists and lack of internal agreement.

In 1935 Price, along with Dudley Joseph Whitney, a farm journalist, and L. Allen Higley, a Wheaton College science professor, formed a Religion and Science Association to create "a united front against the theory of evolution." Among those invited to participate in the association's first—and only— convention were representatives of the three major creationist parties, including Price himself, Rimmer, and one of Dawson's sons, who, like his father, advocated the day-age theory. But as soon as the Price faction discovered that its associates had no intention of agreeing on a short earth history, it bolted the organization, leaving it a shambles.[41]

Shortly thereafter, in 1938, Price and some Seventh-day Adventist friends in the Los Angeles area, several of them physicians associated with the College of Medical Evangelists (now part of Loma Linda University), organized their own Deluge Geology Society and, between 1941 and 1945, published a *Bulletin of Deluge Geology and Related Science*. As described by Price, the group consisted of "a very eminent set of men. . . . In no other part of this round globe could anything like the number of scientifically educated believers in Creation and opponents of evolution be assembled, as here in Southern California."[42] Perhaps the society's most notable achievement was its sponsorship in the early 1940s of a hush-hush project to study giant fossil footprints, believed to be human, discovered in rocks far older than the theory of evolution would allow. This find, the society announced excitedly, thus demolished that theory "at a single stroke" and promised to "*astound the scientific world!*" But despite such activity and the group's religious homogeneity, it, too, soon foundered—on "the same rock," complained a disappointed member, that wrecked the Religion and Science Association, that is "*pre-Genesis time for the earth.*"[43]

By this time creationists were also beginning to face a new problem: the presence within their own ranks of young university-trained scientists who wanted to bring evangelical Christianity more into line with mainstream science. The encounter between the two generations often proved traumatic, as is illustrated by the case of Harold W. Clark (b. 1891). A former student of Price's, he had gone on to earn a master's degree in biology from the University of California and taken a position at a small Adventist college in northern California. By 1940 his training and field experience had convinced him that Price's *New Geology* was "entirely out of date and inadequate" as a text, especially in its rejection of the geological column. When Price learned of this, he angrily accused his former disciple of suffering from "the modern mental disease of university-itis" and of currying the favor of "tobacco-smoking, Sabbath-breaking, God-defying" evolutionists. Despite Clark's protests that he still believed in a literal six-day creation and universal flood, Price kept up his attack for the better part of a decade, at one point addressing a vitriolic pamphlet, *Theories of Satanic Origin*, to his erstwhile friend and fellow creationist.[44]

The inroads of secular scientific training also became apparent in the American Scientific Affiliation (ASA), created by evangelical scientists in 1941.[45] Although the society took no official stand on creation, strict creationists found the atmosphere congenial during the early years of the society. In the late 1940s, however, some of the more progressive members, led by J. Laurence Kulp, a young geochemist on the faculty of Columbia University, began criticizing Price and his followers for their allegedly unscientific effort to squeeze earth history into less than ten thousand years. Kulp, a Wheaton alumnus and member of the Plymouth Brethren, had acquired a doctorate in physical chemistry from Princeton University and gone on to complete all the requirements, except a dissertation, for a Ph.D. in geology. Although initially suspicious of the conclusions of geology regarding the history and antiquity of the earth, he had come to accept them. As one of the first evangelicals professionally trained in geology, he felt a responsibility to warn his colleagues in the ASA about Price's work, which, he believed, had "infiltrated the greater portion of fundamental Christianity in America primarily due to the absence of trained Christian geologists." In what was apparently the first systematic critique of the "new geology" Kulp concluded that the "major propositions of the theory are contra-indicated by established physical and chemical laws." Conservatives within the ASA not unreasonably suspected that Kulp's exposure to "the orthodox geological viewpoint" had severely undermined his faith in a literal interpretation of the Bible.[46]

Before long it became evident that a growing number of ASA members, like Kulp, were drifting from strict to progressive creationism and sometimes on to theistic evolutionism. The transition for many involved immense personal stress, as revealed in the autobiographical testimony of another Wheaton alumnus, J. Frank Cassel:

> First to be overcome was the onus of dealing with a "verboten" term and in a "non-existent" area. Then, as each made an honest and objective consideration of the data, he was struck with the validity and undeniability of datum after datum. As he strove to incorporate each of these facts into his Biblico-scientific frame of reference, he found that—while the frame became more complete and satisfying—he began to question first the feasibility and then the desirability of an effort to refute the total evolutionary concept, and finally he became impressed by its impossibility on the basis of existing data. This has been a heart-rending, soul-searching experience for the committed Christian as he has seen what he had long considered the raison d'être of God's call for his life endeavor fade away, and as he has struggled to release strongly held convictions as to the close limitations of Creationism.

Cassel went on to note that the struggle was "made no easier by the lack of approbation (much less acceptance) of some of his less well-informed colleagues, some of whom seem to question motives or even to imply heresy."[47] Strict creationists, who suffered their own agonies, found it difficult not to conclude that their liberal colleagues were simply taking the easy way out. To both parties a split seemed inevitable.

Creationism abroad

During the decades immediately following the crusade of the 1920s American antievolutionists were buoyed by reports of a creationist revival in Europe, especially in England, where creationism was thought to be all but dead. The Victoria Institute in London, a haven for English creationists in the nineteenth century, had by the 1920s become a stronghold of theistic evolution. When Price visited the institute in 1925 to receive its Langhorne-Orchard Prize for an essay on "Revelation and Evolution," several members protested his attempt to export the fundamentalist controversy to England. Even evangelicals refused to get caught up in the turmoil that engulfed the United States. As historian George Marsden has explained, English evangelicals, always a minority, had developed a stronger tradition of theological toleration than revivalist Americans, who until the twentieth century had never experienced minority status. Thus while the displaced Americans fought to recover their lost position, English evangelicals adopted a nonmilitant live-and-let-live philosophy that stressed personal piety.[48]

The sudden appearance of a small but vocal group of British creationists in the early 1930s caught nearly everyone by surprise. The central figure in this movement was Douglas Dewar (1875–1957), a Cambridge graduate and amateur ornithologist, who had served for decades as a lawyer in the Indian Civil Service. Originally an evolutionist, he had gradually become convinced of the necessity of adopting "a provisional hypothesis of special creation . . . supplemented by a theory of evolution." This allowed him to accept unlimited development within biological families. His published views, unlike those of most American creationists, betrayed little biblical influence. His greatest intellectual debt was not to Moses but to a French zoologist, Louis Vialleton (1859–1929), who had attracted considerable attention in the 1920s for suggesting a theory of discontinuous evolution, which antievolutionists eagerly—but erroneously—equated with special creation.[49]

Soon after announcing his conversion to creationism in 1931, Dewar submitted a short paper on mammalian fossils to the Zoological Society of London, of which he was a member. The secretary of the society subsequently rejected the piece, noting that a competent referee thought Dewar's evidence "led to no valuable conclusion." Such treatment infuriated Dewar and convinced him that evolution had become "a scientific creed." Those who questioned scientific orthodoxy, he complained, "are deemed unfit to hold scientific offices; their articles are rejected by newspapers or journals; their contributions are refused by scientific societies, and publishers decline to publish their books except at the author's expense. Thus the independents are today pretty effectually muzzled." Because of such experiences Dewar and other

British dissidents in 1932 organized the Evolution Protest Movement, which after two decades claimed a membership of two hundred.[50]

Henry M. Morris and the revival of creationism

In 1964 one historian predicted that "a renaissance of the [creationist] movement is most unlikely." And so it seemed. But even as these words were penned, a major revival was under way, led by a Texas engineer, Henry M. Morris (b. 1918). Raised a nominal Southern Baptist, and as such a believer in creation, Morris as a youth had drifted unthinkingly into evolutionism and religious indifference. A thorough study of the Bible following graduation from college convinced him of its absolute truth and prompted him to reevaluate his belief in evolution. After an intense period of soul-searching he concluded that creation had taken place in six literal days, because the Bible clearly said so and "God doesn't lie." Corroborating evidence came from the book of nature. While sitting in his office at Rice Institute, where he was teaching civil engineering, he would study the butterflies and wasps that flew in through the window; being familiar with structural design, he calculated the improbability of such complex creatures developing by chance. Nature as well as the Bible seemed to argue for creation.[51]

For assistance in answering the claims of evolutionists, he found little creationist literature of value apart from the writings of Rimmer and Price. Although he rejected Price's peculiar theology, he took an immediate liking to the Adventist's flood geology and incorporated it into a little book, *That You Might Believe* (1946), the first book, so far as he knew, "published since the Scopes trial in which a scientist from a secular university advocated recent special creation and a worldwide flood." In the late 1940s he joined the American Scientific Affiliation—just in time to protest Kulp's attack on Price's geology. But his words fell largely on deaf ears. In 1953 when he presented some of his own views on the flood to the ASA, one of the few compliments came from a young theologian, John C. Whitcomb, Jr., who belonged to the Grace Brethren. The two subsequently became friends and decided to collaborate on a major defense of the Noachian flood. By the time they finished their project, Morris had earned a Ph.D. in hydraulic engineering from the University of Minnesota and was chairing the civil engineering department at Virginia Polytechnic Institute; Whitcomb was teaching Old Testament studies at Grace Theological Seminary in Indiana.[52]

In 1961 they brought out *The Genesis Flood*, the most impressive contribution to strict creationism since the publication of Price's *New Geology* in 1923. In many respects their book appeared to be simply "a reissue of G. M. Price's views, brought up to date," as one reader described it. Beginning with a testimony to their belief in "the verbal inerrancy of Scripture," Whitcomb and Morris went on to argue for a recent creation of the entire universe, a Fall that triggered the second law of thermodynamics, and a worldwide flood that in one year laid down most of the geological strata. Given this history, they argued, "the last refuge of the case for evolution immediately vanishes away, and the record of the rocks becomes a tremendous witness . . . to the holiness and justice and power of the living God of Creation!"[53]

Despite the book's lack of conceptual novelty, it provoked an intense debate among evangelicals. Progressive creationists denounced it as a travesty on geology that threatened to set back the cause of Christian science a generation, while strict creationists praised it for making biblical catastrophism intellectually respectable. Its appeal, suggested one critic, lay primarily in the fact that, unlike previous creationist works, it "looked *legitimate* as a scientific contribution," accompanied as it was by footnotes and other scholarly appurtenances. In responding to their detractors, Whitcomb and Morris repeatedly refused to be drawn into a scientific debate, arguing that "the real issue is not the correctness of the interpretation of various details of the geological data, but simply what God has revealed in His Word concerning these matters."[54]

Whatever its merits, The Genesis Flood unquestionably "brought about a stunning renaissance of flood geology," symbolized by the establishment in 1963 of the Creation Research Society. Shortly before the publication of his book Morris had sent the manuscript to Walter E. Lammerts (b. 1904), a Missouri-Synod Lutheran with a doctorate in genetics from the University of California. As an undergraduate at Berkeley Lammerts had discovered Price's New Geology, and during the early 1940s, while teaching at UCLA, he had worked with Price in the Creation-Deluge Society. After the mid-1940s, however, his interest in creationism had flagged—until awakened by reading the Whitcomb and Morris manuscript. Disgusted by the ASA's flirtation with evolution, he organized in the early 1960s a correspondence network with Morris and eight other strict creationists, dubbed the "team of ten." In 1963 seven of the ten met with a few other like-minded scientists at the home of a team member in Midland, Michigan, to form the Creation Research Society (CRS).[55]

The society began with a carefully selected eighteen-man "inner-core steering committee," which included the original team of ten. The composition of this committee reflected, albeit imperfectly, the denominational, regional, and professional bases of the creationist revival. There were six Missouri-Synod Lutherans, five Baptists, two Seventh-day Adventists, and one each from the Reformed Presbyterian Church, the Reformed Christian Church, the Church of the Brethren, and an independent Bible church. (Information about one member is not available.) Eleven lived in the Midwest, three in the South, and two in the Far West. The committee included six biologists, but only one geologist, an independent consultant with a master's degree. Seven members taught in church-related colleges, five in state institutions; the others worked for industry or were self-employed.[56]

To avoid the creeping evolutionism that had infected the ASA and to ensure that the society remained loyal to the Price-Morris tradition, the CRS required members to sign a statement of belief accepting the inerrancy of the Bible, the special creation of "all basic types of living things," and a worldwide deluge. It restricted membership to Christians only. (Although creationists liked to stress the scientific evidence for their position, one estimated that "only about five percent of evolutionists-turned-creationists did so on the basis of the overwhelming evidence for creation in the world of nature"; the remaining 95 percent became creationists because they believed in the Bible.) To legitimate its claim to being a scientific society, the CRS published a quarterly journal and limited full membership to persons possessing a graduate degree in a scientific discipline.[57]

At the end of its first decade the society claimed 450 regular members, plus 1,600 sustaining members, who failed to meet the scientific qualifications. Eschewing politics, the CRS devoted itself almost exclusively to education and research, funded "at very little expense, and . . . with no expenditure of public money." CRS-related projects included expeditions to search for Noah's ark, studies of fossil human footprints and pollen grains found out of the predicted evolutionary order, experiments on radiation-produced mutations in plants, and theoretical studies in physics demonstrating a recent origin of the earth. A number of members collaborated in preparing a biology textbook based on creationist principles. In view of the previous history of creation science, it was an auspicious beginning.[58]

While the CRS catered to the needs of scientists, a second, predominantly lay organization carried creationism to the masses. Created in 1964 in the wake of interest generated by *The Genesis Flood*, the Bible-Science Association came to be identified by many with one man: Walter Lang, an ambitious Missouri-Synod pastor who self-consciously prized spiritual insight above scientific expertise. As editor of the widely circulated *Bible-Science Newsletter* he vigorously promoted the Price-Morris line—and occasionally provided a platform for individuals on the fringes of the creationist movement, such as those who questioned the heliocentric theory and who believed that Einstein's theory of relativity "was invented in order to circumvent the evidence that the earth is at rest." Needless to say, the pastor's broad-mindedness greatly embarrassed creationists seeking scientific respectability, who feared that such bizarre behavior would tarnish the entire movement.[59]

Scientific creationism

The creationists revival of the 1960s attracted little public attention until late in the decade, when fundamentalists became aroused about the federally funded Biological Sciences Curriculum Study texts, which featured evolution, and the California State Board of Education voted to require public-school textbooks to include creation along with evolution. This decision resulted in large part from the efforts of two southern California housewives, Nell Segraves and Jean Sumrall, associates of both the Bible-Science Association and the CRS. In 1961 Segraves learned of the U.S. Supreme Court's ruling in the Madalyn Murray case protecting atheist students from required prayers in public schools. Murray's ability to shield her child from religious exposure suggested to Segraves that creationist parents like herself "were entitled to protect our children from the influence of beliefs that would be offensive to our religious beliefs." It was this line of argument that finally persuaded the Board of Education to grant creationists equal rights.[60]

Flushed with victory, Segraves and her son Kelly in 1970 joined an effort to organize a Creation-Science Research Center (CSRC), affiliated with Christian Heritage College in San Diego, to prepare creationist literature suitable for adoption in public schools. Associated with them in this enterprise was Henry Morris, who resigned his position at Virginia Polytechnic Institute to help establish a center for creation research. Because of differences in personalities and objectives, the Segraveses in 1972 left the college, taking the CSRC with them; Morris thereupon set up a new research division at the college, the Institute for Creation Research (ICR), which, he announced with obvious relief, would be "controlled and operated by scientists" and would engage in research and education, not political action. During the 1970s Morris added five scientists to his staff and, funded largely by small gifts and royalties from institute publications, turned the ICR into the world's leading center for the propagation of strict creationism.[61] Meanwhile, the CSRC continued campaigning for the legal recognition of special creation, often citing a direct relationship between the acceptance of evolution and the breakdown of law and order. Its own research, the CSRC announced, proved that evolution fostered "the moral decay of spiritual values which contribute to the destruction of mental health and . . . [the prevalence of] divorce, abortion, and rampant venereal disease."[62]

The 1970s witnessed a major shift in creationist tactics. Instead of trying to outlaw evolution, as they had done in the 1920s, antievolutionists now fought to give creation equal time. And instead of appealing to the authority of the Bible, as Morris and Whitcomb had done as recently as 1961, they consciously downplayed the Genesis story in favor of what they called "scientific creationism." Several factors no doubt contributed to this shift. One sociologist has suggested that creationists began stressing the scientific legitimacy of their enterprise because "their theological legitimation of reality was no longer sufficient for maintaining their world and passing on their world view to their children." But there were also practical considerations. In 1968 the U.S. Supreme Court declared the Arkansas antievolution law unconstitutional, giving creationists reason to suspect that legislation requiring the teaching of biblical creationism would meet a similar fate. They also feared that requiring the biblical account "would open the door to a wide variety of interpretations of Genesis" and produce demands for the inclusion of non-Christian versions of creation.[63]

In view of such potential hazards, Morris recommended that creationists ask public schools to teach "only the scientific aspects of creationism," which in practice meant leaving out all references to the six days of Genesis and Noah's ark and focusing instead on evidence for a recent worldwide catastrophe and on arguments against evolution. Thus the product remained virtually the same; only the packaging changed. The ICR textbook *Scientific Creationism* (1974), for example, came in two editions: one for public schools, containing no references to the Bible, and another for use in Christian schools that included a chapter on "Creation According to Scripture."[64]

In defending creation as a scientific alternative to evolution, creationists relied less on Francis Bacon and his conception of science and more on two new philosopher-heroes: Karl Popper and Thomas Kuhn. Popper required all scientific theories to be falsifiable; since evolution could not be falsified, reasoned the creationists, it was by definition not science. Kuhn described scientific progress in terms of competing models or paradigms rather than the accumulation of objective knowledge. Thus creationists saw no reason why their flood-geology model should not be allowed to compete on an equal scientific basis with the evolution model. In selling this two-model approach to school boards, creationists were advised:

> Sell more SCIENCE. . . . Who can object to teaching more science? What is controversial about that? . . . do not use the word "creationism." Speak only of science. Explain that withholding scientific information contradicting evolution amounts to "censorship" and smacks of getting into the province of religious dogma. . . . Use the "censorship" label as one who is against censoring science. YOU are for science, anyone else who wants to censor scientific data is an old fogey and too doctrinaire to consider.

This tactic proved extremely effective, at least initially. Two state legislatures, in Arkansas and Louisiana, and various school boards adopted the two-model approach, and an informal poll of school-board members in 1980 showed that only 25 percent favored teaching nothing but evolution. In 1982, however, a federal judge declared the Arkansas law, requiring a "balanced treatment" of creation and evolution, to be unconstitutional.[65] Three years later a similar decision was reached regarding the Louisiana law.

Except for the battle to get scientific creationism into public schools, nothing brought more attention to the creationists than their public debates with prominent evolutionists, usually held on college campuses. During the 1970s the ICR staff alone participated in more than a hundred of these contests and, according to their own reckoning, never lost one. Although Morris preferred delivering straight lectures—and likened debates to the bloody confrontations between Christians and lions in ancient Rome—he recognized their value in carrying the creationist message to "more non-Christians and non-creationists than almost any other method." Fortunately for him, an associate, Duane T. Gish, holder of a doctorate in biochemistry from the University of California, relished such confrontations. If the mild-mannered, professorial Morris was the Darwin of the creationist movement, then the bumptious Gish was its Huxley. He "hits the floor running" just like a bulldog, observed an admiring colleague; and "I go for the jugular vein," added Gish himself. Such enthusiasm helped draw crowds of up to five thousand.[66]

Early in 1981 the ICR announced the fulfillment of a recurring dream among creationists: a program offering graduate degrees in various creation-oriented sciences. Besides hoping to fill an anticipated demand for teachers trained in scientific creationism, the ICR wished to provide an academic setting where creationist students would be free from discrimination. Over the years a number of creationists had reportedly been kicked out of secular universities because of their heterodox views, prompting leaders to warn graduate students to keep silent, "because if you don't, in almost 99 percent of the cases you will be asked to leave." To avoid anticipated harassment, several graduate students took to using pseudonyms when writing for creationist publications.[67]

Creationists also feared—with good reason—the possibility of defections while their students studied under evolutionists. Since the late 1950s the Seventh-day Adventist Church had invested hundreds of thousands of dollars to staff its Geoscience Research Institute with well-trained young scientists, only to discover that in several instances exposure to orthodox science had destroyed belief in strict creationism. To reduce the incidence of apostasy, the church established its own graduate programs at Loma Linda University, where George McCready Price had once taught.[68]

To all the world

It is still too early to assess the full impact of the creationist revival sparked by Whitcomb and Morris, but its influence, especially among evangelical Christians, seems to have been immense. Not least, it has elevated the strict creationism of Price and Morris to a position of apparent orthodoxy. It has also endowed creationism with a measure of scientific respectability unknown since the deaths of Guyot and Dawson. Yet it is impossible to determine how much of the creationists' success stemmed from converting evolutionists as opposed to mobilizing the already converted, and how much it owed to widespread disillusionment with established science. A sociological survey of church members in northern California in 1963 revealed that over a fourth of those polled—30 percent of Protestants and 28 percent of Catholics—were already opposed to evolution when the creationist revival began.[69] Broken down by denomination, it showed:

Liberal Protestants	
(Congregationalists, Methodists, Episcopalians, Disciples)	11%
Moderate Protestants	
(Presbyterians, American Lutherans, American Baptists)	29%
Church of God	57%
Missouri-Synod Lutherans	64%
Southern Baptists	72%
Church of Christ	78%
Nazarenes	80%
Assemblies of God	91%
Seventh-day Adventists	94%

Thus the creationists launched their crusade having a large reservoir of potential support.

But has belief in creationism increased since the early 1960s? The scanty evidence available suggests that it has. A nationwide Gallup poll in 1982, cited at the beginning of this paper, showed that nearly as many Americans (44 percent) believed in a recent special creation as accepted theistic (38 percent) or nontheistic (9 percent) evolution. These figures, when compared with the roughly 30 percent of northern California church members who opposed evolution in 1963, suggest, in a grossly imprecise way, a substantial gain in the actual number of American creationists. Bits and pieces of additional evidence lend credence to this conclusion. For example, in 1935 only 36 percent of the students at Brigham Young University, a Mormon school, rejected human evolution; in 1973 the percentage had climbed to 81. Also, during the 1970s both the Missouri-Synod Lutheran and Seventh-day Adventist churches, traditional bastions of strict creationism, took strong measures to reverse a trend toward greater toleration of progressive creationism. In at least these instances, strict creationism did seem to be gaining ground.[70]

Unlike the antievolution crusade of the 1920s, which remained confined mainly to North America, the revival of the 1960s rapidly spread overseas as American creationists and their books circled the globe. Partly as a result of stimulation from America, including the publication of a British edition of *The Genesis Flood* in 1969, the lethargic Evolution Protest Movement in Great Britain was revitalized; and two new creationist organizations, the Newton Scientific Association and the Biblical Creation Society, sprang into existence.[71] On the Continent the Dutch assumed the lead in promoting creationism, encouraged by the translation of books on flood geology and by visits from ICR scientists. Similar developments occurred elsewhere in Europe, as well as in Australia, Asia, and South America. By 1980 Morris's books alone had been translated into Chinese, Czech, Dutch, French, German, Japanese, Korean, Portuguese, Russian, and Spanish. Strict creationism had become an international phenomenon.[72]

Notes

I would like to thank David C. Lindberg for his encouragement and criticism, Rennie B. Schoepflin for his research assistance, and the Graduate School Research Committee of the University of Wisconsin-Madison for financial support during the preparation of this paper. An abridged version appeared as "Creationism in 20th-Century America" in *Science* 218 (1982): 538–544.

1   "Poll Finds Americans Split on Creation Idea," *New York Times*, 29 Aug. 1982, p. 22. Nine percent of the respondents favored an evolutionary process in which God played no part, 38 percent believed God directed the evolutionary process, and 9 percent had no opinion. Regarding Dawson and Guyot, see Edward J. Pfeifer, "United States," in *The Comparative Reception of Darwinism*, ed. Thomas F. Glick (Austin: Univ. of Texas Press, 1974), p. 203; and Asa Gray, *Darwiniana: Essays and Reviews Pertaining to Darwinism*, ed. A. Hunter Dupree (Cambridge: Harvard Univ. Press, 1963), pp. 202–203. In *The Darwinian Revolution: Science Red in Tooth and Claw* (Chicago: Univ. of Chicago Press, 1979), Michael Ruse argues that most British biologists were evolutionists by the mid-1860s, while David L. Hull, Peter D. Tessner, and Arthur M. Diamond point out in "Planck's Principle," *Science* 202 (1978): 721, that more than a quarter of British scientists continued to reject the evolution of species as late as 1869. On the acceptance of evolution among religious leaders see, e.g., Frank Hugh Foster, *The Modern Movement in American Theology: Sketches in the History of American Protestant*

Thought from the Civil War to the World War (New York: Fleming H. Revell Co., 1939), pp. 38–58; and Owen Chadwick, The Victorian Church, Part 2, 2d ed. (London: Adam & Charles Black, 1972), pp. 23–24.

2   William G. McLoughlin, Jr., Modern Revivalism: Charles Grandison Finney to Billy Graham (New York: Ronald Press, 1959), p. 213. In Protestant Christianity Interpreted through Its Development (New York: Charles Scribner's Sons, 1954), p. 227, John Dillenberger and Claude Welch discuss the conservatism of the common people. On the attitudes of premillennialists see Robert D. Whalen, "Millenarianism and Millennialism in America, 1790–1880" (Ph.D. diss., State University of New York at Stony Brook, 1972), pp. 219–229; and Ronald L. Numbers, "Science Falsely So-Called: Evolution and Adventists in the Nineteenth Century," Journal of the American Scientific Affiliation 27 (March 1975): 18–23.

3   Ronald L. Numbers, Creation by Natural Law: Laplace's Nebular Hypothesis in American Thought (Seattle: Univ. of Washington Press, 1977), pp. 89–90; Bernard Ramm, The Christian View of Science and Scripture (Grand Rapids, Mich.: Wm. B. Eerdmans, 1954), pp. 195–198. On the influence of the Scofield Reference Bible see Ernest R. Sandeen, The Roots of Fundamentalism: British and American Millenarianism, 1800–1930 (Chicago: Univ. of Chicago Press, 1971), p. 222.

4   Charles F. O'Brien, Sir William Dawson: A Life in Science and Religion (Philadelphia: American Philosophical Society, 1971). On Guyot and his influence see Numbers, Creation by Natural Law, pp. 91–100. On the popularity of the Guyot-Dawson view, also associated with the geologist James Dwight Dana, see William North Rice, Christian Faith in an Age of Science, 2d ed. (New York: A. C. Armstrong & Son, 1904), p. 101; and Dudley Joseph Whitney, "What Theory of Earth History Shall We Adopt?" Bible Champion 34 (1928): 616.

5   H. L. Hastings, preface to the 1889 edition of The Errors of Evolution: An Examination of the Nebular Theory, Geological Evolution, the Origin of Life, and Darwinism, by Robert Patterson, 3d ed. (Boston: Scriptural Tract Repository, 1893), p. iv. On the Darwinian debate see James R. Moore, The Post-Darwinian Controversies: A Study of the Protestant Struggle to Come to Terms with Darwin in Great Britain and America, 1870–1900 (Cambridge: Cambridge Univ. Press, 1979).

6   G. L. Young, "Relation of Evolution and Darwinism to the Question of Origins," Bible Student and Teacher 11 (July 1909): 41. On anti-Darwinian books see "Evolutionism in the Pulpit," in The Fundamentals, 12 vols. (Chicago: Testimony Publishing Co., 1910–1915), 8:28–30. See also Peter J. Bowler, The Eclipse of Darwinism: Anti-Darwinian Evolution Theories in the Decades around 1900 (Baltimore: Johns Hopkins Univ. Press, 1983).

7   Philip Mauro, "Modern Philosophy," in The Fundamentals 2:85–105; and J. J. Reeve, "My Personal Experience with the Higher Criticism," ibid., 3:98–118.

8   G. Frederick Wright, Story of My Life and Work (Oberlin, Ohio: Bibliotheca Sacra Co., 1916); idem, "The First Chapter of Genesis and Modern Science," Homiletic Review 35 (1898): 392–399; idem, introduction to The Other Side of Evolution: An Examination of Its Evidences, by Alexander Patterson (Chicago: Winona Pub. Co., 1902), pp. xvii–xix.

9   George Frederick Wright, "The Passing of Evolution," in The Fundamentals 7:5–20.

The Scottish theologian James Orr contributed an equally tolerant essay, "Science and Christian Faith," ibid., 4:91–104.

10 Lawrence W. Levine, *Defender of the Faith—William Jennings Bryan: The Last Decade, 1915–1925* (New York: Oxford Univ. Press, 1965), p. 277.

11 Ibid., p. 272. The quotation about America going mad appears in Roland T. Nelson, "Fundamentalism and the Northern Baptist Convention" (Ph.D. diss., University of Chicago, 1964), p. 319. On antievolution legislation see Maynard Shipley, *The War on Modern Science: A Short History of the Fundamentalist Attacks on Evolution and Modernism* (New York: Alfred A. Knopf, 1927); and idem, "Growth of the Anti-Evolution Movement," *Current History* 32 (1930): 330–332. On Bryan's catalytic role see Ferenc Morton Szasz, *The Divided Mind of Protestant America, 1889–1930* (University: Univ. of Alabama Press, 1982), pp. 107–116.

12 Levine, *Defender of the Faith*, pp. 261–265.

13 Ibid., pp. 266–267. Mrs. Bryan's statement appears in Wayne C. Williams, *William Jennings Bryan* (New York: G. P. Putnam, 1936), p. 448.

14 William Jennings Bryan, *In His Image* (New York: Fleming H. Revell Co., 1922), pp. 94, 97–98. "The Menace of Darwinism" appears in this work as chap. 4, "The Origin of Man." Bryan apparently borrowed his account of the evolution of the eye from Patterson, *The Other Side of Evolution*, pp. 32–33.

15 Paolo E. Coletta, *William Jennings Bryan*, vol. 3, *Political Puritan, 1915–1925* (Lincoln: Univ. of Nebraska Press, 1969), p. 230.

16 "Progress of Anti-Evolution," *Christian Fundamentalist* 2 (1929): 13. Bryan's reference to a "scientific soviet" appears in Levine, *Defender of the Faith*, p. 289. Bryan gives the estimate of nine-tenths in a letter to W. A. McRae, 5 Apr. 1924, box 29, Bryan Papers, Library of Congress.

17 "Fighting Evolution at the Fundamentals Convention," *Christian Fundamentals in School and Church* 7 (July–Sept. 1925): 5. The best state histories of the antievolution crusade are Kenneth K. Bailey, "The Enactment of Tennessee's Antievolution Law," *Journal of Southern History* 16 (1950): 472–510; Willard B. Gatewood, Jr., *Preachers, Pedagogues and Politicians: The Evolution Controversy in North Carolina, 1920–1927* (Chapel Hill: Univ. of North Carolina Press, 1966); and Virginia Gray, "Anti-Evolution Sentiment and Behavior: The Case of Arkansas," *Journal of American History* 57 (1970): 352–366. Ferenc Morton Szasz stresses the urban dimension of the crusade in "Three Fundamentalist Leaders: The Roles of William Bell Riley, John Roach Straton, and William Jennings Bryan in the Fundamentalist-Modernist Controversy" (Ph.D. diss., University of Rochester, 1969), p. 351.

18 George Herbert Betts, *The Beliefs of 700 Ministers and Their Meaning for Religious Education* (New York: Abingdon Press, 1929), pp. 26, 44; Milton L. Rudnick, *Fundamentalism and the Missouri Synod: A Historical Study of Their Interaction and Mutual Influence* (St. Louis: Concordia Publishing House, 1966), pp. 88–90; Sandeen, *Roots of Fundamentalism*, pp. 266–268, which discusses the premillennialists. Lutheran reluctance to join the crusade is also evident in Szasz, "Three Fundamentalist Leaders," p. 279. For examples of prominent fundamentalists who stayed aloof from the antievolution controversy see Ned B. Stonehouse, *J. Gresham Machen: A Biographical Memoir* (Grand

Rapids, Mich.: Wm. B. Eerdmans, 1954), pp. 401–402, and William Bryant Lewis, "The Role of Harold Paul Sloan and his Methodist League for Faith and Life in the Fundamentalist-Modernist Controversy of the Methodist Episcopal Church" (Ph.D. diss., Vanderbilt University, 1963), pp. 86–88.

19   Edward Lassiter Clark, "The Southern Baptist Reaction to the Darwinian Theory of Evolution" (Ph.D. diss., Southwestern Baptist Theological Seminary, 1952), p. 154; James J. Thompson, Jr., "Southern Baptists and the Antievolution Controversy of the 1920's," *Mississippi Quarterly* 29 (1975–1976): 65–81; Lefferts A. Loetscher, *The Broadening Church: A Study of Theological Issues in the Presbyterian Church since 1869* (Philadelphia: Univ. of Pennsylvania Press, 1954), p. 111; John L. Morrison, "American Catholics and the Crusade against Evolution," *Records of the American Catholic Historical Society of Philadelphia* 64 (1953): 59–71. Norman F. Furniss, *The Fundamentalist Controversy, 1918–1931* (New Haven: Yale Univ. Press, 1954), includes chapter-by-chapter surveys of seven denominations.

20   T. T. Martin, *Hell and the High School: Christ or Evolution, Which?* (Kansas City: Western Baptist Pub. Co., 1923), pp. 164–165. On Riley see Marie Acomb Riley, *The Dynamic of a Dream: The Life Story of Dr. William B. Riley* (Grand Rapids, Mich.: Wm. B. Eerdmans, 1938), pp. 101–102; and Szasz, *The Divided Mind of Protestant America*, pp. 89–91. George M. Marsden, *Fundamentalism and American Culture: The Shaping of Twentieth-Century Evangelicalism, 1870–1925* (New York: Oxford Univ. Press, 1980), pp. 169–170, stresses the interdenominational character of the antievolution crusade. On the expansion of public education see Kenneth K. Bailey, *Southern White Protestantism in the Twentieth Century* (New York: Harper & Row, 1964), pp. 72–73.

21   Both quotations come from Howard K. Beale, *Are American Teachers Free? An Analysis of Restraints upon the Freedom of Teaching in American Schools* (New York: Charles Scribner's Sons, 1936), pp. 249–251.

22   [William B. Riley], "The Evolution Controversy," *Christian Fundamentals in School and Church* 4 (Apr.–June 1922): 5; Bryan, *In His Image*, p. 94.

23   L. S. K[eyser], "No War against Science—Never!" *Bible Champion* 31 (1925): 413. On the fundamentalist affinity for Baconianism see Marsden, *Fundamentalism and American Culture*, pp. 214–215.

24   William Bateson, "Evolutionary Faith and Modern Doubts," *Science* 55 (1922): 55–61. The creationists' use of Bateson provoked the evolutionist Henry Fairfield Osborn into repudiating the British scientist; see Osborn, *Evolution and Religion in Education: Polemics of the Fundamentalist Controversy of 1922 to 1926* (New York: Charles Scribner's Sons, 1926), p. 29. On proevolution resolutions see Shipley, *War on Modern Science*, p. 384.

25   Heber D. Curtis to W. J. Bryan, 22 May 1923, box 37, Bryan Papers, Library of Congress. Two physicians, Arthur I. Brown of Vancouver and Howard A. Kelly of Johns Hopkins, achieved prominence in the fundamentalist movement, but Kelly leaned toward theistic evolution.

26   William D. Edmondson, "Fundamentalist Sects of Los Angeles, 1900–1930" (Ph.D. diss., Claremont Graduate School, 1969), pp. 276–336; Steward G. Cole, *The History of Fundamentalism* (New York: Richard R. Smith, 1931), pp. 264–265; F. J. B[oyer],

"Harry Rimmer, D.D.," *Christian Faith and Life* 45 (1939): 6–7; "Two Great Field Secretaries—Harry Rimmer and Dr. Arthur I. Brown," *Christian Fundamentals in School and Church* 8 (July–Sept. 1926): 17. Harry Rimmer refers to his medical vocabulary in *The Harmony of Science and Scripture*, 11th ed. (Grand Rapids, Mich.: Wm. B. Eerdmans, 1945), p. 14.

27   Edmondson, "Fundamentalist Sects of Los Angeles," pp. 329–330, 333–334. Regarding the $100 reward, see "World Religious Digest," *Christian Faith and Life* 45 (1939): 215.

28   This and the following paragraphs on Price closely follow my account in " 'Sciences of Satanic Origin': Adventist Attitudes toward Evolutionary Biology and Geology," *Spectrum* 9 (Jan. 1979): 22–24.

29   George McCready Price, *Illogical Geology: The Weakest Point in the Evolution Theory* (Los Angeles: Modern Heretic Co., 1906), p. 9. Four years earlier Price had published his first antievolution book, *Outlines of Modern Science and Modern Christianity* (Oakland, Calif.: Pacific Press, 1902).

30   David Starr Jordan to G. M. Price, 5 May 1911, Price Papers, Andrews University Library.

31   George McCready Price, *The New Geology* (Mountain View, Calif.: Pacific Press, 1923), pp. 637–638. Price first announced the discovery of his law in *The Fundamentals of Geology and Their Bearings on the Doctrine of a Literal Creation* (Mountain View, Calif.: Pacific Press, 1913), p. 119.

32   Charles Schuchert, review of *The New Geology*, by George McCready Price, *Science* 59 (1924): 486–487; Harry Rimmer, *Modern Science, Noah's Ark and the Deluge* (Los Angeles: Research Science Bureau, 1925), p. 28.

33   *Science* 63 (1926): 259.

34   Howard A. Kelly to W. J. Bryan, 15 June 1925; Louis T. More to W. J. Bryan, 7 July 1925; and Alfred W. McCann to W. J. Bryan, 30 June 1925, box 47, Bryan Papers, Library of Congress. Regarding Price, see Numbers, " 'Sciences of Satanic Origin,' " p. 24.

35   Numbers, " 'Sciences of Satanic Origin,' " p. 24; Levine, *Defender of the Faith*, p. 349.

36   W. J. Bryan to Howard A. Kelly, 22 June 1925, box 47, Bryan Papers, Library of Congress. In a letter to the editor of *The Forum* 70 (1923): 1852–1853, Bryan asserted that he had never taught that the world was made in six literal days. I am indebted to Paul M. Waggoner for bringing this document to my attention.

37   W. B. Riley and Harry Rimmer, *A Debate: Resolved, That the Creative Days in Genesis Were Aeons, Not Solar Days* (undated pamphlet); [W. B. Riley], "The Creative Week," *Christian Fundamentalist* 4 (1930): 45; Price, *Outlines*, pp. 125–127; idem, *The Story of the Fossils* (Mountain View, Calif.: Pacific Press, 1954), p. 39. On Rimmer's acceptance of a local flood see Robert D. Culver, "An Evaluation of *The Christian View of Science and Scripture* by Bernard Ramm from the Standpoint of Christian Theology," *Journal of the American Scientific Affiliation* 7 (Dec. 1955): 7.

38   Shipley, "Growth of the Anti-Evolution Movement," pp. 330–332; Szasz, *The Divided Mind of Protestant America*, pp. 117–125.

39   Beale, *Are American Teachers Free?* pp. 228–237; Willard B. Gatewood Jr., ed., *Controversy*

in the Twenties: Fundamentalism, Modernism, and Evolution (Nashville: Vanderbilt Univ. Press, 1969), p. 39. The quotation comes from Shipley, "Growth of the Anti-Evolution Movement," p. 330. See also Judith V. Grabiner and Peter D. Miller, "Effects of the Scopes Trial," Science 185 (1974): 832–837; and Estelle R. Laba and Eugene W. Gross, "Evolution Slighted in High-School Biology," Clearing House 24 (1950): 396–399.

40   Joel A. Carpenter, "Fundamentalist Institutions and the Rise of Evangelical Protestantism, 1929–1942," Church History 49 (1980): 62–75, provides an excellent analysis of this trend. For a typical statement of creationist frustration see George McCready Price, "Guarding the Sacred Cow," Christian Faith and Life 41 (1935): 124–127. The title for this section comes from Henry M. Morris, The Troubled Waters of Evolution (San Diego: Creation-Life Publishers, 1974), p. 13.

41   "Announcement of the Religion and Science Association," Price Papers, Andrews University; "The Religion and Science Association," Christian Faith and Life 42 (1936): 159–160; "Meeting of the Religion and Science Association," ibid., p. 209; Harold W. Clark, The Battle over Genesis (Washington: Review & Herald Publishing Association, 1977), p. 168. On the attitude of the Price faction see Harold W. Clark to G. M. Price, 12 Sept. 1937, Price Papers, Andrews University.

42   Numbers, " 'Sciences of Satanic Origin,' " p. 26.

43   Ben F. Allen to the Board of Directors of the Creation-Deluge Society, 12 Aug. 1945 (courtesy of Molleurus Couperus). Regarding the fossil footprints, see the Newsletters of the Creation-Deluge Society for 19 Aug. 1944 and 17 Feb. 1945.

44   Numbers, " 'Sciences of Satanic Origin,' " p. 25.

45   On the early years of the ASA see Alton Everest, "The American Scientific Affiliation—The First Decade," Journal of the American Scientific Affiliation 3 (Sept. 1951): 33–38.

46   J. Laurence Kulp, "Deluge Geology," ibid., 2, no. 1 (1950): 1–15; "Comment on the 'Deluge Geology' Paper of J. L. Kulp," ibid., 2 (June 1950): 2. Kulp mentions his initial skepticism of geology in a discussion of "Some Presuppositions in Evolutionary Thinking," ibid., 1 (June 1949): 20.

47   J. Frank Cassel, "The Evolution of Evangelical Thinking on Evolution," ibid., 11 (Dec. 1959): 26–27. For a fuller discussion see Ronald L. Numbers, "The Dilemma of Evangelical Scientists," in Evangelicalism and Modern America, ed. George M. Marsden (Grand Rapids, Mich.: Wm. B. Eerdmans, 1984), pp. 150–160.

48   Numbers, " 'Sciences of Satanic Origin,' " p. 25; George Marsden, "Fundamentalism as an American Phenomenon: A Comparison with English Evangelicalism," Church History 46 (1977): 215–232; idem, Fundamentalism and American Culture, pp. 222–226.

49   Douglas Dewar, The Difficulties of the Evolution Theory (London: Edward Arnold & Co., 1931), p. 158; Arnold Lunn, ed., Is Evolution Proved? A Debate between Douglas Dewar and H. S. Shelton (London: Hollis & Carter, 1947), pp. 1, 154; Evolution Protest Movement Pamphlet No. 125 (Apr. 1965). On Vialleton see Harry W. Paul, The Edge of Contingency: French Catholic Reaction to Scientific Change from Darwin to Duhem (Gainesville: University Presses of Florida, 1979), pp. 99–100.

50   Douglas Dewar, "The Limitations of Organic Evolution," *Journal of the Victoria Institute* 64 (1932): 142; "EPM—40 Years On; Evolution—114 Years Off," supplement to *Creation* 1 (May 1972): no pagination.

51   R. Halliburton, Jr., "The Adoption of Arkansas' Anti-Evolution Law," *Arkansas Historical Quarterly* 23 (1964): 283; interviews with Henry M. Morris, 26 Oct. 1980 and 6 Jan. 1981. See also the autobiographical material in Henry M. Morris, *History of Modern Creationism* (San Diego: Master Book Publishers, 1984).

52   Interviews with Morris; Henry M. Morris, introduction to the revised edition, *That You Might Believe* (San Diego: Creation-Life Publishers, 1978), p. 10.

53   John C. Whitcomb, Jr. and Henry M. Morris, *The Genesis Flood: The Biblical Record and Its Scientific Implications* (Philadelphia: Presbyterian & Reformed Pub. Co., 1961), pp. xx, 451.

54   Henry M. Morris and John C. Whitcomb, Jr., "Reply to Reviews in the March 1964 Issue," *Journal of the American Scientific Affiliation* 16 (June 1964): 60. The statement regarding the appearance of the book comes from Walter Hearn, quoted in Vernon Lee Bates, "Christian Fundamentalism and the Theory of Evolution in Public School Education: A Study of the Creation Science Movement" (Ph.D. diss., University of California, Davis, 1976), p. 52. See also Frank H. Roberts, review of *The Genesis Flood*, by Henry M. Morris and John C. Whitcomb, Jr., *Journal of the American Scientific Affiliation* 16 (Mar. 1964): 28–29; J. R. Van de Fliert, "Fundamentalism and the Fundamentals of Geology," ibid., 21 (Sept. 1969): 69–81; and Walter E. Lammerts, "Introduction," Creation Research Society, *Annual*, 1964, no pagination. Among Missouri-Synod Lutherans, John W. Klotz, *Genes, Genesis, and Evolution* (St. Louis: Concordia Publishing House, 1955), may have had an even greater influence than Morris and Whitcomb.

55   Walter E. Lammerts, "The Creationist Movement in the United States: A Personal Account," *Journal of Christian Reconstruction* 1 (Summer 1974): 49–63. The first quotation comes from Davis A. Young, *Creation and the Flood: An Alternative to Flood Geology and Theistic Evolution* (Grand Rapids, Mich.: Baker Book House, 1977), p. 7.

56   Names, academic fields, and institutional affiliations are given in *Creation Research Society Quarterly* 1 (July 1964): [13]; for additional information I am indebted to Duane T. Gish, John N. Moore, Henry M. Morris, Harold Slusher, and William J. Tinkle.

57   *Creation Research Society Quarterly* 1 (July 1964): [13]; [Walter Lang], "Editorial Comments," *Bible-Science Newsletter* 16 (June 1978): 2. Other creationists have disputed the 5-percent estimate.

58   Lammerts, "The Creationist Movement in the United States," p. 63; Duane T. Gish, "A Decade of Creationist Research," *Creation Research Society Quarterly* 12 (June 1975): 34–46; John N. Moore and Harold Schultz Slusher, eds., *Biology: A Search for Order in Complexity* (Grand Rapids, Mich.: Zondervan Publishing House, 1970).

59   Walter Lang, "Fifteen Years of Creationism," *Bible Science Newsletter* 16 (Oct. 1978): 1–3; "Editorial Comments," ibid., 15 (Mar. 1977): 2–3; "A Naturalistic Cosmology vs. a Biblical Cosmology," ibid., 15 (Jan.-Feb. 1977): 4–5; Gerald Wheeler, "The Third National Creation Science Conference," *Origins* 3 (1976): 101–102.

60   Bates, "Christian Fundamentalism," p. 58; "15 Years of Creationism," *Five Minutes with the Bible and Science,* supplement to *Bible-Science Newsletter* 17 (May 1979): 2; Nicholas Wade, "Creationists and Evolutionists: Confrontation in California," *Science* 178 (1972): 724–729. Regarding the BSCS texts see Gerald Skoog, "Topic of Evolution in Secondary School Biology Textbooks: 1900–1977," *Science Education* 63 (1979): 621–640; and "A Critique of BSCS Biology Texts," *Bible-Science Newsletter* 4 (15 Mar. 1966): 1. See also John A. Moore, "Creationism in California," *Daedalus* 103 (1974): 173–189; and Dorothy Nelkin, *The Creation Controversy: Science or Scripture in the Schools* (New York: W. W. Norton, 1982).

61   Henry M. Morris, "Director's Column," *Acts & Facts* 1 (June–July 1972): no pagination; Morris interview, 6 Jan. 1981.

62   Nell J. Segraves, *The Creation Report* (San Diego: Creation-Science Research Center, 1977), p. 17; "15 Years of Creationism," pp. 2–3.

63   Bates, "Christian Fundamentalism," p. 98; Henry M. Morris, "Director's Column," *Acts & Facts* 3 (Sept. 1974): 2. See also Edward J. Larson, "Public Science vs. Popular Opinion: The Creation-Evolution Legal Controversy" (Ph.D. diss., University of Wisconsin-Madison, 1984).

64   Morris, "Director's Column," p. 2; Henry M. Morris, ed., *Scientific Creationism,* General Edition (San Diego: Creation-Life Publishers, 1974).

65   The quotation comes from Russel H. Leitch, "Mistakes Creationists Make," *Bible-Science Newsletter* 18 (Mar. 1980): 2. Regarding school boards, see "Finding: Let Kids Decide How We Got Here," *American School Board Journal* 167 (Mar. 1980): 52; and Segraves, *Creation Report,* p. 24. On Popper's influence see, e.g., Ariel A. Roth, "Does Evolution Qualify as a Scientific Principle?" *Origins* 4 (1977): 4–10. In a letter to the editor of *New Scientist* 87 (21 Aug. 1980): 611, Popper affirmed that the evolution of life on earth was testable and, therefore, scientific. On Kuhn's influence see, e.g., Ariel A. Roth, "The Pervasiveness of the Paradigm," *Origins* 2 (1975): 55–57; Leonard R. Brand, "A Philosophic Rationale for a Creation-Flood Model," ibid., 1 (1974): 73–83; and Gerald W. Wheeler, *The Two-Taled Dinosaur: Why Science and Religion Conflict over the Origin of Life* (Nashville: Southern Publishing Association, 1975), pp. 192–210. For the judge's decision see "Creationism in Schools: The Decision in McLean versus the Arkansas Board of Education," *Science* 215 (1982): 934–943.

66   Henry M. Morris, "Two Decades of Creation: Past and Future," *Impact,* supplement to *Acts & Facts* 10 (Jan. 1981): iii; idem, "Director's Column," ibid., 3 (Mar. 1974): 2. The reference to Gish comes from an interview with Harold Slusher and Duane T. Gish, 6 Jan. 1981.

67   "ICR Schedules M.S. Programs," *Acts & Facts* 10 (Feb. 1981): 1–2. Evidence for alleged discrimination and the use of pseudonyms comes from: "Grand Canyon Presents Problems for Long Ages," *Five Minutes with the Bible and Science,* supplement to *Bible-Science Newsletter* 18 (June 1980): 1–2; interview with Ervil D. Clark, 9 Jan. 1981; interview with Steven A. Austin, 6 Jan. 1981; and interview with Duane T. Gish, 26 Oct. 1980, the source of the quotation.

68   Numbers, " 'Sciences of Satanic Origin,' " pp. 27–28; Molleurus Couperus, "Tensions between Religion and Science," *Spectrum* 10 (Mar. 1980): 74–88.

69   William Sims Bainbridge and Rodney Stark, "Superstitions: Old and New," *Skeptical Inquirer* 4 (Summer, 1980): 20.

70   "Poll Finds Americans Split on Evolution Idea," p. 22; Harold T. Christensen and Kenneth L. Cannon, "The Fundamentalist Emphasis at Brigham Young University: 1935–1973," *Journal for the Scientific Study of Religion* 17 (1978): 53–57; "Return to Conservatism," *Bible-Science Newsletter* 11 (Aug. 1973); 1; Numbers, " 'Sciences of Satanic Origin,' " pp. 27–28.

71   Eileen Barker, "In the Beginning: The Battle of Creationist Science against Evolutionism," in *On the Margins of Science: The Social Construction of Rejected Knowledge*, ed. Roy Wallis, Sociological Review Monograph 27 (Keele: University of Keele, 1979), pp. 179–200, who greatly underestimates the size of the E.P.M. in 1966; [Robert E. D. Clark], "Evolution: Polarization of Views," *Faith and Thought* 100 (1972–1973): 227–229; [idem], "American and English Creationists," ibid., 104 (1977): 6–8; "British Scientists Form Creationist Organization," *Acts & Facts* 2 (Nov.–Dec. 1973): 3; "EPM—40 Years On; Evolution—114 Years Off," supplement to *Creation* 1 (May 1972): no pagination.

72   W.J. Ouweneel, "Creationism in the Netherlands," *Impact*, supplement to *Acts & Facts* 7 (Feb. 1978): i–iv. Notices regarding the spread of creationism overseas appeared frequently in *Bible-Science Newsletter* and *Acts & Facts*. On translations see "ICR Books Available in Many Languages," *Acts & Facts* 9 (Feb. 1980): 2, 7.

PART FOUR

Intelligent design

INTRODUCTION TO PART FOUR

PART THREE OF THIS COLLECTION examined the creationist opposition to evolution. Coming from the ranks of fundamentalist and evangelical Christianity, creationists see Darwinism not only as incompatible with a literal interpretation of the Genesis creation story but also as a threat to traditional sources of meaning and morality.

This unit deals with a new player in the creation-evolution debate, intelligent design. The intelligent design movement, which dates in the US from the mid-1980s, insists that the complexity of life goes beyond what the theory of evolution through natural selection can explain and that therefore a scientific account of the history of life should include the actions of a supernatural agent. Unlike the creationists surveyed in the previous unit, the supporters of intelligent design do not insist that this agent be identified as the Christian God (although it should be noted that many ID advocates are in fact Christian theists). ID supporters also do not uniformly reject evolution, and some even allow for a long history of descent from common ancestors and accept a limited role for natural selection. The common denominator among ID proponents is, however, the assumption that there are some biological processes whose complexity cannot be accounted for through gradual evolution. Evidence of design demands the intervention of an intelligent designer.

The argument from design has a long history, taking shape in the work of both non-Christian (e.g., Plato) and Christian (e.g., Thomas Aquinas) authors. The first selection in this part is taken from one of the most famous Christian versions of this argument, that of Anglican Archdeacon William Paley in his *Natural Theology*, which appeared originally in 1802. Paley observes that if he were to find a watch upon the ground and should be asked how it came to be there, he would, upon discovering the intricate complexity of the watch, have to assume the existence of an intelligent watchmaker. He considers and rejects factors that might weaken his conclusion, such as never having seen a watch made or finding imperfections or superfluous parts in the watch. "There cannot be design without a designer," he insists. "Arrangement, disposition of parts, subserviency of means to an end, relation of instruments to a use imply the presence of intelligence and mind."

Paley applies the argument to the world of nature, where he finds manifestations of design that surpass those of a human contrivance. The selection concludes with his rhapsody on the intricacies of the eye: "Were there no example in the world of contrivance except that of the eye, it would be alone sufficient to support the conclusion which we draw from it, as to the necessity of an intelligent Creator."

This section then pairs essays by biochemist Michael J. Behe and cell biologist Kenneth R. Miller, who directly address one another in their pieces. Both practicing Roman Catholics, Behe and Miller are major adversaries in the contemporary debate about intelligent design. Behe's article "Irreducible Complexity: Obstacle to Darwinian Evolution" appeared in *Debating Design: From Darwin to DNA*, edited by William A. Dembski and Michael Ruse. Miller's article "Answering the Biochemical Argument from Design" was published in *God and Design: The Teleological Argument and Modern Science*, edited by Neil A. Manson.

Behe in his essay advances claims that he made earlier in his book *Darwin's Black Box: The Biochemical Challenge to Evolution* (The Free Press, 1996). He argues that certain biochemical systems are irreducibly complex and cannot be accounted for by Darwin's gradualistic process of natural selection. He defines an irreducibly complex system as "a single system that is necessarily composed of several well-matched, interacting parts that contribute to the basic function, and where the removal of any one of the parts causes the system to effectively cease functioning." Insisting that in such cases one must appeal to purposeful design by an intelligent agent, Behe criticizes as "fainthearted" those who refuse to include non-naturalistic causes in scientific theories. As he declares, "I think science should follow the evidence wherever it seems to lead."

While he cites various examples of molecular machinery that he considers to be irreducibly complex, including the eukaryotic cilium and the bacterial flagellum, Behe illustrates his point by offering the analogy of a mechanical mousetrap that will not function to catch mice without all of its essential parts in place. He insists that the mousetrap is an all-or-nothing system that could not have been formed gradually by "something akin to a Darwinian process." He then addresses what he views as several misconceptions about intelligent design and responds to critics of his ideas by suggesting that their "putative counterexamples" not only "fail to make their case for the sufficiency of natural selection, they show clearly the obstacle that irreducible complexity poses to Darwinism."

Miller targets Behe's central claim that the existence of irreducibly complex systems necessitates the appeal to intelligent design. Pointing to the opportunistic and improvisational nature of evolution, Miller suggests that evolution produces complex organs in a series of fully functional intermediate stages, each of which can be favored by natural selection. In this way, he maintains, a complex system can evolve gradually.

Miller proposes Darwinian explanations of several cellular structures, including the eukaryotic cilium and the bacterial flagellum, to counter Behe's analysis of these systems as irreducibly complex. He also dismantles Behe's mousetrap, arguing that the mousetrap actually provides a perfect example of the way in which natural selection builds complex structures. There are, Miller asserts, alternate, selectable functions for partial assemblies of the five parts of a standard mousetrap. His facetious suggestions include a toothpick, tie-clip, nose ring, door knocker, catapult, and nutcracker.

Miller insists, moreover, that merely because scientists have not yet given step-by-step Darwinian explanations for certain cellular structures, does not mean that they will not do so in the future. In fact, Miller warns, if one believes Behe's claims about the irreducible complexity of biochemical machines, one "might never bother to check, and this is the real scientific danger of his ideas."

Miller ends his article with a section labeled "Paley's ghost," where he dismisses contemporary advocates of intelligent design as attempting to resurrect Paley's nineteenth-century arguments, dressed up in the modern language of biochemistry. In *Darwin's Black Box*, Behe disputes this wholesale identification of his ideas with those of Paley. Acknowledging that he appreciates Paley's argument for design, Behe nevertheless faults the Archdeacon for overreaching by arguing for the existence of the Christian God. Behe insists that his is a minimalist argument for design itself and points out that he leaves the identity of the designer open. Miller remains unconvinced by Behe's protests.

The efforts of intelligent design advocates to introduce the teaching of

ID along with Darwinian evolution in public school science classes have resulted in the 2005 US Federal District Court decision in Pennsylvania, Kitzmiller et al. v. Dover Area School District. Intelligent design was ruled to be a new form of creationism rather than science, and therefore presenting ID as an alternative to evolution in public school science classes was considered to be an unconstitutional breach of the separation of church and state. Other efforts of ID proponents in America involve inserting disclaimers in biology textbooks about the flaws in Darwin's theory of evolution and the attempts of state school boards to set new standards for science education that allow for non-naturalistic explanations.

The decision in Kitzmiller v. Dover, together with the earlier rulings on the "balanced treatment" laws in Arkansas and Louisiana, has been sharply criticized by several philosophers, not for the ruling but for the premises on which the decision was based. For example, Evan Fales argues in the March 2006 edition of *Science and Theology News* that ID is not science not because it appeals to supernatural causes but rather because it fails to provide a comprehensive theory about the designer that has fertility and explanatory power. On these grounds, Behe's reluctance to flesh out the nature of the designer would count against his claim that ID is good science.

Selections in other parts of this anthology are pertinent to this debate about intelligent design. Articles in Parts One and Two that deal with scientific method help to clarify the dispute between Behe and Miller. ID proponents often cite differences of opinion within the scientific community about the mechanisms of evolution as a rationale for admitting ID as an explanation. In their articles in Part Two of this collection, biologist Francisco Ayala and philosopher Michael Ruse acknowledge the existence of contemporary scientific debates about natural selection, but they do not entertain ID as a legitimate scientific option.

In the next section of this anthology, biologist Richard Dawkins enters into dialogue with William Paley, but Dawkins identifies natural selection as a "blind watchmaker." Christian theologians and scientists included in Parts Six and Seven find ID dubious from a religious perspective, accusing proponents of intelligent design of promoting a "God of the gaps," who is invoked to fill gaps in our scientific knowledge, only to be marginalized by new scientific discoveries.

Chapter 10

William Paley

NATURAL THEOLOGY

I State of the argument

IN CROSSING A HEATH, suppose I pitched my foot against a
stone and were asked how the stone came to be there, I might possibly
answer that for anything I knew to the contrary it had lain there forever; nor
would it, perhaps, be very easy to show the absurdity of this answer. But
suppose I had found a watch upon the ground, and it should be inquired how
the watch happened to be in that place, I should hardly think of the answer
which I had before given, that for anything I knew the watch might have always
been there. Yet why should not this answer serve for the watch as well as for the
stone; why is it not as admissible in the second case as in the first? For this
reason, and for no other, namely, that when we come to inspect the watch, we
perceive–what we could not discover in the stone–that its several parts are
framed and put together for a purpose, e.g., that they are so formed and
adjusted as to produce motion, and that motion so regulated as to point out the
hour of the day; that if the different parts had been differently shaped from
what they are, or placed after any other manner or in any other order than that
in which they are placed, either no motion at all would have been carried on in
the machine, or none which would have answered the use that is now served by
it. To reckon up a few of the plainest of these parts and of their offices, all
tending to one result: we see a cylindrical box containing a coiled elastic spring,

which, by its endeavor to relax itself, turns round the box. We next observe a flexible chain–artificially wrought for the sake of flexure–communicating the action of the spring from the box to the fusee. We then find a series of wheels, the teeth of which catch in and apply to each other, conducting the motion from the fusee to the balance and from the balance to the pointer, and at the same time, by the size and shape of those wheels, so regulating that motion as to terminate in causing an index, by an equable and measured progression, to pass over a given space in a given time. We take notice that the wheels are made of brass, in order to keep them from rust; the springs of steel, no other metal being so elastic; that over the face of the watch there is placed a glass, a material employed in no other part of the work, but in the room of which, if there had been any other than a transparent substance, the hour could not be seen without opening the case. This mechanism being observed–it requires indeed an examination of the instrument, and perhaps some previous knowledge of the subject, to perceive and understand it; but being once, as we have said, observed and understood–the inference we think is inevitable, that the watch must have had a maker–that there must have existed, at some time and at some place or other, an artificer or artificers who formed it for the purpose which we find it actually to answer, who completely comprehended its construction and designed its use.

I. Nor would it, I apprehend, weaken the conclusion, that we had never seen a watch made–that we had never known an artist capable of making one–that we were altogether incapable of executing such a piece of workmanship ourselves, or of understanding in what manner it was performed; all this being no more than what is true of some exquisite remains of ancient art, of some lost arts, and, to the generality of mankind, of the more curious productions of modern manufacture. Does one man in a million know how oval frames are turned? Ignorance of this kind exalts our opinion of the unseen and unknown artist's skill, if he be unseen and unknown, but raises no doubt in our minds of the existence and agency of such an artist, at some former time and in some place or other. Nor can I perceive that it varies at all the inference, whether the question arise concerning a human agent or concerning an agent of a different species, or an agent possessing in some respects a different nature.

II. Neither, secondly, would it invalidate our conclusion, that the watch sometimes went wrong or that it seldom went exactly right. The purpose of the machinery, the design, and the designer might be evident, and in the case supposed, would be evident, in whatever way we accounted for the irregularity of the movement, or whether we could account for it or not. It is not necessary that a machine be perfect in order to show with what design it was made: still less necessary, where the only question is whether it were made with any design at all.

III. Nor, thirdly, would it bring any uncertainty into the argument, if there were a few parts of the watch, concerning which we could not discover or had not yet discovered in what manner they conduced to the general effect; or even some parts, concerning which we could not ascertain whether they conduced to that effect in any manner whatever. For, as to the first branch of the case, if by the loss, or disorder, or decay of the parts in question, the movement of the watch were found in fact to be stopped, or disturbed, or retarded, no doubt would remain in our minds as to the utility or intention of these parts, although we should be unable to investigate the manner according to which, or the connection by which, the ultimate effect depended upon their action or assistance; and the more complex the machine, the more likely is this obscurity to arise. Then, as to the second thing supposed, namely, that there were parts which might be spared without prejudice to the movement of the watch, and that we had proved this by experiment, these superfluous parts, even if we were completely assured that they were such, would not vacate the reasoning which we had instituted concerning other parts. The indication of contrivance remained, with respect to them, nearly as it was before.

IV. Nor, fourthly, would any man in his senses think the existence of the watch with its various machinery accounted for, by being told that it was one out of possible combinations of material forms; that whatever he had found in the place where he found the watch, must have contained some internal configuration or other; and that this configuration might be the structure now exhibited, namely, of the works of a watch, as well as a different structure.

V. Nor, fifthly, would it yield his inquiry more satisfaction, to be answered that there existed in things a principle of order, which had disposed the parts of the watch into their present form and situation. He never knew a watch made by the principle of order; nor can he even form to himself an idea of what is meant by a principle of order distinct from the intelligence of the watchmaker.

VI. Sixthly, he would be surprised to hear that the mechanism of the watch was no proof of contrivance, only a motive to induce the mind to think so:

VII. And not less surprised to be informed that the watch in his hand was nothing more than the result of the laws of *metallic* nature. It is a perversion of language to assign any law as the efficient, operative cause of any thing. A law presupposes an agent, for it is only the mode according to which an agent proceeds: it implies a power, for it is the order according to which that power acts. Without this agent, without this power, which are both distinct from itself, the *law* does nothing, is nothing. The expression, "the law of metallic nature," may sound strange and harsh to a philosophic ear; but it seems quite as justifiable as some others which are more familiar to him, such as "the law of vegetable nature," "the law of animal nature," or, indeed, as "the law of nature" in general, when assigned as the cause of phenomena, in exclusion of agency and power, or when it is substituted into the place of these.

VIII. Neither, lastly, would our observer be driven out of his conclusion or from his confidence in its truth by being told that he knew nothing at all about the matter. He knows enough for his argument; he knows the utility of the end; he knows the subserviency and adaptation of the means to the end. These points being known, his ignorance of other points, his doubts concerning other points affect not the certainty of his reasoning. The consciousness of knowing little need not beget a distrust of that which he does know.

II State of the argument continued

Suppose, in the next place, that the person who found the watch should after some time discover that, in addition to all the properties which he had hitherto observed in it, it possessed the unexpected property of producing in the course of its movement another watch like itself–the thing is conceivable; that it contained within it a mechanism, a system of parts–a mold, for instance, or a complex adjustment of lathes, files, and other tools–evidently and separately calculated for this purpose; let us inquire what effect ought such a discovery to have upon his former conclusion.

I. The first effect would be to increase his admiration of the contrivance, and his conviction of the consummate skill of the contriver. Whether he regarded the object of the contrivance, the distinct apparatus, the intricate, yet in many parts intelligible mechanism by which it was carried on, he would perceive in this new observation nothing but an additional reason for doing what he had already done–for referring the construction of the watch to design and to supreme art. If that construction without this property, or, which is the same thing, before this property had been noticed, proved intention and art to have been employed about it, still more strong would the proof appear when he came to the knowledge of this further property, the crown and perfection of all the rest.

II. He would reflect that, though the watch before him were in some sense the maker of the watch which was fabricated in the course of its movements, yet it was in a very different sense from that in which a carpenter, for instance, is the maker of a chair–the author of its contrivance, the cause of the relation of its parts to their use. With respect to these, the first watch was no cause at all to the second; in no such sense as this was it the author of the constitution and order, either of the parts which the new watch contained, or of the parts by the aid and instrumentality of which it was produced. We might possibly say, but with great latitude of expression, that a stream of water ground corn; but no latitude of expression would allow us to say, no stretch of conjecture could lead us to think that the stream of water built the mill, though it were too ancient for us to know who the builder was. What the stream of water does in the affair is neither more nor less than this: by the application of an unintelligent impulse to a mechanism previously arranged, arranged independently of it and arranged by intelligence, an effect is produced, namely, the corn is ground. But the effect results from the arrangement. The force of the stream cannot be said to be the cause or the author of the effect, still less of the arrangement. Understanding and plan in the formation of the mill were not the less necessary for any share which the water has in grinding the corn; yet is this share the same as that which the watch would have contributed to the production of the new watch, upon the supposition assumed in the last section. Therefore,

III. Though it be now no longer probable that the individual watch which our observer had found was made immediately by the hand of an artificer, yet this alteration does not in anywise affect the inference that an artificer had been originally employed and concerned in the production. The argument from design remains as it was. Marks of design and contrivance are no more accounted for now than they were before. In the same thing, we may ask for the cause of different properties. We may ask for the cause of the color of a body, of its hardness, of its heat; and these causes may be all different. We are now asking for the cause of that subserviency to a use, that relation to an end, which we have remarked in the watch before us. No answer is given to this question by telling us that a preceding watch produced it. There cannot be design without a designer; contrivance without a contriver; order without choice; arrangement without anything capable of arranging; subserviency and relation to a purpose without that which could intend a purpose; means suitable to an end, and executing their office in accomplishing that end, without the end ever having been contemplated or the means accommodated to it. Arrangement, disposition of parts, subserviency of means to an end, relation of instruments to a use imply the presence of intelligence and mind. No one, therefore, can rationally believe that the insensible, inanimate watch, from which the watch before us issued, was the proper cause of the mechanism we so much admire in it–could be truly said to have constructed the instrument, disposed its parts, assigned their office, determined their order, action, and mutual dependency, combined their several motions into one result, and that also a result connected with the utilities of other beings. All these properties, therefore, are as much unaccounted for as they were before. [. . .]

The conclusion which the first examination of the watch, of its works, construction, and movement, suggested, was that it must have had, for cause and author of that construction, an artificer who understood its mechanism and designed its use. This conclusion is invincible. A *second* examination presents us with a new discovery. The watch is found, in the course of its movement, to produce another watch similar to itself; and not only so, but we perceive in it a system or organization separately calculated for that purpose. What effect would this discovery have or ought it to have upon our former inference? What, as has already been said, but to increase beyond measure our admiration of the skill which had been employed in the formation of such a machine? Or shall it, instead of this, all at once turn us round to an opposite conclusion, namely, that no art or skill whatever has been concerned in the business, although all other evidences of art and skill remain as they were, and this last and supreme piece of art be now added to the rest? Can this be maintained without absurdity? Yet this is atheism.

III Application of the argument

This is atheism; for every indication of contrivance, every manifestation of design which existed in the watch, exists in the works of nature, with the difference on the side of nature of being greater and more, and that in a degree which exceeds all computation. I mean that the contrivances of nature surpass the contrivances of art in the complexity, subtlety, and curiosity of the mechanism; and still more, if possible, do they go beyond them in number and variety; yet, in a multitude of cases, are not less evidently mechanical, not less evidently contrivances, not less evidently accommodated to their end or suited to their office than are the most perfect productions of human ingenuity.

I know no better method of introducing so large a subject than that of comparing a single thing with a single thing: an eye, for example, with a telescope. As far as the examination of the instrument goes, there is precisely the same proof that the eye was made for vision as there is that the telescope was made for assisting it. They are made upon the same principles, both being adjusted to the laws by which the transmission and refraction of rays of light are regulated. I speak not of the origin of the laws themselves; but such laws being fixed, the construction in both cases is adapted to them. For instance, these laws require, in order to produce the same effect, that rays of light in passing from water into the eye should be refracted by a more convex surface than when it passes out of air into the eye. Accordingly, we find that the eye of a fish, in that part of it called the crystalline lens, is much rounder than the eye of terrestrial animals. What plainer manifestation of design can there be than this difference? What could a mathematical instrument maker have done more to show his knowledge of his principle, his application of that knowledge, his suiting of his means to his end–I will not say to display the compass or excellence of his skill and art, for in these all comparison is indecorous, but to testify counsel, choice, consideration, purpose? [. . .]

V   Application of the argument continued

Every observation which was made in our first chapter concerning the watch may be repeated with strict propriety concerning the eye, concerning animals, concerning plants, concerning, indeed, all the organized parts of the works of nature. As,

I. When we are inquiring simply after the *existence* of an intelligent Creator, imperfection, inaccuracy, liability to disorder, occasional irregularities may subsist in a considerable degree without inducing any doubt into the question; just as a watch may frequently go wrong, seldom perhaps exactly right, may be faulty in some parts, defective in some, without the smallest ground of suspicion from thence arising that it was not a watch, not made, or not made for the purpose asscribed to it. When faults are pointed out, and when a question is started concerning the skill of the artist or the dexterity with which the work is executed, then, indeed, in order to defend these qualities from accusation, we must be able either to expose some intractableness and imperfection in the materials or point out some invincible difficulty in the execution, into which imperfection and difficulty the matter of complaint may be resolved; or, if we cannot do this, we must adduce such specimens of consummate art and contrivance proceeding from the same hand as may convince the inquirer of the existence, in the case before him, of impediments like those which we have mentioned, although, what from the nature of the case is very likely to happen, they be unknown and unperceived by him. This we must do in order to vindicate the artist's skill, or at least the perfection of it; as we must also judge of his intention and of the provisions employed in fulfilling that intention, not from an instance in which they fail but from the great plurality of instances in which they succeed. But, after all, these are different questions from the question of the artist's existence; or, which is the same, whether the thing before us be a work of art or not; and the questions ought always to be kept separate in the mind. So likewise it is in the works of nature. Irregularities and imperfections are of little or no weight in the consideration when that consideration relates simply to the existence of a Creator. When the argument respects his attributes, they are of weight; but are then to be taken in conjunction—the attention is not to rest upon them, but they are to be taken in conjunction with the unexceptional evidences which we possess of skill, power, and benevolence displayed in other instances; which evidences may, in strength, number, and variety, be such and may so overpower apparent blemishes as to induce us, upon the most reasonable ground, to believe that these last ought to be referred to some cause, though we be ignorant of it, other than defect of knowledge or of benevolence in the author. [. . .]

VI The argument cumulative

Were there no example in the world of contrivance except that of the *eye*, it would be alone sufficient to support the conclusion which we draw from it, as to the necessity of an intelligent Creator. It could never be got rid of, because it could not be accounted for by any other supposition which did not contradict all the principles we possess of knowledge–the principles according to which things do, as often as they can be brought to the test of experience, turn out to be true or false. Its coats and humors, constructed as the lenses of a telescope are constructed, for the refraction of rays of light to a point, which forms the proper action of the organ; the provision in its muscular tendons for turning its pupil to the object, similar to that which is given to the telescope by screws, and upon which power of direction in the eye the exercise of its office as an optical instrument depends; the further provision for its defense, for its constant lubricity and moisture, which we see in its socket and its lids, in its glands for the secretion of the matter of tears, its outlet or communication with the nose for carrying off the liquid after the eye is washed with it; these provisions compose altogether an apparatus, a system of parts, a preparation of means, so manifest in their design, so exquisite in their contrivance, so successful in their issue, so precious, and so infinitely beneficial in their use, as, in my opinion, to bear down all doubt that can be raised upon the subject. And what I wish, under the title of the present chapter, to observe is that, if other parts of nature were inaccessible to our inquiries, or even if other parts of nature presented nothing to our examination but disorder and confusion, the validity of this example would remain the same. If there were but one watch in the world, it would not be less certain that it had a maker. If we had never in our lives seen any but one single kind of hydraulic machine, yet if of that one kind we understood the mechanism and use, we should be as perfectly assured that it proceeded from the hand and thought and skill of a workman, as if we visited a museum of the arts and saw collected there twenty different kinds of machines for drawing water, or a thousand different kinds for other purposes. Of this point each machine is a proof independently of all the rest. So it is with the evidences of a divine agency. The proof is not a conclusion which lies at the end of a chain of reasoning, of which chain each instance of contrivance is only a link, and of which, if one link fail, the whole fails; but it is an argument separately supplied by every separate example. An error in stating an example affects only that example. The argument is cumulative in the fullest sense of that term. The eye proves it without the ear; the ear without the eye. The proof in each example is complete; for when the design of the part and the conduciveness of its structure to that design is shown, the mind may set itself at rest; no future consideration can detract anything from the force of the example.

Chapter 11

Michael J. Behe

IRREDUCIBLE COMPLEXITY: OBSTACLE TO DARWINIAN EVOLUTION

A sketch of the intelligent design hypothesis

IN HIS SEMINAL WORK On the Origin of Species, Darwin hoped to explain what no one had been able to explain before – how the variety and complexity of the living world might have been produced by simple natural laws. His idea for doing so was, of course, the theory of evolution by natural selection. In a nutshell, Darwin saw that there was variety in all species. For example, some members of a species are bigger than others, some faster, some brighter in color. He knew that not all organisms that are born will survive to reproduce, simply because there is not enough food to sustain them all. So Darwin reasoned that the ones whose chance variation gives them an edge in the struggle for life would tend to survive and leave offspring. If the variation could be inherited, then over time the characteristics of the species would change, and over great periods of time, perhaps great changes could occur.

It was an elegant idea, and many scientists of the time quickly saw that it could explain many things about biology. However, there remained an important reason for reserving judgment about whether it could actually account for all of biology: the basis of life was as yet unknown. In Darwin's day, atoms and molecules were still theoretical constructs – no one was sure if such things actually existed. Many scientists of Darwin's era took the cell to be a simple glob of protoplasm, something like a microscopic piece of Jell-O. Thus the intricate molecular basis of life was utterly unknown to Darwin and his contemporaries.

In the past hundred years, science has learned much more about the cell and, especially in the past fifty years, much about the molecular basis of life. The discoveries of the double helical structure of DNA, the genetic code, the complicated, irregular structure of proteins, and much else have given us a greater appreciation for the elaborate structures that are necessary to sustain life. Indeed, we have seen that the cell is run by machines – literally, machines made of molecules. There are molecular machines that enable the cell to move, machines that empower it to transport nutrients, machines that allow it to defend itself.

In light of the enormous progress made by science since Darwin first proposed his theory, it is reasonable to ask if the theory still seems to be a good explanation for life. In *Darwin's Black Box: The Biochemical Challenge to Evolution* (Behe 1996), I argued that it is not. The main difficulty for Darwinian mechanisms is that many systems in the cell are what I termed "irreducibly complex." I defined an irreducibly complex system as: a single system that is necessarily composed of several well-matched, interacting parts that contribute to the basic function, and where the removal of any one of the parts causes the system to effectively cease functioning (Behe 2001). As an example from everyday life of an irreducibly complex system, I pointed to a mechanical mousetrap such as one finds in a hardware store. Typically, such traps have a number of parts: a spring, a wooden platform, a hammer, and other pieces. If one removes a piece from the trap, it can't catch mice. Without the spring, or hammer, or any of the other pieces, one doesn't have a trap that works half as well as it used to, or a quarter as well; one has a broken mousetrap, which doesn't work at all.

Irreducibly complex systems seem very difficult to fit into a Darwinian framework, for a reason insisted upon by Darwin himself. In the *Origin*, Darwin wrote that "[i]f it could be demonstrated that any complex organ existed which could not possibly have been formed by numerous, successive, slight modifications, my theory would absolutely break down. But I can find out no such case" (Darwin 1859, 158). Here Darwin was emphasizing that his was a gradual theory. Natural selection had to improve systems by tiny steps, over a long period of time, because if things improved too rapidly, or in large steps, then it would begin to look as if something other than natural selection were driving the process. However, it is hard to see how something like a mousetrap could arise gradually by something akin to a Darwinian process. For example, a spring by itself, or a platform by itself, would not catch mice, and adding a piece to the first nonfunctioning piece wouldn't make a trap either. So it appears that irreducibly complex biological systems would present a considerable obstacle to Darwinian evolution.

The question then becomes, are there any irreducibly complex systems in the cell? Are there any irreducibly complex molecular machines? Yes, there are many. In *Darwin's Black Box*, I discussed several biochemical systems as examples of irreducible complexity: the eukaryotic cilium, the intracellular transport system, and more. Here I will just briefly describe the bacterial flagellum (DeRosier 1998; Shapiro 1995), since its structure makes the difficulty for Darwinian evolution easy to see (Figure 11.1). The flagellum can be thought of as an outboard motor that bacteria use to swim. It was the first truly rotary structure discovered in nature. It consists of a long filamentous tail that acts as a propeller; when it is spun, it pushes against the liquid medium and can propel the bacterium forward. The propeller is attached to the drive shaft indirectly through something called the hook region, which acts as a universal joint. The drive shaft is attached to the motor, which uses a flow of acid or sodium ions from the outside to the inside of the cell to power rotation. Just as an outboard motor has to be kept stationary on a motorboat while the propeller turns, there are proteins that act as a stator structure to keep the flagellum in place. Other proteins act as bushings to permit the drive shaft to pass through the bacterial membrane. Studies have shown that thirty to forty proteins are required to produce a functioning flagellum in the cell. About half of the proteins are components of the finished structure, while the others are necessary for the

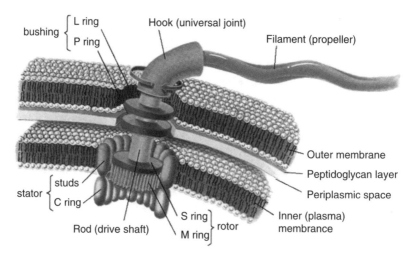

Figure 11.1   The bacterial flagellum. Reproduced from D. Voet and J. G. Voet, *Biochemistry*, 2nd ed. (New York: Wiley, 1995), Figure 34–84, with permission of John Wiley Publishers and Donald Voet, who wished to emphasize that "this is an artist-drawn representation of the flagellum rather than a photo or drawing of an actual flagellum."

construction of the flagellum. In the absence of almost any of the proteins – in the absence of the parts that act as the propeller, drive shaft, hook, and so forth – no functioning flagellum is built.

As with the mousetrap, it is quite difficult to see how Darwin's gradualistic process of natural selection sifting random mutations could produce the bacterial flagellum, since many pieces are required before its function appears. A hook by itself, or a driveshaft by itself, will not act as a propulsive device. But the situation is actually much worse than it appears from this cursory description, for several reasons. First, there is associated with the functioning of the flagellum an intricate control system, which tells the flagellum when to rotate, when to stop, and sometimes when to reverse itself and rotate in the opposite direction. This allows the bacterium to swim toward or away from an appropriate signal, rather than in a random direction that could much more easily take it the wrong way. Thus the problem of accounting for the origin of the flagellum is not limited to the flagellum itself but extends to associated control systems as well.

Second, a more subtle problem is how the parts assemble themselves into a whole. The analogy to an outboard motor fails in one respect: an outboard motor is generally assembled under the direction of a human – an intelligent agent who can specify which parts are attached to which other parts. The information for assembling a bacterial flagellum, however (or, indeed, for assembling any biomolecular machine), resides in the component proteins of the structure itself. Recent work shows that the assembly process for a flagellum is exceedingly elegant and intricate (Yonekura et al. 2000). If that assembly information is absent from the proteins, then no flagellum is produced. Thus, even if we had a hypothetical cell in which proteins homologous to all of the parts of the flagellum were present (perhaps performing jobs other than propulsion) but were missing the information on how to assemble themselves into a flagellum, we would still not get the structure. The problem of irreducibility would remain.

Because of such considerations, I have concluded that Darwinian processes are not promising explanations for many biochemical systems in the cell. Instead, I have noted that, if one looks at the interactions of the components of the flagellum, or cilium, or other irreducibly complex cellular system, they look like they were designed – purposely designed by an intelligent agent. The features of the systems that indicate design are the same ones that stymie Darwinian explanations: the specific interaction of multiple components to accomplish a function that is beyond the individual components. The logical structure of the argument to design is a simple inductive one: whenever we see such highly specific interactions in our everyday world, whether in a mousetrap or elsewhere, we unfailingly find that the systems were intentionally arranged –

that they were designed. Now we find systems of similar complexity in the cell. Since no other explanation has successfully addressed them, I argue that we should extend the induction to subsume molecular machines, and hypothesize that they were purposely designed.

Misconceptions about what a hypothesis of design entails

The hypothesis of Intelligent Design (ID) is quite controversial, mostly because of its philosophical and theological overtones, and in the years since *Darwin's Black Box* was published a number of scientists and philosophers have tried to refute its main argument. I have found these rebuttals to be unpersuasive, at best. Quite the opposite, I think that some putative counterexamples to design are unintentionally instructive. Not only do they fail to make their case for the sufficiency of natural selection, they show clearly the obstacle that irreducible complexity poses to Darwinism. They also show that Darwinists have great trouble recognizing problems with their own theory. I will examine two of those counterexamples in detail a little later in this chapter. Before I do, however, I will first address a few common misconceptions that surround the biochemical design argument.

First of all, it is important to understand that a hypothesis of Intelligent Design has no quarrel with evolution per se – that is, evolution understood simply as descent with modification, but leaving the mechanism open. After all, a designer may have chosen to work that way. Rather than common descent, the focus of ID is on the *mechanism* of evolution – how did all this happen, by natural selection or by purposeful Intelligent Design?

A second point that is often overlooked but should be emphasized is that Intelligent Design can happily coexist with even a large degree of natural selection. Antibiotic and pesticide resistance, antifreeze proteins in fish and plants, and more may indeed be explained by a Darwinian mechanism. The critical claim of ID is not that natural selection doesn't explain *anything*, but that it doesn't explain *everything*.

My book, *Darwin's Black Box*, in which I flesh out the design argument, has been widely discussed in many publications. Although many issues have been raised, I think the general reaction of scientists to the design argument is well and succinctly summarized in the recent book *The Way of the Cell*, published by Oxford University Press and authored by the Colorado State University biochemist Franklin Harold. Citing my book, Harold writes, "We should reject, as a matter of principle, the substitution of intelligent design for the dialogue of chance and necessity (Behe 1996); but we must concede that there are presently no detailed Darwinian accounts of the evolution of any biochemical system, only a variety of wishful speculations" (Harold 2001, 205).

Let me emphasize, in reverse order, Harold's two points. First, as other reviewers of my book have done,[1] Harold acknowledges that Darwinists have no real explanation for the enormous complexity of the cell, only hand-waving speculations, more colloquially known as "just-so stories." I had claimed essentially the same thing six years earlier in *Darwin's Black Box* and encountered fierce resistance – mostly from internet fans of Darwinism who claimed that, why, there were hundreds or thousands of research papers describing the Darwinian evolution of irreducibly complex biochemical systems, and who set up web sites to document them.[2]

As a sufficient response to such claims, I will simply rely on Harold's statement quoted here, as well as the other reviewers who agree that there is a dearth of Darwinian explanations. After all, if prominent scientists who are no fans of Intelligent Design agree that the systems remain unexplained, then that should settle the matter. Let me pause, however, to note that I find this an astonishing admission for a theory that has dominated biology for so long. That Darwinian theory has borne so little fruit in explaining the molecular basis of life – despite its long reign as the fundamental theory of biology – strongly suggests that it is not the right framework for understanding the origin of the complexity of life.

Harold's second point is that there is some principle that forbids us from investigating Intelligent Design, even though design is an obvious idea that quickly pops into your mind when you see a drawing of the flagellum (Figure 11.1) or other complex biochemical system. What principle is that? He never spells it out, but I think the principle probably boils down to this: design appears to point strongly beyond nature. It has philosophical and theological implications, and that makes many people uncomfortable. Because they think that science should avoid a theory that points so strongly beyond nature, they want to rule out intelligent design from the start.

I completely disagree with that view and find it fainthearted. I think science should follow the evidence wherever it seems to lead. That is the only way to make progress. Furthermore, not only Intelligent Design, but *any* theory that purports to explain how life occurred will have philosophical and theological implications. For example, the Oxford biologist Richard Dawkins has famously said that "Darwin made it possible to be an intellectually-fulfilled atheist" (Dawkins 1986, 6). A little less famously, Kenneth Miller has written that "[God] used evolution as the tool to set us free" (Miller 1999, 253). Stuart Kauffman, a leading complexity theorist, thinks Darwinism cannot explain all of biology: "Darwinism is not enough. . . . [N]atural selection cannot be the sole source of order we see in the world" (Kauffman 1995, viii). But Kauffman thinks that his theory will somehow show that we are "at home in the universe." The point, then, is that all theories of origins carry philosophical and theological implications. There is no way to avoid them in an explanation of life.

Another source of difficulty for some people concerns the question, how could biochemical systems have been designed? A common misconception is that designed systems would have to be created from scratch in a puff of smoke. But that isn't necessarily so. The design process may have been much more subtle. In fact, it may have contravened no natural laws at all. Let's consider just one possibility. Suppose the designer is indeed God, as most people would suspect. Well, then, as Kenneth Miller points out in his book, Finding Darwin's God:

> The indeterminate nature of quantum events would allow a clever and subtle God to influence events in ways that are profound, but scientifically undetectable to us. Those events could include the appearance of mutations . . . and even the survival of individual cells and organisms affected by the chance processes of radioactive decay.
>
> (Miller 1999, 241)

Miller doesn't think that guidance is necessary in evolution, but if it were (as I believe), then a route would be open for a subtle God to design life without overriding natural law. If quantum events such as radioactive decay are not governed by causal laws, then it breaks no law of nature to influence such events. As a theist like Miller, that seems perfectly possible to me. I would add, however, that such a process would amount to Intelligent Design, not Darwinian evolution. Further, while we might not be able to detect quantum manipulations, we may nevertheless be able to conclude confidently that the final structure was designed.

Misconceptions concerning supposed ways around the irreducibility of biochemical systems

Consider a hypothetical example where proteins homologous to all of the parts of an irreducibly complex molecular machine first had other individual functions in the cell. Might the irreducible system then have been put together from individual components that originally worked on their own, as some Darwinists have proposed? Unfortunately, this picture greatly oversimplifies the difficulty, as I discussed in Darwin's Black Box (Behe 1996, 53). Here analogies to mousetraps break down somewhat, because the parts of a molecular system have to find each other automatically in the cell. They can't be arranged by an intelligent agent, as a mousetrap is. In order to find each other in the cell, interacting parts have to have their surfaces shaped so that they are very closely matched to each other, as pictured in Figure 11.2. Originally, however, the individually acting components would not have had complementary surfaces. So all of the interacting surfaces of all of the components would first have to be adjusted before they could function together. And only then would the new function of the composite system appear. Thus, I emphasize strongly, *the problem of irreducibility remains, even if individual proteins homologous to system components separately and originally had their own functions.*

Another area where one has to be careful is in noticing that some systems that have extra or redundant components may have an irreducibly complex core. For example, a car with four spark plugs might get by with three or two, but it certainly can't get by with none. Rat traps often have two springs, to give them extra strength. The trap can still work if one spring is removed, but it can't work if both springs are removed. Thus in trying to imagine the origin of a rat trap by Darwinian means, we still have all the problems we had with a mousetrap. A cellular example of redundancy is the hugely complex eukaryotic cilium, which contains about 250 distinct protein parts (Dutcher 1995). The cilium has multiple copies of a number of components, including multiple micro-tubules and dynein arms. Yet a working cilium needs at least one copy of each in order to work, as I pictured in my book (Behe 1996, 60). Thus, like the rat

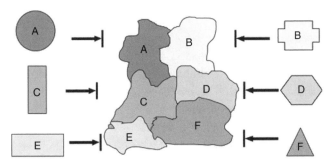

Figure 11.2   The parts of an irreducibly complex molecular machine must have surfaces that are closely matched to each other to allow specific binding. This drawing emphasizes that even if individually acting proteins homologous to parts of a complex originally had separate functions, their surfaces would not be complementary to each other. Thus the problem of irreducibility remains even if the separate parts originally had individual functions. (The blocked arrows indicate that the original protein shapes are not suitable to bind other proteins in the molecular machine.)

trap's, its gradual Darwinian production remains quite difficult to envision. Kenneth Miller has pointed to the redundancy of the cilium as a counter-example to my claim of its irreducibility (Miller 1999, 140–3). But redundancy only delays irreducibility; it does not eliminate it.

Finally, rather than showing how their theory could handle the obstacle, some Darwinists are hoping to get around irreducible complexity by verbal tap dancing. At a debate between proponents and opponents of Intelligent Design sponsored by the American Museum of Natural History in April 2002, Kenneth Miller actually claimed (the transcript is available at the web site of the National Center for Science Education) that a mousetrap isn't irreducibly complex because subsets of a mousetrap, and even each individual part, could still "function" on their own. The holding bar of a mousetrap, Miller observed, could be used as a toothpick, so it still has a "function" outside the mousetrap. Any of the parts of the trap could be used as a paperweight, he continued, so they all have "functions." And since any object that has mass can be a paperweight, then any part of anything has a function of its own. Presto, there is no such thing as irreducible complexity! Thus the acute problem for gradualism that any child can see in systems like the mousetrap is smoothly explained away.

Of course, the facile explanation rests on a transparent fallacy, a brazen equivocation. Miller uses the word "function" in two different senses. Recall that the definition of irreducible complexity notes that removal of a part "causes the *system* to effectively cease functioning." Without saying so, in his exposition Miller shifts the focus from the separate function of the intact *system* itself to the question of whether we can find a different use (or "function") for some of the *parts*. However, if one removes a part from the mousetrap that I have pictured, it can no longer catch mice. The *system* has indeed effectively ceased functioning, so the *system* is irreducibly complex, just as I have written. What's more, the functions that Miller glibly assigns to the parts – paperweight, tooth-pick, key chain, and so forth – have little or nothing to do with the function of the system – catching mice (unlike the mousetrap series proposed by John McDonald, to be discussed later) – so they give us no clue as to how the system's function could arise gradually. Miller has explained precisely nothing.

With the problem of the mousetrap behind him, Miller then moved on to the bacterial flagellum – and again resorted to the same fallacy. If nothing else, one has to admire the breathtaking audacity of verbally trying to turn another severe problem for Darwinism into an advantage. In recent years, it has been shown that the bacterial flagellum is an even more sophisticated system than had been thought. Not only does it act as a rotary propulsion device, it also contains within itself an elegant mechanism used to transport the proteins that make up the outer portion of the machine from the inside of the cell to the outside (Aizawa 1996). Without blinking, Miller asserted that the flagellum is not irreducibly complex because some proteins of the flagellum could be missing and the remainder could still transport proteins, perhaps independently. (Proteins similar – but not identical – to some found in the flagellum occur in the type III secretory system of some bacteria. See Hueck 1998). Again, he was equivocating, switching the focus from the function of the system, acting as a rotary propulsion machine, to the ability of a subset of the system to transport proteins across a membrane. However, taking away the parts of the flagellum certainly destroys the ability of the system to act as a rotary propulsion machine, as I have argued. Thus, contra Miller, the flagellum is indeed irreducibly complex. What's more, the function of transporting proteins has as little directly to do with the function of rotary propulsion as a toothpick has to do with a mousetrap. So discovering the supportive function of transporting proteins tells us precisely nothing about how Darwinian processes might have put together a rotary propulsion machine.

The blood clotting cascade

Having dealt with some common misconceptions about intelligent design, in the next two sections I will examine two systems that were proposed as serious counterexamples to my claim of irreducible complexity. I will show not only that they fail, but also how they highlight the seriousness of the obstacle of irreducible complexity.

In *Darwin's Black Box*, I argued that the blood clotting cascade is an example of an irreducibly complex system (Behe 1996, 74–97). At first glance, clotting seems to be a simple process. A small cut or scrape will bleed for a while and then slow down and stop as the visible blood congeals. However, studies over the past fifty years have shown that the visible simplicity is undergirded by a system of remarkable complexity (Halkier 1992). In all, there are over a score of separate protein parts involved in the vertebrate clotting system. The concerted action of the components results in the formation of a weblike structure at the site of the cut, which traps red blood cells and stops the bleeding. Most of the components of the clotting cascade are involved not in the structure of the clot itself, but in the control of the timing and placement of the clot. After all, it would not do to have clots forming at inappropriate times and places. A clot that formed in the wrong place, such as in the heart or brain, could lead to a heart attack or stroke. Yet a clot that formed even in the right place, but too slowly, would do little good.

The insoluble weblike fibers of the clot material itself are formed of a protein called fibrin. However, an insoluble web would gum up blood flow before a cut or scrape happened, so fibrin exists in the bloodstream initially in a soluble, inactive form called fibrinogen. When the closed circulatory system is breached, fibrinogen is activated by having a piece cut off from one end of two of the three proteins that comprise it. This exposes sticky sites on the protein, which allows them to aggregate. Because of the shape of the fibrin, the molecules aggregate into long fibers that form the meshwork of the clot. Eventually, when healing is completed, the clot is removed by an enzyme called plasmin.

The enzyme that converts fibrinogen to fibrin is called thrombin. Yet the action of thrombin itself has to be carefully regulated. If it were not, then thrombin would quickly convert fibrinogen to fribrin, causing massive blood clots and rapid death. It turns out that thrombin exists in an inactive form called prothrombin, which has to be activated by another component called Stuart factor. But by the same reasoning, the activity of Stuart factor has to be controlled, too, and it is activated by yet another component. Ultimately, the component that usually begins the cascade is tissue factor, which occurs on cells that normally do not come in contact with the circulatory system. However, when a cut occurs, blood is exposed to tissue factor, which initiates the clotting cascade.

Thus in the clotting cascade, one component acts on another, which acts on the next, and so forth. I argued that the cascade is irreducibly complex because, if a component is removed, the pathway is either immediately turned on or permanently turned off. It would not do, I wrote, to postulate that the pathway started from one end, fibrinogen, and then added components, since fibrinogen itself does no good. Nor is it plausible even to start with something like fibrinogen and a nonspecific enzyme that might cleave it, since the clotting would not be regulated and would be much more likely to do harm than good.

So said I. But Russell Doolittle – an eminent protein biochemist, a professor of biochemistry at the University of California-San Diego, a member of the National Academy of Sciences, and a lifelong student of the blood clotting system – disagreed. As part of a symposium discussing my book and Richard Dawkins' *Climbing Mount Improbable* in the *Boston Review*, which is published by the Massachusetts Institute of Technology, Doolittle wrote an essay discussing the phenomenon of gene duplication – the process by which a cell may be provided with an extra copy of a functioning gene. He then conjectured that the components of the blood clotting pathway, many of which have structures that are similar to each other, arose by gene duplication and gradual divergence. This is the common view among Darwinists. Professor Doolittle went on to describe a then-recent experiment that, he thought, showed that the cascade is not irreducible after all. Professor Doolittle cited a paper by Bugge and colleagues (1996a) entitled "Loss of Fibrinogen Rescues Mice from the Pleiotropic Effects of Plasminogen Deficiency." Of that paper, he wrote:

Recently the gene for plaminogen [sic] was knocked out of mice, and, predictably, those mice had thrombotic complications because fibrin clots could not be cleared away. Not long after that, the same workers knocked out the gene for fibrinogen in another line of mice. Again, predictably, these mice were ailing, although in this case hemorrhage was the problem. And what do you think happened when these two lines of mice were crossed? For all practical purposes, the mice lacking both genes were normal! Contrary to claims about irreducible complexity, the entire ensemble of proteins is not needed. Music and harmony can arise from a smaller orchestra.

(Doolittle 1997)

(Again, fibrinogen is the precursor of the clot material itself. Plasminogen is the precursor of plasmin, which removes clots once their purpose is accomplished.) So if one knocks out either one of those genes of the clotting pathway, trouble results; but, Doolittle asserted, if one knocks out both, then the system is apparently functional again. That would be a very interesting result, but it turns out to be incorrect. Doolittle misread the paper.

The abstract of the paper states that "[m]ice deficient in plasminogen and fibrinogen are phenotypically indistinguishable from fibrinogen-deficient mice." In other words, the double mutants have all the problems that the mice lacking just fibrinogen have. Those problems include inability to clot, hemorrhaging, and death of females during pregnancy. Plasminogen deficiency leads to a different suite of symptoms – thrombosis, ulcers, and high mortality. Mice missing both genes were "rescued" from the ill effects of plasminogen deficiency only to suffer the problems associated with fibrinogen deficiency.[3] The reason for this is easy to see. Plasminogen is needed to remove clots that, left in place, interfere with normal functions. However, if the gene for fibrinogen is also knocked out, then clots can't form in the first place, and their removal is not an issue. Yet if clots can't form, then there is no functioning clotting system, and the mice suffer the predictable consequences.

Clearly, the double-knockout mice are not "normal." They are not promising evolutionary intermediates.

The same group that produced the mice missing plasminogen and fibrinogen has also produced mice individually missing other components of the clotting cascade – prothrombin and tissue factor. In each case, the mice are severely compromised, which is *exactly* what one would expect if the cascade is irreducibly complex (Table 11.1).

What lessons can we draw from this incident? The point is certainly not that Russell Doolittle misread a paper, which anyone might do. (Scientists, as a

Table 11.1 Effects of knocking out genes for blood clotting components

Missing Protein	Symptoms	Reference
Plasminogen	Thrombosis, high mortality	Bugge et al. 1995
Fibrinogen	Hemorrhage, death in pregnancy	Suh et al. 1995
Plasminogen/fibrinogen	Hemorrhage, death in pregnancy	Bugge et al. 1996a
Prothrombin	Hemorrhage, death in pregnancy	Sun et al. 1998
Tissue factor	Hemorrhage, death in pregnancy	Bugge et al. 1996b

rule, are not known for their ability to write clearly, and Bugge and colleagues were no exception.) Rather, the main lesson is that irreducible complexity seems to be a much more severe problem than Darwinists recognize, since the experiment Doolittle himself chose to demonstrate that "music and harmony can arise from a smaller orchestra" showed exactly the opposite. A second lesson is that gene duplication is not the panacea that it is often made out to be. Professor Doolittle knows as much about the structures of the clotting proteins and their genes as anyone on Earth, and he is convinced that many of them arose by gene duplication and exon shuffling. Yet that knowledge did not prevent him from proposing utterly nonviable mutants as possible examples of evolutionary intermediates. A third lesson is that, as I had claimed in *Darwin's Black Box*, there are no papers in the scientific literature detailing how the clotting pathway could have arisen by Darwinian means. If there were, Doolittle would simply have cited them.

Another significant lesson that we can draw is that, while the majority of academic biologists and philosophers place their confidence in Darwinism, that confidence rests on no firmer grounds than Professor Doolittle's. As an illustration, consider the words of the philosopher Michael Ruse:

> For example, Behe is a real scientist, but this case for the impossibility of a small-step natural origin of biological complexity has been trampled upon contemptuously by the scientists working in the field. They think his grasp of the pertinent science is weak and his knowledge of the literature curiously (although conveniently) outdated.

For example, far from the evolution of clotting being a mystery, the past three decades of work by Russell Doolittle and others has thrown significant light on the ways in which clotting came into being. More than this, it can be shown that the clotting mechanism does not have to be a one-step phenomenon with everything already in place and functioning. One step in the cascade involves fibrinogen, required for clotting, and another, plaminogen [sic], required for clearing clots away.

(Ruse 1998)

And Ruse goes on to quote Doolittle's passage from the *Boston Review* that I quoted earlier. Now, Ruse is a prominent Darwinist and has written many books on various aspects of Darwiniana. Yet, as his approving quotation of Doolittle's mistaken reasoning shows (complete with his copying of Doolittle's typo-misspelling of "plaminogen"), Ruse has no independent knowledge of how natural selection could have put together complex biochemical systems. As far as the scientific dispute is concerned, Ruse has nothing to add.

Another such example is seen in a recent essay in *The Scientist*, "Not-So-Intelligent Design," by Neil S. Greenspan, a professor of pathology at Case Western Reserve University, who writes (Greenspan 2002), "The Design advocates also ignore the accumulating examples of the reducibility of biological systems. As Russell Doolittle has noted in commenting on the writings of one ID advocate . . ." Greenspan goes on to cite approvingly Doolittle's argument in the *Boston Review*. He concludes, with unwitting irony, that "[t]hese results cast doubt on the claim by proponents of ID that they know which systems exhibit irreducible complexity and which do not." But since the results are precisely the opposite of what Greenspan supposed, the shoe is now on the other foot. This incident casts grave doubt on the claim by Darwinists – both biologists and philosophers – that they know that complex cellular systems are explainable in Darwinian terms. It demonstrates that Darwinists either cannot or will not recognize difficulties for their theory.

The mousetrap

The second counterargument to irreducibility I will discuss here concerns not a biological example but a conceptual one. In *Darwin's Black Box*, I pointed to a common mechanical mousetrap as an example of irreducible complexity. Almost immediately after the book's publication, some Darwinists began proposing ways in which the mousetrap could be built step by step. One proposal that has gotten wide attention, and that has been endorsed by some prominent scientists, was put forward by John McDonald, a professor of biology at the University of Delaware, and can be seen on his web site.[4] His series of traps is shown in Figure 11.3. McDonald's main point was that the trap that I pictured in my book consisted of five parts, yet he could build a trap with fewer parts.

I agree. In fact, I said exactly the same thing in my book. I wrote:

> We need to distinguish between a *physical* precursor and a *conceptual* precursor. The trap described above is not the only system that can immobilize a mouse. On other occasions my family has used a glue trap. In theory at least, one can use a box propped open with a stick that could be tripped. Or one can simply shoot the mouse with a BB gun. However, these are not physical precursors to the standard

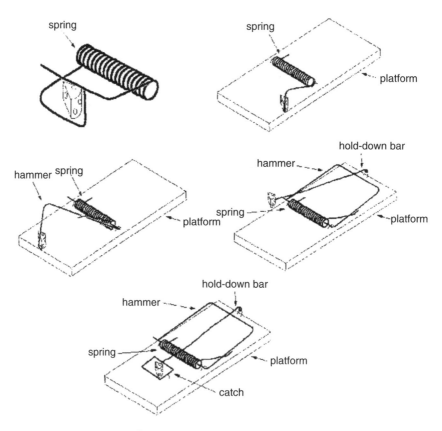

Figure 11.3   A series of mousetraps with an increasing number of parts, as proposed by John McDonald <http://udel.edu/~mcdonald/oldmousetrap.html> and reproduced here with his permission. Yet intelligence is still required to construct one trap from another, as described in the text.

mousetrap since they cannot be transformed, step-by-Darwinian-step, into a trap with a base, hammer, spring, catch, and holding bar.

(Behe 1996, 43)

Thus the point is not that mousetraps can be built in different ways, with different numbers of pieces. (My children have a game at home called "Mouse-trap," which has many, many pieces and looks altogether different from the common mechanical one.) Of course they can. The only question is whether a particular trap can be built by "numerous, successive, slight modifications" to a simple starting point – without the intervention of intelligence – as Darwin insisted that his theory required.

The McDonald traps cannot. Shown at the top of Figure 11.3 are his one-piece trap and his two-piece trap. The structure of the second trap, how-ever, is not a single, small, random step away from the first. First notice that the one-piece trap is not a simple spring – it is shaped in a very special way. In fact, the shape was deliberately chosen by an intelligent agent, John McDonald, to act as a trap. Well, one has to start somewhere. But if the mousetrap series is to have any relevance at all to Darwinian evolution, then intelligence can't be involved at any further point.

Yet intelligence saturates the whole series. Consider what would be necessary to convert the one-piece trap to the "two-piece" trap. One can't just place the first trap on a simple piece of wood and have it work as the second trap does. Rather, as shown in Figure 11.3, the two protruding ends of the spring first have to be reoriented. What's more, two staples (barely visible in Figure 11.3) are added to hold the spring onto the platform so that it can be under tension in the two-piece trap. So we have gone not from a one-piece to a two-piece trap, but from a one-piece to a four-piece trap. Notice also that the placement of the staples in relation to the edge of the platform is critical. If the staples were moved a quarter-inch from where they are, the trap wouldn't work. Finally, consider that, in order to have a serious analogy to the robotic processes of the cell, we can't have an intelligent human setting the mousetrap – the first trap would have to be set by some unconscious charging mechanism. So, when the pieces are rearranged, the charging mechanism too would have to change for the second trap.

It's easy for us intelligent agents to overlook our role in directing the construction of a system, but nature cannot overlook any step at all, so the McDonald mousetrap series completely fails as an analogy to Darwinian evolu-tion. In fact, the second trap is best viewed not as some Darwinian descendant of the first but as a completely different trap, designed by an intelligent agent, perhaps using a refashioned part or two from the first trap.

Each of the subsequent steps in the series suffers from analogous problems, which I have discussed elsewhere.[5]

In his endorsement of the McDonald mousetrap series, Kenneth Miller wrote: "If simpler versions of this mechanical device [the mousetrap] can be shown to work, then simpler versions of biochemical machines could work as well . . . and this means that complex biochemical machines could indeed have had functional precursors."[6] But that is exactly what it doesn't show − if by "precursor" Miller means "Darwinian precursor." On the contrary, McDonald's mousetrap series shows that even if one does find a simpler system to perform some function, that gives one no reason to think that a more complex system performing the same function could be produced by a Darwinian process starting with the simpler system. Rather, the difficulty in doing so for a simple mousetrap gives us compelling reason to think it cannot be done for complex molecular machines.

Future prospects of the intelligent design hypothesis

The misconceived arguments by Darwinists that I have recounted here offer strong encouragement to me that the hypothesis of Intelligent Design is on the right track. After all, if well-informed opponents of an idea attack it by citing data that, when considered objectively, actually demonstrate its force, then one is entitled to be confident that the idea is worth investigating.

Yet it is not primarily the inadequacy of Darwinist responses that bodes well for the design hypothesis. Rather, the strength of design derives mainly from the work-a-day progress of science. In order to appreciate this fact, it is important to realize that the idea of Intelligent Design arose not from the work of any individual but from the collective work of biology, particularly in the last fifty years. Fifty years ago, the cell seemed much simpler, and in our innocence it was easier then to think that Darwinian processes might have accounted for it. But as biology progressed and the imagined simplicity vanished, the idea of design became more and more compelling. That trend is continuing inexorably. The cell is not getting any simpler; it is getting much more complex. I will conclude this chapter by citing just one example, from the relatively new area of proteomics.

With the successful sequencing of the entire genomes of dozens of micro-organisms and one vertebrate (us), the impetus has turned toward analyzing the cellular interactions of the proteins that the genomes code for, taken as a whole. Remarkable progress has already been made. Early in 2002, an exhaustive study of the proteins comprising the yeast proteome was reported. Among other questions, the investigators asked what proportion of yeast proteins work as groups. They discovered that nearly fifty percent of proteins work as complexes of a half-dozen or more, and many as complexes of ten or more (Gavin et al. 2002).

This is not at all what Darwinists had expected. As Bruce Alberts wrote earlier in the article "The Cell as a Collection of Protein Machines":

> We have always underestimated cells. Undoubtedly we still do today. But at least we are no longer as naive as we were when I was a graduate student in the 1960s. Then most of us viewed cells as containing a giant set of second-order reactions. . . .
>
> But, as it turns out, we can walk and we can talk because the chemistry that makes life possible is much more elaborate and sophisticated than anything we students had ever considered. Proteins make up most of the dry mass of a cell. But instead of a cell dominated by randomly colliding individual protein molecules, we now know that nearly every major process in a cell is carried out by assemblies of 10 or more protein molecules. And, as it carries out its biological functions, each of these protein assemblies interacts with several other large complexes of proteins. Indeed, the entire cell can be viewed as a factory that contains an elaborate network of interlocking assembly lines, each of which is composed of a set of large protein machines.
>
> (Alberts 1998)

The important point here for a theory of Intelligent Design is that molecular machines are not confined to the few examples that I discussed in *Darwin's Black Box*. Rather, most proteins are found as components of complicated molecular machines. Thus design might extend to a large fraction of the features of the cell, and perhaps beyond that into higher levels of biology.

Progress in twentieth-century science has led us to the design hypothesis. I expect progress in the twenty-first century to confirm and extend it.

Notes

1   For example, the microbiologist James Shapiro of the University of Chicago declared in *National Review* that "[t]here are no detailed Darwinian accounts for the evolution of any fundamental biochemical or cellular system, only a variety of wishful speculations" (Shapiro 1996, 65). In *Nature*, the University of Chicago evolutionary biologist Jerry Coyne stated, "There is no doubt that the pathways described by Behe are dauntingly complex, and their evolution will be hard to

unravel. . . . [W]e may forever be unable to envisage the first proto-pathways" (Coyne 1996, 227). In a particularly scathing review in *Trends in Ecology and Evolution*, Tom Cavalier-Smith, an evolutionary biologist at the University of British Columbia, nonetheless wrote, "For none of the cases mentioned by Behe is there yet a comprehensive and detailed explanation of the probable steps in the evolution of the observed complexity. The problems have indeed been sorely neglected – though Behe repeatedly exaggerates this neglect with such hyperboles as 'an eerie and complete silence' " (Cavalier-Smith 1997, 162). The Evolutionary biologist Andrew Pomiankowski, writing in *New Scientist*, agreed: "Pick up any biochemistry textbook, and you will find perhaps two or three references to evolution. Turn to one of these and you will be lucky to find anything better than 'evolution selects the fittest molecules for their biological function' " (Pomiankowski 1996, 44). In *American Scientist*, the Yale molecular biologist Robert Dorit averred, "In a narrow sense, Behe is correct when he argues that we do not yet fully understand the evolution of the flagellar motor or the blood clotting cascade" (Dorit 1997, 474).

2   A good example is found on the "World of Richard Dawkins" web site, maintained by a Dawkins fan named John Catalano at <www.world-of-dawkins.com/Catalano/box/published.htm>. It is to this site that the Oxford University physical chemist Peter Atkins was referring when he wrote in a review of *Darwin's Black Box* for the "Infidels" web site: "Dr. Behe claims that science is largely silent on the details of molecular evolution, the emergence of complex biochemical pathways and processes that underlie the more traditional manifestations of evolution at the level of organisms. Tosh! There are hundreds, possibly thousands, of scientific papers that deal with this very subject. For an entry into this important and flourishing field, and an idea of the intense scientific effort that it represents (see the first link above) [sic]" (Atkins 1998).

3   Bugge and colleagues (1996a) were interested in the question of whether plasminogen had any role in metabolism other than its role in clotting, as had been postulated. The fact that the direct effects of plasminogen deficiency were ameliorated by fibrinogen deficiency showed that plasminogen probably had no other role.

4   <http://udel.edu/~mcdonald/oldmousetrap.html>. Professor McDonald has recently designed a new series of traps that can be seen at <http://udel.edu/~mcdonald/mousetrap.html>. I have examined them and have concluded that they involve his directing intelligence to the same degree.

5   M. J. Behe, "A Mousetrap Defended: Response to Critics." <www.crsc.org>

6   <http://biocrs.biomed.brown.edu/Darwin/DI/Mousetrap.html>

References

Aizawa, S. I. 1996. Flagellar assembly in Salmonella typhimurium. *Molecular Microbiology* 19: 1–5.

Alberts, B. 1998. The cell as a collection of protein machines: Preparing the next generation of molecular biologists. *Cell* 92: 291–4.

Atkins, P. W. 1998. Review of Michael Behe's *Darwin's Black Box*. <www.infidels.org/library/modern/peter_atkins/behe.html>.

Behe, M. J. 1996. *Darwin's Black Box: The Biochemical Challenge to Evolution*. New York: The Free Press.

—— 2001. Reply to my critics: A response to reviews of *Darwin's Black Box: The Biochemical Challenge to Evolution*. *Biology and Philosophy* 16: 685–709.

Bugge, T. H., M. J. Flick, C. C. Daugherty, and J. L. Degen. 1995. Plasminogen deficiency causes severe thrombosis but is compatible with development and reproduction. *Genes and Development* 9: 794–807.

Bugge, T. H., K. W. Kombrinck, M. J. Flick, C. C. Daugherty, M. J. Danton, and J. L. Degen. 1996a. Loss of fibrinogen rescues mice from the pleiotropic effects of plasminogen deficiency. *Cell* 87: 709–19.

Bugge, T. H., Q. Xiao, K. W. Kombrinck, M. J. Flick, K. Holmback, M. J. Danton, M. C. Colbert, D. P. Witte, K. Fujikawa, E. W. Davie, and J. L. Degen. 1996b. Fatal embryonic bleeding events in mice lacking tissue factor, the cell-associated initiator of blood coagulation. *Proceedings of the National Academy of Sciences (USA)* 93: 6258–63.

Cavalier-Smith, T. 1997. The blind biochemist. *Trends in Ecology and Evolution* 12: 162–3.

Coyne, J. A. 1996. God in the details. *Nature* 383: 227–8.

Darwin, C. 1859. *The Origin of Species*. New York: Bantam Books.

Dawkins, R. 1986. *The Blind Watchmaker*. New York: Norton.

DeRosier, D. J. 1998. The turn of the screw: The bacterial flagellar motor. *Cell* 93: 17–20.

Doolittle, R. F. A delicate balance. *Boston Review*, February/March 1997, pp. 28–9.

Dorit, R. 1997. Molecular evolution and scientific inquiry, misperceived. *American Scientist* 85: 474–5.

Dutcher, S. K. 1995. Flagellar assembly in two hundred and fifty easy-to-follow steps. *Trends in Genetics* 11: 398–404.

Gavin, A. C., et al. 2002. Functional organization of the yeast proteome by systematic analysis of protein complexes. *Nature* 415: 141–7.

Greenspan, N. S. 2002. Not-so-intelligent design. *The Scientist* 16: 12.

Halkier, T. 1992. *Mechanisms in Blood Coagulation Fibrinolysis and the Complement System*. Cambridge: Cambridge University Press.

Harold, F. M. 2001. *The Way of the Cell*. Oxford: Oxford University Press.

Hueck, C. J. 1998. Type III protein secretion systems in bacterial pathogens of animals and plants. *Microbiology and Molecular Biology Reviews* 62: 379–433.

Kauffman, S. A. 1995. *At Home in the Universe: The Search for Laws of Self-Organization and Complexity*. New York: Oxford University Press.

Miller, K. R. 1999. *Finding Darwin's God: A Scientist's Search for Common Ground between God and Evolution*. New York: Cliff Street Books.

Pomiankowski, A. 1996. The God of the tiny gaps. *New Scientist*, September 14, pp. 44–5.

Ruse, M. 1998. Answering the creationists: Where they go wrong and what they're afraid of. *Free Inquiry*, March 22, p. 28.

Shapiro, J. 1996. In the details . . . what? *National Review*, September 16, pp. 62–5.

Shapiro, L. 1995. The bacterial flagellum: From genetic network to complex architecture. *Cell* 80: 525–7.

Suh, T. T., K. Holmback, N. J. Jensen, C. C. Daugherty, K. Small, D. I. Simon, S. Potter, and J. L. Degen. 1995. Resolution of spontaneous bleeding events but failure of pregnancy in fibrinogen-deficient mice. *Genes and Development* 9: 2020–33.

Sun, W. Y., D. P. Witte, J. L. Degen, M. C. Colbert, M. C. Burkart, K. Holmback, Q. Xiao, T. H. Bugge, and S. J. Degen. 1998. Prothrombin deficiency results in embryonic and neonatal lethality in mice. *Proceedings of the National Academy of Sciences USA* 95: 7597–602.

Yonekura, K., S. Maki, D. G. Morgan, D. J. DeRosier, F. Vonderviszt, K. Imada, and K. Namba. 2000. The bacterial flagellar cap as the rotary promoter of flagellin self-assembly. *Science* 290: 2148–52.

Chapter 12

Kenneth R. Miller

ANSWERING THE BIOCHEMICAL
ARGUMENT FROM DESIGN

ONE OF THE THINGS that makes science such an exhilarating activity is its revolutionary character. As science advances, there is always the possibility that some investigator, working in the field or at a laboratory bench, will produce a discovery or experimental result that will completely transform our understanding of nature. The history of science includes so many examples of such discoveries that in many respects the practice of science has a built-in bias in favor of the little guy, the individual investigator who just might hold the key to our next fundamental scientific advance. Indeed, if there is one dogma in science, it should be that science has no dogma.

What this means, as a practical matter, is that everything in science is open to question. Can we be sure that the speed of light isn't an absolute upper limit? Is it possible that genetic information can be carried by proteins, rather than DNA? Was Einstein correct in his formulation of the theory of general relativity? It is never easy to upset the scientific apple cart, but the practice of science requires, as an absolute, that everything in science be open to question. Everything.

In 1996, Michael Behe took a bold step in this scientific tradition by challenging one of the most useful, productive, and fundamental concepts in all of biology – Charles Darwin's theory of evolution. Behe's provocative claim, carefully laid out in his book, *Darwin's Black Box*, was that whatever else Darwinian evolution can explain successfully, it cannot account for the biochemical complexity of the living cell. As Behe put it: "for the Darwinian theory of evolution to be true, it has to account for the molecular structure of life. It is the purpose of this book to show that it does not" (1996a: 24–5).

As we will see, Behe's argument is crafted around the existence of complex molecular machines found in all living cells. Such machines, he argues, could not have been produced by evolution, and therefore must be the products of intelligent design. . . . This argument has been picked up by a variety of anti-evolution groups around the USA, and has become a focal point for those who would argue that "intelligent design" theory (ID) deserves a place in the science classroom as a scientific alternative to Darwin. What I propose to do in this brief review is to put this line of reasoning to the test. I will examine both the scientific evidence for this claim and the logical structure of the biochemical argument from design, and will pose the most fundamental question one can ask of any scientific hypothesis – does it fit the facts?

An exceptional claim

For nearly more than a century and a half, one of the classic ways to argue against evolution has been to point to an exceptionally complex and intricate structure and then to challenge an evolutionist to "evolve this!" Examples of such challenges have included everything from the optical marvels of the human eye to the chemical defenses of the bombardier beetle. At first glance, Behe's examples seem to fit this tradition. As examples of cellular machinery for which no evolutionary explanations exist he cites the cilia and flagella that produce cell movement, the cascade of blood-clotting proteins, the systems that target proteins to specific sites within the cell, the production of antibodies by the immune system, and the intricacies of biosynthetic pathways.

As he realizes, however, the mere existence of structures and pathways that have not yet been given step-by-step Darwinian explanation does not make much of a case against evolution. Critics of evolution have laid down such challenges before, only to see them backfire when new scientific work provided exactly the evidence they had demanded. Behe himself once made a similar claim when he challenged evolutionists to produce transitional fossils linking the first fossil whales with their supposed land-based ancestors (Behe 1994: 61). Ironically, not one, not two, but three transitional species between whales and land-dwelling Eocene mammals had been discovered by the end of 1994 when his challenge was published (Gould 1994: 8–15).

Given that the business of science is to provide and test explanations, the fact that there are a few things that have, as yet, no published evolutionary explanations is not much of an argument against Darwin. Rather, it means that the field is still active, vital, and filled with scientific challenges. Behe realizes this, and therefore his principal claim for design is quite different. He observes, quite correctly, that science has not explained the evolution of the bacterial flagellum, but then he goes one step further. No such explanation is even *possible*, according to Behe. Why? Because the flagellum has a characteristic that Behe calls "irreducible complexity":

> By irreducibly complex I mean a single system composed of several well-matched, interacting parts that contribute to the basic function, wherein the removal of any one of the parts causes the system to effectively cease functioning.
>
> (Behe 1996a: 39)

Irreducible complexity is the key to Behe's argument against Darwin. Why? Because it opens a chain of reasoning that allows the critic of evolution to reach the conclusion of design. It alone allows one to state that the notion of an evolutionary origin for any complex biochemical structure can be ruled out in principle. To make his point perfectly clear, Behe uses a common mechanical device, the mousetrap, as an example of irreducible complexity:

> A good example of such a system is a mechanical mousetrap. . . . The mousetrap depends critically on the presence of all five of its components; if there were no spring, the mouse would not be pinned to the base; if there were no platform, the other pieces would fall apart; and so on. The function of the mousetrap requires all the pieces: you cannot catch a few mice with just a platform, add a spring and catch a few more mice, add a holding bar and catch a few more. All of the components have to be in place before any mice are caught. Thus the mousetrap is irreducibly complex.
>
> (Behe 1998: 178)

Since every part of the mousetrap must be in place before it is functional, this means that partial mousetraps, ones that are missing one or two parts, are useless — you cannot catch mice with them. Extending the analogy to irreducibly complex biochemical machines, they also are without function until all of their parts are assembled. What this means, of course, is that natural selection could not produce such machines gradually, one part at a time. They would be non-functional until all of their parts were assembled, and natural selection, which can only select functioning systems, would have nothing to work with.

Behe has made this exact point quite clear:

An irreducibly complex system cannot be produced directly by numerous, successive, slight modifications of a precursor system, because any precursor to an irreducibly complex system that is missing a part is by definition nonfunctional. Since natural selection can only choose systems that are already working, then if a biological system cannot be produced gradually it would have to arise as an integrated unit, in one fell swoop, for natural selection to have anything to act on.

(1996b: 39)

In Behe's view, this observation, in and of itself, makes the case for design. If the biochemical machinery of the cell cannot be produced by natural selection, then there is only one reasonable alternative – design by an intelligent agent. Lest anyone doubt his claim for the absolute impossibility that evolution might have produced such machinery, Behe assures his readers that the immense scientific literature on evolution contains not a single example to the contrary:

There is no publication in the scientific literature – in prestigious journals, specialty journals, or books – that describes how the

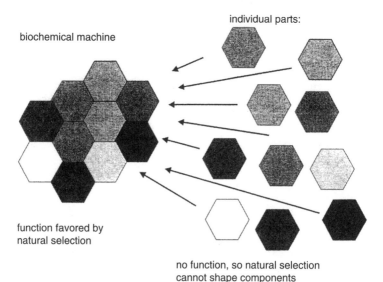

Figure 12.1 The Biochemical Argument from Design

Note: According to the biochemical argument from design, natural selection could not produce an irreducibly complex biochemical machine because its individual parts are, by definition, without any selectable function.

molecular evolution of any real, complex, biochemical system
either did occur or even might have occurred.

(1996a: 185)

Powerful stuff. The great power of Behe's argument is that it claims to have
discovered, in the biochemical machinery of the living cell, a new property
(irreducible complexity) that makes it possible to rule out, even in principle,
any possibility that evolution could have produced it. The next question we
should ask is simple – is he right?

Mr Darwin's workshop

If Behe's arguments have a familiar ring to them, they should. They mirror the
classic "Argument from Design," articulated so well by William Paley nearly
200 years ago in his book *Natural Theology*. Darwin was well aware of the argument, so much so that he devoted special care to answering it when he wrote *On
the Origin of Species*. Darwin's answer, in essence, was that evolution produces
complex organs in a series of fully functional intermediate stages. If each of the
intermediate stages can be favored by natural selection, then so can the whole
pathway. Is there something different about biochemistry, a reason why
Darwin's answer would not apply to the molecular systems that Behe cites?

In a word, no.

In 1998, Siegfried Musser and Sunney Chan described the evolutionary
development of the cytochrome c oxidase proton pump, a complex, multi-part
molecular machine that plays a key role in energy transformation by the cell. In
human cells, the pump consists of six proteins, each of which is necessary for
the pump to function properly. It would seem to be a perfect example of
irreducible complexity. Take one part away from the pump, and it no longer
works. And yet these authors were able to produce, in impressive detail, "an
evolutionary tree constructed using the notion that respiratory complexity and
efficiency progressively increased throughout the evolutionary process"
(Musser and Chan 1998: 517).

How is this possible? If you believed Michael Behe's assertion that
biochemical machines were irreducibly complex, you might never bother to
check, and this is the real scientific danger of his ideas. Musser and Chan did
check, and found that two of the six proteins in the proton pump were quite
similar to a bacteria enzyme known as the cytochrome bo_3 complex. Could this
mean that part of the proton pump evolved from a working cytochrome bo_3
complex? Certainly.

An ancestral two-part cytochrome bo_3 complex would have been fully functional, albeit in a different context, but that context would indeed have allowed natural selection to favor its evolution. How can we be sure that this "half" of the pump would be any good? By reference to modern organisms that have full, working versions of the cytochrome bo$_3$ complex. Can we make the same argument for the rest of the pump? Well, it turns out that each of the pump's major parts is closely related to working protein complexes found in micro-organisms. Evolution assembles complex biochemical machines, as Musser and Chan proposed, from smaller working assemblies that are adapted to fit novel functions. The multiple parts of complex biochemical machines are themselves assembled from smaller, working machines developed by natural selection, as shown in Figure 12.2.

What of the statement that there is no publication anywhere describing how the "molecular evolution of any real, complex, biochemical system either did occur or even might have occurred?" Simply put, that statement is not correct.

In 1996, Enrique Meléndez-Hevia and his colleagues published, in the *Journal of Molecular Evolution*, a paper entitled "The puzzle of the Krebs citric acid cycle: Assembling the pieces of chemically feasible reactions, and opportunism in the design of metabolic pathways during evolution" (Meléndez-Hevia *et al.* 1996). The Krebs cycle is *real, complex, and biochemical*, and this paper does exactly

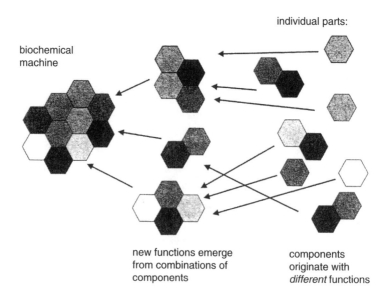

Figure 12.2 The Evolution of Biochemical Machines

Note: A Darwinian view of the evolution of complex biochemical machines requires that their individual parts and components have selectable functions.

what Behe says cannot be done, even in principle – it presents a feasible proposal for its evolution from simpler biochemical systems. This paper, as well as
a subsequent review of the Krebs cycle by other authors (Huynen et al. 1999),
shows that the scheme indicated in Figure 12.2 is a perfectly adequate model to
account for biochemical complexity.

These are not isolated examples. Recently Martino Rizzotti published a
series of detailed, step-by-step hypotheses for the evolution of a wide variety of
cellular structures, including the bacterial flagellum and the eukaryotic cilium
(Rizzotti 2000). I do not claim, even for a moment, that every one of Rizzotti's
explanations represents the final word on the evolution of these structures.
Nonetheless, any validity one might have attached to the claim that the literature
lacks such explanations vanishes upon inspection.

What all of this means, of course, is that two principal claims of the ID
movement are disproved, namely that it is impossible to present a Darwinian
explanation for the evolution of a complex biochemical system, and that no
such papers appear in the scientific literature. It is possible, and such papers do
exist.

Getting to the heart of the matter

To fully explore the scientific basis of the biochemical argument from design,
we should investigate the details of some of the very structures used in Behe's
book as examples of irreducibly complex systems. One of these is the eukaryotic cilium, an intricate whip-like structure that produces movement in cells as
diverse as green algae and human sperm. And,

> Just as a mousetrap does not work unless all of its constituent parts
> are present, ciliary motion simply does not exist in the absence of
> microtubules, connectors, and motors. Therefore we can conclude
> that the cilium is irreducibly complex.
>
> (Behe 1996a: 65)

Remember Behe's statement that the removal of any one of the parts of an
irreducibly complex system effectively causes the system to stop working? The
cilium provides us with a perfect opportunity to test that assertion. If it is
correct, then we should be unable to find examples of functional cilia anywhere
in nature that lack the cilium's basic parts. Unfortunately for the argument, that
is not the case. Nature presents many examples of fully functional cilia that are
missing key parts. One of the most compelling is the eel sperm flagellum
(Figure 12.3), which lacks at least three important parts normally found in the

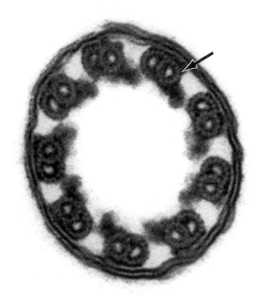

Figure 12.3 A Living Contradiction to "Irreducible Complexity"

Note: A cross-section of an eel sperm flagellum. In other organisms, this "irreducibly complex" structure includes a central pair of microtubules, spokes linking the central pair to the outer doublets, and dynein outer arms linking the doublets. Each of these structures is missing in the eel sperm flagellum (the arrow shows the location of one of these missing dynein arms), and yet the structure is fully functional. From Woolley (1997: 91).

cilium: the central doublet, central spokes, and the dynein outer arm (Woolley 1997).

This leaves us with two points to consider. First, a wide variety of motile systems exist that are missing parts of this supposedly irreducibly complex structure. Second, biologists have known for years that each of the major components of the cilium, including proteins tubulin, dynein, and actin, have distinct functions elsewhere in the cell that are unrelated to ciliary motion.

Given these facts, what is one to make of the core argument of biochemical design – namely, that the parts of an irreducibly complex structure have no functions on their own? The key element of the claim was that "any precursor to an irreducibly complex system that is missing a part is by definition nonfunctional." But the individual parts of the cilium, including tubulin, the motor protein dynein, and the contractile protein actin, are fully functional elsewhere in the cell. What this means, of course, is that a selectable function exists for each of the major parts of the cilium, and therefore that the argument is wrong.

Whips and syringes

In many ways, the "poster child" for irreducible complexity has been the bacterial flagellum. The well-matched parts of this ion-driven rotary engine pose, in the view of many critics, an insurmountable challenge to Darwinian evolution. Once again, however, a close examination of this remarkable biochemical machine tells a quite different story.

To begin with, there is more than one type of "bacterial flagellum." Flagella found in the archaebacteria are clearly not irreducibly complex. Recent research has shown that the flagellar proteins of these organisms are closely related to a group of cell surface proteins known as the Class IV pilins (Jarrel et al. 1996). Since these proteins have a well-defined function that is not related to motility, the archael flagella fail the test of irreducible complexity.

Clearly, when he speaks of the bacterial flagellum, Behe refers to flagella found in the eubacteria. Representations of eubacterial flagella appear in Darwin's Black Box (Behe 1996a: 71) and have been used by Dr Behe in a number of public presentations. Surely these structures must fit the test of irreducible complexity? Ironically, they don't.

In 1998 the flagella of eubacteria were discovered to be closely related to a non-motile cell membrane complex known as the Type III secretory apparatus (Hueck 1998). These complexes play a deadly role in the cytotoxic (cell-killing) activities of bacteria such as Yersinia pestis, the bacterium that causes bubonic plague. When these bacteria infect an organism, bacteria cells bind to host cells, and then pump toxins directly through the secretory apparatus into the host cytoplasm. Efforts to understand the deadly effects of these bacteria on their hosts led to molecular studies of the proteins in the Type III apparatus, and it quickly became apparent that at least ten of them are homologous to proteins that form part of the base of the bacterial flagellum (Hueck 1998: 410).

This means that a portion of the whip-like bacterial flagellum functions as the "syringe" that makes up the Type III secretory apparatus. In other words, a subset of the proteins of the flagellum is fully functional in a completely different context – not motility, but the deadly delivery of toxins to a host cell. This observation falsifies the central claim of the biochemical argument from design – namely, that a subset of the parts of an irreducibly complex structure must be "by definition nonfunctional." Here are ten proteins from the flagellum that are missing not just one part but more than forty, and yet they are fully functional in the Type III apparatus.

Disproving design

If the biochemical argument from design is a scientific hypothesis, as its proponents claim, then it should make specific predictions that are testable in scientific terms. The most important prediction of the hypothesis of irreducible complexity is shown in Figure 12.4, and it is that components of irreducibly complex structures should not have functions that can be favored by natural selection.

As we have seen, a subset of the proteins from the flagellum does indeed have a selectable function in Type III secretion. However, we can make a more general statement about many of the components of the eubacterial flagellum (see Figure 12.5). Proteins that make up the flagellum itself are closely related to a variety of cell surface proteins, including the pilins found in a variety of bacteria. A portion of the flagellum functions as an ion channel, and ion channels are found in all bacterial cell membranes. Part of the flagellar base is functional in protein secretion, and, once again, all bacteria possess membrane-bound protein secretory systems. Finally, the heart of the flagellum is an ion-driven rotary motor, a remarkable piece of protein machinery that converts ion movement into rotary movement that makes flagellar movement possible. Surely this part of the flagellum must be unique? Not at all. All bacteria possess a membrane protein complex known as the ATP synthase that uses ion movements to produce ATP. How does the synthase work? It uses the energy of ion movements to produce rotary motion. In short, at least four key elements of the eubacterial flagellum have other selectable functions in the cell that are unrelated to motility.

These facts demonstrate that the one system most widely cited as the premier example of irreducible complexity contains individual parts that have selectable functions. What this means, in scientific terms, is that the hypothesis of irreducible complexity is falsified. The Darwinian explanation of complex systems, however, is supported by the same facts.

One might, of course, raise the objection that I have not provided a detailed, step-by-step explanation of the evolution of the flagellum. Isn't such an explanation required to dispose of the biochemical argument from design?

In a word, no. Not unless the argument has allowed itself to be reduced to a mere observation that an evolutionary explanation of the eubacterial flagellum has yet to be written. I would certainly agree with such a statement. However, the contention made by Behe is quite different from this – it is that evolution cannot explain the flagellum in principle (because its multiple components have no selectable function). By demonstrating the existence of such functions, even in just a handful of components, we have invalidated the argument.

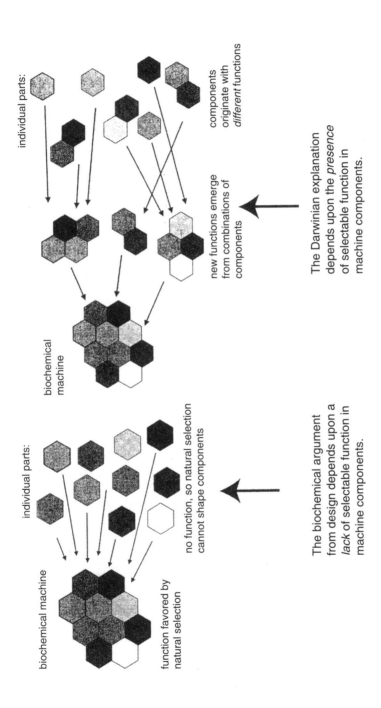

individual parts:

components originate with *different* functions

new functions emerge from combinations of components

biochemical machine

The Darwinian explanation depends upon the *presence* of selectable function in machine components.

individual parts:

biochemical machine

function favored by natural selection

no function, so natural selection cannot shape components

The biochemical argument from design depends upon a *lack* of selectable function in machine components.

Figure 12.4 Putting Design to the Test

Note: The biochemical argument from design makes a specific, testable prediction about the components of "irreducibly complex" structures. That prediction is that individual portions of such machines should not have selectable functions. The Darwinian explanation for such structures makes a contrary prediction – namely, that components of the machine should have such functions. The scientific literature provides more than enough evidence to distinguish between the two alternatives.

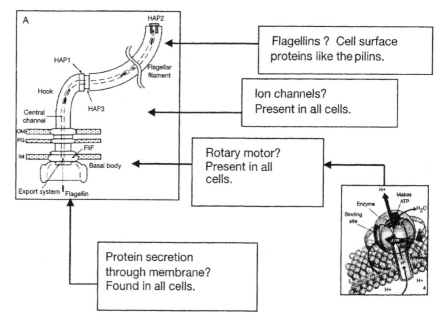

Figure 12.5 A Reducible Flagellum

Note: At least four components of the eubacterial flagellum have selectable functions that are unrelated to motility.

Caught in the mousetrap

Why does the biochemical argument from design collapse so quickly upon close inspection? I would suggest that this is because the logic of the argument itself is flawed. Consider, for example, the mechanical mousetrap as an analogy of irreducibly complex systems. Behe has written that a mousetrap does not work if even one of its five parts is removed. However, with a little ingenuity, it turns out to be remarkably easy to construct a working mousetrap *after* removing one of its parts, leaving just four. In fact, Professor John McDonald of the University of Delaware has taken this several steps further, posting drawings on a website that show how a mousetrap may be constructed with just three, two, or even just one part. McDonald's mousetrap plans are available at: *http://udel.edu/~mcdonald/mousetrap.html.*

Behe has responded to these simpler mousetraps by pointing out, quite correctly, that human intervention and ingenuity are needed to construct the simpler mousetraps, and therefore they do not present anything approaching a model for the "evolution" of the five-part trap. However, his response overlooks the crucial question: are subsets of the five-part trap useful (selectable) in different contexts? Considering the following examples: for my personal use I sometimes wear a tie clip consisting of just three parts (platform, spring, and hammer) and use a key chain consisting of just two (platform and hammer). It is possible, in fact, to imagine a host of uses for parts of the "irreducibly complex" mousetrap, some of which are listed in Figure 12.6.

The meaning of this should be clear. If portions of a supposedly irreducibly complex mechanical structure are fully functional in different contexts, then the central claim built upon this concept is incorrect. If bits and pieces of a machine are useful for different functions, it means that natural selection could indeed produce elements of a biochemical machine for different purposes. The mousetrap example provides, unintentionally, a perfect analogy for the way in which natural selection builds complex structures.

Breaking the chain

Critics of evolution are fond of claiming that they have "discovered" evidence of intelligent design in biochemical systems, suggesting that they have found positive evidence of the work of the designer. Behe himself uses such language when he writes:

Individual parts of a supposedly irreducibly complex machine are fully functional for different purposes. Examples:

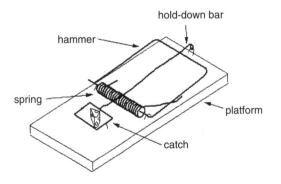

tie clip (3)
key ring (2)
refrigerator clip (3 + 1
clipboard holder (2)
door knocker (3)
paperweight (1)
kindling block (1)
catapult (4)
nutcracker (3)
nose ring (2)
fish hook (1)
toothpick (1)

Figure 12.6 A Reducible Mousetrap

Note: There are alternate, selectable functions for partial assemblies of the five parts of a standard mousetrap. The numbers in parentheses indicate the number of parts required for each function. For example, just one part (the hold-down bar) is required for a toothpick. Three parts are needed for a tie-clip (base, spring, and hammer). A refrigerator clip can be fashioned from the same three parts by adding one additional part (a magnet).

The result of these cumulative efforts to investigate the cell – to investigate life at the molecular level – is a loud, clear, piercing cry of "design!" The result is so unambiguous and so significant that it must be ranked as one of the greatest achievements in the history of science. The discovery rivals those of Newton and Einstein, Lavoisier and Schrödinger, Pasteur, and Darwin.

(1996a: 232–3)

What, exactly, is the source of this "loud, piercing cry"? It turns out not to be any direct evidence, but rather a chain of reasoning – begining with the observation of "irreducible complexity" and leading, step by step, to a conclusion of design (see below) – that is well-removed from experimental evidence:

What is the "evidence" for design?

What follows is the logical chain of reasoning leading from the observation of biochemical complexity to the conclusion of intelligent design.

1 *Observation*: the cell contains biochemical machines in which the loss of a single component may abolish function. *Definition*: such machines are therefore said to be "irreducibly complex."

2 *Assertion*: any irreducibly complex structure that is missing a part is by definition non-functional, leaving natural selection with nothing to select for.

3 *Conclusion*: therefore, irreducibly complex structures *could not* have been produced by natural selection.

4 *Secondary conclusion*: therefore, such structures must have been produced by another mechanism. Since the only credible alternate mechanism is intelligent design, the very existence of such structures must be evidence of intelligent design.

When the reasoning behind the biochemical argument from design is laid out in this way, it becomes easy to spot the logical flaw in the argument. The first statement is true – the cell does indeed contain any number of complex molecular machines in which the loss of a single part may affect function.

However, the second statement, the assertion of non-functionality, is demonstrably false. As we have seen, the individual parts of many such machines do indeed have well-defined functions within the cell. Once this is realized, the logic of the argument collapses. If the assertion in the second statement is shown to be false, the chain of reasoning is broken and both conclusions are falsified.

The cell does not contain biochemical evidence of design.

Paley's ghost

Paley's twenty-first century followers claim that the ID movement is based upon new discoveries in molecular biology, and represents a novel scientific movement that is worthy of scientific and educational attention. Couched in the modern language of biochemistry, Behe's formulation of Paley represents the best hope of the movement to establish its views as scientifically legitimate. As we have seen in this brief review, however, it is remarkably easy to answer each of his principal claims.

This analysis shows that the "evidence" used by modern advocates of intelligent design to resurrect Paley's early nineteenth-century arguments is neither novel nor new. Indeed, their only remaining claim against Darwin is that they cannot imagine how evolution might have produced such systems. Time and time again, other scientists, unpersuaded by such self-serving pessimism, have shown (and published) explanations to the contrary. When closely examined, even the particular molecular machines employed by the movement as examples of "irreducible complexity" turn out to be incorrect. Finally, the logic of the argument itself turns out to have an obvious and fatal flaw.

Behe argues that anti-religious bias is the reason the scientific community resists the explanation of design for his observations:

> Why does the scientific community not greedily embrace its startling discovery? Why is the observation of design handled with intellectual gloves? The dilemma is that while one side of the elephant is labeled intelligent design, the other side might be labeled God.
>
> (1996a: 232)

I would suggest that the actual reason is much simpler. The scientific community has not embraced the explanation of design because it is quite clear, on the basis of the evidence, that it is wrong.

References

Behe, M. (1998) "Intelligent design theory as a tool for analyzing biochemical systems," in W. Dembski (ed.) *Mere Creation*, Downers Grove, Illinois: Inter-Varsity Press.

—— (1996a) *Darwin's Black Box*, New York: The Free Press.

—— (1996b) "Evidence for intelligent design from biochemistry," from a speech delivered at the Discovery Institute's "God and Culture" conference, 10 August 1996. Available online at the Discovery Institute website: *www.discovery.org/crsc*.

—— (1994) "Experimental support for regarding functional classes of proteins to be highly isolated from each other," in J. Buell and V. Hearn (eds) *Darwinism: Science or Philosophy?*, Houston, Texas: The Foundation for Thought and Ethics.

Gould, S.J. (1994) "Hooking Leviathan by its past," *Natural History* May: 8–15.

Hueck, C.J. (1998) "Type III protein secretion systems in bacterial pathogens of animals and plants," *Microbiology and Molecular Biology Review* 62: 379–433.

Huynen, M.A., Dandekar, T., and Bork, P. (1999) "Variation and evolution of the citric acid cycle: A genomic perspective," *Trends in Microbiology* 7: 281–91.

Jarrel, K.F., Bayley, D.P., and Kostyukova, A.S. (1996) "The archael flagellum: A unique motility structure," *Journal of Bacteriology* 178: 5,057–64.

Meléndez-Hevia, E., Waddell, T.G., and Cascante, M. (1996) "The puzzle of the Krebs citric acid cycle: Assembling the pieces of chemically feasible reactions, and opportunism in the design of metabolic pathways during evolution," *Journal of Molecular Evolution* 43: 293–303.

Musser, S.M. and Chan, S.I. (1998) "Evolution of the cytochrome c oxidase proton pump," *Journal of Molecular Evolution* 46: 508–20.

Rizzotti, M. (2000) *Early Evolution: From the Appearance of the First Cell to the First Modern Organisms*, Basel: Birkhauser.

Woolley, D.M. (1997) "Studies on the eel sperm flagellum," *Journal of Cell Science* 110: 85–94.

Naturalism

INTRODUCTION TO PART FIVE

PART THREE OF THIS VOLUME surveyed the thought of creationists who on religious grounds challenge the compatibility of God
and evolution. Part Four examined thinkers who find Darwinian natural
selection unable to account for the complexity of life and hence propose to
include in a scientific theory the actions of an intelligent designer.

This section surveys thinkers who question the compatibility of God and
evolution from the other end of the spectrum, namely, the perspective of
atheistic naturalism. For these authors, Darwin's theory of natural selection
is a self-sufficient explanatory mechanism that rules out any talk of God,
purpose, or design.

Biologist Richard Dawkins is one of the most eloquent advocates of
this viewpoint. This part includes excerpts from two of Dawkins's books,
*The Blind Watchmaker: Why the Evidence of Evolution Reveals a Uni-
verse without Design* and *River out of Eden: A Darwinian View of Life*.
Dawkins borrows the watchmaker image in the title of the first work from
the famous version of the argument from design crafted by Archdeacon
William Paley in his *Natural Theology*, an extract of which is included in
Part Four of this collection. Dawkins credits Paley with a proper reverence
for the complexity of the living world but finds Paley's traditional religious
appeal to the existence of an intelligent deity "wrong, gloriously and
utterly wrong." According to Dawkins, it took Darwin's discovery of natural selection to provide an alternative explanation for the "apparent

design" observed by Paley. Since natural selection has no purpose in mind, Dawkins labels it the "blind" watchmaker and utters his famous assessment that "Darwin made it possible to be an intellectually fulfilled atheist."

In the second piece Dawkins raises the problem of evil as a major impediment to the coherence of Christian claims about an intelligent and benevolent deity. Reflecting the influence of philosopher Daniel Dennett, Dawkins introduces two technical terms, "reverse engineering," analyzing an object with a view to determining its purpose and "utility function," that which is maximized. Asking what God's utility function was in designing the struggle for survival between the cheetah and the antelope, Dawkins concludes, among several facetious suggestions, that this creator is at best "a sadist who enjoys spectator blood sports." If, however, one realizes that the "true utility function of life" is DNA survival, Dawkins maintains, the "problem of suffering" is placed in a different interpretive context. As he remarks, the universe we observe "has precisely the properties we should expect if there is, at bottom, no design, no purpose, no evil and no good, nothing but blind, pitiless indifference." In short, "DNA neither knows nor cares. DNA just is. And we dance to its music."

The next selections are taken from philosopher Daniel Dennett's book *Darwin's Dangerous Idea: Evolution and the Meanings of Life*. Dennett maintains that Darwin's theory of evolution is dangerous because the mechanism proposed by Darwin, natural selection, is an algorithmic process, a mindless, mechanical, automatic procedure that does not require intelligent supervision and challenges our most fundamental assumptions about values and meaning. Resembling "universal acid," Darwin's idea cannot be confined within biology but leaks out into cosmology, psychology, human culture, ethics, politics, and religion. Although Darwin did not pursue the far-reaching implications of his theory for other disciplines, Dennett sees the corrosive effects of Darwinism as inevitable and faults other thinkers for what he calls "failed campaigns" to contain Darwin's idea within a merely partial revolution.

Dennett credits Darwin with inverting the traditional cosmic pyramid that pictured a top-down causal chain, a "mind-first" scheme with God at the peak. Darwin was instead offering the world a "get-rich-*slow* scheme, a scheme for creating Design out of Chaos without the aid of Mind." To help elucidate this claim Dennett invokes the concepts of "skyhooks" and "cranes." He maintains that Darwin's idea of evolution by natural selection eliminates the need to appeal to imaginary supernatural skyhooks as the driving force of the universe, when the real lifters in Design Space are cranes. The apparent design of our universe is the result of brute, mechanical, algorithmic climbing, of the operation of impersonal physical laws, not of some intervention by any power from on high.

Pointing out that those who yearn for skyhooks call those who settle for cranes "reductionists," Dennett vigorously defends what he calls "good" reductionism, the "commitment to non-question-begging science without any cheating by embracing mysteries or miracles at the outset." In fact, Darwin's dangerous idea, which Dennett has earlier deemed "the single best idea anyone has ever had," is "reductionism incarnate."

The next two selections offer the critical responses of philosophers Mary Midgley and Michael Ruse to the views of Dennett and Dawkins. Midgley's piece appeared first in *Alas, Poor Darwin: Arguments Against Evolutionary Psychology*, edited by Hilary Rose and Steven Rose and was later published in her own book, *The Myths We Live By*. Midgley addresses Dennett's claim that Darwin's idea acts as a universal acid that eats through traditional concepts in a variety of fields. Accusing Dennett of overreaching, she praises Darwin for refusing to inflate his theory beyond its use in biology. To Dennett's labeling of Darwin's theory as "dangerous," she tartly comments that ideas do indeed become dangerous "to honesty, to intelligibility, to all the proper purposes of thought" if they are overextended. Her remarks here parallel the concerns that she expresses in her article in Part One of this collection, where she warns against the claims of omnicompetence advanced by some for science.

The selection from Michael Ruse comes from his article "Methodological Naturalism under Attack," in *Intelligent Design Creationism and Its Critics: Philosophical, Theological, and Scientific Perspectives*, edited by Robert T. Pennock. In the extract included here, Ruse comments that there are "materialists, atheists, naturalists, and evolutionists" such as Dawkins and Dennett who "see everything as a united package deal." Ruse, however, suggests that one can separate atheism and evolutionism by drawing a distinction between two forms of naturalism, methodological and metaphysical. According to Ruse, metaphysical naturalism, which considers the world to be as we see it and that there is nothing more, does entail atheism. In contrast, the methodological naturalist, while insisting that theological references have no place in science *per se*, is not committed to a denial of God's existence. Hence one cannot, on the grounds of science alone, claim to be able to rule out God, purpose, and meaning.

Parts Six and Seven of this anthology survey the work of Christian theologians and scientists who challenge the assumption shared by creationists and atheistic naturalists that God and evolution cannot be reconciled. Proposing models of God in an evolutionary world, they offer new thinking on design, purpose, and suffering that sets them apart from creationists and ID proponents on the one hand and atheistic naturalists on the other.

Chapter 13

Richard Dawkins

THE BLIND WATCHMAKER

W E ANIMALS ARE THE MOST complicated things in the known universe. The universe that we know, of course, is a tiny fragment of the actual universe. There may be yet more complicated objects than us on other planets, and some of them may already know about us. But this doesn't alter the point that I want to make. Complicated things, everywhere, deserve a very special kind of explanation. We want to know how they came into existence and why they are so complicated. The explanation, as I shall argue, is likely to be broadly the same for complicated things everywhere in the universe; the same for us, for chimpanzees, worms, oak trees and monsters from outer space. On the other hand, it will not be the same for what I shall call 'simple' things, such as rocks, clouds, rivers, galaxies and quarks. These are the stuff of physics. Chimps and dogs and bats and cockroaches and people and worms and dandelions and bacteria and galactic aliens are the stuff of biology.

The difference is one of complexity of design. Biology is the study of complicated things that give the appearance of having been designed for a purpose. Physics is the study of simple things that do not tempt us to invoke design. At first sight, man-made artefacts like computers and cars will seem to provide exceptions. They are complicated and obviously designed for a purpose, yet they are not alive, and they are made of metal and plastic rather than of flesh and blood. [Here] they will be firmly treated as biological objects.
[. . .]

We wanted to know why we, and all other complicated things, exist. And we can now answer that question in general terms, even without being able to comprehend the details of the complexity itself. To take an analogy, most of us don't understand in detail how an airliner works. Probably its builders don't comprehend it fully either: engine specialists don't in detail understand wings, and wing specialists understand engines only vaguely. Wing specialists don't even understand wings with full mathematical precision: they can predict how a wing will behave in turbulent conditions, only by examining a model in a wind tunnel or a computer simulation – the sort of thing a biologist might do to understand an animal. But however incompletely we understand how an airliner works, we all understand by what general process it came into existence. It was designed by humans on drawing boards. Then other humans made the bits from the drawings, then lots more humans (with the aid of other machines designed by humans) screwed, rivetted, welded or glued the bits together, each in its right place. The process by which an airliner came into existence is not fundamentally mysterious to us, because humans built it. The systematic putting together of parts to a purposeful design is something we know and understand, for we have experienced it at first hand, even if only with our childhood Meccano or Erector set.

What about our own bodies? Each one of us is a machine, like an airliner, only much more complicated. Were we designed on a drawing board too, and were our parts assembled by a skilled engineer? The answer is no. It is a surprising answer, and we have known and understood it for only a century or so. When Charles Darwin first explained the matter, many people either wouldn't or couldn't grasp it. I myself flatly refused to believe Darwin's theory when I first heard about it as a child. Almost everybody throughout history, up to the second half of the nineteenth century, has firmly believed in the opposite – the Conscious Designer theory. Many people still do, perhaps because the true, Darwinian explanation of our own existence is still, remarkably, not a routine part of the curriculum of a general education. It is certainly very widely misunderstood.

The watchmaker of my title is borrowed from a famous treatise by the eighteenth-century theologian William Paley. His *Natural Theology – or Evidences of the Existence and Attributes of the Deity Collected from the Appearances of Nature*, published in 1802, is the best-known exposition of the 'Argument from Design', always the most influential of the arguments for the existence of a God. It is a book that I greatly admire, for in his own time its author succeeded in doing what I am struggling to do now. He had a point to make, he passionately believed in it, and he spared no effort to ram it home clearly. He had a proper reverence for the complexity of the living world, and he saw that it demands a very special kind of explanation. The only thing he got wrong – admittedly quite a big thing! –

was the explanation itself. He gave the traditional religious answer to the riddle, but he articulated it more clearly and convincingly than anybody had before. The true explanation is utterly different, and it had to wait for one of the most revolutionary thinkers of all time, Charles Darwin.

Paley begins *Natural Theology* with a famous passage:

> In crossing a heath, suppose I pitched my foot against a *stone*, and were asked how the stone came to be there; I might possibly answer, that, for anything I knew to the contrary, it had lain there for ever: nor would it perhaps be very easy to show the absurdity of this answer. But suppose I had found a *watch* upon the ground, and it should be inquired how the watch happened to be in that place; I should hardly think of the answer which I had before given, that for anything I knew, the watch might have always been there.

Paley here appreciates the difference between natural physical objects like stones, and designed and manufactured objects like watches. He goes on to expound the precision with which the cogs and springs of a watch are fashioned, and the intricacy with which they are put together. If we found an object such as a watch upon a heath, even if we didn't know how it had come into existence, its own precision and intricacy of design would force us to conclude

> that the watch must have had a maker: that there must have existed, at some time, and at some place or other, an artificer or artificers, who formed it for the purpose which we find it actually to answer; who comprehended its construction, and designed its use.

Nobody could reasonably dissent from this conclusion, Paley insists, yet that is just what the atheist, in effect, does when he contemplates the works of nature, for:

> every indication of contrivance, every manifestation of design, which existed in the watch, exists in the works of nature; with the difference, on the side of nature, of being greater or more, and that in a degree which exceeds all computation.

Paley drives his point home with beautiful and reverent descriptions of the dissected machinery of life, beginning with the human eye, a favourite example which Darwin was later to use and which will reappear throughout this book. Paley compares the eye with a designed instrument such as a telescope, and concludes that 'there is precisely the same proof that the eye was made for vision, as there is that the telescope was made for assisting it'. The eye must have had a designer, just as the telescope had.

Paley's argument is made with passionate sincerity and is informed by the best biological scholarship of his day, but it is wrong, gloriously and utterly wrong. The analogy between telescope and eye, between watch and living organism, is false. All appearances to the contrary, the only watchmaker in nature is the blind forces of physics, albeit deployed in a very special way. A true watchmaker has foresight: he designs his cogs and springs, and plans their interconnections, with a future purpose in his mind's eye. Natural selection, the blind, unconscious, automatic process which Darwin discovered, and which we now know is the explanation for the existence and apparently purposeful form of all life, has no purpose in mind. It has no mind and no mind's eye. It does not plan for the future. It has no vision, no foresight, no sight at all. If it can be said to play the role of watchmaker in nature, it is the blind watchmaker.

I shall explain all this, and much else besides. But one thing I shall not do is belittle the wonder of the living 'watches' that so inspired Paley. On the contrary, I shall try to illustrate my feeling that here Paley could have gone even further. When it comes to feeling awe over living 'watches' I yield to nobody. I feel more in common with the Reverend William Paley than I do with the distinguished modern philosopher, a well-known atheist, with whom I once discussed the matter at dinner. I said that I could not imagine being an atheist at any time before 1859, when Darwin's Origin of Species was published. 'What about Hume?', replied the philosopher. 'How did Hume explain the organized complexity of the living world?', I asked. 'He didn't', said the philosopher. 'Why does it need any special explanation?'

Paley knew that it needed a special explanation; Darwin knew it, and I suspect that in his heart of hearts my philosopher companion knew it too. In any case it will be my business to show it here. As for David Hume himself, it is sometimes said that that great Scottish philosopher disposed of the Argument from Design a century before Darwin. But what Hume did was criticize the logic of using apparent design in nature as positive evidence for the existence of a God. He did not offer any alternative explanation for apparent design, but left the question open. An atheist before Darwin could have said, following Hume: 'I have no explanation for complex biological design. All I know is that God isn't a good explanation, so we must wait and hope that somebody comes up with a better one.' I can't help feeling that such a position, though logically sound, would have left one feeling pretty unsatisfied, and that although atheism might have been logically tenable before Darwin, Darwin made it possible to be an intellectually fulfilled atheist. I like to think that Hume would agree, but some of his writings suggest that he underestimated the complexity and beauty of biological design. The boy naturalist Charles Darwin could have shown him a thing or two about that, but Hume had been dead 40 years when Darwin enrolled in Hume's university of Edinburgh. [. . .]

[C]umulative selection can manufacture complexity while single-step selection cannot. But cumulative selection cannot work unless there is some minimal machinery of replication and replicator power, and the only machinery of replication that we know seems too complicated to have come into existence by means of anything less than many generations of cumulative selection! Some people see this as a fundamental flaw in the whole theory of the blind watchmaker. They see it as the ultimate proof that there must originally have been a designer, not a blind watchmaker but a far-sighted supernatural watchmaker. Maybe, it is argued, the Creator does not control the day-to-day succession of evolutionary events; maybe he did not frame the tiger and the lamb, maybe he did not make a tree, but he did set up the original machinery of replication and replicator power, the original machinery of DNA and protein that made cumulative selection, and hence all of evolution, possible.

This is a transparently feeble argument, indeed it is obviously self-defeating. Organized complexity is the thing that we are having difficulty in explaining. Once we are allowed simply to postulate organized complexity, if only the organized complexity of the DNA/protein replicating engine, it is relatively easy to invoke it as a generator of yet more organized complexity. . . . But of course any God capable of intelligently designing something as complex as the DNA/protein replicating machine must have been at least as complex and organized as that machine itself. Far more so if we suppose him additionally capable of such advanced functions as listening to prayers and forgiving sins. To explain the origin of the DNA/protein machine by invoking a supernatural Designer is to explain precisely nothing, for it leaves unexplained the origin of the Designer. You have to say something like 'God was always there', and if you allow yourself that kind of lazy way out, you might as well just say 'DNA was always there', or 'Life was always there', and be done with it. [. . .]

Chapter 14

Richard Dawkins

GOD'S UTILITY FUNCTION

CHARLES DARWIN LOST his [faith] with the help of [a wasp]: "I cannot persuade myself," Darwin wrote, "that a beneficent and omnipotent God would have designedly created the Ichneumonidae with the express intention of their feeding within the living bodies of Caterpillars." Actually Darwin's gradual loss of faith, which he downplayed for fear of upsetting his devout wife Emma, had more complex causes. His reference to the Ichneumonidae was aphoristic. The macabre habits to which he referred are shared by their cousins the digger wasps. . . . A female digger wasp not only lays her egg in a caterpillar (or grasshopper or bee) so that her larva can feed on it but, according to Fabre and others, she carefully guides her sting into each ganglion of the prey's central nervous system, so as to paralyze it but not kill it. This way, the meat keeps fresh. It is not known whether the paralysis acts as a general anesthetic, or if it is like curare in just freezing the victim's ability to move. If the latter, the prey might be aware of being eaten alive from inside but unable to move a muscle to do anything about it. This sounds savagely cruel but as we shall see, nature is not cruel, only pitilessly indifferent. This is one of the hardest lessons for humans to learn. We cannot admit that things might be neither good nor evil, neither cruel nor kind, but simply callous—indifferent to all suffering, lacking all purpose.

We humans have purpose on the brain. We find it hard to look at anything without wondering what it is "for," what the motive for it is, or the purpose behind it. When the obsession with purpose becomes pathological it is called paranoia—reading malevolent purpose into what is actually random bad luck. But this is just an exaggerated form of a nearly universal delusion. Show us almost any object or process, and it is hard for us to resist the "Why" question—the "What is it for?" question.

The desire to see purpose everywhere is a natural one in an animal that lives surrounded by machines, works of art, tools and other designed artifacts; an animal, moreover, whose waking thoughts are dominated by its own personal goals. A car, a tin opener, a screwdriver and a pitchfork all legitimately warrant the "What is it for?" question. Our pagan forebears would have asked the same question about thunder, eclipses, rocks and streams. Today we pride ourselves on having shaken off such primitive animism. If a rock in a stream happens to serve as a convenient steppingstone, we regard its usefulness as an accidental bonus, not a true purpose. But the old temptation comes back with a vengeance when tragedy strikes—indeed, the very word "strikes" is an animistic echo: "Why, oh why, did the cancer/earthquake/hurricane have to strike my child?" And the same temptation is often positively relished when the topic is the origin of all things or the fundamental laws of physics, culminating in the vacuous existential question "Why is there something rather than nothing?"

I have lost count of the number of times a member of the audience has stood up after a public lecture I have given and said something like the following: "You scientists are very good at answering 'How' questions. But you must admit you're powerless when it comes to 'Why' questions." Prince Philip, Duke of Edinburgh, made this very point when he was in an audience at Windsor addressed by my colleague Dr. Peter Atkins. Behind the question there is always an unspoken but never justified implication that since science is unable to answer "Why" questions, there must be some other discipline that is qualified to answer them. This implication is, of course, quite illogical.

I'm afraid that Dr. Atkins gave the Royal Why fairly short shrift. The mere fact that it is possible to frame a question does not make it legitimate or sensible to do so. There are many things about which you can ask, "What is its temperature?" or "What color is it?" but you may not ask the temperature question or the color question of, say, jealousy or prayer. Similarly, you are right to ask the "Why" question of a bicycle's mudguards or the Kariba Dam, but at the very least you have no right to *assume* that the "Why" question deserves an answer when posed about a boulder, a misfortune, Mt. Everest or the universe. Questions can be simply inappropriate, however heartfelt their framing.

Somewhere between windscreen wipers and tin openers on the one hand and rocks and the universe on the other lie living creatures. Living bodies and their organs are objects that, unlike rocks, seem to have purpose written all over them. Notoriously, of course, the apparent purposefulness of living bodies has dominated the classic Argument from Design, invoked by theologians from Aquinas to William Paley to modern "scientific" creationists.

The true process that has endowed wings and eyes, beaks, nesting instincts and everything else about life with the strong illusion of purposeful design is now well understood. It is Darwinian natural selection. Our understanding of this has come astonishingly recently, in the last century and a half. Before Darwin, even educated people who had abandoned "Why" questions for rocks, streams and eclipses still implicitly accepted the legitimacy of the "Why" question where living creatures were concerned. Now only the scientifically illiterate do. But "only" conceals the unpalatable truth that we are still talking about an absolute majority. [. . .]

I now want to introduce two technical terms, "reverse engineering" and "utility function." In this section, I am influenced by Daniel Dennett's superb book *Darwin's Dangerous Idea*. Reverse engineering is a technique of reasoning that works like this. You are an engineer, confronted with an artifact you have found and don't understand. You make the working assumption that it was designed for some purpose. You dissect and analyze the object with a view to working out what problem it would be good at solving: "If I had wanted to make a machine to do so-and-so, would I have made it like this? Or is the object better explained as a machine designed to do such-and-such?"

The slide rule, talisman until recently of the honorable profession of engineer, is in the electronic age as obsolete as any Bronze Age relic. An archaeologist of the future, finding a slide rule and wondering about it, might note that it is handy for drawing straight lines or for buttering bread. But to assume that either of these was its original purpose violates the economy assumption. A mere straight-edge or butter knife would not have needed a sliding member in the middle of the rule. Moreover, if you examine the spacing of the graticules you find precise logarithmic scales, too meticulously disposed to be accidental. It would dawn on the archaeologist that, in an age before electronic calculators, this pattern would constitute an ingenious trick for rapid multiplication and division. The mystery of the slide rule would be solved by reverse engineering, employing the assumption of intelligent and economical design.

"Utility function" is a technical term not of engineers but of economists. It means "that which is maximized." Economic planners and social engineers are rather like architects and real engineers in that they strive to maximize something. Utilitarians strive to maximize "the greatest happiness for the greatest number" (a phrase that sounds more intelligent than it is, by the way). Under this umbrella, the utilitarian may give long-term stability more or less priority at the expense of short-term happiness, and utilitarians differ over whether they measure "happiness" by monetary wealth, job satisfaction, cultural fulfillment or personal relationships. Others avowedly maximize their own happiness at the expense of the common welfare, and they may dignify their egoism by a philosophy that states that general happiness will be maximized if one takes care of oneself. By watching the behavior of individuals throughout their lives, you should be able to reverse-engineer their utility functions. If you reverse-engineer the behavior of a country's government, you may conclude that what is being maximized is employment and universal welfare. For another country, the utility function may turn out to be the continued power of the president, or the wealth of a particular ruling family, the size of the sultan's harem, the stability of the Middle East or maintaining the price of oil. The point is that more than one utility function can be imagined. It isn't always obvious what individuals, or firms, or governments are striving to maximize. But it is probably safe to assume that they are maximizing something. This is because *Homo sapiens* is a deeply purpose-ridden species. The principle holds good even if the utility function turns out to be a weighted sum or some other complicated function of many inputs.

Let us return to living bodies and try to extract their utility function. There could be many but, revealingly, it will eventually turn out that they all reduce to one. A good way to dramatize our task is to imagine that living creatures were made by a Divine Engineer and try to work out, by reverse engineering, what the Engineer was trying to maximize: What was God's Utility Function?

Cheetahs give every indication of being superbly designed for something, and it should be easy enough to reverse-engineer them and work out their utility function. They appear to be well designed to kill antelopes. The teeth, claws, eyes, nose, leg muscles, backbone and brain of a cheetah are all precisely what we should expect if God's purpose in designing cheetahs was to maximize deaths among antelopes. Conversely, if we reverse-engineer an antelope we find equally impressive evidence of design for precisely the opposite end: the survival of antelopes and starvation among cheetahs. It is as though cheetahs had been designed by one deity and antelopes by a rival deity. Alternatively, if there is only one Creator who made the tiger and the lamb, the cheetah and the gazelle, what is He playing at? Is He a sadist who enjoys spectator blood sports? Is He trying to avoid overpopulation in the mammals of Africa? Is He maneuvering to maximize David Attenborough's television ratings? These are all intelligible utility functions that might have turned out to be true. In fact, of course, they are all completely wrong. We now understand the single Utility Function of life in great detail, and it is nothing like any of those. . . .

[T]he true utility function of life, that which is being maximized in the natural world, is DNA survival. But DNA is not floating free; it is locked up in living bodies and it has to make the most of the levers of power at its disposal.

DNA sequences that find themselves in cheetah bodies maximize their survival by causing those bodies to kill gazelles. Sequences that find themselves in gazelle bodies maximize their survival by promoting opposite ends. But it is DNA survival that is being maximized in both cases. [. . .]

[W]hen the utility function—that which is being maximized—is DNA survival, this is not a recipe for happiness. So long as DNA is passed on, it does not matter who or what gets hurt in the process. It is better for the genes of Darwin's ichneumon wasp that the caterpillar should be alive, and therefore fresh, when it is eaten, no matter what the cost in suffering. Genes don't care about suffering, because they don't care about anything.

If Nature were kind, she would at least make the minor concession of anesthetizing caterpillars before they are eaten alive from within. But Nature is neither kind nor unkind. She is neither against suffering nor for it. Nature is not interested one way or the other in suffering, unless it affects the survival of DNA. It is easy to imagine a gene that, say, tranquilizes gazelles when they are about to suffer a killing bite. Would such a gene be favored by natural selection? Not unless the act of tranquilizing a gazelle improved that gene's chances of being propagated into future generations. It is hard to see why this should be so, and we may therefore guess that gazelles suffer horrible pain and fear when they are pursued to the death—as most of them eventually are. The total amount of suffering per year in the natural world is beyond all decent contemplation. During the minute it takes me to compose this sentence, thousands of animals are being eaten alive; others are running for their lives, whimpering with fear; others are being slowly devoured from within by rasping parasites; thousands of all kinds are dying of starvation, thirst and disease. It must be so. If there is ever a time of plenty, this very fact will automatically lead to an increase in population until the natural state of starvation and misery is restored.

Theologians worry away at the "problem of evil" and a related "problem of suffering." On the day I originally wrote this paragraph, the British newspapers all carried a terrible story about a bus full of children from a Roman Catholic school that crashed for no obvious reason, with wholesale loss of life. Not for the first time, clerics were in paroxysms over the theological question that a writer on a London newspaper (*The Sunday Telegraph*) framed this way: "How can you believe in a loving, all-powerful God who allows such a tragedy?" The article went on to quote one priest's reply: "The simple answer is that we do not know why there should be a God who lets these awful things happen. But the horror of the crash, to a Christian, confirms the fact that we live in a world of real values: positive and negative. If the universe was just electrons, there would be no problem of evil or suffering."

On the contrary, if the universe were just electrons and selfish genes, meaningless tragedies like the crashing of this bus are exactly what we should expect, along with equally meaningless *good* fortune. Such a universe would be neither evil nor good in intention. It would manifest no intentions of any kind. In a universe of blind physical forces and genetic replication, some people are going to get hurt, other people are going to get lucky, and you won't find any rhyme or reason in it, nor any justice. The universe we observe has precisely the properties we should expect if there is, at bottom, no design, no purpose, no evil and no good, nothing but blind, pitiless indifference. As that unhappy poet A. E. Housman put it:

> For Nature, heartless, witless Nature
> Will neither know nor care.

DNA neither knows nor cares. DNA just is. And we dance to its music.

Chapter 15

Daniel C. Dennett

DARWIN'S DANGEROUS IDEA

Is nothing sacred?

WE USED TO SING a lot when I was a child, around the campfire at summer camp, at school and Sunday school, or gathered around the piano at home. One of my favorite songs was "Tell Me Why." . . .

> Tell me why the stars do shine,
> Tell me why the ivy twines,
> Tell me why the sky's so blue.
> Then I will tell you just why I love you.

> Because God made the stars to shine,
> Because God made the ivy twine,
> Because God made the sky so blue.
> Because God made you, that's why I love you.

This straightforward, sentimental declaration still brings a lump to my throat—so sweet, so innocent, so reassuring a vision of life!

And then along comes Darwin and spoils the picnic. Or does he? . . . From the moment of the publication of *Origin of Species* in 1859, Charles Darwin's fundamental idea has inspired intense reactions ranging from ferocious condemnation to ecstatic allegiance, sometimes tantamount to religious zeal.

Darwin's theory has been abused and misrepresented by friend and foe alike. It has been misappropriated to lend scientific respectability to appalling political and social doctrines. It has been pilloried in caricature by opponents, some of whom would have it compete in our children's schools with "creation science," a pathetic hodgepodge of pious pseudo-science.[1]

Almost no one is indifferent to Darwin, and no one should be. The Darwinian theory is a scientific theory, and a great one, but that is not all it is. The creationists who oppose it so bitterly are right about one thing: Darwin's dangerous idea cuts much deeper into the fabric of our most fundamental beliefs than many of its sophisticated apologists have yet admitted, even to themselves.

The sweet, simple vision of the song, taken literally, is one that most of us have outgrown, however fondly we may recall it. The kindly God who lovingly fashioned each and every one of us (all creatures great and small) and sprinkled the sky with shining stars for our delight—that God is, like Santa Claus, a myth of childhood, not anything a sane, undeluded adult could literally believe in. That God must either be turned into a symbol for something less concrete or abandoned altogether.

Not all scientists and philosophers are atheists, and many who are believers declare that their idea of God can live in peaceful coexistence with, or even find support from, the Darwinian framework of ideas. Theirs is not an anthropomorphic Handicrafter God, but still a God worthy of worship in their eyes, capable of giving consolation and meaning to their lives. Others ground their highest concerns in entirely secular philosophies, views of the meaning of life that stave off despair without the aid of any concept of a Supreme Being—other than the Universe itself. Something is sacred to these thinkers, but they do not call it God; they call it, perhaps, Life, or Love, or Goodness, or Intelligence, or Beauty, or Humanity. What both groups share, in spite of the differences in their deepest creeds, is a conviction that life does have meaning, that goodness matters.

But can any version of this attitude of wonder and purpose be sustained in the face of Darwinism? From the outset, there have been those who thought they saw Darwin letting the worst possible cat out of the bag: nihilism. They thought that if Darwin was right, the implication would be that nothing could be sacred. To put it bluntly, nothing could have any point. Is this just an overreaction? What exactly are the implications of Darwin's idea—and, in any case, has it been scientifically proven or is it still "just a theory"?

Perhaps, you may think, we could make a useful division: there are the parts of Darwin's idea that really are established beyond any reasonable doubt, and then there are the speculative extensions of the scientifically irresistible parts. Then—if we were lucky—perhaps the rock-solid scientific facts would have no stunning implications about religion, or human nature, or the meaning of life, while the parts of Darwin's idea that get people all upset could be put into quarantine as highly controversial extensions of, or mere interpretations of, the scientifically irresistible parts. That would be reassuring.

But alas, that is just about backwards. There are vigorous controversies swirling around in evolutionary theory, but those who feel threatened by Darwinism should not take heart from this fact. Most—if not quite all—of the controversies concern issues that are "just science"; no matter which side wins, the outcome will not undo the basic Darwinian idea. That idea, which is about as secure as any in science, really does have far-reaching implications for our vision of what the meaning of life is or could be.

In 1543, Copernicus proposed that the Earth was not the center of the universe but in fact revolved around the Sun. It took over a century for the idea to sink in, a gradual and actually rather painless transformation. (The religious reformer Philipp Melanchthon, a collaborator of Martin Luther, opined that "some Christian prince" should suppress this madman, but aside from a few such salvos, the world was not particularly shaken by Copernicus himself.) The Copernican Revolution did eventually have its own "shot heard round the world": Galileo's *Dialogue Concerning the Two Chief World Systems*, but it was not published until 1632, when the issue was no longer controversial among scientists. Galileo's projectile provoked an infamous response by the Roman Catholic Church, setting up a shock wave whose reverberations are only now dying out. But in spite of the drama of that epic confrontation, the idea that our planet is not the center of creation has sat rather lightly in people's minds. Every schoolchild today accepts this as the matter of fact it is, without tears or terror.

In due course, the Darwinian Revolution will come to occupy a similarly secure and untroubled place in the minds—and hearts—of every educated person on the globe, but today, more than a century after Darwin's death, we still have not come to terms with its mind-boggling implications. Unlike the Copernican Revolution, which did not engage widespread public attention until the scientific details had been largely sorted out, the Darwinian Revolution has had anxious lay spectators and cheerleaders taking sides from the outset, tugging at the sleeves of the participants and encouraging grandstanding. The scientists themselves have been moved by the same hopes and fears, so it is not surprising that the relatively narrow conflicts among theorists have often been not just blown up out of proportion by their adherents, but seriously distorted in the process. Everybody has seen, dimly, that a lot is at stake.

Moreover, although Darwin's own articulation of his theory was monumental, and its powers were immediately recognized by many of the scientists and other thinkers of his day, there really were large gaps in his theory that have only recently begun to be properly filled in. The biggest gap looks almost comical in retrospect. In all his brilliant musings, Darwin never hit upon the central concept, without which the theory of evolution is hopeless: the concept of a *gene*. Darwin had no proper unit of heredity, and so his account of the process of natural selection was plagued with entirely reasonable doubts about whether it would work. Darwin supposed that offspring would always exhibit a sort of blend or average of their parents' features. Wouldn't such "blending inheritance" always simply average out all differences, turning everything into uniform gray? How could diversity survive such relentless averaging? Darwin recognized the seriousness of this challenge, and neither he nor his many ardent supporters succeeded in responding with a description of a convincing and well-documented mechanism of heredity that could combine traits of parents while maintaining an underlying and unchanged identity. The idea they needed was right at hand, uncovered ("formulated" would be too strong) by the monk Gregor Mendel and published in a relatively obscure Austrian journal in 1865, but, in the best-savored irony in the history of science, it lay there unnoticed until its importance was appreciated (at first dimly) around 1900. Its triumphant establishment at the heart of the "Modern Synthesis" (in effect, the synthesis of Mendel and Darwin) was eventually made secure in the 1940s, thanks to the work of Theodosius Dobzhansky, Julian Huxley, Ernst Mayr, and others. It has taken another half-century to iron out most of the wrinkles of that new fabric.

The fundamental core of contemporary Darwinism, the theory of DNA-based reproduction and evolution, is now beyond dispute among scientists. It demonstrates its power every day, contributing crucially to the explanation of planet-sized facts of geology and meteorology, through middle-sized facts of ecology and agronomy, down to the latest microscopic facts of genetic engineering. It unifies all of biology and the history of our planet into a single grand story. Like Gulliver tied down in Lilliput, it is unbudgeable, not because of some one or two huge chains of argument that might—hope against hope—have weak links in them, but because it is securely tied by hundreds of thousands of threads of evidence anchoring it to virtually every other area of human knowledge. New discoveries may conceivably lead to dramatic, even "revolutionary" shifts in the Darwinian theory, but the hope that it will be "refuted" by some shattering breakthrough is about as reasonable as the hope that we will return to a geocentric vision and discard Copernicus.

Still, the theory is embroiled in remarkably hot-tempered controversy, and one of the reasons for this incandescence is that these debates about scientific matters are usually distorted by fears that the "wrong" answer would have intolerable moral implications. So great are these fears that they are carefully left unarticulated, displaced from attention by several layers of distracting rebuttal and counter-rebuttal. The disputants are forever changing the subject slightly, conveniently keeping the bogeys in the shadows. It is this misdirection that is mainly responsible for postponing the day when we can all live as comfortably with our new biological perspective as we do with the astronomical perspective Copernicus gave us.

Whenever Darwinism is the topic, the temperature rises, because more is at stake than just the empirical facts about how life on Earth evolved, or the correct logic of the theory that accounts for those facts. One of the precious things that is at stake is a vision of what it means to ask, and answer, the question "Why?" Darwin's new perspective turns several traditional assumptions upside down, undermining our standard ideas about what ought to count as satisfying answers to this ancient and inescapable question. Here science and philosophy get completely intertwined. Scientists sometimes deceive themselves into thinking that philosophical ideas are only, at best, decorations or parasitic commentaries on the hard, objective triumphs of science, and that they themselves are immune to the confusions that philosophers devote their lives to dissolving. But there is no such thing as philosophy-free science; there is only science whose philosophical baggage is taken on board without examination.

The Darwinian Revolution is both a scientific and a philosophical revolution, and neither revolution could have occurred without the other. . . . [I]t was the philosophical prejudices of the scientists, more than their lack of scientific evidence, that prevented them from seeing how the theory could actually work, but those philosophical prejudices that had to be overthrown were too deeply entrenched to be dislodged by mere philosophical brilliance. It took an irresistible parade of hard-won scientific facts to force thinkers to take seriously the weird new outlook that Darwin proposed. Those who are still ill-acquainted with that beautiful procession can be forgiven their continued allegiance to the pre-Darwinian ideas. And the battle is not yet over; even among the scientists, there are pockets of resistance.

Let me lay my cards on the table. If I were to give an award for the single best idea anyone has ever had, I'd give it to Darwin, ahead of Newton and Einstein and everyone else. In a single stroke, the idea of evolution by natural selection unifies the realm of life, meaning, and purpose with the realm of space and time, cause and effect, mechanism and physical law. But it is not just a wonderful scientific idea. It is a dangerous idea. My admiration for Darwin's magnificent idea is unbounded, but I, too, cherish many of the ideas and ideals that it *seems* to challenge, and want to protect them. For instance, I want to protect the campfire song, and what is beautiful and true in it, for my little grandson and his friends, and for their children when they grow up. There are many more magnificent ideas that are also jeopardized, it seems, by Darwin's idea, and they, too, may need protection. The only good way to do this— the only way that has a chance in the long run—is to cut through the smokescreens and look at the idea as unflinchingly, as dispassionately, as possible. [. . .]

Natural selection as an algorithmic process

[. . .]

[Darwin] presents his principle as deducible by a formal argument—if the conditions are met, a certain outcome is *assured*.[2] Here is [his] summary . . ., with some key terms in boldface.

> **If**, during the long course of ages and under varying conditions of life, organic beings vary at all in the several parts of their organization, and I think this cannot be disputed; **if** there be, owing to the high geometric powers of increase of each species, at some age, season, or year, a severe struggle for life, and this certainly cannot be disputed; **then**, considering the infinite complexity of the relations of all organic beings to each other and to their conditions of existence, causing an infinite diversity in structure, constitution, and habits, to be advantageous to them, **I think it would be a most extraordinary fact if no variation ever had occurred useful to each being's own welfare,** in the same way as so many variations have occurred useful to man. But **if** variations useful to any organic being do occur, **assuredly** individuals thus characterized will have the best chance of being preserved in the struggle for life; and from the strong principle of inheritance they will tend to produce offspring similarly characterized. This principle of preservation, I have called, for the sake of brevity, Natural Selection.
>
> [*Origin*, p. 127 (facs. ed. of 1st ed.).]

The basic deductive argument is short and sweet, but Darwin himself described *Origin of Species* as "one long argument." That is because it consists of two sorts of demonstrations: the logical demonstration that a certain sort of process would necessarily have a certain sort of outcome, and the empirical demonstration that the requisite conditions for that sort of process had in fact been met in nature. He bolsters up his logical demonstration with thought experiments— "imaginary instances" (*Origin*, p. 95)—that show how the meeting of these conditions might actually account for the effects he claimed to be explaining, but his whole argument extends to book length because he presents a wealth of hard-won empirical detail to convince the reader that these conditions have been met over and over again. [. . .]

Darwin appreciated that only a relentlessly detailed survey of the evidence for the historical processes he was postulating would—or should—persuade scientists to abandon their traditional convictions and take on his revolutionary vision, even if it was in fact "deducible from first principles."

From the outset, there were those who viewed Darwin's novel mixture of detailed naturalism and abstract reasoning about processes as a dubious and inviable hybrid. It had a tremendous air of plausibility, but so do many get-rich-quick schemes that turn out to be empty tricks. Compare it to the following stock-market principle: Buy Low, Sell High. This is guaranteed to make you wealthy. You cannot fail to get rich if you follow this advice. Why doesn't it work? It does work—for everybody who is fortunate enough to act according to it, but, alas, there is no way of determining that the conditions are met until it is too late to act on them. Darwin was offering a skeptical world what we might call a get-rich-*slow* scheme, a scheme for creating Design out of Chaos without the aid of Mind.

The theoretical power of Darwin's abstract scheme was due to several features that Darwin quite firmly identified, and appreciated better than many of his supporters, but lacked the terminology to describe explicitly. Today we could capture these features under a single term. Darwin had discovered the power of an *algorithm*. An algorithm is a certain sort of formal process that can be counted on—logically—to yield a certain sort of result whenever it is "run" or instantiated. Algorithms are not new, and were not new in Darwin's day. Many familiar arithmetic procedures, such as long division or balancing your checkbook, are algorithms, and so are the decision procedures for playing perfect tic-tac-toe, and for putting a list of words into alphabetical order. What is relatively new—permitting us valuable hindsight on Darwin's discovery—is the theoretical reflection by mathematicians and logicians on the nature and power of algorithms in general, a twentieth-century development which led to the birth of the computer, which has led in turn, of course, to a much deeper and more lively understanding of the powers of algorithms in general.

The term *algorithm* descends, via Latin (*algorismus*) to early English (*algorisme* and, mistakenly therefrom, *algorithm*), from the name of a Persian mathematician, Mûusâ al-Khowârizm, whose book on arithmetical procedures, written about 835 A.D., was translated into Latin in the twelfth century by Adelard of Bath or Robert of Chester. The idea that an algorithm is a foolproof and somehow "mechanical" procedure has been present for centuries, but it was the pioneering work of Alan Turing, Kurt Gödel, and Alonzo Church in the 1930s that more or less fixed our current understanding of the term. Three key features of algorithms will be important to us, and each is somewhat difficult to define. Each, moreover, has given rise to confusions (and anxieties) that continue to beset our thinking about Darwin's revolutionary discovery, so we will have to revisit and reconsider these introductory characterizations several times before we are through:

(1)   *substrate neutrality*: The procedure for long division works equally well with pencil or pen, paper or parchment, neon lights or skywriting, using any symbol system you like. The power of the procedure is due to its *logical* structure, not the causal powers of the materials used in the instantiation, just so long as those causal powers permit the prescribed steps to be followed exactly.

(2)   *underlying mindlessness*: Although the overall design of the procedure may be brilliant, or yield brilliant results, each constituent step, as well as the transition between steps, is utterly simple. How simple? Simple enough for a dutiful idiot to perform—or for a straightforward mechanical device to perform. The standard textbook analogy notes that algorithms are *recipes* of sorts, designed to be followed by *novice* cooks. A recipe book written for great chefs might include the phrase "Poach the fish in a suitable wine until almost done," but an algorithm for the same process might begin, "Choose a white wine that says 'dry' on the label; take a corkscrew and open the bottle; pour an inch of wine in the bottom of a pan; turn the burner under the pan on high; . . ."—a tedious breakdown of the process into dead-simple steps, requiring no wise decisions or delicate judgments or intuitions on the part of the recipe-reader.

(3)   *guaranteed results*: Whatever it is that an algorithm does, it always does it, if it is executed without misstep. An algorithm is a foolproof recipe.

It is easy to see how these features made the computer possible. *Every computer program is an algorithm*, ultimately composed of simple steps that can be executed with stupendous reliability by one simple mechanism or another. Electronic circuits are the usual choice, but the power of computers owes nothing (save speed) to the causal peculiarities of electrons darting about on silicon chips. The very same algorithms can be performed (even faster) by devices shunting photons in glass fibers, or (much, much slower) by teams of people using paper and pencil. . . .

What Darwin discovered was not really *one* algorithm but, rather, a large class of related algorithms that he had no clear way to distinguish. We can now reformulate his fundamental idea as follows:

Life on Earth has been generated over billions of years in a single branching tree—the Tree of Life—by one algorithmic process or another.

[. . .]

Here, then, is Darwin's dangerous idea: the algorithmic level *is* the level that best accounts for the speed of the antelope, the wing of the eagle, the shape of the orchid, the diversity of species, and all the other occasions for wonder in the world of nature. It is hard to believe that something as mindless and mechanical as an algorithm could produce such wonderful things. No matter how impressive the products of an algorithm, the underlying process always consists of nothing but a set of individually mindless steps succeeding each other without the help of any intelligent supervision; they are "automatic" by definition: the workings of an automaton. They feed on each other, or on blind chance—coin-flips, if you like—and on nothing else. Most algorithms we are familiar with have rather modest products: they do long division or alphabetize lists or figure out the income of the Average Taxpayer. Fancier algorithms produce the dazzling computer-animated graphics we see every day on television, transforming faces, creating herds of imaginary ice-skating polar bears, simulating whole virtual worlds of entities never seen or imagined before. But the actual biosphere is much fancier still, by many orders of magnitude. Can it really be the outcome of nothing but a cascade of algorithmic processes feeding on chance? And if so, who designed that cascade? Nobody. It is itself the product of a blind, algorithmic process. As Darwin himself put it, in a letter to the geologist Charles Lyell shortly after publication of *Origin*, "I would give absolutely nothing for the theory of Natural Selection, if it requires miraculous additions at any one stage of descent. . . . If I were convinced that I required such additions to the theory of natural selection, I would reject it as rubbish . . ." (F. Darwin 1911, vol. 2, pp. 6–7).

According to Darwin, then, evolution is an algorithmic process. Putting it this way is still controversial. One of the tugs-of-war going on within evolutionary biology is between those who are relentlessly pushing, pushing, pushing towards an algorithmic treatment, and those who, for various submerged reasons, are resisting this trend. It is rather as if there were metallurgists around who were disappointed by the algorithmic explanation of annealing. "You mean that's all there is to it? No submicroscopic Superglue specially created by the heating and cooling process?" Darwin has convinced all the scientists that evolution, like annealing, *works*. His radical vision of *how* and *why* it works is still somewhat embattled, largely because those who resist can dimly see that their skirmish is part of a larger campaign. If the game is lost in evolutionary biology, where will it all end?

[. . .]

Universal acid

[. . .]

Darwin began his explanation in the middle, or even, you might say, at the end: starting with the life forms we presently see, and showing how the patterns in today's biosphere could be explained as having arisen by the process of natural selection from the patterns in yesterday's biosphere, and so on, back into the very distant past. He started with facts that everyone knows: all of today's living things are the offspring of parents, who are the offspring of grandparents, and so forth, so everything that is alive today is a branch of a genealogical family, which is itself a branch of a larger clan. He went on to argue that, if you go back far enough, you find that all the branches of all the families eventually spring from common ancestral limbs, so that there is a single Tree of Life, all the limbs, branches, and twigs united by descent with modification. The fact that it has the branching organization of a tree is crucial to the explanation of the sort of process involved, for such a tree could be created by an automatic, recursive process: first build an x, then modify x's descendants, then modify those modifications, then modify the modifications of the modifications. . . . If Life is a Tree, it could all have arisen from an inexorable, automatic rebuilding process in which designs would accumulate over time.

Working backwards, starting at or near "the end" of a process, and solving the next-to-last step before asking how it could have been produced, is a tried and true method of computer programmers, particularly when creating programs that use recursion. Usually this is a matter of practical modesty: if you don't want to bite off more than you can chew, the right bite to start with is often the finishing bite, if you can find it. Darwin found it, and then very cautiously worked his way back, skirting around the many grand issues that his investigations stirred up, musing about them in his private notebooks, but postponing their publication indefinitely. (For instance, he deliberately avoided discussing human evolution in Origin; see the discussion in R. J. Richards 1987, pp. 160ff.) But he could see where all this was leading, and, in spite of his near-perfect silence on these troubling extrapolations, so could many of his readers. Some loved what they thought they saw, and others hated it.

Karl Marx was exultant: "Not only is a death blow dealt here for the first time to 'Teleology' in the natural sciences but their rational meaning is empirically explained" (quoted in Rachels 1991, p. 110). Friedrich Nietzsche saw—through the mists of his contempt for all things English—an even more

cosmic message in Darwin: God is dead. If Nietzsche is the father of existentialism, then perhaps Darwin deserves the title of grandfather. Others were less
enthralled with the thought that Darwin's views were utterly subversive to
sacred tradition. Samuel Wilberforce, Bishop of Oxford, whose debate with
Thomas Huxley in June 1860 was one of the most celebrated confrontations
between Darwinism and the religious establishment . . . said in an anonymous
review:

> Man's derived supremacy over the earth; man's power of articulate
> speech; man's gift of reason; man's free-will and responsibility
> . . .—all are equally and utterly irreconcilable with the degrading
> notion of the brute origin of him who was created in the image of
> God. . . .
>
> [Wilberforce 1860.]

When speculation on these extensions of his view arose, Darwin wisely chose
to retreat to the security of his base camp, the magnificently provisioned and
defended thesis that began in the middle, with life already on the scene, and
"merely" showed how, once this process of design accumulation was under
way, it could proceed without any (further?) intervention from any Mind. But,
as many of his readers appreciated, however comforting this modest disclaimer
might be, it was not really a stable resting place.

Did you ever hear of universal acid? This fantasy used to amuse me and
some of my schoolboy friends—I have no idea whether we invented or
inherited it, along with Spanish fly and saltpeter, as a part of underground
youth culture. Universal acid is a liquid so corrosive that it will eat through
anything! The problem is: what do you keep it in? It dissolves glass bottles and
stainless-steel canisters as readily as paper bags. What would happen if you
somehow came upon or created a dollop of universal acid? Would the whole
planet eventually be destroyed? What would it leave in its wake? After everything had been transformed by its encounter with universal acid, what would
the world look like? Little did I realize that in a few years I would encounter an
idea—Darwin's idea—bearing an unmistakable likeness to universal acid: it
eats through just about every traditional concept, and leaves in its wake a
revolutionized world-view, with most of the old landmarks still recognizable,
but transformed in fundamental ways.

Darwin's idea had been born as an answer to questions in biology, but it
threatened to leak out, offering answers—welcome or not—to questions in
cosmology (going in one direction) and psychology (going in the other direction). If redesign could be a mindless, algorithmic process of evolution, why
couldn't that whole process itself be the product of evolution, and so forth, all

the way down? And if mindless evolution could account for the breathtakingly clever artifacts of the biosphere, how could the products of our own "real" minds be exempt from an evolutionary explanation? Darwin's idea thus also threatened to spread *all the way up*, dissolving the illusion of our own authorship, our own divine spark of creativity and understanding.

Much of the controversy and anxiety that has enveloped Darwin's idea ever since can be understood as a series of failed campaigns in the struggle to contain Darwin's idea within some acceptably "safe" and merely partial revolution. Cede some or all of modern biology to Darwin, perhaps, but hold the line there! Keep Darwinian thinking out of cosmology, out of psychology, out of human culture, out of ethics, politics, and religion! In these campaigns, many battles have been won by the forces of containment: flawed applications of Darwin's idea have been exposed and discredited, beaten back by the champions of the pre-Darwinian tradition. But new waves of Darwinian thinking keep coming. They seem to be improved versions, not vulnerable to the refutations that defeated their predecessors, but are they sound extensions of the unquestionably sound Darwinian core idea, or might they, too, be perversions of it, and even more virulent, more dangerous, than the abuses of Darwin already refuted?

Opponents of the spread differ sharply over tactics. Just where should the protective dikes be built? Should we try to contain the idea within biology itself, with one post-Darwinian counterrevolution or another? Among those who have favored this tactic is Stephen Jay Gould, who has offered several different revolutions of containment. Or should we place the barriers farther out? To get out bearings in this series of campaigns, we should start with a crude map of the pre-Darwinian territory. As we shall see, it will have to be revised again and again to make accommodations as various skirmishes are lost.

Darwin's assault on the cosmic pyramid

A prominent feature of Pre-Darwinian world-views is an overall top-to-bottom map of things. This is often described as a Ladder; God is at the top, with human beings a rung or two below (depending on whether angels are part of the scheme). At the bottom of the Ladder is Nothingness, or maybe Chaos, or maybe Locke's inert, motionless Matter. Alternatively, the scale is a Tower, or, in the intellectual historian Arthur Lovejoy's memorable phrase (1936), a Great Chain of Being composed of many links. John Locke's argument has already drawn our attention to a particularly abstract version of the hierarchy, which I will call the Cosmic Pyramid:

God

Mind

Design

Order

Chaos

Nothing

(Warning: each term in the pyramid must be understood in an old-fashioned, pre-Darwinian sense!)

Everything finds its place on one level or another of the Cosmic Pyramid, even blank nothingness, the ultimate foundation. Not all matter is Ordered, some is in Chaos; only some Ordered matter is also Designed; only some Designed things have Minds, and of course only one Mind is God. God, the first Mind, is the source and explanation of everything underneath. (Since everything thus *depends on* God, perhaps we should say it is a chandelier, hanging from God, rather than a pyramid, supporting Him.)

What is the difference between Order and Design? As a first stab, we might say that Order is mere regularity, mere pattern; Design is Aristotle's *telos*, an exploitation of Order for a purpose, such as we see in a cleverly designed artifact. The solar system exhibits stupendous Order, but does not (apparently) have a purpose—it isn't for anything. An eye, in contrast, is for seeing. Before Darwin, this distinction was not always clearly marked. Indeed, it was positively blurred:

> In the thirteenth century, Aquinas offered the view that natural bodies [such as planets, raindrops, volcanos] act as if guided toward a definite goal or end "so as to obtain the best result." This fitting of means to ends implies, argued Aquinas, an intention. But, seeing as natural bodies lack consciousness, they cannot supply that intention themselves. "Therefore some intelligent being exists by whom all natural things are directed to their end; and this being we call God."
>
> [Davies 1992, p. 200.]

Hume's Cleanthes, following in this tradition, lumps the adapted marvels of the living world with the regularities of the heavens—it's *all* like a wonderful clockwork to him. But Darwin suggests a division: Give me Order, he says, and time, and I will give you Design. Let me start with regularity—the mere purposeless, mindless, pointless regularity of physics—and I will show you a process that eventually will yield products that exhibit not just regularity but purposive design. (This was just what Karl Marx thought he saw when he declared that Darwin had dealt a death blow to Teleology: Darwin had *reduced* teleology to nonteleology, Design to Order.)

Before Darwin, the difference between Order and Design didn't loom large, because in any case it all came down from God. The whole universe was His artifact, a product of His Intelligence, His Mind. Once Darwin jumped into the middle with his proposed answer to the question of how Design could arise from mere Order, the rest of the Cosmic Pyramid was put in jeopardy. Suppose we accept that Darwin has explained the Design of the bodies of plants and animals (including our own bodies—we have to admit that Darwin has placed us firmly in the animal kingdom). Looking up, if we concede to Darwin our bodies, can we keep him from taking our minds as well? . . . Looking down, Darwin asks us to give him Order as a premise, but is there anything to keep him from stepping down a level and giving himself an algorithmic account of the origin of Order out of mere Chaos? . . .

The vertigo and revulsion this prospect provokes in many was perfectly expressed in an early attack on Darwin, published anonymously in 1868:

> In the theory with which we have to deal, Absolute Ignorance is the artificer; so that we may enunciate as the fundamental principle of the whole system, that, IN ORDER TO MAKE A PERFECT AND BEAUTIFUL MACHINE, IT IS NOT REQUISITE TO KNOW HOW TO MAKE IT. This proposition will be found, on careful examination, to express, in condensed form, the essential purport of the Theory, and to express in a few words all Mr. Darwin's meaning; who, by a strange inversion of reasoning, seems to think Absolute Ignorance fully qualified to take the place of Absolute Wisdom in all the achievements of creative skill.
>
> [MacKenzie 1868.]

Exactly! Darwin's "strange inversion of reasoning" was in fact a new and wonderful way of thinking, completely overturning the Mind-first way that John Locke "proved" and David Hume could see no way around. John Dewey nicely described the inversion some years later, in his insightful book *The Influence of Darwin on Philosophy*: "Interest shifts . . . from an intelligence that shaped things once for all to the particular intelligences which things are even now shaping" (Dewey 1910, p. 15). But the idea of treating Mind as an effect rather than as a First Cause is too revolutionary for some—an "awful stretcher" that their own minds cannot accommodate comfortably. This is as true today as it was in 1860, and it has always been as true of some of evolution's best friends as of its foes. For instance, the physicist Paul Davies, in his recent book *The Mind of God*, proclaims that the reflective power of human minds can be "no trivial detail, no minor by-product of mindless purposeless forces" (Davies 1992, p. 232). This is a most revealing way of expressing a familiar denial, for it betrays an ill-examined prejudice. Why, we might ask Davies, would its being a by-product of mindless, purposeless forces make it trivial? Why couldn't the most important thing of all be something that arose from unimportant things? Why should the importance or excellence of *anything* have to rain down on it from on high, from something more important, a gift from God? Darwin's inversion suggests that we abandon that presumption and look for sorts of excellence, of worth and purpose, that can emerge, bubbling up out of "mindless, purposeless forces."

Alfred Russel Wallace, whose own version of evolution by natural selection arrived on Darwin's desk while he was still delaying publication of *Origin*, and whom Darwin managed to treat as codiscoverer of the principle, never quite got the point.[3] Although at the outset Wallace was much more forthcoming on the subject of the evolution of the human mind than Darwin was willing to be, and stoutly maintained at first that human minds were no exception to the rule that all features of living things were products of evolution, he could not see the "strange inversion of reasoning" as the key to the greatness of the great idea. Echoing John Locke, Wallace proclaimed that "the marvelous complexity of forces which appear to control matter, if not actually to constitute it, are and must be mind-products" (Gould 1985, p. 397). When, later in his life, Wallace converted to spiritualism and exempted human consciousness altogether from the iron rule of evolution, Darwin saw the crack widen and wrote to him: "I hope you have not murdered too completely your own and my child" (Desmond and Moore 1991, p. 569).

But was it really so inevitable that Darwin's idea should lead to such revolution and subversion? "It is obvious that the critics did not wish to understand, and to some extent Darwin himself encouraged their wishful thinking" (Ellegård 1956). Wallace wanted to ask what the *purpose* of natural selection might be, and though this might seem in retrospect to be squandering the fortune he and Darwin had uncovered, it was an idea for which Darwin himself often expressed sympathy. Instead of reducing teleology all the way to purposeless Order, why couldn't we reduce all mundane teleology to a single purpose: God's purpose? Wasn't this an obvious and inviting way to plug the dike? Darwin was clear in his own mind that the variation on which the process of natural selection depended *had* to be unplanned and undesigned, but the process itself might have a purpose, mightn't it? In a letter in 1860 to the American naturalist Asa Gray, an early supporter, Darwin wrote, "I am inclined to look at everything as resulting from *designed* [emphasis added] laws, with the details whether good or bad, left to the working out of what we may call chance" (F. Darwin 1911, vol. 2, p. 105).

Automatic processes are themselves often creations of great brilliance. From today's vantage point, we can see that the inventors of the automatic transmission and the automatic door-opener were no idiots, and their genius lay in seeing how to create something that could do something "clever" without having to think about it. Indulging in some anachronism, we could say that, to some observers in Darwin's day, it seemed that he had left open the possibility that God did His handiwork by designing an automatic design-maker. And to some of these, the idea was not just a desperate stopgap but a positive improvement on tradition. The first chapter of Genesis describes the successive waves of Creation and ends each with the refrain "and God saw that it was good." Darwin had discovered a way to eliminate this retail application of Intelligent Quality Control; natural selection would take care of that without further intervention from God. (The seventeenth-century philosopher Gottfried Wilhelm Leibniz had defended a similar hands-off vision of God the Creator.) As Henry Ward Beecher put it, "Design by wholesale is grander than design by retail" (Rachels 1991, p. 99). Asa Gray, captivated by Darwin's new idea but trying to reconcile it with as much of his traditional religious creed as possible, came up with this marriage of convenience: God intended the "stream of variations" and foresaw just how the laws of nature He had laid down would prune this stream over the eons. As John Dewey later aptly remarked, invoking yet another mercantile metaphor, "Gray held to what may be called design on the installment plan" (Dewey 1910, p. 12).

[. . .]

The tools for R and D: skyhooks or cranes?

The work of R and D is not like shoveling coal; it is somehow a sort of "intellectual" work, and this fact grounds the other family of metaphors that has both enticed and upset, enlightened and confused, the thinkers who have confronted Darwin's "strange inversion of reasoning": the apparent attribution of intelligence to the very process of natural selection that Darwin insisted was not intelligent.

Was it not unfortunate, in fact, that Darwin had chosen to call his principle "natural selection," with its anthropomorphic connotations? Wouldn't it have been better, as Asa Gray suggested to him, to replace the imagery about "nature's Guiding Hand" with a discussion of the different ways of winning life's race (Desmond and Moore 1991, p. 458)? Many people just didn't get it, and Darwin was inclined to blame himself: "I must be a very bad explainer," he said, conceding: "I suppose 'natural selection' was a bad term" (Desmond and

Moore 1991, p. 492). Certainly this Janus-faced term has encouraged more than a century of heated argument. A recent opponent of Darwin sums it up:

> Life on Earth, initially thought to constitute a sort of prima facie case for a creator, was, as a result of Darwin's idea, envisioned merely as being the outcome of a process and a process that was, according to Dobzhansky, "blind, mechanical, automatic, impersonal," and, according to de Beer, was "wasteful, blind, and blundering." But as soon as these criticisms [sic] were leveled at natural selection, the "blind process" itself was compared to a poet, a composer, a sculptor, Shakespeare—to the very notion of creativity that the idea of natural selection had originally replaced. It is clear, I think, that there was something very, very wrong with such an idea.
>
> [Bethell 1976.]

Or something very, very right. It seems to skeptics like Bethell that there is something willfully paradoxical in calling the process of evolution the "blind watchmaker" (Dawkins 1986a), for this takes away with the left hand ("blind") the very discernment, purpose, and foresight it gives with the right hand. But others see that this manner of speaking—and we shall find that it is not just ubiquitous but irreplaceable in contemporary biology—is just the right way to express the myriads of detailed discoveries that Darwinian theory helps to expose. There is simply no denying the breathtaking brilliance of the designs to be found in nature. Time and again, biologists baffled by some apparently futile or maladroit bit of bad design in nature have eventually come to see that they have underestimated the ingenuity, the sheer brilliance, the depth of insight to be discovered in one of Mother Nature's creations. Francis Crick has mischievously baptized this trend in the name of his colleague Leslie Orgel, speaking of what he calls "Orgel's Second Rule: Evolution is cleverer than you are." (An alternative formulation: Evolution is cleverer than Leslie Orgel!)

Darwin shows us how to climb from "Absolute Ignorance" (as his outraged critic said) to creative genius without begging any questions, but we must tread very carefully, as we shall see. Among the controversies that swirl around us, most if not all consist of different challenges to Darwin's claim that he can take us all the way to here (the wonderful world we inhabit) from there (the world of chaos or utter undesignedness) in the time available without invoking anything beyond the mindless mechanicity of the algorithmic processes he had proposed. Since we have reserved the vertical dimension of the traditional Cosmic Pyramid as a measure of (intuitive) designedness, we can dramatize the challenge with the aid of another fantasy item drawn from folklore.

skyhook, orig. Aeronaut. An imaginary contrivance for attachment to the sky; an imaginary means of suspension in the sky.

[*Oxford English Dictionary.*]

The first use noted by the OED is from 1915: "an aeroplane pilot commanded to remain in place (aloft) for another hour, replies 'the machine is not fitted with skyhooks.' " The skyhook concept is perhaps a descendant of the *deus ex machina* of ancient Greek dramaturgy: when second-rate playwrights found their plots leading their heroes into inescapable difficulties, they were often tempted to crank down a god onto the scene, like Superman, to save the situation supernaturally. Or skyhooks may be an entirely independent creation of convergent folkloric evolution. Skyhooks would be wonderful things to have, great for lifting unwieldy objects out of difficult circumstances, and speeding up all sorts of construction projects. Sad to say, they are impossible.

There are cranes, however. Cranes can do the lifting work our imaginary skyhooks might do, and they do it in an honest, non-question-begging fashion. They are expensive, however. They have to be designed and built, from everyday parts already on hand, and they have to be located on a firm base of existing ground. Skyhooks are miraculous lifters, unsupported and insupportable. Cranes are no less excellent as lifters, and they have the decided advantage of being real. Anyone who is, like me, a lifelong onlooker at construction sites will have noticed with some satisfaction that it sometimes takes a small crane to set up a big crane. And it must have occurred to many other onlookers that in principle this big crane could be used to enable or speed up the building of a still more spectacular crane. Cascading cranes is a tactic that seldom if ever gets used more than once in real-world construction projects, but in principle there is no limit to the number of cranes that could be organized in series to accomplish some mighty end.

Now imagine all the "lifting" that has to get done in Design Space to create the magnificent organisms and (other) artifacts we encounter in our world. Vast distances must have been traversed since the dawn of life with the earliest, simplest self-replicating entities, spreading outward (diversity) and upward (excellence). Darwin has offered us an account of the crudest, most rudimentary, stupidest imaginable lifting process—the wedge of natural selection. By taking tiny—the tiniest possible—steps, this process can gradually, over eons, traverse these huge distances. Or so he claims. At no point would anything miraculous—from on high—be needed. Each step has been accomplished by brute, mechanical, algorithmic climbing, from the base already built by the efforts of earlier climbing.

It does seem incredible. Could it really have happened? Or did the process need a "leg up" now and then (perhaps only at the very beginning) from one sort of skyhook or another? For over a century, skeptics have been trying to find a proof that Darwin's idea just can't work, at least not *all the way*. They have been hoping for, hunting for, praying for skyhooks, as exceptions to what they see as the bleak vision of Darwin's algorithm churning away. And time and again, they have come up with truly interesting challenges—leaps and gaps and other marvels that do seem, at first, to need skyhooks. But then along have come the cranes, discovered in many cases by the very skeptics who were hoping to find a skyhook.

It is time for some more careful definitions. Let us understand that a *skyhook* is a "mind-first" force or power or process, an exception to the principle that all design, and apparent design, is ultimately the result of mindless, motiveless mechanicity. A *crane*, in contrast, is a subprocess or special feature of a design process that can be demonstrated to permit the local speeding up of the basic, slow process of natural selection, *and* that can be demonstrated to be itself the predictable (or retrospectively explicable) product of the basic process. Some cranes are obvious and uncontroversial; others are still being argued about, very fruitfully. . . . [L]et me point to [an] example.

It is now generally agreed among evolutionary theorists that *sex* is a crane. That is, species that reproduce sexually can move through Design Space at a much greater speed than that achieved by organisms that reproduce asexually. Moreover, they can "discern" design improvements along the way that are all but "invisible" to asexually reproducing organisms (Holland 1975). This cannot be the *raison d'être* of sex, however. Evolution cannot see way down the road, so anything it builds must have an immediate payoff to counterbalance the cost. As recent theorists have insisted, the "choice" of reproducing sexually carries a huge *immediate* cost: organisms send along only 50 percent of their genes in any one transaction (to say nothing of the effort and risk involved in securing a transaction in the first place). So the *long-term* payoff of heightened efficiency, acuity, and speed of the redesign process—the features that make sex a magnificent crane—is as nothing to the myopic, local competitions that must determine which organisms get favoured in the very next generation. Some other, short-term, benefit must have maintained the positive selection pressure required to make sexual reproduction an offer few species could refuse. There are a variety of compelling—and competing—hypotheses that might solve this puzzle, which was first forcefully posed for biologists by John Maynard Smith (1978). For a lucid introduction to the current state of play, see Matt Ridley 1993. [. . .]

Who's afraid of reductionism?

Reductionism is a dirty word, and a kind of 'holistier than thou' self-righteousness has become fashionable.
—RICHARD DAWKINS 1982, p. 113

The term that is most often bandied about in these conflicts, typically as a term of abuse, is "reductionism." Those who yearn for skyhooks call those who eagerly settle for cranes "reductionists," and they can often make reductionism seem philistine and heartless, if not downright evil. But like most terms of abuse, "reductionism" has no fixed meaning. The central image is of somebody claiming that one science "reduces" to another: that chemistry reduces to physics, that biology reduces to chemistry, that the social sciences reduce to biology, for instance. The problem is that there are both bland readings and preposterous readings of any such claim. According to the bland readings, it is possible (and desirable) to unify chemistry and physics, biology and chemistry, and, yes, even the social sciences and biology. After all, societies are composed of human beings, who, as mammals, must fall under the principles of biology that cover all mammals. Mammals, in turn, are composed of molecules, which must obey the laws of chemistry, which in turn must answer to the regularities of the underlying physics. No sane scientist disputes this bland reading; the assembled Justices of the Supreme Court are as bound by the law of gravity as is any avalanche, because they are, in the end, also a collection of physical objects. According to the preposterous readings, reductionists want to abandon the principles, theories, vocabulary, laws of the higher-level sciences, in favor of the lower-level terms. A reductionist dream, on such a preposterous reading, might be to write "A Comparison of Keats and Shelley from the Molecular Point of View" or "The Role of Oxygen Atoms in Supply-Side Economics," or "Explaining the Decisions of the Rehnquist Court in Terms of Entropy Fluctuations." Probably nobody is a reductionist in the preposterous sense, and everybody should be a reductionist in the bland sense, so the "charge" of reductionism is too vague to merit a response. If somebody says to you, "But that's so reductionistic!" you would do well to respond, "That's such a quaint, old-fashioned complaint! What on Earth did you have in mind?"

I am happy to say that in recent years, some of the thinkers I most admire have come out in defense of one or another version of reductionism, carefully circumscribed. The cognitive scientist Douglas Hofstadter, in *Gödel Escher Bach*, composed a "Prelude . . . Ant Fugue" (Hofstadter 1979, pp. 275–336) that is an analytical hymn to the virtues of reductionism in its proper place. George C. Williams, one of the pre-eminent evolutionists of the day, published "A Defense of Reductionism in Evolutionary Biology" (1985). The zoologist

Richard Dawkins has distinguished what he calls hierarchical or gradual reductionism from precipice reductionism; he rejects only the precipice version (Dawkins 1986b, p. 74).[4] More recently the physicist Steven Weinberg, in *Dreams of a Final Theory* (1992), has written a chapter entitled "Two Cheers for Reductionism," in which he distinguishes between uncompromising reductionism (a bad thing) and compromising reductionism (which he ringingly endorses). Here is my own version. We must distinguish reductionism, which is in general a good thing, from *greedy reductionism*, which is not. The difference, in the context of Darwin's theory, is simple: greedy reductionists think that everything can be explained without cranes; good reductionists think that everything can be explained without skyhooks.

There is no reason to be compromising about what I call good reductionism. It is simply the commitment to non-question-begging science without any cheating by embracing mysteries or miracles at the outset. (For another perspective on this, see Dennett 1991a, pp. 33–39.) *Three* cheers for that brand of reductionism—and I'm sure Weinberg would agree. But in their eagerness for a bargain, in their zeal to explain too much too fast, scientists and philosophers often underestimate the complexities, trying to skip whole layers or levels of theory in their rush to fasten everything securely and neatly to the foundation. That is the sin of greedy reductionism, but notice that it is only when overzealousness leads to falsification of the phenomena that we should condemn it. In itself, the desire to reduce, to unite, to explain it all in one big overarching theory, is no more to be condemned as immoral than the contrary urge that drove Baldwin to his discovery. It is not wrong to yearn for simple theories, or to yearn for phenomena that no simple (or complex!) theory could ever explain; what is wrong is zealous misrepresentation, in either direction.

Darwin's dangerous idea is reductionism incarnate,[5] promising to unite and explain just about everything in one magnificent vision. Its being the idea of an *algorithmic* process makes it all the more powerful, since the substrate neutrality it thereby possesses permits us to consider its application to just about anything. It is no respecter of material boundaries. It applies, as we have already begun to see, even to itself. The most common fear about Darwin's idea is that it will not just explain but *explain away* the Minds and Purposes and Meanings that we all hold dear. People fear that once this universal acid has passed through the monuments we cherish, they will cease to exist, dissolved in an unrecognizable and unlovable puddle of scientistic destruction. This cannot be a sound fear; a *proper* reductionistic explanation of these phenomena would leave them still standing but just demystified, unified, placed on more secure foundations. We might learn some surprising or even shocking things about these treasures, but unless our valuing these things was based all along on confusion or mistaken identity, how could increased understanding of them diminish their value in our eyes?

A more reasonable and realistic fear is that the greedy abuse of Darwinian reasoning might lead us to deny the existence of real levels, real complexities, real phenomena. By our own misguided efforts, we might indeed come to discard or destroy something valuable. We must work hard to keep these two fears separate, and we can begin by acknowledging the pressures that tend to distort the very description of the issues. For instance, there is a strong tendency among many who are uncomfortable with evolutionary theory to exaggerate the amount of disagreement among scientists ("It's just a theory, and there are many reputable scientists who don't accept this"), and I must try hard not to overstate the compensating case for what "science has shown." Along the way, we will encounter plenty of examples of genuine ongoing scientific disagreement, and unsettled questions of fact. There is no reason for me to conceal or downplay these quandaries, for no matter how they come out, a certain amount of corrosive work has already been done by Darwin's dangerous idea, and can never be undone.

We should be able to agree about one result already. Even if Darwin's relatively modest idea about the origin of species came to be rejected by science—yes, utterly discredited and replaced by some vastly more powerful (and currently unimaginable) vision—it would still have irremediably sapped conviction in any reflective defender of the tradition expressed by Locke. It has done this by opening up new possibilities of imagination, and thus utterly destroying any illusions anyone might have had about the soundness of an argument such as Locke's *a priori* proof of the inconceivability of Design without Mind. Before Darwin, this was inconceivable in the pejorative sense that no one knew how to take the hypothesis seriously. Proving it is another matter, but the evidence does in fact mount, and we certainly can and must take it seriously. So whatever else you may think of Locke's argument, it is now as obsolete as the quill pen with which it was written, a fascinating museum piece, a curiosity that can do no real work in the intellectual world today.

[. . .]

Notes

1   I will not devote any space [here] to cataloguing the deep flaws in creationism, or supporting my peremptory condemnation of it. I take that job to have been admirably done by Kitcher 1982, Futuyma 1983, Gilkey 1985, and others.

2   The ideal of a deductive (or "nomologico-deductive") science, modeled on Newtonian or Galilean physics, was quite standard until fairly recently in the philosophy

of science, so it is not surprising that much effort has been devoted to devising and criticizing various axiomatizations of Darwin's theory—since it was presumed that in such a formalization lay scientific vindication. The idea, introduced in this section, that Darwin should be seen, rather, as postulating that evolution is an algorithmic process, permits us to do justice to the undeniable *a priori* flavor of Darwin's thinking without forcing it into the Procrustean (and obsolete) bed of the nomologico-deductive model. See Sober 1984a and Kitcher 1985a.

3   This fascinating and even excruciating story has been well told many times, but still the controversies rage. Why did Darwin delay publication in the first place? Was his treatment of Wallace generous or monstrously unfair? The unsettled relations between Darwin and Wallace are not just a matter of Darwin's uneasy conscience about how he handled Wallace's innocent claim-jumping correspondence; as we see here, the two were also separated by vast differences in insight and attitude about the idea they both discovered. For particularly good accounts, see Desmond and Moore 1991; Richards 1987, pp. 159–61.

4   See also his discussion of Lewontin, Rose, and Kamin's (1984) idiosyncratic version of reductionism—Dawkins aptly calls it their "private bogey"—in the second edition of *The Selfish Gene* (1989a), p. 331.

5   Yes, incarnate. Think about it: would we want to say it was reductionism *in spirit*?

Bibliography

Bethell, Tom. 1976. "Darwin's Mistake." *Harper's Magazine*, February, pp. 70–75.

Darwin, Charles. 1859. *On the Origin of Species by Means of Natural Selection*. London: Murray.

Darwin, Francis. 1911. *The Life and Letters of Charles Darwin*, 2 vols. New York: Appleton. (Originally published in 1887, in 3 vols., by Murray in London.)

Davies, Paul. 1992. *The Mind of God*. New York: Simon & Schuster.

Dawkins, Richard. 1982. *The Extended Phenotype: The Gene as the Unit of Selection*. Oxford and San Francisco: Freeman.

——— . 1986a. *The Blind Watchmaker*. London: Longmans.

——— . 1986b. "Sociobiology: The New Storm in a Teacup." In Steven Rose and Lisa Appignanese, eds., *Science and Beyond* (Oxford: Blackwell), pp. 61–78.

——— . 1989a. *The Selfish Gene* (2nd ed.) Oxford: Oxford University Press.

Dennett, Daniel C. 1991a. *Consciousness Explained*. Boston: Little, Brown.

Desmond, Adrian, and Moore, James. 1991. *Darwin*. London: Michael Joseph.

Dewey, John. 1910. *The Influence of Darwin on Philosophy*. New York: Holt, 1910. Reprint ed., Bloomington: Indiana University Press, 1965.

Ellegård, Alvar. 1956. "The Darwinian Theory and the Argument from Design." *Lychnos*, pp. 173–92.

Futuyma, Douglas. 1982. *Science on Trial: The Case for Evolution*. New York: Pantheon.

Galilei, Galileo. 1632. *Dialogue Concerning the Two Chief World Systems*. Florence.

Gilkey, Langdon. 1985. *Creationism on Trial: Evolution and God at Little Rock*. San Francisco: Harper & Row.

Gould, Stephen Jay. 1985. *The Flamingo's Smile*. New York: Norton.

Hofstadter, Douglas. 1979. *Gödel Escher Bach*. New York: Basic Books.

Holland, John. 1975. *Adaptation in Natural and Artificial Systems*. Ann Arbor: University of Michigan Press.

Hume, David. 1779. *Dialogues Concerning Natural Religion*. London.

Kitcher, Philip. 1982. *Abusing Science*. Cambridge, Mass.: MIT Press.

———. 1985a. "Darwin's Achievement." In N. Rescher, ed., *Reason and Rationality in Science* (Lanham, Md.: University Press of America), pp. 127–89.

Lewontin, Richard; Rose, Steven; and Kamin, Leon. 1984. *Not in our Genes: Biology, Ideology and Human Nature*. New York: Pantheon.

Locke, John. 1690. *Essay Concerning Human Understanding*. London.

Lovejoy, Arthur O. 1936. *The Great Chain of Being: A Study of the History of an Idea*. New York: Harper & Row.

Mackenzie, Robert Beverley. 1868. *The Darwinian Theory of the Transmutation of Species Examined* (published anonymously "By a Graduate of the University of Cambridge"). Nisbet & Co. (Quoted in a review, *Athenaeum*, no. 2102, February 8, p. 217.)

Maynard Smith, John. 1978. *The Evolution of Sex*. Cambridge: Cambridge University Press.

Rachels, James. 1991. *Created from Animals: The Moral Implications of Darwinism*. Oxford: Oxford University Press.

Richards, Robert J. 1987. *Darwin and the Emergence of Evolutionary Theories of Mind and Behavior*. Chicago: University of Chicago Press.

Ridley, Matt. 1993. *The Red Queen: Sex and the Evolution of Human Nature*. New York: Macmillan.

Sober, Elliot. 1984a. *The Nature of Selection: Evolutionary Theory in Philosophical Focus*. Cambridge, Mass.: MIT Press.

Weinberg, Steven. 1992. *Dreams of a Final Theory*. New York: Pantheon.

Wilberforce, Samuel. 1860. "Is Mr Darwin a Christian?" (review of *Origin*, published anonymously). *Quarterly Review*, vol. 108, July, pp. 225–64.

Williams, George C. 1985. "A Defense of Reductionism in Evolutionary Biology." *Oxford Surveys in Evolutionary Biology*, vol. 2, pp. 1–27.

Chapter 16

Mary Midgley

THE QUEST FOR A UNIVERSAL ACID

IS IT POSSIBLE to provide any stricter, more formal kind of unity than the convergence that results from discussing a single world and a single range of experience? The great rationalist thinkers of the seventeenth century were obsessed by the ambition to drill all thought into a single formal system. Descartes himself, as well as Spinoza and Leibniz, tried inexhaustibly to mend the mind/body gap by building abstract metaphysical systems powered by arguments akin to their favoured models of thought, logic and mathematics. They were answered, however, by empiricists such as Locke and Hume who pointed out how disastrously this project ignores the huge element of contingency that pervades all experience. We are not terms in an abstract calculation but real concrete beings. We do not live in a pure world of necessary connections but in one shaped, over countless ages, by countless events of which we know very little. We deal with this pervasive contingency by ways of thinking – such as historical methods – which provide crucial forms for our understanding of this strange world, but which cannot be reduced to a single form.

Although both rationalists and empiricists tried to claim a monopoly for their own chosen forms of thinking it has become clear, from Kant's time onward, that the tool-bench of thought must allow for a wider variety of methods. The subject-matter is far more radically complex than the seventeenth century supposed. It cannot be drilled to show a single empire. Daniel Dennett, however, persistently tries to dodge this awkward fact by imposing uniformity. He describes what he calls Darwin's 'dangerous idea' – that is, the idea of development by natural selection – as a 'universal acid . . . it eats through just about every traditional concept and leaves in its wake a revolutionised world view, with most of the old land-marks still recognisable, but transformed in fundamental ways'.[1] This is, however, evidently a selective acid, trained to eat only other people's views while leaving his own ambitious project untouched:

> Darwin's dangerous idea is reductionism incarnate, promising to unite and explain just about everything in one magnificent vision. Its being the idea of an algorithmic process makes it all the more powerful, since the substrate neutrality it thereby possesses permits us to consider its application to just about anything . . . [including] all the achievements of human culture – language, art, religion, ethics, science itself.[2]

He sees this as a revolutionary move. Yet this attempt to frame a Grand Universal Theory of Everything is markedly old-fashioned. It flows from just the same kind of casual, misplaced confidence that led physicists of the Aristotelian school to extend purposive reasoning beyond the sphere of human conduct, where it worked well, to explain the behaviour of stones, where it did not. Still more damagingly for Dennett's claims, it also resembles closely the vast metaphysical structures that Herbert Spencer built by extrapolating evolutionary ideas to all possible subject-matters, thus producing, as his followers admiringly said, 'the theory of evolution dealing with the universe *as a whole*, from gas to genius'.[3] Darwin, though he remained polite in public, hated 'magnificent visions' of this kind. As he wrote in his *Autobiography*,

> I am not conscious of having profited in my work from Spencer's writings. His deductive manner of treating every subject is wholly opposed to my frame of mind. His conclusions never convince me. . . . They partake more of the nature of definitions than of laws of nature.[4]

In short, Darwin understood that large ideas do indeed become dangerous if they are inflated beyond their proper use: dangerous to honesty, to intelligibility, to all the proper purposes of thought. For him the concept of natural selection was strictly and solely a biological one and even in biology he steadily rejected the claim that it was a universal explanation. He re-emphasised this point strongly in the sixth edition of the *Origin*:

As my conclusions have lately been much misrepresented, and it has been stated that I attribute the modification of species exclusively to natural selection, I may be permitted to remark that in the first edition of this work, and subsequently, I placed in a most conspicuous position – namely at the close of the Introduction – the following words: '*I am convinced that natural selection has been the main, but not the exclusive, means of modification*'. This has been of no avail. Great is the power of steady misrepresentation.[5]

[. . .]

Notes

1   Daniel Dennett, *Darwin's Dangerous Idea* (Harmondsworth: Penguin, 1996), p. 63.
2   Ibid., pp. 82 and 144.
3   Edward Clodd, Spencer's follower and interpreter, thus triumphantly described his achievement. See A. C. Armstrong, *Transitional Eras in Thought, with Special Reference to the Present Age* (New York: Macmillan, 1904), p. 48.
4   *The Autobiography of Charles Darwin, 1809–1882, with Original Omissions Restored,* ed. Nora Barlow (New York: Harcourt, Brace and World, 1958), p. 109, emphasis mine.
5   Ibid., 6th edn, 1872, p. 395.

Chapter 17

Michael Ruse

METHODOLOGICAL NATURALISM UNDER ATTACK

[...]

THERE ARE EVOLUTIONISTS—notably Richard Dawkins (1995, 1996), Daniel Dennett (1995), and William Provine (1989)—who are materialists, atheists, naturalists, and evolutionists, and who see everything as a united package deal. But these men do not speak for all evolutionists or all naturalists. Those of us—for I am one—who are unwilling to be pinned into the corner of atheistic evolutionism point historically to the fact that there have been distinguished evolutionists who were practicing Christians. In this century, notably the two leading evolutionists, Sir Ronald Fisher (1950) in England and Theodosius Dobzhansky (1967) in America, were both absolutely and completely committed to the idea of Jesus as their Savior. Philosophically, those of us who would separate atheism and evolutionism suggest that simply using a catch-all term "naturalism" conceals subtleties in peoples' approaches. . . .

[E]volutionists who want to divorce their science from supposedly atheistic implications invite one to draw a distinction between two forms of naturalism. On the one hand, one has what one might call "metaphysical naturalism": this indeed is a materialistic, atheistic view, for it argues that the world is as we see it and that there is nothing more. On the other hand, one has a notion or a practice that can properly be called "methodological naturalism":

although this is the working philosophy of the scientist, it is in no sense atheistic as such. The methodological naturalist is the person who assumes that the world runs according to unbroken law; that humans can understand the world in terms of this law; and that science involves just such understanding without any reference to extra or supernatural forces like God. Whether there are such forces or beings is another matter entirely and simply not addressed by methodological naturalism. Hence, although indeed evolution as we understand it is a natural consequence of methodological naturalism, given the facts of the world as they can be discovered, in no sense is the methodological naturalist thereby committed to the denial of God's existence. It is simply that the methodological naturalist insists that, inasmuch as one is doing science, one avoid all theological or other religious references. In particular, one denies God a role in the creation.

This is not to say that God did not have a role in the creation, but simply that, qua science, that is qua an enterprise formed through the practice of methodological naturalism, science has no place for talk of God. Just as, for instance, if one were to go to the doctor one would not expect any advice on political matters, so if one goes to a scientist one does not expect any advice on or reference to theological matters. The physician may indeed have very strong political views, which one may or may not share. But the politics are irrelevant to the medicine. Similarly, the scientist may or may not have very strong theological views, which one may or may not share. But inasmuch as one is going to the scientist for science, theology can and must be ruled out as irrelevant. [. . .]

References

Dawkins, R. 1995. *A River Out of Eden*. New York: Basic Books.
———. 1996. *Climbing Mount Improbable*. New York: Norton.
Dennett, D. C. 1995. *Darwin's Dangerous Idea*. New York: Simon and Schuster.
Dobzhansky, T. 1967. *The Biology of Ultimate Concern*. New York: The New American Library.
Fisher, R. A. 1950. *Creative Aspects of Natural Law: The Eddington Memorial Lecture*. Cambridge: Cambridge University Press.
Provine, W. 1989. Evolution and the foundation of ethics. *Science, Technology, and Social Progress*. Bethlehem, Pa.: Lehigh University Press.

PART SIX

Evolutionary theism

INTRODUCTION TO PART SIX

THOSE ARGUING FOR THE COMPATIBILITY of God and evolution are a very diversified group, coming from a variety of denominational identities as well as spanning the range of theological positions from traditionalists to revisionists. While they thus differ in many respects, they are united in opposing creationism and intelligent design at one end of the spectrum as promoting a "God of the gaps" and atheistic naturalism at the other for suggesting that evolution rules out God.

The evolutionary theists included in this section modify traditional models of the God-world relationship in light of views of reality coming to us from contemporary science. They are confident that a Christian doctrine of God can accommodate an evolutionary world-view.

The first selection in this part is physicist Howard J. Van Till's essay "The Creation: Intelligently Designed or Optimally Equipped?" which appeared in the journal *Theology Today*. Van Till, who comes from the Reformed tradition, addresses concerns of evangelical Christians that adhering to evolution will compromise their faith in God. He criticizes the usual framing of the creation/evolution debate as an either/or choice between special creationism and evolutionary naturalism and suggests that there is a way beyond this impasse. He speaks of a fully gifted creation that is "thoughtfully conceptualized" and "optimally equipped" by the creator with a "robust and gapless formational economy" that is "robust enough to make possible the evolutionary continuity envisioned by cosmologists and biologists." With this concept he challenges the view of creationists and ID proponents that there are gaps in the creation's formational economy that require episodes of special creation or intelligent design. He also challenges the view of atheistic naturalists that such a robust formational economy rules out the activity of a Creator-God. Van Till utilizes the royal metaphor of a king and his subjects to picture the creative and generous activity of God, who he pictures "calling upon the creation to employ its creaturely capabilities to bring about a fruitful outcome."

The second selection is biochemist and Anglican theologian Arthur Peacocke's article "Biological Evolution—A Positive Theological Appraisal," which was published in *Evolutionary and Molecular Biology: Scientific Perspectives on Divine Action*, edited by Robert John Russell, William R. Stoeger, and Francisco J. Ayala. Calling Darwinism the "disguised friend" of Christian theology, Peacocke surveys various themes and characteristics of biological evolution and pairs them with theological reflections that he finds compatible with these scientific observations. He pictures God as an immanent Creator, continuously creating in and through the processes of the natural world. Peacocke's perspective is, however, that of a panentheist and not a pantheist in that he sees the whole universe as contained within God but considers that God exists apart from the world. He illustrates God's immanence and transcendence by appealing to the metaphor of the relationship of a composer to a musical composition. The composer not only transcends the music that he or she creates but is also found within it.

Peacocke claims that there is no need to postulate any special action of God supplementing natural processes. At most one can say that God exerts a "whole-part" constraint upon the interconnected and interdependent system of the cosmos, serving as its "ultimate boundary condition." Peacocke acknowledges that a Christian doctrine of God must come to terms with the ubiquity of pain and suffering in the world. He concludes that a Creator God must both delight in the whole tapestry of the created order, in its "warp and woof," and suffer "in, with, and under the creative processes of the world with their costly unfolding in time."

The next essay, Protestant theologian Jürgen Moltmann's "God's Kenosis in the Creation and Consummation of the World," is taken from *The Work of Love: Creation as Kenosis*, edited by John Polkinghorne. Moltmann surveys Jewish and Christian kenotic theology, which emphasizes God's self-emptying, self-limitation, and vulnerability, as relevant for an understanding of God's presence and activity in the cosmos that coheres with contemporary scientific accounts of experiences of nature. Christian reflection on God has focused on the presence of God in Jesus Christ and his history. Taking their lead from Philippians 2:5–II, Christian theologians have interpreted the becoming-human of Jesus Christ as a kenosis for the sake of the redemption of humankind. As the biblical text proclaims, God's Son "emptied himself, taking the form of a servant" and "humbled himself and became obedient unto death, even death on the cross." Another Christian resource that Moltmann finds pertinent is the interpretation of Christ's kenosis within the context of the Trinity. He maintains that kenotic self-surrender is God's trinitarian nature and should be considered the mark not only of the inner life of the Trinity, the reciprocal kenosis of the divine persons in relation to one another, but also of God's relation with the world, the creation, reconciliation, and redemption of all things. Jewish thinking about God has centered on the Shekinah, God's indwelling presence in the midst of the Israelites, pictured by theologians as a self-humiliation and willingness to suffer with the exiled people. Kenotic thought is related to creation through the Jewish Kabbalistic concept of zimzum, a divine self-contraction in order to provide space for the created world.

Drawing together these resources from Jewish and Christian kenotic theology, Moltmann speaks of a God whose self-limitation allows for the creation and salvation of an independent world and whose power is defined not by coercion but by long-suffering, persuasive, and patient love. Such a view, he claims, allows for an evolving universe with an open future of possibilities.

The last piece in this section is Roman Catholic theologian Elizabeth A. Johnson's article "Does God Play Dice? Divine Providence and Chance," which was published in *Theological Studies*. Challenging Albert Einstein's famous remark denying that God plays dice with the universe, Johnson affirms that divine providence is compatible with genuine randomness and further claims that this compatibility "can shed light on the incomprehensible, gracious mystery of God." She retrieves the view of Thomas Aquinas that God as primary cause is working through secondary causes in the natural world and elucidates this notion of dual agency by focusing on the dynamic idea of participation that she finds at the heart of Aquinas's vision of the God-world relationship. In this context, Johnson pictures God as active not only through the regularities of the laws of nature but also through chance occurrences, which she describes as themselves secondary causes with their own integrity.

The God who works through chance is in turn a risk-taking God. Like Moltmann, Johnson appeals to divine kenosis in salvation and speaks of a vulnerable God who is involved in the suffering of the created world. Such a God is a God of love, "a self-emptying, self-offering, delighting, exploring, suffering, sovereign Love, transcendent wellspring of all possibilities who acts immanently through the matrix of the freely evolving universe."

Chapter 18

Howard J. Van Till

THE CREATION: INTELLIGENTLY DESIGNED OR OPTIMALLY EQUIPPED?

The shaping of questions and strategies

Matters of heritage and context

EACH OF THE CONTRIBUTIONS to this issue of THEOLOGY TODAY has a focus of concern that has been influenced by the author's particular intellectual and spiritual odyssey. My own concerns and priorities have developed in the North American context, in which an attitude of antagonism and mutual mistrust has developed between two important portions of the population: the intellectual/scientific community and the more conservative portion of the Christian community.[1] On the one hand, a large portion of the Christian community has come to adopt a very skeptical attitude toward the results of scientific theorizing regarding the formational history of the universe—theorizing that appears to contradict certain beliefs derived from a particular reading of the biblical text. On the other hand, a large portion of the scientific community has assumed an equally skeptical attitude toward Christianity, in part because the Christian faith is so frequently identified with some form of episodic creationism—a concept of the universe's formational history that is at odds with natural science's reading of the empirical evidence.

Within this North American context, my own theological roots extend deeply into the soil of the Calvinist heritage, especially as it has been expressed in the Netherlands. The names of Abraham Kuyper, Herman Bavinck, and Louis Berkhof can still be heard in our denominational discourse. From childhood on, most of us were taught to place high value on thoughtfully-articulated theological principles and well-examined philosophical foundations. We were taught by example to look beneath the superficial details of an issue and to examine the presuppositions on which a particular position was founded.

Given that background, as soon as I became familiar with the resurgent creation/evolution debate I had the sense that there was something radically wrong about it and I began to puzzle over just what its shortcomings might be. That puzzlement, along with an intense interest in the natural sciences, ultimately led to my becoming deeply involved, as a Christian trained in physics, in reflections on the character of the creation and of God's creative action.

One of the more obvious shortcomings of the common creation/evolution debate is evident when it is framed as a simple either/or choice between only two comprehensive positions: "episodic creationist theism" and "evolutionary naturalism." Before dealing with the substance of the issues, let me here clarify my use of some important terminology. By *episodic creationist theism* (often called *special creationism* and often presented as entailing a commitment to an Ussher-style, young-earth chronology), I mean to denote the belief that the formation of certain physical structures and life forms now found in the creation was accomplished by occasional episodes of extraordinary divine action in which God imposed those structures and forms on matter. The term *naturalism* will be used in this essay to represent the comprehensive, atheistic worldview based on the presumption that the natural world is all there is. In this worldview, nature is presumed to be a self-existent and closed system that requires no transcendent Creator to act as the source of its being and leaves no opportunity for divine action of any sort within it. More specifically, the term *evolutionary naturalism* here denotes a naturalistic worldview in which the scientific concept of evolutionary development in the formational history of the universe is taken to play a major role in warranting its credibility over against episodic creationist theism.

Presented as a simple either/or choice, the creation/evolution debate suffers the fatal flaw commonly called "the fallacy of many questions." The issue under debate is very broad in scope and includes a lengthy list of questions that span a diversity of categories—scientific methodology, empirical evidence, interpretive strategies, metaphysical presuppositions, theological principles, faith commitments, and the like. However, each of the two contestants in the debate—episodic creationism and evolutionary naturalism—brings but one package of answers to this long list of categorially diverse questions and demands that its package be adopted in its entirety at the exclusion of the other. Such a demand is, of course, grossly unfair. Answers to each of the many questions at issue deserve to be evaluated on their own terms, not to be presented as non-negotiable components of some "no-options package deal."

The return of Paley's argument from design

Recognizing the shortcomings of young-earth episodic creationism and yet desiring to offer a theistic perspective that would be apologetically effective in theism's engagement with evolutionary naturalism, some Christians have become proponents of an approach they wish to call "intelligent design theory."[2] The basic strategy of the intelligent design movement is as follows: Select and consider, in the light of information drawn from the natural sciences, specific life forms and biotic subsystems. Ask the question, "Can one now, with the science of the day, construct a complete and credible account of how that particular life form or biotic subsystem first came to be actualized in a Darwinian gradualist fashion?[3] If not, the intelligent design theorists argue, then it must be the outcome, not of mindless, purposeless, naturalistic, evolutionary processes, but of "intelligent design." The precise meaning of "intelligent design" is not always apparent, but it most often entails the combination of both thoughtful conceptualization and the first assembly of a new form by extra-natural means.

In contrast to the young-earth episodic creationist movement with its transparently inadequate treatment of both the biblical text and empirical data, this particular form of skepticism toward evolution demands a more careful critique, some of which will appear later in this essay. As I engage in discussion, both formal and informal, with Christians in search of a defensible position somewhere in the vast conceptual space between young-earth creationism and evolutionary naturalism, I find that many Christians, some scholars included, find the argumentation of intelligent design proponents to be very attractive. My own measure of that position is mixed—positive in regard to some of its elements, negative in regard to others. With them, I reject young-earth creationism for numerous biblical, theological, and scientific reasons. And with them, I reject evolutionary naturalism because of its denial of a Creator-God. However, in contrast to the proponents of intelligent design, I find no warrant for rejecting the possibility (or, stated more strongly, the likelihood) that the creation has been gifted with all of the self-organizational and transformational capabilities needed to make something like the macroevolutionary scenario viable. In fact, I have argued elsewhere that I find a great deal of encouragement for envisioning such a robustly gifted creation in early Christian writings, especially in the reflections of Augustine on the early chapters of Genesis.[4]

The goal of articulating a well-informed faith

In all of my reflections on the character of the creation and on divine action within it, my goal is to articulate a perspective that is at once faithful to historic Christian doctrine and well-informed by the natural sciences. Given the way in which the North American community continues to puzzle over both the credibility and the theological relevance of evolutionary theorizing, I continue to search for ways in which faithful Christians might perceive the fruits of divine action expressed in the course of creation's formational history. In so doing, my strategy is twofold: (1) to encourage the conservative Christian community to re-examine its concept of divine creative action and to develop a more appreciative attitude toward scientific investigation regarding the creation's gifts for self-organization and transformation, and (2) to encourage persons outside of the Christian faith to consider a contemporary articulation of historic Christianity that welcomes the fruits of scientific theorizing performed with procedural competence, professional integrity, and intellectual humility.

One of the hazards of this approach is that each of the two communities being addressed is inclined to perceive the message as a threat to its own apologetic strategy. If episodic creationist theism, for instance, perceives its defense of the Christian faith to depend on demonstrating the need for episodes of special creation in the formational history of the universe, then any encouragement to consider evolutionary continuity as an acceptable possibility will appear to constitute a call to "give away the store." And if the proponents of evolutionary naturalism take comfort in their belief that the defeat of episodic creationism constitutes a lasting victory over all forms of Christian theism, then any encouragement to consider the viability of an evolving creation perspective will be viewed as an unwelcome threat to the simple either/or format of the creation/evolution debate. Herein lies a deep irony of the debate: The two diametrically opposed parties—episodic creationism and evolutionary naturalism—agree to promote the idea that a simple either/or debate is meaningful.

The formational economy of the universe

The need for a reexamination of fundamental questions

In spite of the numerous shortcomings of the creation/evolution debate, it does stimulate us to re-examine some profoundly important questions. For example: In the awareness of what has been learned through modern scientific investigation regarding the manner and history of creaturely action, how might we now speak about the character of divine creative activity and about our apprehension of it? What does God, specifically in the role of Creator, do? And how do we come to be aware of the Creator's action? What are its distinguishing marks? Focusing on the diverse phenomena that comprise the formational history of the Creation, how might we distinguish between the Creator's action and the action of creatures in the actualization of novel structures and life forms in the course of time?

Although there is within the Christian community a diversity of concepts concerning divine action, I presume that there would be general agreement on at least the following propositions regarding God's action as Creator: (1) that as Creator, God gave being to the creation "in the beginning"—often taken to be the beginning of time as we know it; and (2) that God continues to sustain the creation in its being from moment to moment. Were God to cease acting as Creator, the creation would not merely decline in some quality, but it would cease to be. In other words, historic Christian theology sees the existence of the universe to be radically dependent on God's creative action at all times, at this moment no less than at the first moment of its existence. What has traditionally been taken to be the evidence for this creative action? Quite simply, the existence of ourselves and the creation of which we are members. If no Creator, then no creation. In the context of a theistic worldview, the evidence of divine creative action is both obvious and undeniable—we are here.

But there are, of course, alternatives to this line of thought. Naturalistic worldviews, for instance, presume that the universe is self-existent and needs no Creator to serve as the divine Source of its existence. In the context of a commitment to naturalism, then, the existence of the universe is evidence only for the existence of the universe—nothing more to be said. Fortunately for us, it might be argued, the universe happens to exist and we are in it. Furthermore, in the more specific context of *evolutionary* naturalism, the universe that happens to exist also happens to satisfy all of the requisite conditions and to possess all of the requisite capabilities—a truly astounding list, we are beginning to realize— to make possible our formation in time from the more elementary units of matter present in the early universe. We are here, says naturalism, not as the outcome of a Creator's intention, but by a remarkable fortuity.

What rejoinder does Christian theism have against these bold assertions of naturalism? What apologetic strategy, for instance, would effectively engage evolutionary naturalism and, presumably, defeat its claims that we are nothing more than amusing artifacts of the self-organizational powers that the universe just happens to possess? One of the most commonly employed strategies among conservative North American Christians is to counter by asserting that the type of evolutionary development of life forms that evolutionary naturalism presumes to be possible did not, in fact, occur. Why not? Because, it is argued, such continuous formational development is, in actuality, impossible. And if evolution is impossible, then evolutionary naturalism is false and episodic creationist theism, the only other possibility offered in the creation/evolution debate, must be true.

From this formulation (I would classify it as a tragic misformulation) of the issue proceeds the familiar shouting match between episodic creationist theism and evolutionary naturalism. A considerable portion of the debate has been carried out in the court of scientific theorizing and has focused on whether the empirical evidence favors (1) the concept of evolutionary continuity in the formational history of all inanimate structures and life forms, or (2) the concept of radical discontinuities of the sort that could be bridged only by episodes of special creation or of intelligent design. Once the issue is framed in this way, a peculiar—and, I would argue, inverted—scoring system falls into place: Evidence for the functioning of natural processes that make unbroken evolutionary continuity appear plausible is credited to evolutionary naturalism, while the credibility of Christian theism, on the other hand, appears to depend on the absence or inadequacy of certain natural form-producing processes. This apologetic strategy places some Christian scientists in the awkward position of looking for evidence that God has withheld from the creation certain crucial capabilities for self-organization or transformation so that macroevolutionary continuity would be impossible. Searching for evidence of gifts withheld from the creation strikes me as precisely the opposite of what the enterprise of Christian scientific scholarship ought to be doing.

An important definition

In order to see more clearly what the underlying issues are, I have found it helpful to define a concept that I call the "formational economy" of the universe. By the *formational economy of the universe* I mean the set of all of the dynamic capabilities of matter and material, physical, and biotic systems that contribute to the actualization of both inanimate structures and biotic forms in the course of the universe's formational history. Special attention would be drawn to capabilities for self-organization and transformation.

Elementary particles called quarks, for instance, possess the capabilities to interact in such a way as to form nucleons (protons and neutrons). Nucleons, in turn, have the capacities to interact and organize, by such processes as thermonuclear fusion, into progressively larger atomic nuclei. Nuclei and electrons have the dynamic capability to interact and organize into atoms. On the macroscopic scale, vast collections of atoms interact to form the inanimate structures of interest to astronomy—galaxies, stars, and planets. On the microscopic scale, atoms interact chemically to form molecules; molecules interact to form more complex molecules. Some molecular ensembles are presumed to possess the capabilities to organize into the fundamental units that constitute living cells and organisms. Organisms and environments interact and organize into eco-systems. All of these organizational and transformational capabilities together comprise the *formational economy* of the universe.

The robust formational economy principle

With this concept defined and named, I believe that we can now approach questions regarding the formational history of the creation in a way that will allow us to rise above the self-perpetuating din of the usual creation/evolution debate. I would begin by posing the question, "What is the character or scope of the creation's formational economy?" More specifically, is the formational economy of the universe sufficiently robust (that is, does it possess all of the requisite capabilities) to make possible the actualization in time of all of the inanimate structures and biotic forms that have ever existed? The natural sci-ences, as now practiced, presume the answer to be, "Yes." Furthermore, the manner of historical actualization is judged to entail an unbroken continuity of increasingly complex and diverse life forms.

On the other hand, a substantial portion of the North American Christian community presumes the answer to our question to be, "No." Episodic cre-ationism, for instance, is well known for its insistence not only that its concept of special creation episodes is a "clear teaching" of the Bible (conveyed unambiguously by its inerrant text) and one of the fundamental "deliverances of the faith," but also that unbroken evolutionary continuity is physically impossible. Strategies for warranting such beliefs vary considerably, but the claim that evolutionary continuity is impossible is ordinarily grounded in an appeal (by what standards is another question) to the empirical evidence.

Typical argumentation purporting to take a person from empirical evi-dence to an episodic creationist conclusion would include the following: (1) The fossil record fails to support the idea of Darwinian gradual development of new forms. On the contrary, it is argued, it supports the concept of the "sudden appearance" of new "kinds" of creatures, just as the Bible would lead a faithful reader to expect. (2) The second law of thermodynamics precludes the devel-opment of more complex organisms from simpler forms of life or the devel-opment of any life form from non-living matter; a variant on this argument would be to assert that the second law precludes the spontaneous generation of the "new genetic information" that any novel life form would necessarily require. (3) The only kind of genetic transformation that can be demonstrated empirically is variation within biblical "kinds," and there is no empirical warrant for extrapolating from these microevolutionary variations to the full-scale macroevolutionary transformation presumed possible by contemporary biology. (4) Finally, according to some proponents of intelligent design theory, it is now possible to point to specific life forms and biotic subsystems that could not possibly have come to be assembled by "natural" means.[5]

One common theme in these and other episodic creationist or intelligent design theorist appeals to empirical science is that it is possible to identify notable gaps in our knowledge about the formational history of the universe. On that point, we must agree. There are indeed *epistemological* gaps to which the episodic creationists and intelligent design theorists can call attention. We do not now have the scientific competence to say in full detail and with certainty just how each form of life came to be actualized in the course of time. We do not know precisely what role each creaturely capability for self-organization or transformation has played in actualizing the diversity of life forms and biotic subsystems that we now see. Even more seriously, we *cannot* now demonstrate the sufficiency of known creaturely capabilities to make the full macroevolutionary scenario of unbroken genealogical continuity possible. Thus, the episodic creationist is technically correct in saying that there are epistemological gaps of the sort that stand in the way of natural science saying that a detailed theory of biotic evolution has been "proved" in the strict, logical sense of the term.

But the "provability" of a particular evolutionary scenario is not, in fact, the issue. The truth is, as philosophers of science have long been reminding us, that *all* scientific theories are necessarily underdetermined by the empirical data. The word, "proof," in the strict, logical sense, has no place in the world of scientific theory evaluation. There will always be more than one possible scientific account for any natural phenomenon. Epistemological gaps and the unprovability of scientific theories are permanent features of the scientific landscape. The goal of scientific theorizing is not to prove, by appeal to empirical data and unassailable logic alone, one theory correct and all others false. Rather, the goal is to construct a theoretical account that is, in the context of all relevant empirical data at hand and within the bounds of certain presuppositions regarding the character of the universe and its formational history, the most adequate account conceivable at a particular time.

One of the questions of the moment, then, concerns the status of those epistemological gaps. In the context of theorizing about the formational history of the universe, contemporary natural science ordinarily presumes that these gaps in our knowledge could, in principle, be filled at some time in the future. The scientific community fully expects that further research will provide the basis for more adequate and comprehensive theories regarding the formational history of the universe and the life forms that inhabit it. One of the most basic—but seldom explicitly stated—presuppositions of the natural sciences, especially relevant to the formulation of theories regarding the formational history of the universe, is that *the formational economy of the universe is sufficiently robust to make possible the actualization of all inanimate structures and all life forms that have ever appeared in the course of time.* I call this proposition the *robust formational economy principle.* In my judgment, it is not only one of the most fundamental presuppositions of the natural sciences but also the fundamental "sticking point" for a large portion of North American Christians in their assessment of evolutionary theorizing.

The role of apologetics

Why would this principle be seen as a sticking point? Why would it be perceived by millions of North American Christians as being incompatible, say, with Christian belief regarding God's creative action? Is it the case, for instance, that God might be incapable of giving being to a creation so richly gifted with formational capabilities? I would presume that the answer of all Christians would be, "Surely not!" We creatures would have to be arrogant beyond measure (an ever present danger) to declare God incapable of so gifting creation. What, then, is the basis for the widespread Christian rejection of the robust formational economy principle? One major reason for its rejection, as noted above, is the belief that the concept of episodic creation (which presumes the presence of substantial gaps in the creation's formational economy) is both a "clear teaching of the Bible" and a fundamental "deliverance of the faith."

But suppose a person were to set those "in house" concerns aside for the moment (important as they might be to many Christians). Suppose one wished to eschew any appeal either to Scripture or to widely-held Christian beliefs and sought instead to develop an apologetic strategy that appealed only to empirical evidence and sound reasoning, so that even a vocal proponent of naturalism would have to pay attention? This is, I believe, one of the principal goals of the contemporary intelligent design movement. Consequently, to ignore the role of apologetic considerations would be to close one's eyes to a major driving force for the movement.

Now, the goal of effective apologetic engagement with the preachers of naturalism is itself a noble one. However, it is imperative that the apologetic strategy employed in defense of the Christian faith be built on a foundation formed not by the preconceptions of naturalism but by the historic Christian theological heritage. Christian apologetic strategy must be shaped by foundational Christian theological commitments, not by the presuppositions of the opposition. The question is, then, what are the foundational theological propositions on which the intelligent design movement builds its case? Or, to entertain an even more problematic possibility, is their case built not on a consciously-examined theological foundation but simply as a reaction to the offensive naturalistic rhetoric of the day?

Intelligent design theory and its apologetic engagement with evolutionary naturalism

The naturalistic challenge

If contemporary intelligent design theory does function primarily as an apologetic reaction to naturalism, what is the nature of the challenge to which it is responding? Specifically, what is the most common form in which the naturalistic challenge to belief in a Creator is presented, and what is the particular concept of divine creative action that it presumes to discredit?

Perhaps the best way to answer this question is to look at an example of the rhetoric of evolutionary naturalism—rhetoric that elicits from many Christians not only an intensified antagonism toward naturalism but also the presumption that ownership of the robust formational economy principle should be ceded to that atheistic worldview. The recent book, *Darwin's Dangerous Idea*,[6] by philosopher Daniel C. Dennett, provides a more than ample supply of such rhetoric.

Dennett focuses much of his attention on the matter of "design." How do things that we see in the world around us, especially living things, he asks, come to exhibit *design*, whether in their internal workings or in their adaptation to the peculiarities of some natural environment? The term "design," as Dennett employs it, functions most commonly as the generic category for any feature of the world, especially of its life forms, that is likely to give an observer the impression (by Dennett's measure, a false impression) of being the outcome of an intentional action by an intelligent agent, such as one would recognize in "a cleverly designed artifact" of human craftsmanship.

Dennett is especially critical of the eighteenth-century style of natural theology with its apologetic strategy of arguing from claims (stated in the conceptual vocabulary of the natural sciences) for the empirical detection of "design" in the universe to the (religiously significant) conclusion of the existence of a Designer.

> The overwhelming favorite among purportedly scientific arguments for religious conclusions, then and now, was one version or another of the Argument from Design: among the effects we can

objectively observe in the world, there are many that are not (cannot be, for various reasons) mere accidents; they must have been designed to be as they are, and there cannot be design without a Designer; therefore, a Designer, God, must exist (or have existed), as the source of all these wonderful effects.[7]

It is, I believe, important to note here that the concept of "Designer," as it was most commonly employed in the eighteenth century by clergyman William Paley and others, was based on the artisan metaphor. One person, the artisan, did both the conceptualization and the construction of what was intended. Paley's watchmaker, for instance, did both the planning and the fabrication of the watch. Paley's Designer (like his watchmaker) was taken to possess both a mind (to conceptualize, or intend) and the divine equivalent of "hands" (the power to manipulate raw materials into the intended form).

The design concept under Dennett's critical scrutiny entails not only the claim that thoughtful conceptualization would be required for a particular sort of outcome but also the presumption that the actualization of what was first conceptualized would require the action of an "intelligent" agent capable of imposing structure or form on relatively inert materials—at least on materials not equipped with the requisite capabilities for self-organization or transformation into the conceptualized form. Typical of the rhetoric offered by proponents of triumphalist naturalism, Dennett rejects the need for either of these two elements. What appears in nature to be designed, according to Dennett, requires neither thoughtful conceptualization nor extra-natural assembly.

The need for thoughtful conceptualization is dismissed by Dennett with facile ease simply by presuming that one can take for granted the self-existence of a universe complete with a robust economy of formational capabilities. Questions regarding the need for extra-natural assembly are handled in a somewhat more reasoned manner. Here Dennett calls upon the natural sciences and their growing awareness of the powers for self-organization and transformation that contribute to the formational economy of the universe. Presuming the robust formational economy principle to be warranted, Dennett forcefully rejects the "Handicrafter-God" of both episodic creationism and the argument from design. He characterizes such approaches as ill-conceived attempts to inject supernatural explanations into circumstances where natural explanations would suffice. In Dennett's colorful metaphor, he sees no need to appeal to a "skyhook" (the top-down action of some higher power) when a "crane" (the bottom-up action of some extant natural mechanism) is able to do the job of lifting a biotic system to new heights of configurational complexity:

The skyhook concept is perhaps a descendant of the *deus ex machina* of ancient Greek dramaturgy: when second-rate playwrights found their plots leading their heroes into inescapable difficulties, they were often tempted to crank down a god onto the scene, like Superman, to save the situation supernaturally. . . . [A] *skyhook* is a "mind-first" force or power or process, an exception to the principle that all design, and apparent design, is ultimately the result of mindless, motiveless mechanicity. A *crane*, in contrast, is a subprocess or special feature of a design process that can be demonstrated to permit the local speeding up of the basic, slow process of natural selection, *and* that can be demonstrated to be itself the predictable (or retrospectively explicable) product of the basic process.[8]

What, then, is the essence of the naturalistic challenge? As I read Dennett, whose perspective I find to be representative of modern evolutionary naturalism, the thrust of his challenge to theism is this: *If there are no gaps in the formational economy of the universe, then what need is there for a Creator?* Implicit in this challenge is the presumption that, in order to establish the need for a Creator, one would have to demonstrate that the actualization (assembly from constituent parts) of some particular structures or life forms could have been accomplished only by an irruptive divine act. What is being challenged most specifically here is the interventionist concept of divine creative action in the formational history of the universe—the idea that certain novel life forms or "irreducibly complex" biotic subsystems could have come to be actualized only as the outcome of a form-imposing divine intervention.[9]

Is divine intervention necessary for the universe's formational development?

Dennett's "hit list"—composed of those belief systems that he presumes will collapse under the weight of his attack—includes episodic creationism and intelligent design theory, both of which presume that the robust formational economy principle is not warranted and that material, physical, and biotic systems do not have the requisite capabilities to make macroevolutionary continuity possible. His strategy is to argue that what is taken by theists to be evidence of design (especially in the sense of manifesting some quality of form that could have been assembled only by extra-natural means) has been grossly misread. From Dennett's perspective, those qualities of form are the product, not of divine imposition, but of natural *algorithmic processes*—material, physical, and biotic processes whose outcome, no matter how complex in appearance, proceeds from the actions of basic material units (atoms, molecules, cells) behaving in accordance with relatively simple rules.

> Here, then, is Darwin's dangerous idea: the algorithmic level is the level that best accounts for the speed of the antelope, the wing of the eagle, the shape of the orchid, the diversity of species, and all the other occasions for wonder in the world of nature. . . . No matter how impressive the products of an algorithm, the underlying process always consists of nothing but a set of individually mindless steps succeeding each other without the help of any intelligent supervision. . . .[10]

No "intelligent supervision" is necessary, says Dennett. No episodes of miraculous special creation in the course of time are needed in order to actualize novel forms. No imposition of form by an act of supernatural assembly is needed. Why not? Because the universe has all of the requisite capabilities for self-organization and transformation. There are no gaps in the formational economy of the universe. And, if no gaps, then what need for a Creator?

Why the emphasis on a gapless formational economy? Because what Dennett takes to be the "creationist" position is one that insists on the need for episodes of *special* divine creative action in order to bridge those presumed gaps. Dennett's attack is directed toward episodic creationists, well known for their resistance to the concept of a gapless formational economy and of evolutionary continuity.

> The resistance comes from those who think there must be some discontinuities somewhere, some skyhooks, or moments of Special Creation, or some other sort of miracles, between the prokaryotes and the finest treasures in our libraries.[11]

> For over a century, skeptics have been trying to find a proof that Darwin's idea just can't work, at least not *all the way*. They have been hoping for, hunting for, praying for skyhooks, as exceptions to what they see as the bleak vision of Darwin's algorithm churning away. And time and again, they have come up with truly interesting challenges—leaps and gaps and other marvels that do seem, at first, to need skyhooks. But then along have come the cranes, discovered in many cases by the very skeptics who were hoping to find a skyhook.[12]

Is divine intervention necessary for the universe's daily functioning?

There is something puzzling to me about the way in which empirical support functions in the strategy for warranting belief in the existence of gaps in the universe's formational economy. The bottom line in all appeals for empirical support for this belief is necessarily an argument of the following form: The first appearance of form X cannot at this moment be fully accounted for in terms of what we now know regarding the self-organizational or transformational capacities of material, physical, and biotic systems. This *epistemological* gap is then taken to be sufficient warrant for believing that there exists a corresponding *ontological* gap—the requisite formational capability is missing in the formational economy of the universe. There is, I believe, no way to escape the recognition that this is an appeal to ignorance in which one begins with the statement, "Given our present state of knowledge regarding natural processes, we do not know with certainty how form X could have been assembled by natural means," and then moves to the conclusion, "Therefore form X must have been assembled by extra-natural means."

Why am I puzzled by this strategy of warranting belief in ontological gaps by appeal to epistemological gaps? Mostly because of the inconsistency with which it is employed. To illustrate the inconsistency, suppose we were to define the *functional economy* of the universe to be the set of all active capabilities of material, physical, and biotic systems that contribute to the normal functioning of the universe at any time. Needless to say, this functional economy is no less impressive than the universe's formational economy. Just try to consider for a moment all of the properties and capabilities that the universe must possess in order for us to experience only one day of our life.

With that attempt under way, think of the following questions: Do we at this time know all of the elements of this functional economy? Can we now give a complete natural account of everything that material, physical, and biotic systems presently do? Given the obvious fact that we must confess some degree of ignorance in the face of both of these questions, are we then, as Christians, inclined to claim that these epistemological gaps warrant the presumption of corresponding ontological gaps? Do we, as Christians, judge that we are warranted in presuming that God is daily bridging gaps in the functional economy of the creation with extraordinary divine action in order to effect outcomes that we do not yet fully understand in terms of creaturely action? Setting aside for the moment the question of occasional miraculous acts that God might choose to perform for special purposes, is extraordinary divine action also necessary for the daily operation of the creation? In other words, is extraordinary divine action really quite ordinary?

To the best of my knowledge, most Christians—including episodic creationists—would answer these questions in the negative. As far as the daily functioning of the universe is concerned, we see no need to jump from the recognition of our ignorance regarding numerous particular elements in the creation's functional economy to the conclusion that divine interventions are a necessary supplement to an inadequate set of creaturely actions. Or, to say it more formally, when we consider the creation's functional economy, we see no need to take epistemological gaps as conclusive evidence for the existence of corresponding ontological gaps. This leaves the question: If this move from epistemological to ontological gaps is not done in regard to the creation's *functional* economy, then why would one proceed in this manner in regard to the creation's *formational* economy? Why the inconsistency here?

Numerous reasons could be suggested, but it is difficult to assess their relative importance. Nonetheless, my personal judgment would be that a major contributing factor is the widespread belief that an episodic creationist picture of God's creative action is both a "clear teaching of the Bible" and one of the fundamental "deliverances of the faith." Beneath the surface of appeals to an empirical basis for belief in either episodic creation or intelligent design lies a set of beliefs (relatively unexamined, I suspect) regarding both biblical and traditional support for an interventionist concept of divine creative action. From this underlying concept of divine creative action proceeds the evidentialist apologetic strategy commonly employed in the debate with naturalism. It would seem, therefore, that the interventionist concept of divine creative action that prevails among the proponents both of episodic creationist theism and of evolutionary naturalism has set the unfruitful agenda of the contemporary creation/evolution debate. Hence, the importance of encouraging a theological reexamination of the concept of divine action in the physical world that is also the object of scientific scrutiny.

The optimally-gifted creation perspective

Distinguishing conceptualization from actualization

As I reflect upon the ongoing shouting match between proponents of evolutionary naturalism and of episodic creationist theism (or of intelligent design theory), I have come to the conclusion that any advancement in understanding, especially of the historic Christian theological perspective, is unlikely unless both parties agree to distinguish between the issues of (1) thoughtful conceptualization and (2) mode of actualization. The two substantive questions that need to be distinguished from one another are these: (1) Does the universe, in the totality of its properties and dynamic capabilities (in other words, its formational and functional economies), display the marks of having been thoughtfully conceptualized or does it bear the marks of being the sort of unconceptualized entity that just happens to exist? (2) Whether thoughtfully conceptualized or not, is the formational economy of the universe sufficiently robust to make possible the actualization (in this context "actualization" means "assembly from the requisite elementary components") of all physical struc- tures and life forms by means of self-organization and transformation in the course of time?

Both the either/or format of the creation/evolution debate and the apologetic strategy modeled by proponents of intelligent design theory have been built on the presumption that the answers to these two questions are inextricably coupled in one particular way. According to Phillip Johnson, for instance, an authentically theistic perspective on evolution is impossible because evolution and metaphysical naturalism cannot be isolated from one another. In Johnson's own words,

> I think that most theistic evolutionists accept as scientific the claim that natural selection performed the creating, but would like to reject the accompanying metaphysical doctrine that the scientific understanding of evolution excludes design and purpose. The problem with this way of dividing things is that the metaphysical statement is no mere embellishment but the essential foundation for the scientific claim.[13]

William Provine, a vocal proponent of naturalism, heartily agrees with Johnson's claim regarding the incompatability of evolution and theistic religion. Johnson takes this agreement as confirmatory of his rhetorical strategy. "Provine and I have become very friendly adversaries, because our agreement about how to define the question is more important than our disagreement on how to answer it."[14] (I would have expected their religious differences to be far more important than their agreement on rhetorical strategy.)

Proponents of evolutionary naturalism (like Johnson's sparring partner Provine, for instance) presume that their case is to be won by amassing evi- dence for the robustness of the universe's formational economy. As we noted earlier, the essence of the naturalistic challenge is this: If there are no gaps in the universe's formational economy, then what need is there for a Creator? The response of episodic creationists and intelligent design theorists to this challenge is to say, in effect, "Then there must be demonstrable gaps in the creation's formational economy. We think we have found some of them. There- fore, some form of extra-natural assembly (such as fiat creation or its more subtle intelligent design variant) is essential for the formation of at least some life forms or biotic subsystems, and naturalism is thereby discredited."

The two parties in the popular debate categorically disagree, of course, on whether or not the robust formational economy principle is true, but they nonetheless appear to agree that if it is true, then naturalism wins, or at least appears more likely to be true than does Christian theism. As I see it, that agreement constitutes a tragedy of major proportions for the Christian witness to a scientifically literate world. It implies that the apologetic contest between theism and naturalism is to be settled on the basis of the mode by which life-forms came to be actualized in time. The credibility of theism is presumed by both parties to be closely linked with the possibility of demonstrating a need for occasional episodes of divine creative action of the extra-natural assembly variety. If that need could be conclusively demonstrated, it would falsify both the robust formational economy principle and evolutionary naturalism. In fact, as I have already intimated, some proponents of intelligent design theory see little distinction between these two concepts, presuming that the robust for-mational economy principle and evolutionary naturalism are, for all practical purposes, equivalent.

To illustrate this last point, consider the following sample of the rhetoric of Phillip Johnson. In a published exchange of views regarding the place of divine intervention in the course of creation's formational history, I challenged John-son to articulate his conception of "just what biological history would have been like if left to natural phenomena without 'super-natural assistance'." His candid and very telling reply was,

> If God had created a lifeless world, even with oceans rich in amino acids and other organic molecules, and thereafter had left matters alone, life would not have come into existence. If God had done nothing but create a world of bacteria and protozoa, it would still be a world of bacteria and protozoa. Whatever may have been the case in the remote past, the chemicals we see today have no observ-able tendency or ability to form complex plants and animals. Per-sons who believe that chemicals unassisted by intelligence can combine to create life, or that bacteria can evolve by natural pro-cesses into complex animals, are making an a priori assumption that nature has the resources to do its own creating. I call such persons metaphysical *naturalists*.[15]

I can only take this to mean that, from Johnson's perspective, only a meta-physical naturalist would presume the truth of the robust formational economy principle. If that were so, then the credibility of theism could be convincingly established by demonstrating the existence of gaps in the formational economy of the universe.

The credibility of naturalism, on the other hand, is often presumed to be established by demonstrating that the actualization of all life forms can be accomplished "naturally," that is, without episodes of special creation in time. Implicit in this line of argumentation is the astounding presumption that the truth of the robust formational economy principle warrants the rejection of the idea that the being of the universe bears the marks of having been thoughtfully conceptualized. One can readily see why proponents of evolutionary naturalism would be eager to grant this presumption, but it is exceptionally difficult for me to see why it would be attractive to a Christian. Why would a Christian be inclined to reject the possibility that a creation thoughtfully conceptualized by God could well also be a creation generously gifted by God with a robust and gapless formational economy?

Should not creationists have high expectations for the creation?

It is clear, then, that the status of the robust formational economy principle in relationship to both evolutionary naturalism and Christian theism must be reexamined. The popular debate is structured around the presumption that this principle is the offspring of naturalism and that if Christian theism is to survive, it must now slay the dragon named "the robust formational economy principle."

But is that actually the case? Suppose that we, as scientifically-informed Christians, were to address anew, in the contemporary context, the question regarding the mode in which the physical structures and life-forms of the creation have come to be actualized in time. Suppose, furthermore, that we were to adopt the position generally held in the scientific community that the answer is, "Yes, the robust formational economy principle is likely to be true." Would the adoption of such a presupposition place the Christian apologist in a position of weakness or disadvantage, as is commonly believed? Emphatically not, I would argue. Recognizing that such an approach might take many persons, both within and outside of the Christian community, by surprise, let me explain how I have come to adopt this stance.

All Christians are authentic "creationists" in the full *theological* sense of that term. We are all committed to the biblically-informed and historic Christian doctrine of creation that affirms that everything that is not God is part of a creation that has being only because God has given it being and continues to sustain it. As a creation, the universe is neither a divine being nor a self-existent entity that has its being independent of divine creative action. This theological core of the doctrine of creation sets Judeo-Christian theism in bold distinction from both pantheism (all is God) and naturalism (all is nature).

It is important here, I believe, to remind ourselves that the being of every creature—that is, every member of the creation, whether animate or inanimate—is defined not only by its "creaturely properties" but also by its characteristic array of "creaturely capabilities" to act and interact in particular ways, often in accordance with patterns—whether deterministic or probabilistic—that are empirically accessible to the natural sciences. Christians committed to the doctrine of creation recognize all of these "creaturely capabilities" (all of the remarkable things, for instance, that fundamental particles, atoms, molecules, and cells are capable of doing) as God's "gifts of dynamic being" to the several members of creation. A creature can do no more than what God has gifted it with the capacities to do.

From this creationist perspective, then, each discovery of a creaturely capability—including every discovery contributed by the natural sciences—provides the theist with an occasion for expressing awe regarding the Creator's unfathomable creativity (in thoughtfully conceptualizing the gifts to be given) and unlimited generosity (in actually granting this rich array of gifts of being to the creation). Furthermore, given the creationist orientation here described, I would argue that the Judeo-Christian theist should be inclined to have exceedingly high expectations regarding the character of creation's formational and functional economies. Since the richness of these creaturely economies is to be seen as a manifestation of the creativity and the generosity of the Creator, we have every reason to have high expectations for the fullness of being that is resident in the integrated set of creaturely capabilities with which God has gifted creation for the purposes of both formational development and moment-by-moment functioning. This high expectation is affirmed each time the empirical sciences come to an awareness of another member of these dynamic economies.

Note carefully what I have just said. All Christians hold that the creation is "designed" in the fundamental sense of having been *thoughtfully conceptualized* by a Creator possessing unimaginable creativity. But if that creativity is beyond human comprehension, as we should expect, then the mode by which particular structures and forms are to be actualized in the course of time is also likely to be far more wondrous than we could imagine. Therefore, those epistemological gaps of which I spoke earlier provide no sufficient basis whatsoever for presuming the existence of corresponding ontological gaps in the formational economy of the creation.

The fully-gifted creation: both thoughtfully conceptualized and optimally equipped

Drawing from a number of biblical and theological considerations, I envision a creation brought into being in nascent form, brimming not only with awesome potentialities—for being organized into an astounding array of both physical structures and biotic forms—but also with a robust set of dynamic pathways for achieving them by the exercise of their creaturely capacities.

Drawing also from the vocabulary of the natural sciences, I envision a creation brought into being by God and gifted not only with a rich "potentiality space" of possible structures and life forms but also with the capabilities for realizing these potentialities by means of self-organization into nucleons, atoms, molecules, galaxies, nebulae, stars, planets, plants, animals, and the like. To say it in another way, I believe that the universe in its present form is to be seen as a potentiality of the creation that has been actualized by the exercise of its God-given creaturely capabilities.

For this to be possible, however, the creation's formational economy must be astoundingly robust and gapless—lacking none of the resources or capabilities necessary to make possible the sort of continuous actualization of new structures and life forms as now envisioned by the natural sciences. The optimally-equipped character of the universe's formational economy is, I believe, a vivid manifestation of the fact that it is the product, not of mere accident or happenstance, as the worldview of naturalism would have it, but of intention. In other words, the universe bears the marks of being the product of thoughtful conceptualization for the accomplishment of some purpose. From the Christian perspective, this comes as no surprise whatsoever because the formational economy of the universe—every creaturely capability that contributes to it—is a symbol both of God's creativity and of God's generosity.

How is divine creative action manifested?

Among Christians in North America, there appears to be a strong desire for conceiving of divine creative action in a way that would provide a basis for expecting it to be empirically distinguishable from "natural" action. In the minds of many, an appeal to divine action becomes convincing only if it can be demonstrated to have made a difference of the empirically discernible sort. In essence, evidentialist apologetics is presumed to provide the most substantive and convincing reasons to believe.

The question before us, then, is, *What is the character of that creative activity and how does it become manifest to those who have eyes to see it?* When I speak of divine creative action, however, I am inclined to speak of it not in the Aristotelian vocabulary of cause and effect, but in the royal metaphor (frequently employed in Scripture) of creative word and creaturely response. Cause and effect language seems to encourage images of God acting like creatures, only more powerfully. Matter is coerced to assume new forms. Word and response language focuses more attention on matters of authority and accountability. The king speaks, the king's subjects carry out his wishes.

I believe that God acts by calling upon the creation to employ its creaturely capabilities to bring about a fruitful outcome, and that *the fruitful character of creation's formational history is the manifestation of that divine calling*. This is, I believe, the same kind of divine action that we ask for when we pray for God's "blessing" on the work of the surgical team as we prepare for a journey into the operating room—we ask that God act in such a way that the actions of God's creatures (from the medical staff in the hospital to the molecules in our cells) will lead to a fruitful outcome.

In the contemporary discussion of issues regarding natural science and Christian faith, the question of empirical detectability often arises. Is God's action of blessing, for instance, empirically detectable as the "effect" of some non-creaturely "cause" that overpowers creatures in such a way that the outcome is clearly beyond the realm of creaturely possibility? I think not. If that were the sort of divine action that we were expecting in response to our pre-surgery prayer, why not skip the surgery and avoid both the pain and the expense? The kind of divine action we pray for is discernible only by those who have eyes (of faith) to see it. The natural sciences have no instruments with which to measure the level or effectiveness of God's blessing.

Reflect for a moment on the way modern astrophysics and cosmology describe (within the limits of a very restricted conceptual vocabulary) the processes from time $t = 0$ until now. Some nascent, non-material form of energy (whose ultimate source of being lies beyond the competence of science to identify) employs its capabilities for self-organization (capabilities that are in no way self-explanatory) to form the fundamental particles and their four distinct forces of interaction, from which also proceed such macroscopic forms as galaxies, stars, and planets. How could the universe's formational economy be so robust as to make this astrophysical drama a possibility? Only, I believe, as an outcome of God's thoughtful conceptualization and effective will to give being to the creation first conceptualized.

And how could it be that the outcome of this exercise of creaturely capabilities has been so astonishingly fruitful? Even if we could comprehend all of the things that atoms and molecules could do, how could it be that the outcome of their actions could lead to the vast array of astronomical and biotic forms that now comprise the universe? Only, I believe, as the outcome of God's continuing blessing on those creaturely capabilities.

Do I expect to find particular instances in which God's action in the course of cosmic formative history is empirically discernible? Do I expect to catch God in the act of coercing atoms and molecules into doing things differently from what they might otherwise have done (as if I could even know that)? No, I do not. I can observe what creatures have done, but God's act of calling for that particular creaturely action is beyond my empirical grasp. Though I can empirically detect the creaturely response, I cannot record the divine creative word that called for it. Furthermore, what I observe creatures to be doing in response to that creative word is not something of which they were never capable, but rather it is a fruitful exercise of the very God-given capabilities that constitute their being.

Intelligently designed or optimally equipped?

The question posed in the title of this essay is an invitation to choose between two differing visions regarding the character of the creation, the nature of divine creative action, and the effective reasons for the fruitful outcome of the creation's formational history. Some have chosen a perspective that presumes the existence of gaps in the creation's formational economy—gaps to be bridged by occasional episodes of form-imposing divine intervention. My own choice strongly favors the concept of a creation optimally gifted by the creator with a robust and gapless formational economy—yes, even robust enough to make possible the evolutionary continuity envisioned by cosmologists and biologists.

Nearly every time that I have presented this perspective to a Christian audience someone expresses the fear that it represents a form of deism, with its concept of a distant and inactive God. I find the frequency of this concern very intriguing. Is it telling us something about how we Christians today are inclined to think about divine action? Has our concept of divine creative action been unduly affected by the "special effects" industry? Perhaps so.

But the "optimally-gifted creation perspective" is not at all inclined toward deism. I think the quickest way to dispel that fear is to ask the following question: Has orthodox Christian theology ever suggested that God is able and/ or willing to act in the world only within gaps in either the formational economy or the operational economy of the Creation? To the best of my knowledge the answer is a resounding no. Therefore, if the presence of such gaps is not required to "make room" for divine action, then the absence of such gaps is no loss whatsoever. End of story.

From the vantage point of believing that God gave being to a creation in which the robust formational economy principle is true, God is still as free as ever to act in any way that is consistent with God's nature and will. The optimally-gifted creation, complete with a gapless formational economy, does not in any way hinder God from acting as God wills to act. As I have said on numerous occasions, the question at issue is not, "Does God act in or interact with the creation," but rather, "What is the character of the creation in which God acts and with which God interacts?" I believe that it is an optimally-gifted creation.

Does this perspective crowd God or divine action out of the picture? Does this perspective entail too high a view of the creation's dynamic capabilities or too lofty a view of the Creator's creativity and generosity? I, for one, think not.

Notes

1   The term *conservative* has many meanings. As employed here, the term is meant to call attention to that substantial portion of the North American Christian community that places great emphasis on the role of the biblical text in providing clear, fixed, and normative answers to a broad spectrum of questions, including questions regarding the character and timetable of the creation's formational history. The early chapters of Genesis, for instance, would be viewed as a concise chronicle of particular divine acts by which God brought into being new physical, astronomical, geological, and biotic forms—a faithful reading of the text that must be conserved over against the challenges of modern evolutionary science.

2   Representative literature written from this perspective includes books by law professor Philip E. Johnson, *Darwin on Trial* (Downers Grove: InterVarsity, 1991) and *Reason in the Balance* (Downers Grove: InterVarsity, 1995); an essay collection edited by philosophy professor J. P. Moreland, *The Creation Hypothesis* (Downers Grove: InterVarsity, 1994); and the book, *Darwin's Black Box* (New York: The Free Press, 1996) by biochemist Michael J. Behe. A list of active intelligent design proponents would also include Stephen Meyer, Paul Nelson, and William Dembski.

3   In *Darwin's Black Box*, Behe further restricts the science of the day to the conceptual vocabulary of biochemistry.

4   Howard J. Van Till, "Basil, Augustine, and the Doctrine of Creation's Functional Integrity," in *Science and Christian Belief* 8 (1996) 21–38.

5   For an example of this type of argumentation see Behe's book, *Darwin's Black Box*.

6   Daniel C. Dennett, *Darwin's Dangerous Idea* (New York: Touchstone, 1995). For a more extensive critique of this work see my essay, "No Place for a Small God," in *How Large is God?*, ed. John Marks Templeton (Philadelphia: Templeton Foundation, 1997).

7   Dennett, *Darwin's Dangerous Idea*, 28.

8   Ibid., 74, 76.

9   Divine *intervention* is another term that has numerous meanings. In this context, it

denotes the concept of an extraordinary divine act in which God directly causes members of the creation (atoms, molecules, cells, or organisms, for instance) to assume a configuration that they would not otherwise have been able to achieve by the employment of their ordinary capabilities for self-organization or transformation. Thus, divine intervention of this character is presumed to "make a difference" (a phrase commonly employed in the books by Phillip Johnson) of the empirically detectable sort.

10   Dennett, *Darwin's Dangerous Idea*, 59.
11   Ibid., 136.
12   Ibid., 75–76.
13   Phillip E. Johnson, *Darwin on Trial*, 2d ed. (Downers Grove: InterVarsity, 1993), 168.
14   Ibid., 165.
15   *First Things* (June/July 1993), 38.

Chapter 19

Arthur Peacocke

BIOLOGICAL EVOLUTION —
A POSITIVE
THEOLOGICAL APPRAISAL

Darwinism appeared, and, under the disguise of a foe, did the work of a friend. It has conferred upon philosophy and religion an inestimable benefit, by shewing us that we must choose between two alternatives. Either God is everywhere present in nature, or He is nowhere.

(Aubrey Moore, in the 12th edition of Lux Mundi, 1891, p. 73).

1 Introduction

IT[1] **WOULD, NO DOUBT**, come as a surprise to many of the biologically-cultured "despisers of the Christian religion," to learn that, as increasingly thorough historical investigations are showing,[2] the nineteenth-century reaction to Darwin in theological and ecclesiastical circles was much more positive and welcoming than the legends propagated by both popular and academic biological publications are prepared to admit. Furthermore, the scientific reaction was also much more negative than usually depicted, those skeptical of Darwin's ideas including initially *inter alia* the leading comparative anatomist of his day, Richard Owen (a Cuverian), and the leading geologist, Charles Lyell. Many theologians deferred judgment, but the proponents of at least one strand in theology in nineteenth-century England chose to intertwine their insights closely with the Darwinian—that "catholic" revival in the Church of England of a stress on the doctrine of the Incarnation and its extension into the sacraments and so of a renewed sense of the sacramentality of nature and

God's immanence in the world. I have summarized elsewhere[3] some of this history, not only in Britain but also in France, Germany, and America—suffice it to say that more of the nineteenth-century theological reaction to Darwin was constructive and reconciling in temper than practically any biological authors today will allow.

That is perhaps not surprising in view of the background to at least T. H. Huxley's aggressive propagation of Darwin's ideas and his attacks on Christianity, namely that of clerical restriction on, and opportunities for, biological scientists in England in the nineteenth century. His principal agenda was the establishment of science as a profession independent of ecclesiastical control—and in this we can sympathize. So it is entirely understandable that the present *Zeitgeist* of biological science is that of viewing "religion" as the opposition, if no longer in any way a threat. This tone saturates the writings of the biologists Richard Dawkins and Stephen Gould and many others—and even philosophers such as Daniel Dennett. Indeed, the strictures of Jacques Monod in his 1970 publication *Le hasard et la nécessité*, especially in its English translation *Chance and Necessity*, could be said to be one of the strongest attacks in this century, in the name of science, on belief in God and in the universe having any attributable meaning and purpose. His remarks on this are well known and widely quoted.

Perhaps this has polarized the scene, but what I find even more surprising, and less understandable, is the way in which the "disguised friend" of Darwinism, and more generally of evolutionary ideas, has been admitted (if at all) only grudgingly, with many askance and sidelong looks, into the parlors of Christian theology. I believe it is vital for this churlishness to be rectified in this last decade of the twentieth century if the Christian religion (indeed any religion) is to be believable and have intellectual integrity enough to command even the attention, let alone the assent, of thoughtful people in the beginning of the next millennium.

2 Biological evolution and God's relation to the living world

We shall consider in this section various features and characteristics of biological evolution and any theological reflections to which they may give rise.

2.1 Continuity and emergence

A notable aspect of the scientific account of the natural world in general is the seamless character of the web that has been spun on the loom of time: the process appears as continuous from its cosmic "beginning," in the "hot big bang," to the present and at no point do modern natural scientists have to invoke any non-natural causes to explain their observations and inferences about the past. Their explanations are usually in terms of concepts, theories and mechanisms which they can confirm by, or infer from, present-day experiments, or reasonably infer by extrapolating from principles themselves confirmable by experiment. In particular, the processes of biological evolution also display a continuity, which although at first a conjecture of Darwin (and, to be fair, of many of his predecessors), is now thoroughly validated by the established universality of the genetic code and by the study of past and present species of DNA nucleotide sequences and of amino acid sequences in certain widely-distributed proteins.

The process that has occurred can be characterized also as one of *emergence*, for new forms of matter, and a hierarchy of organization of these forms, appear in the course of time. These new forms have new properties, behaviors and networks of relations which necessitate not only specific methods of investigation but also the development of new epistemologically irreducible concepts in order to describe and refer to them. To these new organizations of matter it is, very often, possible to ascribe new levels of what can only be called "reality": that is, the epistemology implies at least a putative ontology. In other words new kinds of reality may be said to "emerge" in time. Notably, on the surface of the Earth, new forms of living matter (that is, living organisms) have come into existence by this continuous process—that is what we mean by evolution.[4]

What the scientific perspective of the world, especially the living world, inexorably impresses upon us is a *dynamic* picture of entities and structures involved in continuous and incessant change and process without ceasing. Any static conception of the way in which God sustains and holds the cosmos in being is therefore precluded, for new entities, structures, and processes appear in the course of time, so that God's action as Creator is both past and present: it is continuous. The scientific perspective of a cosmos, and in particular that of the biological world, as in development all the time must re-introduce into our understanding of God's creative relation to the world a dynamic element which was, even if obscured by the assigning of "creation" to an event in the past, always implicit in the Hebrew conception of a "living God," dynamic in action. Any notion of God as Creator must now take into account that God is continuously creating, continuously giving existence to, what is new; God is *semper Creator*, and the world is a *creatio continua*. The traditional notion of God *sustaining* the world in its general order and structure now has to be enriched by a dynamic and creative dimension—the model of God sustaining and giving continuous existence to a process which has a creativity built into it by God. God is creating at every moment of the world's existence in and through the perpetually-endowed creativity of the very stuff of the world. God indeed makes "things make themselves," as Charles Kingsley put it in *The Water Babies.* . . .

Thus it is that the scientific perspective, and especially that of biological evolution, impels us to take more seriously and more concretely than hitherto the notion of the immanence of God-as-Creator—God is the Immanent Creator *creating in and through the processes of the natural order.* I would urge that all this has to be taken in a very strong sense. If one asks where do we see God-as-Creator during, say, the processes of biological evolution, one has to reply: "The processes themselves, as unveiled by the biological sciences, *are* God-acting-as-Creator, God *qua* Creator."[5] God gives existence in divinely-created time to a process that itself brings forth the new: thereby God is creating. This means we do not have to look for any extra supposed gaps in which, or mechanisms whereby, God might be supposed to be acting as Creator in the living world.

The model of musical composition for God's activity in creation is, I would suggest, particularly helpful here. There is no doubt of the "transcendence" of the composer in relation to the music he or she creates—the composer gives it existence and without the composer it would not be at all. So the model properly reflects, as do all those of artistic creativity, that transcendence of God as Creator of all-that-is which, as the "listeners" to the music of creation, we wish to aver. Yet, when we are actually listening to a musical work, say, a Beethoven piano sonata, then there are times when we are so deeply absorbed in it that, for a moment we are thinking Beethoven's musical thoughts with him. In such moments the

> Music is heard so deeply
> That it is not heard at all, but you are the music
> While the music lasts[6]

Yet if anyone were to ask at that moment, "*Where* is Beethoven now?"—we could only reply that Beethoven-*qua*-composer was to be found only in the music itself. The music would in some sense be Beethoven's inner musical thought rekindled in us and we would genuinely be encountering Beethoven-*qua*-composer. This very closely models, I am suggesting, God's immanence in creation and God's self-communication in and through the processes by means of which God is creating. The processes revealed by the sciences, especially evolutionary biology, are in themselves God-acting-as-Creator. There is no need to look for God as some kind of *additional* factor supplementing the processes of the world. God, to use language usually applied in sacramental theology, is "in, with, and under" all-that-is and all-that-goes-on.

2.2 The mechanism of biological evolution

There appear to be no serious biologists who doubt that natural selection is a factor operative in biological evolution—and most would say it is by far the most significant one. At one end of the spectrum authors like Dawkins argue cogently for the all-sufficiency of natural selection in explaining the course of biological evolution. Certainly he has illustrated by his "biomorph" computer program how the counter-intuitive creativity of evolution could be generated by the interplay of chance events operating in a law-like framework—this is, in the case of biological evolution, the interplay between mutational events in the DNA of the genome with the environment of the phenotype to which it gives rise. This was well illustrated by Dawkins[7] with his program in which two-dimensional patterns of branching lines, "biomorphs," are generated by random changes in a defined number of features combined with a reproduction and selection procedure. It was striking how subtle, varied and complex were the "biomorph" patterns after surprisingly few "generations," that is, reiterations of the procedure. Such computer simulations go a long way toward making it clear how it is that the complexity and diversity of biological organisms could arise through the operation of the apparently simple principles of natural selection.

However, other biologists are convinced that, even when the subtleties of natural selection are taken into account, it is not the whole story; and some even go so far as to say that natural selection alone cannot account for speciation, the formation of distinctly new species.

What is significant about all these proposals[8] is that they are all operating entirely within a naturalistic framework—to use Dennett's graphic designation, they are all "cranes" and not "skyhooks"[9]—and, moreover, they assume a basically Darwinian process to be operating, even when they disagree about its speed and smoothness (e.g., the presence or absence of the sudden "saltations" proposed by Gould). That being so, it has to be recognized that the history of life on Earth involves chance in a way unthinkable before Darwin. There is a creative interplay of "chance" and law apparent in the evolution of living matter by natural selection. However what we mean by "chance" in this context first needs closer examination.

Events are unpredictable by us in basically two ways:

1. They can be unpredictable because we can never possess the necessary detailed knowledge with the requisite accuracy at this microlevel of description. In such cases talk of the role of "chance" can mean either: (A) we cannot determine accurately the microparameters of the initial conditions determining the macroevents (e.g., the forces on a tossed coin) while often knowing the overall constraints that must operate on the system as a whole (e.g., the

symmetry constraints making for equal probabilities of heads and tails); or (B) the observed events are the outcome of the crossing of two independent causal chains, accurate knowledge of which is unattainable both with respect to the chains themselves and to their point of intersection.

2. At the subatomic level events can also be inherently unpredictable because of the operation of the Heisenberg Uncertainty Principle.

Events of type (1) and (2), unpredictable as they are, can produce effects at the macroscopic level which operate in a law-like framework which delimits the scope of the consequent events or provides them with new and unexpected outcomes. Both ways of viewing the matter are pertinent to biological evolution, which depends on a process in which changes occur in the genetic-information carrying material (DNA) that are random with respect to the biological needs of the organisms possessing the DNA—in particular, random with respect to its need to produce progeny for the species to survive. What we call "chance" is involved both at the level of the mutational event in the DNA itself (1A and/or 2), and in the intersecting of two causally unrelated chains of events (1B). The biological niche in which the organism exists then filters out, by the processes of natural selection, those changes in the DNA that enable the organisms possessing them to produce more progeny in an entirely law-like fashion.

The interplay between "chance," at the molecular level of the DNA, and "law" or "necessity" at the statistical level of the population of organisms tempted Jacques Monod, in *Chance and Necessity*[10] to elevate "chance" to the level almost of a metaphysical principle whereby the universe might be interpreted. As is well known, he concluded that the "stupendous edifice of evolution" is, in this sense, rooted in "pure chance" and that therefore all inferences of direction or purpose in the development of the biological world, in particular, and of the universe, in general, must be false. As Monod saw it, it was the purest accident that any particular creature came into being, in particular *Homo sapiens*, and no direction or purpose or meaning could ever be expected to be discerned in biological evolution. A creator God, for all practical purposes, might just as well not exist, since everything in evolution went on in an entirely uncontrolled and fortuitous manner.

The responses to this thesis—mainly from theologically informed scientists and some philosophers, rather than from theologians—have been well surveyed and analyzed by Bartholomew.[11] I shall pursue here what I consider the most fruitful line of reflection on the processes that Monod so effectively brought to our attention—a direction that I began to pursue[12] in response to Monod and which has been further developed by the statistically-informed treatment of Bartholomew.

There is no reason to give the randomness of a molecular event the metaphysical status that Monod attributed to it. The involvement of "chance" at the level of mutation in the DNA does not, of itself, preclude these events from displaying trends and manifesting inbuilt propensities at the higher levels of organisms, populations, and eco-systems. To call the mutation of the DNA a "chance" event serves simply to stress its randomness with respect to biological consequence. As I have earlier put it (in a response later supported and amplified by others):

> Instead of being daunted by the role of chance in genetic mutations as being the manifestation of irrationality in the universe, it would be more consistent with observation to assert that the full gamut of the potentialities of living matter could be explored only through the agency of the rapid and frequent randomization which is possible at the molecular level of the DNA.[13]

This role of "chance," or rather randomness (or "free experiment") at the microlevel is what one would expect if the universe were so constituted that all the potential forms of organization of matter (both living and non-living) which it contains might be thoroughly explored. Indeed, since Monod first published his book in 1970, there have been the developments in theoretical and molecular biology and physical biochemistry of the Brussels and Göttingen schools. They demonstrated that it is the interplay of chance and law that is in fact creative within time, for it is the combination of the two which allows new forms to emerge and evolve—so that natural selection appears to be opportunistic. As in many games, the consequences of the fall of the dice depend very much on the rules of the game.[14] It has become increasingly apparent that it is chance operating within a law-like framework that is the basis of the inherent creativity of the natural order, its ability to generate new forms, patterns and organizations of matter and energy. If all were governed by rigid law, a repetitive and uncreative order would prevail; if chance alone ruled, no forms, patterns or organizations would persist long enough for them to have any identity or real existence and the universe could never be a cosmos and susceptible to rational inquiry. It is the combination of the two which makes possible an ordered universe capable of developing within itself new modes of existence (cf. Dawkins' biomorphs). The "rules" are what they are because of the "givenness" of the properties of the physical environment and of the other already evolved living organisms with which the organism in question interacts.

This givenness, for a theist, can only be regarded as an aspect of the God-endowed features of the world. The way in which what we call "chance" operates within this "given" framework to produce new structures, entities and processes can then properly be seen as an eliciting of the potentialities that the physical cosmos possessed *ab initio*. Such potentialities a theist must regard as written into creation by the Creator's intention and purpose and must conceive as gradually being actualized by the operation of "chance" stimulating their coming into existence. One might say that the potential of the "being" of the world is made manifest in the "becoming" that the operation of chance makes actual. God is the ultimate ground and source of both law ("necessity") and "chance."[15]

For a theist, God must now be seen as acting to create in the world through what we call "chance" operating within the created order, each stage of which constitutes the launching pad for the next. The Creator, it now seems, is unfolding the divinely-endowed potentialities of the universe, in and through a process in which these creative possibilities and propensities (see next section), inherent by God's own intention within the fundamental entities of that universe and their interrelations, become actualized within a created temporal development shaped and determined by those selfsame God-given potentialities.[16]

2.3 Trends in evolution?

Are there any trends or discernable directions in evolution? This is a notoriously loaded question, which human beings are only too ready to answer on the basis of their own believed significance in the universe grounded on their own importance to themselves! Is there any objective, non-anthropocentrically biased evidence for directions or at least trends in biological evolution? Biologists have been especially cautious not to answer this question affirmatively, not least because they do not wish to give premature hostages to those seeking to gain a foothold for claiming some kind of "skyhook," such as divine action, intervention even, directing the course of evolution. Evolution is best depicted biologically not as a kind of Christmas tree, with *Homo sapiens* accorded an angelic position crowning the topmost frond, but rather as a bush—"Life is a copiously branching bush, continually pruned by the grim reaper of extinction, not a ladder of predictable progress."[17] Nevertheless, G. G. Simpson can affirm that "Within the framework of the evolutionary history of life there have been not one but many different kinds of progress."[18] While admitting that such lines of "progress" can be traced in the evolutionary "bush," other biologists would be more neutral.

The question of more general significance that is being addressed in relation to the biological evolutionary story is, it would seem, Are there any particular properties and functions attributable to living organisms which could be said to be in themselves helpful for evolution to occur because they are advantageous in natural selection (for survival of progeny) of organisms poss-essing them? Simpson's suggested list seems to fulfil this criterion and so it could be said that the evolutionary process manifests what Karl Popper[19] has called a "propensity" in nature for such properties to appear. He argued that a greater frequency of occurrence of a particular kind of event may be used as a test of whether or not there is inherent in a sequence of events (equivalent to throws of a die) a tendency or propensity to realize the event in question. He has pointed out that the *realization of possibilities*, which may be random, *depend on the total situation within which the possibilities are being actualized* so that "there exist weighted possibilities which are *more than mere possibilities*, but tendencies or propensities to become real"[20] and that these "propensities in physics are properties of *the whole situation* and sometimes even of the particular way in which a situation changes. And the same holds of the propensities in chemistry, in biochemistry, and in biology."[21] I suggest that there *are* propensities, in this Popperian sense, in evolution towards the possession of certain character-istics, propensities that are inherently built into an evolutionary process based on natural selection of the best procreators. Such properties naturally enhance survival for procreation in certain widely-occurring environments.

Among the plethora of such properties of living organisms which might in some circumstance or another be advantageous in natural selection, there are a number which characterize *Homo sapiens* and are pertinent to our wider concerns in this paper. . . . They are as follows.

1. *Complexity*. The human brain is the most complex natural system known to us in the universe. Is there a propensity to complexity in *biological*[22] evolution? There certainly seems to be, and "increasing complexity" was included in Simpson's list (see n. 18) as characteristic of it. What significance is to be attributed to this? Is it simply that biological "evolution is a process of divergence and wandering rather than an inexorable progression towards increasing complexity" so that evolution "*permits* the emergence of new complexity, but does not in any particular case necessitate it"?[23]

The fact is that there *has* been, taking biological evolution as a whole, an emergence of increasingly complex organisms, even if in some evolutionary lines there has been a loss of complexity and so of organization. So, on Popper's criterion enunciated above, we would be correct in saying that there is a pro-pensity towards increased complexity in the evolution of living organisms. Saunders and Ho[24] identify the basis of this tendency to be the process by which a self-organizing system optimizes its organization with respect to locally defined requirements for fitness. Even if it cannot be predicated as inevitable in any particular evolutionary line, there has been an overall trend towards and an increase in complexity along particular lines in biological evolution, so that it is right to be speak of a propensity for this to occur.

The need for *organization* for survival was beautifully demonstrated by H. A. Simon[25] who showed that the simplest modular organization of, say, the structure of a watch, so that each module had a limited stability, led to an enormous increase in survivability during manufacture in the face of random destructive events. Hence the increases we observe during evolution in complexity and organization (subsumed under "complexity" from now on) in the biological world are entirely intelligible as contributing to success in natural selection and are not at all mysterious in the sense of requiring some non-naturalistic explanation.

2. *Information-processing and -storage ability.* The more capable an organism is of receiving, recording, and analyzing signals and using the information to make predictions useful for survival about changes in its environment, the better chance it will have of surviving under the pressures of natural selection in a wide variety of habitats. In other words, there is a propensity towards the formation of systems having the functions we now recognize in nervous systems and brains. Such ability for information-processing and -storage is indeed the necessary, if not sufficient, condition for the emergence of consciousness.

3. *Pain and suffering.* This sensitivity to, this sentience of, its surroundings inevitably involves an increase in its ability to experience pain, which constitutes the necessary biological warning signals of danger and disease, so that it is impossible readily to envisage an increase of information-processing ability without an increase in the sensitivity of the signal system of the organism to its environment. Hence an increase in "information-processing" capacity, with the advantages it confers in natural selection, cannot but have as its corollary an increase, not only in the level of consciousness, but also in the experience of pain. Insulation from the surrounding world in the biological equivalent of three-inch nickel steel would be a sure recipe for preventing the development of consciousness!

Each increase in sensitivity, and eventually of consciousness, as evolution proceeds inevitably heightens and accentuates awareness both of the beneficent, life-enhancing, and of the inimical, life-diminishing, elements in the world in which the organism finds itself. The stakes for joy and pain are, as it were, continuously being raised, and the living organism learns to discriminate between them, so that pain and suffering, on the one hand, and consciousness of pleasure and well-being, on the other, are emergents in the world. Thus there can be said to be a propensity for them to occur. From a purely naturalistic viewpoint, the emergence of pain and its compounding as suffering as consciousness increases seem to be inevitable aspects of any conceivable developmental process that would be characterized by a continuous increase in ability to process and store information coming from the environment, for this entails an increase in sensitivity, hence in vulnerability, and consequently in suffering as consciousness (minimally the sum of the brain states reflecting it all) ramifies. In the context of natural selection, pain has an energizing effect and suffering is a goad to action: they both have survival value for creatures continually faced with new problematic situations challenging their survival.[26] In relation to any theological reflections, it must be emphasized that pain and suffering are present in biological evolution as a necessary condition for survival of the individual long before the appearance of human beings on the scene. So the presence of pain and suffering cannot be the result of any particular human failings, though undoubtedly human beings experience them with a heightened sensitivity and, more than any other creatures, inflict them on each other.

4. *Self-consciousness and language.* If an information-processing and -storage system can also monitor its own state at any moment, then it has at least the basis for communicating what that state is to other similar systems. Hence, provided the physical apparatus for communicating has also evolved, the capacity for language becomes possible, especially in the most highly developed of such systems. In other words, there is an inbuilt propensity for the acquisition of language and so for developing the necessary basis for *self*-consciousness. This would be an advantage in natural selection, for it is the basis of complex social cooperation in the creatures that possess it (apparently supremely *Homo sapiens*) with all the advantages this gives against predators and in gaining food.[27]

Given an immanentist understanding of God's presence "in, with, and under" the processes of biological evolution adopted up to this point, can God be said to be implementing any purpose in biological evolution? Or is the whole process so haphazard, such a matter of happenstance, such a matter of what Monod and Jacob called bricolage (tinkering), that no meaning, least of all a divinely intended one, can be discerned in the process?

I have given reasons above for postulating that there are propensities in evolution towards the possession of certain characteristics, propensities that are inherently built into an evolutionary process based on natural selection, for they naturally enhance survival for procreation in a wide range of environments. Thus it is that the evolutionary process is characterized by propensities towards increase in complexity, information-processing and -storage, consciousness, sensitivity to pain, and even self-consciousness (a necessary prerequisite for social development and the cultural transmission of knowledge down the generations). Some successive forms, along some branch or "twig" (à la Gould), have a distinct probability of manifesting more and more of these characteristics. However, the actual physical form of the organisms in which these propensities are actualized and instantiated is contingent on the history of the confluence of disparate chains of events, including the survival of the mass extinctions that have occurred (96% of all species in the Permo-Triassic one[28]).

So it is not surprising that recent re-interpretation of the fossils of very early (*circa* 530 million years ago) soft-bodied fauna found in the Burgess shale of Canada show that, had any larger proportion of these survived and prevailed, the actual forms of contemporary, evolved creatures would have been very much more disparate in anatomical *plans* than those now observed to exist—albeit with a very great diversity in the few surviving designs.[29] But even had these particular organisms, unique to the Burgess shale, been the progenitors of subsequent living organisms, the same propensities towards complexity, etc., would also have been manifest in *their* subsequent evolution, for these "propensities" simply reflect the advantages conferred in natural selection by these features. The same considerations apply to the arbitrariness and contingency of the mass extinctions, which Gould also strongly emphasizes. So that, providing there had been enough time, a complex organism with consciousness, self-consciousness, social and cultural organization (that is, the basis for the existence of "persons") would have been likely eventually to have evolved and appeared on the Earth (or on some other planet amenable to the emergence of living organisms), though no doubt with a physical form very different from *Homo sapiens*. There can, it seems to me (*pace* Stephen Gould[30]) be overall direction and implementation of divine purpose through the interplay of chance and law without a deterministic plan fixing all the details of the structure(s) of what emerges possessing personal qualities. Hence the emergence of self-conscious persons capable of relating personally to God can still be regarded as an intention of God continuously creating through the processes of that to which God has given an existence of this contingent kind and not some other. It certainly must have been possible since it actually happened—with us!

I see no need to postulate any *special* action of God—along the lines, say, of some divine manipulation of mutations at the quantum level (as proposed by others . . .)—to ensure that persons emerge in the universe, and in particular on Earth. Not to coin a phrase, "I have no need of that hypothesis!"[31] If there are any such influences by God shaping the direction of evolutionary processes at specific points—for which I see no evidence (how could we know?) and no theological need—I myself could only envisage them as being through God's whole-part constraint on all-that-is affecting the confluence of what, to us, would be independent causal chains. Such specifically-directed constraints I would envisage as possible by being exerted upon the whole interconnected and interdependent system of the whole Earth in the whole cosmos which is in and present to God, who is therefore its ultimate boundary condition and therefore capable of shaping the occurrence of particular patterns of events, if God chooses to do so.[32]

2.4 The ubiquity of pain, suffering and death

The biological inevitability of the experience of pain in any creature that is going to be aware of—and can gain information from—its environment and thereby avoid dangers has already been emphasized. The pain associated with breakdown of health due to general organic causes also appears to be simply a concomitant of being a complex organized system containing internal as well as external sensors. When pain is experienced by a conscious organism, the attribution of "suffering" becomes appropriate and *a fortiori*, with self-consciousness the suffering of others also becomes a burden. The ubiquity of pain and suffering in the living world appears to be an inevitable consequence of creatures acquiring those information-processing and -storage systems, so advantageous in natural selection, which we observe as nerves and brains in the later stages of evolution.

New patterns can only come into existence in a finite universe ("finite" in the sense of the conservation of matter-energy) if old patterns dissolve to make place for them. This is a condition of the creativity of the process—that is, of its ability to produce the new—which at the biological level we observe as new forms of life only through death of the old. For the death of individuals is essential for release of food resources for new arrivals, and species simply die out by being ousted from biological "niches" by new ones better adapted to survive and reproduce in them. Thus, biological death of the individual is the prerequisite of the creativity of the biological order, that creativity which eventually led to the emergence of human beings. At this biological level we discover the process to be one of "natural selection," but it is possible to discern cognate processes occurring also at other levels.

For complex living structures can only have a finite chance of coming into existence if they are not assembled *de novo*, as it were, from their basic subunits, but emerge through the accumulation of changes in simpler forms, as demonstrated by H. A. Simon in his classic paper.[33] Having come on to the scene, they can then survive, because of the finitude of their life spans, only by building pre-formed complex chemical structures into their fabric through imbibing the materials of other living organisms. For the chemist and biochemist there is the same kind of difficulty in conceiving how complex material structures, especially those of the intricacy of living organisms, could be assembled otherwise than from less complex units, as there is for the mathematician of conceiving of a universe in which the analytic laws of arithmetic were inapplicable. So there is a kind of *structural* logic about the inevitability of living organisms dying and preying on each other—for we cannot conceive, in a lawful, non-magical universe, of any way whereby the immense variety of developing, biological, structural complexity might appear, except by utilizing structures already existing, either by way of modification (as in biological evolution) or of incorporation (as in feeding).[34] The statistical logic is inescapable: new forms of matter arise only through the dissolution of the old; new life only through death of the old. It would seem that the law of "new life through death of the old" (J. H. Fabre's "sublime law of sacrifice"[35]) is inevitable in a world composed of common "building blocks" (atoms, etc.).

But death not only of individuals but of whole species has also occurred on the Earth during the periods of mass extinction which are now widely attributed to chance extraterrestrial collisions of the planet with comet showers, asteroids or other bodies. These could be cataclysmic and global in their effects and have been far more frequent than previously imagined. This adds a further element of sheer contingency to the history of life on the Earth.

The theist cannot ignore these features of the created order. Any theodicy has to come to terms with the obliteration of far more species than now exist on the Earth. The spontaneity and fecundity of the biological world is gained at the enormous price of universal death and of pain and suffering during life.[36] Yet individual living creatures scarcely ever commit suicide in any way that might be called intentional. Let us pay attention to this positive aspect first.

The natural world is immensely variegated in its hierarchies of levels of entities, structures, and processes, in its "being," and abundantly diversifies with a cornucopian fecundity in its "becoming" in time. From the unity in this diversity and the richness of the diversity itself, one may adduce,[37] respectively, both the essential oneness of its source of being, namely the one God the Creator, and the unfathomable richness of the unitive being of that Creator God. But now we must reckon more directly with the diversity itself. The forms even of non-living matter throughout the cosmos as it appears to us are even more diverse than what we can now observe immediately on the Earth. Furthermore the multiply-branching bush of terrestrial biological evolution appears to be primarily opportunist in the direction it follows and, in so doing, produces the enormous variety of biological life on this planet.

We can only conclude that, if there is a Creator, least misleadingly described in terms of "personal" attributes, then that Creator intended this rich multiformity of entities, structures, and processes in the natural world and, if so, that such a Creator God takes what, in the personal world of human experience, could only be called "delight" in this multiformity of what he has created—and not only in what Darwin, called "the most exalted object which we are capable of conceiving, namely the production of the higher animals."[38] The existence of the whole tapestry of the created order, in its warp and woof, and in the very heterogeneity and multiplicity of its forms must be taken to be the Creator's intention. We can only make sense of that, utilizing our resources of personal language, if we say that God has something akin to "joy" and "delight" in creation. We have a hint of this in the satisfaction attributed to God as Creator in the first chapter of *Genesis*: "And God saw everything he had made, and behold, it was very good."[39] This naturally leads to the idea of the "play" of God in creation on which I have expanded elsewhere,[40] in relation to Hindu thought as well as to that of Judaism and Christianity.

But now for the darker side. The ubiquity of pain, suffering and death as the means of creation through biological evolution entails, for any concept of God which is morally acceptable and coherent, that if God is immanently present in and to natural processes, in particular those that generate conscious and self-conscious life, then we cannot but infer that God suffers in, with, and under the creative processes of the world with their costly unfolding in time.

Rejection of the notion of the impassibility of God has, in fact, been a feature of the Christian theology of recent decades. There has been an increasing assent to the idea that it is possible to speak consistently of *a God who suffers eminently and yet is still God, and a God who suffers universally and yet is still present uniquely and decisively in the sufferings of Christ.*[41]

As Paul Fiddes points out in his survey and analysis of this change in theological perspective, the factors that have promoted the view that God suffers are new assessments of "the meaning of love [especially, the love of God], the implications of the Cross of Jesus, the problem of [human] suffering, and the structure of the world."[42] It is this last-mentioned—the "structure of the world"—on which the new perspectives of the biological sciences bear by revealing the world processes to be such, as described above, that involvement in them by the immanent Creator has to be regarded as involving suffering on the Creator's part. God, we find ourselves having to conjecture, suffers the "natural" evils of the world along with ourselves because—we can but tentatively suggest at this stage—God purposes *inter alia* to bring about a greater good thereby, namely, the kingdom of free-willing, loving persons in communion with God and with each other.[43]

Because sacrificial, self-limiting, self-giving action on behalf of the good of others is, in human life, the hallmark of love, those who believe in Jesus the Christ as the self-expression of God's own self have come to see his life as their ultimate warrant for asserting that God is essentially "Love," insofar as any one word can accurately refer to God's nature. Jesus' own teaching concerning God as "Abba," Father, and the conditions for entering the "Kingdom of God" pointed to this too, but it was the person of Jesus and what happened to him that finally, and early, established in the Christian community this perception of God as self-offering Love.

On their, and subsequent Christians', understanding Jesus the Christ is the definitive communication from God to humanity of the deep meaning of what God has been effecting in creation—and that is precisely what the Prologue to

John's Gospel says in terms of God the Word/*Logos* active in creation and as now manifest in the person of Jesus the Christ.

As we saw above, it may be inferred, however tentatively, from the character of the natural processes of creation that God has to be seen as suffering in, with, and under these selfsame processes with their costly unfolding in time. But if God was present in and one with Jesus the Christ, then we have to conclude that *God* also suffered in and with him in his passion and death. The God whom Jesus therefore obeyed and expressed in his life and death is indeed a "crucified God,"[44] and the cry of dereliction can be seen as an expression of the anguish also of God in and through creation. If Jesus is indeed the self-expression of God in a human person, then the tragedy of his actual human life can be seen as a drawing back of the curtain to unveil a God suffering in and with the sufferings of created humanity and so, by a natural extension, with those of all creation, since humanity is an evolved part of it. The suffering of God, which we could glimpse only tentatively in the processes of creation, is in Jesus the Christ concentrated into a point of intensity and transparency which reveals it to all who focus on him.

[. . .]

Notes

1   General and theological reflections on biological evolution will appear below in this font, scientific accounts in this font. Some of the phrasing in this paper follows sections of my *Theology for a Scientific Age* [henceforth *TSA*] (London: SCM Press. Minneapolis: Fortress Press, 2nd enlarged ed., 1993), and my *Creation and the World of Science* [henceforth *CWS*] (Oxford: Clarendon Press, 1979).

2   E.g., J. R. Moore, *The Post-Darwinian Controversies: a study of the Protestant struggle to come to terms with Darwin in Great Britain and America* (Cambridge: Cambridge University Press, 1979); J. R. Lucas, "Wilberforce and Huxley: a legendary encounter," *The Historical Journal* 22.2 (1979): 313–30, J. V. Jensen, "Return to the Huxley-Wilberforce Debate," *Brit. J. Hist. Sci.* 21 (1988): 161–79.

3   Arthur Peacocke, "Biological Evolution and Christian Theology—Yesterday and Today," in *Darwinism and Divinity*, ed. John Durant (Oxford: Blackwell, 1985), 101–30.

4   Even the "origin of life," that is the appearance of living matter on the surface of the Earth some four and a half billion years ago, can be subsumed within this seamless web of the operation of processes at least now intelligible to and entirely conformable with the sciences, if inevitably never entirely provable by repeatable experiments—the situation with all the historical natural sciences (cosmology, geology, evolutionary biology). Studies on dissipative systems (the Brussels school) have shown how interlocking systems involving feedback can, entirely in accord with

the second law of thermodynamics, undergo transitions to more organized and more complex forms, provided such systems are open, non-linear and far from equilibrium. All these conditions would have been satisfied by many systems of chemical reactions present on the Earth during its first billion years of existence. Furthermore, with our increasing knowledge of how molecular patterns can be copied in present living systems, it is now possible to make plausible hypotheses concerning how early forms of nucleic acids and/or proteins might have formed self-replicating molecular systems (e.g., the "hypercycle" of the Göttingen school). Such systems can be shown to multiply at the expense of less efficient rival ones (q.v., Peacocke, *The Physical Chemistry of Biological Organization* (Oxford: Clarendon Press, 1983), chap.5). These studies indicate the inevitability of the appearance of more organized self-replicating systems, the properties of atoms and molecules being what they are; but what form of organization would be adopted is not strictly predictable (by us, at least) since it depends on fluctuations (M. Eigen, "The Self-Organization of Matter and the Evolution of Biological Macromolecules," *Naturwissenschaften* 58 (1971): 465–523).

5   This is not pantheism, for it is the action of God that is identified with the creative processes of nature, not God's own self.

6   T. S. Eliot, "The Dry Salvages," *The Four Quartets* (London: Faber & Faber, 1944), II. 210–12, p. 33.

7   Richard Dawkins, *The Blind Watchmaker* (Harlow: Longmans, 1986).

8   Some considerations other than natural selection which, it is claimed, are needed to be taken into account are thought to be:

1. The "evolution of evolvability" (Daniel C. Dennett, *Darwin's Dangerous Idea* (London and New York: Allen Lane, Penguin, 1995), 222 and n. 20, for references.), in particular the constraints and selectivity effected by self-organizational principles which shape the possibilities of elaboration of structures and even direct its course (Stuart A. Kauffman, *The Origins of Order: Self-organization and Selection in Evolution* (Oxford Univ. Press, New York and London, 1993); idem, *At Home in the Universe* (Penguin Books, London, 1995); B. C. Goodwin, *How the Leopard Changed Its Spots: the evolution of complexity* (New York: Scribner's Sons, 1994));

2. The "genetic assimilation" of C. H. Waddington (*The Strategy of the Genes: a discussion of some aspects of theoretical biology* (London: Allen and Unwin, 1957);

3. How an organism might evolve is a consequence of itself, its state at any given moment, historical accidents, as well as its genotype and environment (R. C. Lewontin, "Gene, Organism and Environment," in *Evolution from Molecules to Man*, D. S. Bendall, ed. (Cambridge: Cambridge University Press, 1983), 273–85);

4. The innovative behavior of an individual living creature in a particular environment can be a major factor on its survival and selection and so in evolution (A. Hardy, *The Living Stream* (London: Collins, 1985), 161ff., 189ff.);

5. "Top-down causation" operates in evolution (D. T. Campbell, "Downward Causation in Hierarchically Organized Systems," in *Studies in the Philosophy of Biology: reduction and related problems*, F. J. Ayala and T. Dobzhansky, eds. (London: MacMillan, 1974), 179–86) and does so more by a flow of information between organism and environment and between different levels (q.v., *TSA*, 59) than by any obvious material or energetic causality;

6. The "silent" substitutions in DNA are more frequent than non-silent ones (with an effect on the phenotype); in other words, the majority of molecular evolutionary change is immune to natural selection (M. Kimura, "The Neutral Theory of Evolution," *Sci. Amer.* 241(1979): 98–126);

7. The recent re-introduction of *group* (alongside that of *individual*) selection in a unified theory of natural selection as operating at different levels in a nested hierarchy of units, groups of organisms being regarded as "vehicles" of selection (D. S. Wilson and E. Sober, "Reintroducing group selection to the human behavioral sciences," *Behavioral and Brain Sciences* 17 (1994): 585–654);

8. Long-term changes in the genetic composition of a population resulting from "molecular drive," the process in which mutations spread through a family and through a population as a consequence of a variety of mechanisms of non-reciprocal DNA transfer, thereby inducing the gain or loss of a variant gene in an individual's lifetime, leading to non-Mendelian segregation ratios (G. A. Dover, "Molecular Drive in Multigene Families: how biological novelties arise, spread and are assimilated," *Trends in Genetics* 2 (1986): 159–65).

9. An emphasis on the context of adaptive change (or, in many cases, non-change) in species regarded as existing in interlocking hierarchies of discrete biological entities (genes, populations, species, eco-systems, etc.) in a physical environment (N. Eldredge, *Reinventing Darwin: the great evolutionary debate* (London: Wiedenfeld and Nicolson, 1996).

9   A crane "is a sub-process or feature of a design process that can be demonstrated to permit the local speeding up of the basic, slow process of natural selection, *and* that can be demonstrated to be itself the predictable (or retrospectively explicable) product of the basic process" (Daniel C. Dennett, *Darwin's Dangerous Idea* (London & New York: Allen Lane, Penguin, 1995), 76). Cranes include sex and the Baldwin Effect. Dennett means by a skyhook "a 'mind-first' force or power or process, an exception to the principle that all design, and apparent design, is ultimately the result of mindless, motiveless mechanicity" (ibid.).

10   Jacques Monod, *Chance and Necessity* (London: Collins, 1972).

11   David J. Bartholomew, *God of Chance* (London: SCM Press, 1984).

12   Peacocke, "Chance, Potentiality and God," *The Modern Churchman*, 17 (New Series 1973): 13–23; idem, in *Beyond Chance and Necessity*, ed. J. Lewis (London: Garnstone Press, 1974), 13–25; idem, "Chaos or Cosmos," *New Scientist*, 63 (1974): 386–89; and *CWS*, chap. 3.

13   CWS, 94.

14   R. Winkler and M. Eigen, *Laws of the Game* (New York: Knopf, 1981. London: Allen Lane, 1982).

15   D. J. Bartholomew in his *God of Chance* has urged that God and chance are not only logically compatible, as the foregoing has argued, but that there are "positive reasons for supposing that an element of pure chance would play a constructive role in creating a richer environment than would otherwise be possible" (97). He argues that "chance offers the potential Creator many advantages which it is difficult to envisage being obtained in any other way" (97). Since in many natural processes, often utilized by human beings, chance processes can in fact lead to

determinate ends—for many of the laws of nature are statistical—"there is every reason to suppose that a Creator wishing to achieve certain ends might choose to reach them by introducing random processes whose macro-behavior would have the desired character" (98). Thus the determinate ends to which chance processes could lead might well be "to produce intelligent beings capable of interaction with their Creator" (98). For this it would be necessary, he suggests, to have an environment in which chance provides the stimulus and testing to promote intellectual and spiritual evolution.

16 Cf., *CWS*, 105–6.

17 S. J. Gould, *Wonderful Life: the Burgess shale and the nature of history* (London and New York: Penguin Books, 1989), 35. Gould's principle thesis, on the basis of his interpretation of the Burgess shale, of the role of contingency in evolution as rendering impossible any generalizations about trends in evolution, has recently been strongly contraverted and refuted by Simon Conway-Morris, F.R.S., Professor of Evolutionary Palaeobiology at the University of Cambridge, England, who has spent most of his research life on the contents of the Burgess shale, in *The Crucible of Creation* (Oxford: Oxford University Press, 1998).

18 G. G. Simpson, *The Meaning of Evolution* (New Haven: Bantam Books, Yale Univ. Press, 1971), 236. He instances the kinds of "progress" (prescinding from any normative connotation) as: the tendency for living organisms to expand to fill all available spaces in the livable environments; the successive invasion and development by organisms of new environmental and adaptive spheres; increasing specialization with its corollary of improvement and adaptability; increase in the general energy or maintained level of vital processes; protected reproduction-care of the young; individualization, increasing complexity, and so forth.

19 Karl Popper, *A World of Propensities* (Bristol: Thoemmes, 1990).

20 Ibid., 12.

21 Ibid., 17.

22 There certainly seems to be such a propensity in non-living matter, for in those parts of the universe where the temperature is low enough for molecules to exist in sufficient proximity to interact, there is a tendency for more and more complex molecular systems to come into existence and this process is actually driven, in the case of reactions that involve association of molecules to more complex forms, by the tendency to greater overall randomization, that is, as a manifestation of the Second Law (q.v., Peacocke, *The Physical Chemistry of Biological Organization* (Oxford: Clarendon Press, 1983), section 2.7). Such systems, if open and if they also exhibit feedback properties, can become "dissipative" and undergo sharp changes of regime with the appearance of new patterns in space and time. In other words, even in these non-living systems, there is an increase in complexity in the entities involved in certain kinds of natural process. This appears to be an example of "propensity" in Popper's sense.

23 W. McCoy, "Complexity in Organic Evolution," *J. Theor. Biol.*, 68 (1977): 457. J. Maynard Smith, *Towards a Theoretical Biology, vol. 2, Sketches*, C. H. Waddington, ed.,

(Edinburgh: Edinburgh University Press, 1969), 88–89, has pointed out, "All one can say is that since the first living organisms were presumably very simple, then if any large change in complexity has occurred in any evolutionary lineage, it must have been in the direction of increasing complexity . . . 'Nowhere to go but up' . . . Intuitively one feels that the answer to this is that life soon became differentiated into various forms, living in different ways, and that within such a complex eco-system there would always be some way of life open which called for a more complex phenotype. This would be a self-perpetuating process. With the evolution of new species, further ecological niches would open up, and the complexity of the most complex species would increase."

24   P. T. Saunders and M.-W. Ho, "On the Increase in Complexity in Evolution," J. Theor. Biol., 63 (1976): 375–84. But see also W. McCoy, "Complexity in Organic Evolu-tion" and C. Castrodeza, "Evolution, Complexity and Fitness," J. Theor. Biol., 71 (1978): 469–71, for different views.

25   H. A. Simon, "The architecture of complexity," Proc. Amer. Phil. Soc., 106 (1962): 467–82.

26   Holmes Rolston (Science and Religion: a critical survey, New York: Random House, 1987) has developed this characteristic of biological evolution in what he calls "cruciform naturalism" (289ff). Sentience, he argues, evolves with a capacity to separate the "helps" from the "hurts" of the world: with sentience there appears caring (287). With the appearance of life, organisms can now view events as "pro-" or "anti-life" and values and "dis-values" appear—the world becomes a "theater of meanings" and nature may be variously judged as "hostile," "indifferent," and "hospitable" (244). "The step up that brings more drama brings more suffering" (288). But "pain is an energizing force" so that "where pain fits into evolutionary theory, it must have, on statistical average, high survival value, with this selected for, and with a selecting against counterproductive pain" (288). "Suffering . . . moves us to action" and "all advances come in contexts of problem solving, with a central problem in sentient life the prospect of hurt. In the evolution of caring, the organ-ism is quickened to its needs" (288). "Suffering is a key to the whole, not intrinsic-ally, not as an end in itself, but as a transformative principle, transvalued into its opposite" (288).

27   It is interesting to note that Richard Dawkins, too, in his River Out of Eden (London: Weidenfeld and Nicolson, 1995) includes (151ff) amongst the thresholds that will be crossed naturally in "a general chronology of a life explosion on any planet, anywhere in the universe. . . . thresholds that any planetary replication bomb can be expected to pass," those for high-speed information-processing (no. 5, achieved by possession of a nervous system), consciousness (no. 6, concurrent with brains), and language (no. 7). This list partly corresponds to the "propensities" referred to in the text.

28   Gould, Wonderful Life, 306, citing David M. Raup.

29   Ibid., 49.

30   Ibid., 51 and passim.

31   My basically theological and philosophical objections to the location of divine

action in quantum events—in evolution, and elsewhere in the natural world (including that of the human brain)—may be summarized as follows.

1. This hypothesis assumes that if God does act to alter quantum events (e.g., in the present context, quantum events in DNA that constitute mutations), this would still be a "hands on" intervention by God in the very processes to which God has given existence, even if we never, in principal, could detect this divine action. It would imply that these processes without such intervention were inadequate to effect God's creative intentions if operating in the way God originally made and sustains them in existence.

2. Yet one of the principal reasons, certainly for a scientist and those influenced by the scientific perspective, for adducing from the nature of these processes the existence of a Creator God is their inherent rationality, consistency and creativity in themselves.

3. If one does not assume, with most physicists, that there are "hidden variables," that quantum events are indeed ontologically indeterminate within the restrictions of deterministic equations governing their probability—then God cannot know definitely the precise outcome of any quantum event because God can only know that which it is logically possible to know (and God knows everything in this category—that is what constitutes God's omniscience). Ontological indeterminacy at the quantum level precludes such precise knowledge for God to have. Thus God could not know (logically could not know) the outcome of the interference by God in the quantum events which this hypothesis postulates and could not effect the divine purposes thereby.

4. For the overall probabilistic relationships which govern statistically the ontologically indeterministic quantum events to be obeyed, if God were to alter one such event in a particular way, then many others would also have to be changed so that we, the observers, detected no abrogation of the overall statistics, as the hypothesis assumes. So it is certainly no tidy, neat way to solve the problem and one wonders where the chain of necessary alterations would end.

5. Finally, in any case, the hypothesis is otiose if God is regarded as creating in evolution, as elsewhere, through the very processes, themselves creative, to which God gives existence and which God continuously sustains in existence.

This is why I think there is no need of this hypothesis in this evolutionary context—or indeed in that of any other (e.g., as a way God might affect human brain states and so thoughts).

32 For a fuller exposition of this approach, see TSA, 157–65; and, more particularly and recently, "God's Interaction with the World: The Implications of Deterministic 'Chaos' and of Interconnected and Interdependent Complexity," in Chaos and Complexity, R. J. Russell, N. Murphy, and A. Peacocke, eds. (Vatican City State: Vatican Observatory, Berkeley, Calif.: Center for Theology and the Natural Sciences, 1995), 263–87.

33 H. A. Simon, "The architecture of complexity."

34 The depiction of this process as "nature, red in tooth and claw" (a phrase from Tennyson that actually pre-dates Darwin's proposal of evolution through natural selection) is a caricature, for, as many biologists have pointed out (e.g., G. G. Simpson in The Meaning of Evolution (New Haven: Bantam Books, Yale University Press,

1971 edition), 201), natural selection is not even in a figurative sense the outcome of struggle, as such. Natural selection involves many factors that include better integration with the ecological environment, more efficient utilization of available food, better care of the young, more cooperative social organization—and better capacity for surviving such "struggles" as do occur (remembering that it is in the interest of any predator that their prey survive as a species!).

35   Quoted by C. E. Raven, *Natural Religion and Christian Theology*, 1951 Gifford Lectures, Series 1, *Science and Religion* (Cambridge: Cambridge University Press, 1953), 15.

36   Cf., Dawkins' epithet, "DNA neither knows nor cares. DNA just is. And we dance to its music" (*River out of Eden*, 133).

37   *TSA*, chap. 8, section 1.

38   C. Darwin, *The Origin of Species* (London: Thinkers Library, Watts, 6th ed.), 408. As Charles Darwin himself put it in a famous passage at the end of one edition of this work: "It is interesting to contemplate a tangled bank, clothed with many plants of many kinds, with birds singing on the bushes, with various insects flitting about, and with worms crawling through the damp earth, and to reflect that these elaborately constructed forms, so different from each other, and dependent upon each other in so complex a manner, have all been produced by laws acting around us. . . . There is grandeur in this view of life, with its several powers, having been originally breathed by the creator into a few forms or into one; and that, whilst this planet has gone cycling on according to the fixed law of gravity, from so simple a beginning endless forms most beautiful and most wonderful have been, and are being evolved."

39   *Genesis* 1:31.

40   *CWS*, 108–11.

41   Paul S. Fiddes, *The Creative Suffering of God* (Oxford: Clarendon Press, 1988), 3 (emphasis in the original).

42   Ibid., 45 (see also all of chap. 2).

43   I hint here at my broad acceptance of John Hick's "Irenaean" theodicy in relation to "natural" evil (q.v., "An Irenaean Theodicy," in *Encountering Evil*, ed. Stephen T. Davis (Edinburgh: T. & T. Clark, 1981), 39–52; and his earlier *Evil and the God of Love* (London: MacMillan, 1966), especially chapters 15 and 16); and the position outlined by Brian Hebblethwaite in chapter 5 ("Physical suffering and the nature of the physical world") of his *Evil, Suffering and Religion* (London: Sheldon Press, 1976).

44   The title of Jürgen Moltmann's profound book, *The Crucified God* (London: SCM Press, 1974).

Chapter 20

Jürgen Moltmann

GOD'S KENOSIS IN THE CREATION AND CONSUMMATION OF THE WORLD

... faith in [love's] triumph is neither more nor less than faith in the Creator Himself — faith that He will not cease from His handiwork nor abandon the object of His love.

Love's Endeavour, Love's Expense, p. 63

AS A THEOLOGIAN, I should like to begin this contribution with an account of Christian and Jewish kenotic theology, and shall then go on to ask about its possible relevance for an understanding of God's presence and activity in the cosmos. A theological doctrine of creation is not a religious cosmology that enters the lists in competition with the cosmologies of physics. But it has to be compatible with physical cosmologies.[1] The theological account of experiences of God is different from the scientific account of experiences of nature. But if we bring them into dialogue with each other, two things soon emerge. First, theologians have a particular preference for the 'great scientific narratives', with their unique and unrepeatable histories, because these narratives correspond to their own histories with God. The one narrative is the development of the expanding cosmos since the 'Big Bang'; the other the evolution of life in 'the phylogenetic tree'. Second, theologians have a particular interest in a natural phenomenon for which scientists have no great liking: 'contingency'. We know from the unpredictable fortuities in human life and in our own personal biographies that these can put paid to our plans, for both good and ill. Sociologists such as Jürgen Habermas and Hermann Lübbe therefore actually see the very function of religion as being "the mastery of contingency." So in developing a theology of nature, we ask about God's presence in the history of nature and in the chance events that herald a future which cannot be extrapolated from the past and present of the cosmos. We shall see whether here Christian and Jewish kenotic theology can sharpen our insight.

1 Christian theology of the kenosis of Christ

Christian experience of God springs from perception of the presence of God in Jesus Christ and his history. According to the hymn that Paul quotes in Philippians 2:5–11, Christ's history was understood as a kenosis for the sake of the redemption of God-forsaken men and women:

> Have this mind among yourselves, which is also in Christ Jesus;
> who, though he was in the form of God,
> did not count equality with God a thing to be grasped,
> but *emptied himself*, taking the form of a servant,
> being born like another.
> And being found in human form
> he humbled himself and became obedient unto death,
> even death on the cross. Therefore God has highly exalted him. . . .

The history of Christ which the first part of this hymn describes begins with the 'divine form' of the Son of God in heaven and ends with the 'form of a servant' on the cross at Golgotha. The becoming-human of Christ presupposes his 'self-emptying' of his divine form and results in his 'humbling of himself', his self-humiliation. God's Son becomes human and mortal. He becomes the servant of human beings and dies on the cross. He does all this out of 'obedience' to God the Father. I shall not go here into the many individual exegetical problems,[2] but shall turn directly to the theological ones.

1. *Early Lutheran theology* tried to understand this kenosis of the Son of God in the light of the christological doctrine of Christ's two natures.[3] Christ's kenosis means that in becoming human Christ renounces the attributes of divine majesty, so that he is not almighty, omnipresent, and omniscient, but becomes 'like another human being', which is to say a limited being, who encounters other human beings in a human way. But it was only in respect of his human nature that he 'renounced' (as the Gießen theologians said) these divine attributes, or 'concealed' them (as the seventeenth-century Tübingen theologians explained). Neither group was prepared to talk about a kenosis of the divinity of the eternal Logos. They merely wished to make room for the true and real humanity of Christ's life on earth.

In the nineteenth century the Lutheran 'kenotics' (Sartorius, Liebner, Hofmann, Thomasius, Frank, and Geß) initiated a new approach and, following patristic theology, took as subject of Philippians 2 not the Christ-who-has-become-human, but the Christ-in-his-becoming-human. His kenosis does not relate only to the attributes of majesty inherent in his divine nature; it already appertains to the divine being of the eternal Logos itself. Out of a self-limitation of the divine proceeds, as Thomasius taught, the Son of God-human being. His human form, which is the form of a servant, takes the place of his original divine form. But if nothing divine encounters other human beings in the incarnate Son of God, how could they then recognize him as the Christ of God? The kenotics replied — though admittedly with some degree of embarrassment — by postulating a dichotomy in the divine attributes: the incarnate Son of God 'renounces' the divine attributes of majesty related to the world, but retains the inward attributes that constitute God's essential nature: truth, holiness, love. For the act of kenosis is an act of God's free love for men and women.

To split the attributes of the Godhead in this way, as presupposition for the incarnation and the kenosis of the Son of God, remained so unsatisfactory that the nineteenth-century Lutheran kenotics found no successors. But they had detected a problem, for all that. The attributes of deity related to the world (omnipotence, omnipresence, omniscience, immortality, impassibility, and immutability) derive from Aristotle's general metaphysics. They have little to do with God's attributes according to the history of God to which the Bible testifies. So they cannot, either, be the attributes of the God in whom people believe 'for Christ's sake', and whom they therefore call 'the Father of Jesus Christ'. For that God 'was in Christ', according to Paul (2 Cor. 5:19), 'dwells' in Christ, according to the Gospel of John (14:11), and is 'worshiped' in the Son.

This brings us to the other attempt at understanding Christ's kenosis.

2. *Hans Urs von Balthasar* interprets the kenosis, not in the framework of the christological doctrine of the two natures, but in the context of the doctrine of the Trinity.[4] It is the essential nature of the eternal Son of the eternal Father to be 'obedient' in complete love and self-surrender, just as it is the essential nature of the eternal Father to communicate himself to the Son in complete love. If the incarnate Son becomes 'obedient' to the will of the eternal Father to the point of death on the cross, then what he does on earth is no different from what he does in heaven, and what he does in time is no different from what he does in eternity. So in 'the form of a servant' he is not denying his divine form, nor does he conceal it or renounce it; he reveals it. In his obedience he realizes on earth his eternal relationship to the Father. By virtue of the love for the Father which is intrinsic to his nature, in his obedience to the point of death on the cross he is completely one with the Father. For it is not just that he 'empties' himself 'to' the human being, and in the human being to the being of a servant, and in human mortality to the cruel death on the cross; in these things he 'empties' himself in obedience to the will of his divine Father in heaven. So kenosis is not a self-limitation and not a self-renunciation on God's part; it is

the self-realization of the self-surrender of the Son to the Father in the trinitarian life of God. By virtue of limitless love, the inner life of the Trinity takes its impress from the reciprocal kenosis of the divine persons in relation to one another. The Son by virtue of his self-surrender exists wholly in the Father, the Father wholly in the Son, the Spirit wholly in the Father and the Son. Kenotic self-surrender is God's trinitarian nature, and is therefore the mark of all his works 'outwards' (the creation, reconciliation, and redemption of all things).

The inner-trinitarian kenosis is part of the inner-trinitarian *perichoresis*, in Latin: *circuminsessio*. The theological tradition used this concept to interpret the unity of God the Father and Jesus the Son of God as a unity, without mixing and without separating. The one is in the other, as the Gospel of John says of Jesus: "I am in the Father, and the Father is in me" (14:11). They are not one subject or one substance, but one community by their mutual indwelling in each other. Each person of the Trinity is in ecstasy out of itself in the other. "The Father is totally in the Son and totally in the Spirit. The Son is totally in the Father and totally in the Spirit. The Holy Spirit is totally in the Father, totally in the Son," says the Council of Florence (1438–1445). Seen from the other side, one may say that the divine persons of the Trinity become habitable for each other in their mutual perichoresis, giving each other open life-space for their mutual indwelling. Each trinitarian person is then not only subject of itself but also room for the other. In the perichoresis of the eternal Trinity we find therefore not only three persons but also three "broad rooms." It is not by chance that one of the secret names of God according to the Jewish tradition is MAKOM, "broad place" (see also Job 36:16; Psalm 18:19; 31:9).

This attempt to explain the kenosis of Christ as it is described in Philippians 2 by drawing on trinitarian doctrine goes beyond the interpretations of the nineteenth-century kenotics and is the next logical step. But it completely dispenses with the attributes of God that are related to the world and understood metaphysically, and uses solely the mutual inner-trinitarian relations of the Son to the Father and of the Father to the Son, as seen in the second part of the hymn. This premises that the world of human beings and death does not exist outside God, but that from the very beginning it lies within the mystery of the Trinity: the Father creates the world out of love for the Son — the Son redeems the world from sin and death through his emptying of himself out of love for the Father. If conversely we wanted to see the world outside the triune God, we should have to conjoin these inner-trinitarian relationships with God's relationships to the world; and then either go back, after all, to talking about the metaphysical attributes (omnipotence, immutability, etc.) or, alternatively, reform these world-related divine attributes in a biblical and christological sense. We have the kenotics to thank for at last having made the contradiction plain: the God who is metaphysically described in negative terms cannot suffer and cannot change; the God of the biblical history, in contrast, is 'faithful', but he can also 'repent' — 'be sorry' — be full of passion and mercy. And for that reason he is able to love and to suffer.[5]

We shall come back at the end of this essay to a new formulation of the divine attributes in relation to the world, and I shall offer some suggestions.

2 Jewish theology of God's Shekinah

In the idea of the Shekinah — God's 'indwelling' — we find the Old Testament presupposition for the Christian idea of Christ's kenosis, and its Jewish equivalent.[6]

God's promise, "I will dwell in the midst of the Israelites," is already implicit in the covenant made with the chosen people: "I will be your God and you shall be my people."[7] The eternal, infinite God whom even the heavens cannot contain "comes down" (Exod. 3:8), so as "to dwell" among his powerless little people. Israel's history tells about this indwelling of God in vivid and pictorial terms. God led his people out of slavery in Egypt into the liberty of the promised land, and went ahead of them in "the pillar of cloud by day" and "the pillar of fire" by night. He dwelled in the Ark of the Covenant (the transportable altar of God's wandering people) until David brought the Ark to Mount Zion, where King Solomon then built the Temple for it. In the Holy of Holies of the Temple, the "indwelling" of God among the Israelites was present.

But what happened to the Shekinah when in 587 B.C. the Babylonians destroyed city and Temple? Did God withdraw his earthly indwelling to his eternal presence in heaven? That would have been the end of his covenant, and the death of the people of Israel. Or did his Shekinah go into Babylonian exile with the captured people, remaining "in the midst of the Israelites" even though it was now homeless, humiliated, exiled, and exposed to the persecutions of the powerful nations? This second answer has kept Israel's faith in God alive in destruction and exile down to the present day. Ever since, God's Shekinah has been the comrade on the way and the companion in suffering of the homeless Israelites. The people suffer persecution and exile, and God's indwelling suffers with them. "In all their afflictions he was afflicted" (Isa. 63:9). Out of these Israelite experiences of God's Shekinah in its shared suffering later rabbinic literature conceived the theology of God's self-humiliation.[8] This theology led to the hope that at the end, with the redemption of the people from its suffering, God's Shekinah itself will be redeemed from the suffering it endures with the people, and with them will return to its eternal home.

This brings us to the theological interpretations of Israel's experiences of the Shekinah.

1. In his theology of Israel's prophets, *Abraham Heschel* developed out of Israel's experience of the Shekinah and its Sh'ma prayer to the One God a 'bipolar concept' of that One God. In history, God exists in a twofold presence: in heaven and in his exiled people, unlimited and limited, infinite and finite, free from suffering and death, while at the same time suffering and dying with his people.[9]

2. *Franz Rosenzweig* interpreted Israel's experience of the Shekinah with the help of Hegel's dialectic as a "self-differentiation in God": "God himself cuts himself off from himself, he gives himself away to his people, he suffers with their sufferings, he goes with them into the misery of the foreign land, he wanders with their wanderings."[10] He talked about a "divine suffering" on the part of "the banished God," who makes himself in need of redemption in fellowship with his people. This "redemption of God" is the homecoming of the departed Shekinah to the fullness of the One God. Something of this takes place in every Sh'ma Israel prayer, for in the acknowledgment of the One God, God himself is "united," according to Rosenzweig. God will be finally redeemed and united when the One God becomes the All-One God, and is "all in all," as he says with 1 Corinthians 15:28. Then heaven and earth will become God's dwelling place and all created being will participate in the indwelling livingness and glory. Max Jammer quotes a Jewish midrash that says: "We do not know whether God is the space of his world, or whether his world is his space."[11] The Christian answer is to draw on the idea of perichoresis — that is to say, mutual interpenetration: just as the person "who abides in love abides in God and God in him" (1 John 4:16), so in the consummation God will find space in the finite world in a divine way, and the finite world will find space in God in a 'worldly' way. That is a reciprocal interpenetration, in which the differences are not intermingled but where the distances are gathered up and ended.

3 Is the creation of the world linked with an act of kenosis on God's part?

In the next two sections we shall turn to the creation of the world and the history of creation, asking about the possible interpretation and meaning of the kenosis idea for the presence of God and his future in creation and in the preservation of the world.

In our hymns we find two verses in which the Creator and sustainer of the world is conceived of in "the form of a servant" which Christ assumes. Luther writes:

> Er äußert sich all seiner G'walt,
> wird niedrig und gering,

und nimmt an sich ein's Knecht's Gestalt,
der Schöpfer aller Ding.

And W. H. Vanstone:

Thou art God, no monarch Thou
thron'd in easy state to reign.
Thou art God, whose arms of love
aching, spent, the world sustain.

In his Christmas hymn Luther sees in "the self-emptying Christ" the Creator of the world, while Vanstone sees in the sustainer of the world "the crucified God." With these figures of speech, both writers express the conviction that the creation and sustaining of the world are not simply works of the almighty God, but that in them God gives and communicates himself, and is thus himself present in his works.

a. Is creation an act of *divine self-definition*? If in his freedom God resolves to create a being who is not divine, who can co-exist with his own divine being, then this resolve does not affect the created being only; it touches God's own being too. He determines himself to be the Creator who lets a creation co-exist with himself.[12] Logically speaking, God's self-determination to be the Creator precedes the act of creation. God determines himself before he determines the world. It is therefore correct to see God's self-determination to be the Creator of a non-divine world as already a self-limitation on God's part: (1) out of his infinite possibilities God realizes this particular one, and renounces all others; (2) God's determination to be Creator is linked with the consideration for his creation that allows it space and time and its own movement, so that it is not crushed by the divine reality or totally absorbed by it. By differentiating himself as Creator from a created world, God creates a reality that is not divine but is not Nothing either, and preserves it by distancing himself from it. How can a finite world co-exist with the infinite God? Does it set a limit to the limitless God, or does God limit himself? If this limit or frontier between infinity and finitude is already 'fore-given' to God, then God is not infinite. If God is in his very essence infinite, then any such limit or frontier exists only through his self-limitation. That makes it possible for a finite world to co-exist with God. This self-limitation of God's which is given with the differentiation between Creator and creation is viewed in theology as the first act of grace. For the limitation of his infinity and omnipresence is itself an act of his omnipotence. Only God can limit God.

b. Is creation an act of *divine self-contraction*? Before God went out of himself in order to create a non-divine world, he withdrew himself into himself in order to make room for the world and to concede it a space. That was Isaac

Luria's idea. He called it zimzum. According to the Kabbala, the infinite Holy One, the One whose light primordially filled the whole universe, withdrew his light and concentrated it wholly on his own substance, thereby creating empty space.[13] God withdrew his omnipresence in order to concede space for the presence of the creation. In this way creation comes into being in the space of God's kenosis. In the dispute between Newton, with his idea about absolute space, and Leibniz, with his notion of relative spaces, Henry More introduced into the discussion this Jewish-kabbalistic idea of makom-kadosh, though without perceiving the possibility it offered for solving this dispute about the concept of space.[14] Gershom Scholem took up Luria's zimzum idea, using it to provide new explanatory grounds for the Jewish-Christian concept of the creatio ex nihilo: "Where God withdraws himself from himself to himself, he can call something forth which is not of divine essence or divine being."[15] Speaking metaphorically, when God contracts himself in order creatively to go out of himself, then in his self-contraction he gathers together his creative energies. It may be noted in passing that in interpreting the 'Big Bang' (Urknall), similar metaphors are used scientifically to explain the primal impetus (Urschwung).

c. Is creation an act of divine self-humiliation? Many Christian theologians from Nicholas of Cusa down to Emil Brunner have seen in the fact that God commits himself to this finite and fragile creation a first act of self-humiliation on God's part, an act continued in his descent to his people Israel and reaching its nadir in Christ's self-surrender to death on the cross.[16] "The Lamb slain from the foundation of the world" (Rev. 18:8) is a symbol to show that there was already a cross in the heart of God before the world was created and before Christ was crucified on Golgotha. From the creation, by way of reconciliation, right down to the redemption, God's self-humiliation and self-emptying deepen and unfold. Why? Because the creation proceeds from God's love, and this love respects the particular existence of all things, and the freedom of the human beings who have been created. A love that gives the beloved space, allows them time, and expects and demands of them freedom is the power of lovers who can withdraw in order to allow the beloved to grow and to come. Consequently it is not just self-giving that belongs to creative love; it is self-limitation too; not only affection, but respect for the unique nature of the others as well. If we apply this perception to the Creator's relation to those he has created, what follows is a restriction of God's omnipotence, omnipresence, and omniscience for the sake of conceding room to live to those he has created.

Hans Jonas took up the zimzum idea early on, linking it first with the evolutionary world picture, and later also with experiences of death in Auschwitz.[17] For him 'omnipotence' is a meaningless concept, because almighty power is power without an object, and would therefore be a power-less power. "Power is a relational term," and links a dominating subject with a dominated object. God's creative power therefore includes a "self-renunciation of unlimited power" for the sake of created beings. If God as Creator commits himself to this world, he at the same time delivers himself up to this "world-in-its-becoming." Whatever happens to it, happens to God too. As Creator, God becomes part of the fate of the world. Hans Jonas calls this fate "the odyssey of the universe." God becomes dependent on the world, as the world is dependent on him. They share a common history.

Kierkegaard detected similar lines of thought in Hegel's idea of world history as "God's biography," and maintained in opposition that only almighty power can limit itself, can give itself and withdraw itself, in order to make the recipient independent; so that in the divine act of self-humiliation we also have to respect an act of God's omnipotence. We might put it epigrammatically and say that God never appears mightier than in the act of his self-limitation, and never greater than in the act of his self-humiliation.

What is true of the self-limitation of omnipotence in God's love for those he has created can also be said about the other metaphysical attributes of his divinity: omnipresence, omniscience, inviolability, and self-sufficiency. God does not know everything in advance because he does not will to know everything in advance. He waits for the response of those he has created, and lets their future come. God is not incapable of suffering; he opens himself in his Shekinah for the sufferings of his people, and in the incarnation of the Son for the sufferings of the love which is to redeem the world. In a certain way God thus becomes dependent on the response of his beloved creatures. In Christian theology one would not go so far as to declare God "in need of redemption" together with his people Israel; but nevertheless, God has laid the sanctification of his Name and the doing of his will in the hands of human beings, and thus also, in its way, the coming of his kingdom. It must be viewed as part of God's self-humiliation that God does not desire to be without those he has created and loves, and therefore waits for them to repent and turn back, leaving them time, so that he may come to his kingdom together with them.

4 The preservation and consummation of creation through God's patience and the driving energies of his spirit

If the creation of a world not divine is already linked with a kenotic self-limitation on God's part, how much more can this then be said about its preservation for its consummation! In his relation to the world, God is not almighty in the sense that as *causa prima* he effects everything in everything through the *causae secundae* — good and evil, becoming and passing away, genesis and dissolution. The person who assumes that this is the way in which God "so wondrously reigneth" ends up with the unanswerable theodicy question: If God is almighty, why evil? Either he is omnipotent and effects everything, in which case he is not good; or he is good, but then he cannot be almighty. If we start from God's kenosis, we discover his almighty power in his almighty suffering patience, as Russian Orthodox theology says. It is not God's power that is almighty. What is almighty is his love, about which Paul says: "Love is long-suffering and kind. . . . It bears all things, believes all things, hopes all things, endures all things" (1 Cor. 13:4, 7). In this eulogy of love, Paul heaps up the words invoking the 'all'. Through the power of his patience God sustains this world with its contradictions and conflicts. As we know from human history, patience is the most powerful action because it has time, whereas acts of violence never have time and can therefore win only short-term victories. Patience is superior to violence. God does not sustain and rule the world like an autocrat or a dictator, who permits no freedom; he is more like a suffering servant who bears the world with its guilt and its griefs as Atlas carries the world on his shoulders. (Cf. Exod. 19:4; Num. 11:12; Deut. 1:31; Isa. 66:12; 53:4; Matt. 8:17; Heb. 1:3. God's conservation of the creation is in biblical language again and again expressed by God's carrying of the world. As God's creation, the world doesn't exist per se, but per Deum.) To put it without these metaphors: God acts in the history of nature and human beings through his patient and silent presence, by way of which he gives those he has created space to unfold, time to develop, and power for their own movement. We look in vain for God in the history of nature or in human history if what we are looking for are special divine interventions. Is it not much more that God waits and awaits, that — as process theology rightly says — he 'experiences' the history of the world and human beings, that he is "patient and of great goodness," as Psalm 103:8 puts it? Israel's psalms never tire of praising God's great goodness and patience. It is because of his steadfast goodness that "we are not consumed" (Lam. 3:22 AV) — "not yet cut off," to follow Luther's translation. "Waiting" is never disinterested passivity, but the highest form of interest in the other. Waiting means expecting, expecting means inviting, inviting means attracting, alluring, and enticing. By doing this, the waiting and awaiting one keeps an open space for the other, gives the other time, and creates possibilities of life for the other. This is what the theological tradition called creatio continua and what differentiates the ongoing creation from the creatio originalis in the beginning and from the creatio nova in the end.

But why should God bear and endure the world with its contradictions and conflicts and catastrophes? According to Aristotelian metaphysics, which have been taken over by Christian theology down to the present day, God is the supreme reality (summum ens) and pure act (actus purus). All reality derives from, and is caused by, the highest reality, which is God, and therefore points towards this divine reality. Consequently God must also be the power who is all-efficacious in everything. It was only with Kierkegaard and Heidegger that a new idea began to take shape: "higher than actuality stands *possibility*."[18] And all actuality is nothing other than 'realized possibility'. Possibility can become actuality, but actuality never again becomes possibility.

If we put these two modalities of being together with the two modes of time, future and past, then future is the sphere of possibilities but past the realm of actuality. So the future is 'higher' than the past, because in history the future turns into irreversible past, whereas the past never again becomes future. If we switch over from the metaphysics of reality to a metaphysics of possibility, we can then view divine Being as the supreme possibility, as the source of possibilities, and as the transcendental making-possible of the possible. In the theology of time, what corresponds is the future as the transcendent source of time, as Georg Picht has shown, following Heidegger.[19]

If we apply this to our problem, it means that the God who in patience bears and endures the history of nature and human beings, allows time and gives time, and in so doing makes possible ever-new possibilities, which are either realized or not realized, and can be used for further development but also for annihilation. All systems of matter and life are complex systems with a fixed actuality/past and, in each case, a specifically open scope of future/possibility. Their present is the interface between the two times in which more complex structures of reality can be built up. With them there also grow in each case the scope of possibilities. But there can be negative realizations of possibilities too, through which these open systems destroy themselves.

It is in the gift of future and the stream of new possibilities that we have to perceive God's activity in the history of open systems of matter and life — and it is out of these open systems that the world we know exists. This means, not least, that all open systems point beyond themselves to the sphere of what they can be, and are read theologically as true symbols of that future in which they are in God and God is in them, when they will participate unhindered in God's indwelling fullness of possibility without being destroyed by it, and become that for which God has destined them. The goal of God's kenosis in the creation and preservation of the world is that future which we describe with the symbols of the kingdom of God and the new creation, or 'world without end'.

Notes

1   My attempt at a doctrine of creation that is compatible with the natural sciences may be found in *God in Creation: An Ecological Doctrine of Creation* (Gifford Lectures 1984–85), trans. Margaret Kohl (London, 1985).

2   For the exegetical questions I may point to the excellent study by O. Hofius, *Der Christushymnus Phil 2,6–11. Untersuchungen zur Gestalt und Aussage eines urchristlichen Psalms* (Tübingen, 1976).

3   I should also like to recommend here P. Althaus's article "Kenosis," in RGG[3], III, pp. 1244–46, which is brief but very informative.

4   H. Urs von Balthasar, *Mysterium Paschale* in *Mysterium Salutis*, III, 2 (Einsiedeln, 1964), pp. 133–326. I should also like to draw attention to the fruitfulness of the kenosis idea for Christian-Buddhist dialogue. See J. Cobb, Jr., ed., *The Emptying God: A Buddhist-Jewish-Christian Conversation* (New York, 1990). My dialogue with Masao Abe may also be found in this volume.

5   I have described the transformation of the metaphysically determined attribute of *immutabilitas Dei* into the biblically based faithfulness of God in my book *Theology of Hope*, trans. J. W. Leitch (London, 1967), and the transformation of the metaphysically determined attribute of the *impassibilitas Dei* into the passibility of love in *The Crucified God*, trans. R. A. Wilson and J. Bowden (London, 1974).

6   The standard work is A. M. Goldberg, *Untersuchungen über die Vorstellung von der Schechinah in der frühen rabbinischen Literatur* (Berlin, 1969).

7   B. Janowski, " 'Ich will in eurer Mitte wohnen' Struktur and Genese der exilischen Shekina-Theologie," in *Gottes Gegenwart in Israel. Beiträge zur Theologie des Alten Testaments* (Neukirchen, 1993), pp. 119–47.

8   P. Kuhn, *Gottes Selbsterniedrigung in der Theologie der Rabbinen* (Munich, 1968). God carries Israel with its guilt "like a servant" (p. 84).

9   A. Heschel, *The Prophets* (New York, 1962), ch. 18: "Religion of Sympathy," pp. 307–13.

10   F. Rosenzweig, *Der Stern der Erlösung*, 3rd ed. (Heidelberg, 1954), II, 3, pp. 192–94 (*The Star of Redemption*, trans. W. W. Hallo [London, 1971]). The quotation is translated directly from the German.

11   Quoted by Max Jammer in *Concepts of Space* (Cambridge, Mass., 1954; Oxford, 1955).

12   K. Barth, *Church Dogmatics*, III, 1, section 42 (Edinburgh, 1960), pp. 330ff.

13   G. Scholem, "Schöpfung aus Nichts und Selbstverschränkung Gottes," in *Eranos Jahrbuch* 25 (1956): 87–119.

14   For more detail see J. Moltmann, *God in Creation*, ch. 6: "The Space of Creation," pp. 140–57, esp. 153–57.

15   G. Scholem, "Schöpfung aus Nichts," p. 117; see also his *Major Trends in Jewish Mysticism* (New York, 1954; London, 1955).

16   E. Brunner, *Dogmatics*, vol. 2, trans. O. Wyon (London, 1952), p. 20: "This, however, means that God does not wish to occupy the whole of space Himself, but that He wills to make room for other forms of existence. In so doing He limits Himself. . . . The *kenosis* which reaches its paradoxical climax in the cross of Christ, began with the Creation of the world."

17   H. Jonas, *Zwischen Nichts und Ewigkeit. Zur Lehre vom Menschen* (Göttingen, 1963), pp. 55–62 (with reference to the doctrine of evolution); F. Stern and H. Jonas, *Reflexionen finsterer Zeit* (Tübingen, 1984), pp. 63–86: Der Gottesbegriff nach Auschwitz: "So that the world might be, and might exist for itself, God renounced

his own being; he divested himself of his divinity in order to receive it again from the odyssey of time, laden with the fortuitous harvest of unforeseeable temporal experience, transfigured, or perhaps also distorted by them. . . . Only with creation out of nothing do we have the unity of the divine principle together with its *self-restriction*, which gives *space* for the existence and autonomy of a world" (pp. 68, 83).

18   M. Heidegger, *Being and Time*, trans. J. Macquarrie and E. Robinson (London, 1962), p. 63; cf. also p. 378: "The primary phenomenon of primordial and authentic temporality is the future."

19   G. Picht, "Die Zeit und die Modalitäten," in *Hier und Jetzt: Philosophieren nach Auschwitz und Hiroshima*, vol. 1 (Stuttgart, 1980), pp. 362–74.

Chapter 21

Elizabeth A. Johnson

DOES GOD PLAY DICE? DIVINE PROVIDENCE AND CHANCE

IN EVERY AGE theology interacts directly or indirectly with the view of the world prevalent in its culture, including knowledge of the world gained through observation or experimental means. Although certain encounters of theology with this "scientific" intelligence have been shot through with hostility, the history of theology may also be read to disclose how dialogue with technically learned insights about the world has enkindled new religious wisdom, inspired appealing metaphors, and provided a context for new interpretation of religious tradition.[1] In any event, theology's interaction with science is essential to make religious faith both credible and relevant within a particular generation's view of the world and how it works.

In the last two decades of the 20th century, dialogue between theology and science has entered into a newly flourishing state thanks to the emergence of a somewhat less dogmatic, more hermeneutical temper in each discipline, as well as the desire of certain key players to engage the questions of the other.[2] Significant for Catholic theology was the solid encouragement Pope John Paul II gave to this dialogue in a 1987 message:

> The scientific disciplines are endowing us with an understanding and appreciation of our universe as a whole and of the incredibly rich variety of intricately related processes and structures which constitute its animate and inanimate components. . . . The vitality

and significance of theology for humanity will in a profound way be reflected in its ability to incorporate these findings.[3]

Continuing, the papal message presented an interesting list of possibilities:

> If the cosmologies of the ancient Near Eastern world could be purified and assimilated into the first chapters of Genesis, might contemporary cosmology have something to offer to our reflections upon creation? Does an evolutionary perspective bring any light to bear upon theological anthropology, the meaning of the human person as the *imago Dei*, the problem of Christology—and even upon the development of doctrine itself? What, if any, are the eschatological implications of contemporary cosmology, specially in light of the vast future of our universe? Can theological method fruitfully appropriate insights from scientific methodology and the philosophy of science?[4]

Gently childing theological research and teaching for being less than enthusiastic about pursuing these questions, the pope concluded by urging dialogue that can bring mutual benefit to both parties:

> Science can purify religion from error and superstition; religion can purify science from idolatry and false absolutism. Each can draw the other into a wider world, a world in which both can flourish.[5]

In sum, theological reflection today should endeavor to speak about God's relation not to an ancient nor medieval nor Newtonian world, but to the dynamic, emergent, self-organizing universe that contemporary natural and biological sciences describe.

This is not an easy world to comprehend or to comprise within a religious perspective. One of the most challenging discoveries has to do with the natural occurrence of chance, seemingly more intrinsic to the evolutionary development of the world than ever before thought to be the case. Albert Einstein's famous remark denying that God plays dice with the universe is in fact an expression of his religiously based refusal to accept the uncertainty of events encountered at the heart of quantum reality. Subsequently, however, the indispensable role played by random events operating within a law-like framework has received greater appreciation. Now the theological search is on for language, models, and metaphors that will give expression to faith experience in ways coherent with this fundamental scientific insight.

In this article I will engage the particular question of how God's providential activity can be affirmed in a world where chance plays a more essential role than ever before imagined. The conclusion, that divine providence is compatible with genuine randomness and that this compatibility in turn can shed light on the incomprehensible, gracious mystery of God, will be arrived at in three steps. First I will describe the relevant scientific data essential for understanding the problem; next I will retrieve the Thomistic notion of dual agency; and finally I will explore the interface between the two. In no way does this analysis exhaust the topic nor does my proposal resolve the debate. Rather, it simply traces and attempts to contribute to the issue out of the heritage of the Thomistic tradition.

Science: the interplay of law and chance

By almost any measure, 20th-century science has brought to an end the mechanistic view of the world associated with Newtonian physics and has replaced it with a dynamic, open-ended view of the world in which some events are in principle unpredictable, although in retrospect they may make sense. This holds true for events at very small and very large magnitudes of space as well as for events through the long reaches of time.

At the infinitesimal level of the atom and its subatomic particles, quantum mechanics uncovers a realm where time, space, and matter itself behave according to laws whose very functioning have uncertainty built into them. Statistical probability lends a measure of order to this realm, but precise subatomic events do not seem to occur according to any discernible regularity. For example, while it can be predicted that a certain mass of radioactive uranium will decompose within a given time, there is no way to predict which atom will decompose next, or why.[6] Furthermore, as the Heisenberg uncertainty principle asserts, a human observer cannot simultaneously plot both the position and velocity of a subatomic particle, for by charting one we disturb the other. Does this human inability to nail down and predict subatomic events point to the poor state of our equipment or rather to an ontological indeterminacy in reality itself? Many philosophers of science argue for the latter. Judging from the realm of the infinitesimally small, the fundamental building blocks of the world are neither mechanically preprogrammed nor utterly chaotic, but spontaneous within an orderly system.

At the macro level of nonlinear, dynamical systems such as weather, chaos theory explores how very slight changes in initial conditions are ramified to produce massive effects.[7] A butterfly fluttering its wings in Beijing may set up an air current that amplifies upward through different levels of intensity to produce a major storm in New York a week later. While the ramifications of change through chaotic, nonlinear systems are regular enough to be traced in mathematical equations, the number of initial conditions that effect each system is so immense and their confluence so unique that human observation will never get a total handle on them. We will never have a completely accurate weather forecast earlier than a week ahead, and this is due not to the limitation of our instruments but to the nature of the weather system itself. Being intrinsically unpredictable in an epistemological sense, dynamical systems thus represent a form of "structured randomness" in the world.[8] Does this indicate an ontological indeterminacy in the dynamical systems themselves? Many philosophers of science think so.

The immensely long evolution of the cosmos from the Big Bang to the present and still evolving clusters of galaxies, as well as the evolution of matter on earth from nonorganic to living states and from simple life to human consciousness is another story fraught with the subtle interplay between chance and law.[9] To stay with the example of life on earth, mutations in genes caused by the sun's ultraviolet rays or exposure to chemicals issue in variations on life forms. Natural selection then rewards the ones that adapt best to their environment and reproduce. On and on goes this process of a hundred thousand variables, dead ends, and breakthroughs. Roll back the clock to before the appearance of life on earth and then let it roll again. Would humanity appear as we are now? Scientists are virtually unanimous in saying "no," so multiple and diverse are the factors that combined to produce our species. Intelligent life would probably develop, for the matter of the universe has the potential to evolve into complex structures (brains) from which consciousness emerges. But it would be a group with a different genetic history, even a different physical appearance.

The emergence of human mind sheds light on a wondrous ability of matter, namely its capacity so to organize itself as to bring forth the truly new from within itself. Beginning with the featureless state right after the Big Bang, a rich diversity of physical systems and forms have emerged in a long, complex sequence of self-ordering processes even to the point where mind emerges from matter—and seeks to understand the process by which it came to be! This evolutionary interpretation of mind as emergent within the process of matter's self-organization leads to a holistic, nondualistic idea of the human person. Not a composite of the isolatable elements of material body and spiritual but somehow substantial mind, the human being is a single entity whose physical structure enables and supports the emergence of mind. As Paul Davies graphically puts it, mind is not some sort of extra ingredient glued onto brains at some stage of evolution; it did not require any factors external to the world itself.[10] Rather, consciousness is a power that emerges gradually in and through the increasing complexity of those intricately ramified and interlaced structures we call brains. We are the universe become conscious of itself. Material, physical reality is much richer in its possibilities than we are accustomed to think.

Taken together, scientific understandings of the indeterminism of physical systems at the quantum level, the unpredictability of chaotic systems at the macro level, and the random emergence of new forms through the evolutionary process itself undermine the idea that there is a detailed blueprint or unfolding plan according to which the world was designed and now operates. Rather, the stuff of the world has an innate creativity in virtue of which the new continuously emerges through the interplay of chance and law: "there is no detailed blueprint, only a set of laws with an inbuilt facility for making interesting things happen."[11] The genuinely random intersects with deep-rooted regularities, issuing in a new situation which, when regularized, becomes in turn the basis for a new play of chance. The world develops, then, neither according to anarchy nor according to teleology, but purposively if unpredictably. Physical phenomena are constrained in an orderly way, but themselves give rise to novelty due to the intrinsic indeterminism and openness of physical processes.

In this construal of nature's constitutive dynamic, it becomes clear that the classical idea of the laws of nature also requires revision. These are now understood to be descriptive rather than prescriptive, that is, abstract descriptions read off from regularities in the universe that approximate what we observe, rather than rules that preexist platonically apart from the universe, operating to dictate or enforce behavior.[12] The laws of nature approximate the relationships in nature but do not comprehend them to their depths, which remain forever veiled. Nature itself is a mystery.

Furthermore, the laws of nature require the workings of chance if matter is to explore its full range of possibilities and emerge toward richness and complexity. Without chance, the potentialities of this universe would go unactualized. The movement of particles at the subatomic level, the initial conditions of nonlinear dynamic systems, the mutation of genes in evolutionary history, all are necessary for the universe's becoming, though none can be predicted or controlled. It seems that the full gamut of the potentialities of matter can be explored only through the agency of rapid and frequent randomization. This role of chance is what one would expect if the universe were so constituted as to be able to explore all the potential forms of the organization of matter, both living and nonliving, which it contains.

It can even be seen in retrospect that the emergence of human nature as we know it requires such an infrastructure. There is a deep compatibility between the autonomous ways physical, chemical, and biological systems operate though the interplay of law and chance on the one hand, and human consciousness and freedom on the other. These particular human qualities (consciousness and freedom) are intensely concentrated states of tendencies (purposiveness and chance) found throughout the universe in natural forms. The radical freedom of natural systems to explore and discover themselves is the condition for the possibility of the emergence of free and conscious human beings as part of the universe.

The capacity to form a world is there from the beginning in the fundamental constitution of matter. Chance's role is to enable matter to explore these potentialities. No chance, no evolution of the universe. If it were not such an impossible oxymoron, chance might even be called a law of nature itself. Chance, consequently, is not an alternative to law, but the very means whereby law is creative. The two are strongly interrelated and the universe evolves through their interplay.

On balance, the general character of the world as we know it from contemporary science calls for a more subtle notion of overall design, one that incorporates the occurrence of the genuinely novel and unpredictable in the context of laws that underdetermine what occurs. Great possibilities are left open.

God's action in the world: theological options

This contemporary view of the world, which enjoys wide allegiance in the scientific community and is not contingent on particular, disputed points, provides a uniquely new context in which to understand God's creative and providential action. The traditional model of God as king and ruler, gifted with attributes of omniscience and omnipotence, who in creating and sustaining the world preprograms its development, who establishes its laws of nature but sets them aside to intervene miraculously when the occasion warrants—this monarchical model is less and less seriously imaginable. The potentiality of matter, the complexity of self-organizing systems, the potent unpredictability of evolution, the operation of chance within underdetermined laws, the presence of chaos and novelty, the interdependent processes of the world in becoming, all are putting pressure on the classical idea of God and divine action in the world.

Engaging this new question, recent theology has itself self-organized into a range of options. In his 1989–90 Gifford Lectures, Ian Barbour delineates eight different schools of thought on the issue, each of which has its strengths and shortcomings. Classical theology understands God to be omnipotent, omniscient, unchanging sovereign who relates to the world as ruler to kingdom. The Deist option sees God as designer of a law-abiding world to which God relates as clockmaker to clock. Neo-Thomist theology predicates God as primary cause working through secondary causes, on the analogy of an artisan with tools. The kenotic position perceives God as voluntarily self-limiting divine power in order to participate vulnerably in the life of the world, the way a parent enables a child to grow. Since existentialist theology sees God acting only in personal life, it has no model of God's relation to the world. Linguistic theology discerns God as the agent whose intention is carried out in the overall development of the cosmos, the whole then being interpreted as the one, all-encompassing action of God. The option for the theme of embodiment sees the world as God's body to which God relates intimately as a person does to one's own body. Process theology sees God as a creative participant in the cosmic community, with a divine leadership role to play.[13]

In addition to these positions described by Barbour, there is also another, not uncommon view of God's relation to the world that springs from a more closely literal interpretation of the Bible, understanding God to act directly in the events of the world as an individual, personal player. In dialogue with contemporary science this position argues ingeniously that, thanks to the indeterminism of reality at the quantum level, God's direct intervention in any instance does not transgress the laws of nature. Rather, the natural system itself is "gappy" and open to outside influence without being violated.[14] Thus God can answer prayer, arranging, for example, that the sun shines on the church picnic as a result of God's setting certain initial conditions in the weather pattern a week ahead, and can do so without violating the laws of nature. The difficulty with this position, however, is that it confuses a gap, something missing in the ontological structure of natural systems, with indeterminacy, the openness of natural systems to a variety of outcomes. This openness of matter, however, is an intrinsic part of the working of nature and necessary for its creative development. In principle there are no gaps in the universe, which is complete on its own level.

Evaluating the current state of discussion in 1991, Owen Thomas, editor of a major volume on divine action, argues that while each position contributes some insight, only neo-Thomism and process theology are genuinely adequate as they alone give a philosophically satisfying and coherent account of how both divine and creaturely agents are fully active in one unified event.[15] How, in either case, can we conceive of the play of chance in the providential guidance of the world? Process theology would appear to have the advantage in this question with its understanding of how God continuously lures the world to its goal. In this ongoing process, God prehends every new event into the divine consequent nature and gives new initial aims to every ongoing experience on the basis of what has already transpired. Since God and the world are in process together, not only does chance not threaten divine control over the universe, as it does in the classical model, but chance positively enriches divine experience. At the same time it provides opportunity for God's ongoing providential guidance in the giving of new initial aims to actual occasions impacted by chance.

Neo-Thomism, with its roots in a medieval and thus scientifically static view of the world, would seem less able to account for the occurrence of genuinely random events. Assessing its strengths and weaknesses, Barbour notes as a problem its difficulty in moving away from divine determinism to allow for the genuinely random to occur.[16] My own wager at this point, however, is that Aquinas's own thought is not all that closed to the possibility that chance may factor into divine creative and providential action. In fact, it seems to me that Aquinas's insight into how God acts in the world fairly resonates with potential to account for the play of chance.

Aquinas and the integrity of created systems

At the heart of Aquinas's vision of the nature of created reality is the evocative idea of participation. In creating the world, God, whose essence is the very livingness of Being (*esse*), gives a share in that being to what is other than Godself:

> Whatever is of a certain kind through its essence is the proper cause of what is of such a kind by participation. Thus, fire is the cause of all things that are afire. Now, God alone is actual being through divine essence itself, while other beings are actual beings through participation.[17]

As to ignite is the proper effect of fire, so too is the sharing of being the proper effect of the Mystery of Being. Hence, all that exists participates in its own way in divine being through the very gift of creaturely existence. It is not as if God and creatures stood as uncreated and created instantiations of "being" which is held in common by both (a frequent misunderstanding). Rather, the mystery of God is the livingness of Being who freely shares being while creatures participate. Nor is the gift of being given only once in the instant when a creature begins to exist, but continuously in a ceaseless act of divine creation. To cite another fiery analogy, every creature stands in relation to God as the air to the light of the sun. For as the sun is light-giving by its very nature, while the air is illuminated only so long as the sun shines, so also God alone simply exists (divine essence is *esse*) while every creature exists insofar as it participates in being (creaturely essence is not *esse*).[18]

This notion of participation affects the understanding of both God and the world. Continuously creating and sustaining, the life-giving Spirit of God is in all things not as part of their essence but as the innermost source of their being, power, and action. There is, in other words, a constitutive presence of God at the heart of things. Conversely, in its own created being and doing, the world continuously participates in the livingness of the One who is sheer, exuberant aliveness. The universe, in other words, is a sacrament. Every excellence it exhibits is a participation in that quality which supereminently exists in the incomprehensible mystery of God. Take the key example of goodness. Since "it befits divine goodness that other things should be partakers therein,"[19] every created good is a good by participation in the One who is good by essence. It follows that "in the whole sphere of creation there is no good that is not a good participatively."[20] In having their own good, creatures share in a way coherent with their own finite reality in divine goodness which is infinite. Indeed for Aquinas, this is the basis for any speech about the transcendent mystery of God at all, for in knowing the excellence of the world we may speak analogically about the One in whose being it shares.

One of the strengths of Aquinas's vision is the autonomy he grants to created existence through its participation in divine being. He is so convinced of the transcendent mystery of God (*esse ipsum subsistens*) and so clear about the sui generis way God continuously creates the world into being that he sees no threat to divinity in allowing creatures the fullest measure of agency according to their own nature. In fact, it is a measure of the creative power of God to raise up creatures who participate in divine being to such a degree that they are also creative and sustaining in their own right. A view to the contrary would diminish not only creatures but also their Creator: "to detract from the perfection of creatures is to detract from the perfection of divine power."[21] This is a genuinely noncompetitive view of God and the world. According to its dynamism, nearness to God and genuine creaturely autonomy grow in direct rather than inverse proportion. That is, God is not glorified by the diminishment of the creature but by the creature's flourishing in the fullness of its powers. The nature of created participation in divine being is such that it grants creatures their own integrity, without reserve.[22]

This participatory relationship has strong implications for the question of agency. The power of creaturely forces and agents to act and cause change in the world is a created participation in the uncreated power of the One who is pure act. Conversely, God's generous goodness and wisdom are seen especially in the creation of a world with its own innate agency. As is the case with created things' participation in divine being and goodness, so too with agency. God's action is not part of the creature's essential action, which has its own creaturely integrity. Rather, God's act giving creatures their very nature is what makes creaturely act possible at all in its own created autonomy. Technically, God is primary cause of the world, the unfathomable Source of being who continuously creates and sustains it, while creatures are secondary causes, moved movers who receive from God their form and power to act with independence.[23]

These two causes are not two species of the same genus, not two different types of causes united by the commonality of causing. They operate on completely different levels (itself an inadequate analogy), one being the cause of all causes and the other participating in this power. In this system of thought it is incoherent to think of God as working in the world apart from secondary causes, or beside them, or in addition to them, or even in competition with them. God's act does not supply something that is missing from a creaturely act or rob it of its power so that it is only a sham cause. Rather, the mystery of God acts by divine essence, power, and presence in and through the acts of finite agents which have genuine causal efficacy in their own right. It is not the case that divine and finite agents are complementary, each contributing distinct elements to the one outcome. Instead, God acts wholly through and in the finite agents that also act wholly in the event. As a result, the one effect issues from both primary and secondary causes simultaneously, with each cause, however, standing in a fundamentally different relationship to the effect. God makes the world, in other words, in the process of things acting as themselves.

Working in this tradition, Karl Rahner argues that even in the creation of the human soul divine causality does not insert itself into the finite causal series but, through the power given to matter to evolve toward spirit, enables human parents to transcend themselves in the creation of a genuinely other person.[24] Rahner among others also appeals to the doctrine of the Incarnation, wherein the divine and human are united while remaining distinct, and to the doctrine of grace, wherein the Spirit brings wholeness to human beings without violating their freedom or responsibility, as paradigms for the God-world relationship. It seems to me that it is so easy to forget this, slipping God into the web of interactions as though the divine were simply a bigger and better secondary cause. But the distinction between primary and secondary causality enables thought to hold firm to the mystery of the Godness of God and the integrity of creatures, seeing both acting in a unique *concursus*.

In Aquinas's discussion of divine governance of the world, this idea of double agency with respect to efficient causality is correlated with final causality to provide the grid for his understanding of providence. It would seem, he objects with a curiously modern ring, that the universe does not need to be governed by God, for the processes of the world seem to accomplish their purpose on their own and without any interference. However, he replies, this very self-direction is itself an imprint (*impressio*) from God, for in giving creatures their own being God gives them a natural inclination whereby through their own natural actions they tend toward the good. This dynamic tendency is genuinely part of their own nature but it also expresses God's purposes. While endowing creatures with their intrinsic nature and ways of acting, God leaves them free to follow the strivings of their natural inclination which aims them toward the good. Since all good is a participation in divine goodness, we can affirm that the universe as a whole tends toward the ultimate good which is God. While in scholastic categories this is summed up in the notion that God is immanent in the universe as final cause, Aquinas also finds this view resonating in the biblical depiction of Sophia or Holy Wisdom, who reaches from one end of the world to the other, ordering all things sweetly and mightily (Wisdom 8:1).[25]

Let us draw all of these threads together to see how they might deliver an interpretive view of how God acts providentially in the world. As Aquinas explains, the way God is governor of things matches the way God is their cause. As God is primary cause of the world as a whole and in every detail, endowing all created beings with their own participation in divine being (enabling them to exist), in divine agency (empowering them to act), and in divine goodness (drawing them toward their goal), so too God graciously guides the world toward its end in and through the natural workings of the processes found in creation as a whole. Immanent in these processes, divine providential purposes come to fruition by means of purposes inherent in creatures themselves.

Why is this fitting? Aquinas argues in a particularly insightful reply that those forms of governing are best that communicate a higher perfection to the governed. Now there is more excellence in a thing's being a cause in relation to others than in its not being a cause. Consequently, God governs in such a way as to empower creatures to be causes toward others. Indeed, "If God were to govern alone, the capacity to be causes would be missing from creatures,"[26] to the detriment of their flourishing and their Creator's glory. Looked at another way, if God did everything directly so that created causes did not really affect anything, this would be a less powerful God. For it shows more power to give others a causative capability than to do everything oneself.[27] Thus God is everywhere present and active, continuously interacting with the world to implement divine purpose while granting creatures and created systems a full measure of being and efficacy. This is a both/and sensibility that guarantees the integrity of the created causal nexus while affirming the gracious and intentional immanence of the transcendent God active within worldly purposiveness.

Divine purpose is accomplished in a *concursus* or flowing together of divine and creaturely act in which the latter mediates the former. This means that the world necessarily hides divine providential action from us. God's act is not a discrete object that can be isolated and known as a finite constituent of the world, for its very nature is transcendent mystery while its mode of operation transpires immanently in and through created causes. At the same time, faith affirms that the world, far from being merely a stage for divine action, is itself a sacrament of God's providential action, which is sweet and strong within every cause so that everything may truly contribute to the realization of the goal.

Providence and chance

Bringing contemporary science's view of the creative role of chance within law-like structure into dialogue with Aquinas's understanding of the God-world relation yields interesting results. The latter's conviction of the integrity of natural causes, while formulated within a largely static worldview, accommodates evolutionary science with almost surprising ease. For the basic principle remains the same: God's providential guidance is accomplished in and through the free working of secondary causes. Indeed, for Aquinas the understanding that God's providential activity is exercised in and through secondary causes includes rather than excludes chance, contingency, and freedom of choice: "It is not the function of divine providence to impose necessity on things ruled by it."[28] Rather, random occurrences themselves are secondary causes with their own integrity. Science may describe these secondary causes in different ways today, but they still function theologically as the means by which God fulfills divine purpose.

As we have seen, the process of creation is described by the natural sciences as one in which new qualities and modes of existence continuously emerge out of simpler forms of matter by the operation of natural laws. These laws of nature are ingenious and felicitous in that they enable matter and energy to self-organize in unexpectedly remarkable ways from clouds of dust and gas to galaxies and solar systems, and from nonorganic matter to life to mind. Multilayered and underdetermined, these laws reflect the universe's potential to create richness and complexity spontaneously, from within, in a process whose inherent openness precludes detailed fixing in advance. As secondary causes, they realize God's purposes. In the words of astrophysicist and theologian William Stoeger, reflective of the Neo-Thomistic consensus, "God is always acting through the deterministic and indeterministic interrelationships and regularities of physical reality which our models and laws imperfectly describe."[29]

Today's science has discovered that chance is an essential element in the continuous working out of these laws of nature. "In the beginning" the Creator endows the material of this world with one set of potentialities rather than another. These are then unveiled by chance exploring their gamut in an inevitable yet indeterminate evolutionary process. Indeed, in retrospect, this seems to be the only way in which all of matter's potentialities might eventually, given enough time and space, be actualized. Consequently, chance is not an alternative to law, but the very means whereby law is creative. The two are strongly interrelated and the universe evolves through their interplay. If this is the kind of universe created by the Holy Mystery who is God, then faith can affirm that God works not only through the deep regularities of the laws of nature but also through chance occurrence which has its own, genuinely random integrity. God uses chance, so to speak, to ensure variety, resilience, novelty, and freedom in the universe, right up to humanity itself. Absolute Holy Mystery dwells within, encompasses, empowers the evolutionary process, making the world through the process of things being themselves, thus making the world through chance and its genuinely irregular character. If God works through chance, then the natural creativity of chance itself can be thought of as a mode of divine creativity in which it participates. And the gracious mystery of God can be glimpsed as the Source not only of deep regularities in the universe, but also of novelty. The future remains genuinely open: God does not act like a bigger and better secondary cause to determine chance atomic events or initial conditions of chaotic systems. Randomness is real, for God respects the structure of creation while at the same time weaving events into providential patterns toward the realization of the whole. Divine sovereignty and creaturely freedom, of which chance is one instance, do not compete.

Risk-taking God

How does this interpretation of providence working through chance in turn influence classical understanding of divine attributes? With this question we reach a frontier where scientific insight in dialogue with Christian faith is providing the occasion for new forays into the doctrine of God. In these explorations theology today seems to be making bolder use of its own particular wisdom of Christology and pneumatology than did early modern theologians caught on the cusp of scientific atheism's first attacks.[30] The appeal today is to God's gracious action expressed in Incarnation and the gift of grace as the basic paradigm of the God-world relationship.

The creating God is also the redeeming God whose self-emptying Incarnation into the vagaries of history reveals the depths of divine Love, and is also the sanctifying God whose self-gift in grace brings wholeness to the brokenness of sinful hearts and situations without violating human freedom. Could it not be the case that, rather than being uncharacteristic of the mystery of God, divine kenosis revealed in the human history of salvation is what is most typical of God's ways, and therefore also distinguishes God's working in the natural world? Could it not be that God's being edged out of the world and onto the cross, in Bonhoeffer's profound intuition, also refers to the cost of divine vulnerability in creation?[31] Could it not be that since the human world is on a continuum with the micro world, only mediated by more complex biological matter, the best way to understand God's action in the indeterminacy of the natural world is by analogy with how divine initiative relates to human freedom?

If so, and an eminently coherent case can be made for this position, then divine perfection is ultimately a perfection of relationality and love rather than of self-sufficiency and control. Consequently, omnipotence unfailingly manifests itself not as coercive "power over" but as sovereign love which empowers. Exercising this power, God's providential guidance eschews pre-ordaining or imposing exact sequences of events but rather makes itself known as the patient, subtle presence of a gracious Creator who achieves divine purpose through the free play of created processes. Indeed, it is quite likely that Love is able to work only in such a way, out of respect for the beloved. It should be noted that the basic difference between process theology and Thomism regarding God's self-limitation of omnipotence is that for process thought this is a metaphysical necessity while for Thomism it is a free and voluntary act of love.

Divine governance involves God in waiting upon the world, so to speak, patiently acting through its natural processes including unpredictable, uncontrollable random events to bring about the emergence of the new while consistently urging the whole toward fullness of life. Even more can be said. With the development of nerves and brains, suffering in both the natural and human world becomes a terrifying consequence of the free play of randomness. Indwelling the world with the power of providential love, the gracious mystery of God is involved in suffering with the beloved creation as new life is created through death. Not the monarch but the lover becomes the paradigm.[32]

In the course of thinking upon these things, theologians are finding it helpful to imagine new metaphors to capture the nuances of God's providential relation to the workings of chance. As might be suspected, these images are drawn more from artistic creativity and the relationship of love than from the classical model of an artisan working with inert tools. No one of these metaphors, of course, is adequate but each sheds a little light. They also point quite directly to the importance of responsible human action in cooperation with God's providential purpose. Among them: God is like a master theatrical improvisor in live performance, amplifying and embroidering each theme as it presents itself; like a choreographer composing steps in tandem with the creative insights of the whole dance troupe; like a composer of a fugue, starting with a simple line of melody and weaving a complex structure by endlessly folding it back upon itself; like a jazz player, inspired by the spirit of the audience and the night to improvise riffs upon a basic melody; like a designer who sets the rules of a game that includes wild cards and then lets it play. In every instance the image is arrived at through the logic set out in W. Norris Clarke's evocative passage:

> [W]hat must the "personality" or "character" be like of a Creator in whose image this astounding universe of ours is made, with its prodigal abundance of energy, its mind-boggling complexity, yet simplicity, its fecundity of creative spontaneity, its ever surprising fluid mixture of law and chance, etc. Must not the "personality" of such a Creator be one charged not only with unfathomable power and energy, but also with dazzling imaginative creativity? Such a creator must be a kind of daring Cosmic Gambler who loves to work with both law and chance, a synthesis of apparent opposites—of power and gentleness, a lover of both law and order and of challenge and spontaneity.[33]

Key biblical images for Creator Spirit, namely, dynamic wind, fire, and water, also express the moving, playing, unpredictable qualities of the God to whom chance is not a rival.

In dialogue with contemporary science, theology understands that the Creator God is neither a maker of clocks nor an instigator of anarchy, but the one ceaselessly at work bringing overall direction and order to the free play of the undetermined realms of matter and spirit, "an Improviser of unsurpassed ingenuity."[34] In this evolutionary world, the essential role of genuine randomness does not contradict God's providential care but somehow illumines it. To use Christopher Mooney's lovely phrasing,

> Wave packets propagate and collapse, sparrows fall to the ground, humans freely decide for good or for ill; yet hairs of the head nevertheless get numbered, elusive quantum particles eventually statistically stabilize, and "where sin increased, grace abounded all the more."[35]

The world develops in an economy of divine superabundance, gifted with its own freedoms in and through which God's gracious purpose is accomplished. "The Love that moves the sun and the other stars,"[36] it now appears, is a self-emptying, self-offering, delighting, exploring, suffering, sovereign Love, transcendent wellspring of all possibilities who acts immanently through the matrix of the freely evolving universe.

Notes

1   For historical background of the theology-science exchange, see Ernan McMullin, "Natural Science and Belief in a Creator: Historical Notes," in Robert Russell, William Stoeger, and George Coyne, ed., *Physics, Philosophy, and Theology: A Common Quest for Understanding* (Vatican City: Vatican Observatory, 1988) 49–79; and Michael Buckley, "The Newtonian Settlement and the Origins of Aetheism," ibid. 81–102.

2   See results of dialogue in Ted Peters, ed., *Cosmos as Creation: Theology and Science in Consonance* (Nashville: Abingdon, 1989); David Burrell, ed., *God and Creation: An Ecumenical Symposium* (Notre Dame: University of Notre Dame, 1990); and Robert Russell, Nancey Murphy, and C. J. Isham, ed., *Quantum Cosmology and the Laws of Nature: Scientific Perspectives on Divine Action* (Vatican City: Vatican Observatory; and Berkeley: Center for Theology and the Natural Sciences, 1993). Ian Barbour's Gifford Lectures explore the theology-science encounter in illuminating detail: *Religion in an Age of Science*, 2 vols. (San Francisco: Harper and Row, 1990–91). Individuals who have scholarly credentials in both science and theology and whose work helpfully reflects this dialogue include John Polkinghorne (see, e.g., his *One World: The Interaction of Science and Theology* [Princeton: Princeton University, 1986]) and Arthur Peacocke (see, e.g., his *Theology for a Scientific Age: Being and Becoming—Natural, Divine and Human* [Minneapolis: Fortress, 1993]).

3   Papal message reprinted in Robert Russell et al., ed., *John Paul II on Science and Religion: Reflections on the New View from Rome* (Vatican City: Vatican Observatory, 1990) M 1–M 14, at M 5.

4   Ibid. M 11.

5   Ibid. M 13.

6   For general background written for the non-specialist, see John Polkinghorne, *The Quantum World* (Princeton: Princeton University, 1984); and C. J. Isham, "Quantum Theories of the Creation of the Universe," in Russell et al., ed., *Quantum Cosmology* 49–89.

7   For a general introduction, see James Gleick, *Chaos: Making a New Science* (New York: Penguin, 1987); a key refutation of the idea that chaos amounts to blind, purposeless chance is the volume of Ilya Prigogine and Isabelle Stengers, *Order Out of Chaos* (New York: Bantam, 1984).

8   Term used by John Polkinghorne, "The Laws of Nature and the Laws of Physics," in Russell et al., ed., *Quantum Cosmology* 437–48.

9   Helpful scientific introductions include Carl Sagan, *Cosmos* (New York: Ballantine, 1980); Stephen Jay Gould, *Wonderful Life: The Burgess Shale and the Nature of History* (New York: Norton, 1989); and Edmund O. Wilson, *The Diveristy of Life* (New York: Norton, 1992). For religious reflections on this data, see Robert Jastrow, *God and the Astronomers* (New York: Norton, 1978); Paul Davies, *God and the New Physics* (New York: Simon and Schuster, 1983); and Arthur Peacocke, *God and the New Biology* (San Francisco: Harper and Row, 1986).

10   Paul Davies, "The Intelligibility of Nature," in Russell et al., ed., *Quantum Cosmology*

145–61, at 152; see also George Ellis, "The Theology of the Anthropic Principle," ibid. 367–405.

11 Paul Davies, *The Cosmic Blueprint* (New York: Simon & Schuster, 1988) 202.

12 See William Stoeger, "Contemporary Physics and the Ontological Status of the Laws of Nature," in Russell et al., ed., *Quantum Cosmology* 209–34.

13 Ian Barbour, *Religion in an Age of Science* 1:243–70, with chart on 244. See also the organizing schema by Robert Russell, "Introduction," in Russell et al., ed., *Quantum Cosmology* 4–10.

14 Representative of this group is William Alston, "Divine Action, Human Freedom, and the Laws of Nature," in Russell et al., ed., *Quantum Cosmology* 185–207.

15 Owen Thomas, "Recent Thoughts on Divine Agency," in *Divine Action*, ed. Brian Hebblethwaite and Edward Henderson (Edinburgh: T. & T. Clark, 1991) 35–50. See Thomas's own edited volume, *God's Activity in the World: The Contemporary Problem* (Chico, Calif.: Scholars, 1983).

16 Ian Barbour, *Religion in an Age of Science* 1:249–50.

17 Thomas Aquinas, *Summa contra gentiles* 3, chap. 66.7 (hereafter cited as SCG; the edition used is translated by Vernon Bourke [Garden City, N.Y.: Doubleday, 1956]). Aquinas's extended discussion of divine governance can be found in SCG 3, especially chaps. 64–77, and his *Summa theologiae* 1, qq. 103–109 (hereafter cited as ST; the edition used is translated by the English Dominicans [New York: Benziger, 1956]).

18 ST 1, q. 104, a. 1.

19 ST 1, q. 19, a. 2.

20 ST 1, q. 103, a. 2.

21 SCG 3.69.15.

22 For further explanation of this position, see Piet Schoonenberg, "God or Man: A False Dilemma," in his *The Christ* (New York: Seabury, 1971) 13–49.

23 For explanation of this point, see Etienne Gilson, "The Corporeal World and the Efficacy of Secondary Causes," in Owen Thomas, ed., *God's Activity* 213–30. Gilson stresses how strong Aquinas is on the integrity of secondary causes, using Aristotle to combat the Platonism of Avicenna. See also David Burrell, *Aquinas: God and Action* (Notre Dame: University of Notre Dame, 1979).

24 Karl Rahner, *Hominization: The Evolutionary Origin of Man as a Theological Problem* (New York: Herder & Herder, 1965); see also his essays "Christology within an Evolutionary View of the World," in *Theological Investigations* 5 (New York: Seabury, 1975) 157–92; and "The Unity of Spirit and Matter in the Christian Understanding of Faith," in *Theological Investigations* 6 (New York: Crossroad, 1982) 153–77.

25 ST 1, q. 103, a. 8.

26 ST 1, q. 103, a. 6.

27 ST 1, q. 105, a. 5.

28 SCG 3.72.7; see also 3.73 and 74.

29 William Stoeger, "Contemporary Physics" 234.

30 See the magisterial study by Michael J. Buckley, *At the Origins of Modern Atheism* (New Haven: Yale University, 1987), who concludes: "It is not without some sense of

wonder that one records that the theologians bracketed religion in order to defend religion" (345).

31   Dietrich Bonhoeffer, *Letters and Papers from Prison* (New York: Macmillan, 1953) 219 (letter of July 16, 1944). For development of the idea of divine kenosis in creation, see Jürgen Moltmann, *God in Creation* (San Francisco: Harper and Row, 1985); and John B. Cobb and Christopher Ives, ed., *The Emptying God* (Maryknoll, N. Y.: Orbis, 1990). In the latter collection, the pitfalls and strengths of this idea for subordinated groups are explored by Catherine Keller, "Scoop up the Water and the Moon is in Your Hands: On Feminist Theology and Dynamic Self-Emptying" 102–15.

32   Peter Hodgson, *God in History: Shapes of Freedom* (Nashville: Abingdon, 1989) develops this idea with depth and lucidity; Sallie McFague, *Models of God: Theology for an Ecological, Nuclear Age* (Philadelphia: Fortress, 1987), and *The Body of God: An Ecological Theology* (Minneapolis: Fortress, 1993) gives it imaginative depth. Cf. Elizabeth Johnson, *SHE WHO IS: The Mystery of God in Feminist Theological Discourse* (New York: Crossroad, 1992) 224–72.

33   W. Norris Clarke, "Is a Natural Theology Still Possible Today?" in Russell et al., ed., *Physics, Philosophy, and Theology* 103–23, at 121. The theme of improvisation is stressed by Peter Geach, *Providence and Evil* (Cambridge: Cambridge University, 1977). The model of a fugue is developed by Arthur Peacocke, *Theology for a Scientific Age* 173–77, and that of the game by Paul Davies, *God and the New Physics.* Jazz is my suggestion.

34   Arthur Peacocke, *Intimations of Reality* (Notre Dame: University of Notre Dame, 1984) 73.

35   Christopher Mooney, "Theology and the Heisenberg Uncertainty Principle," a paper delivered to the Catholic Theological Society of America in June 1992 and summarized in *Catholic Theological Society of America Proceedings* 47 (1992) 130–32; the citation is taken from p. 62 of the original unpublished paper, and the biblical reference is to Romans 5:21.

36   Dante, *The Divine Comedy: Paradise,* trans. Dorothy Sayers and Barbara Reynolds (Harmondsworth, England: Penguin, 1962) canto 33, line 145.

PART SEVEN

Reformulations of tradition

INTRODUCTION TO PART SEVEN

THE THEOLOGIANS INCLUDED IN THIS section are revisionists who offer dramatic new models for conceiving of God's presence in an evolutionary world. Not satisfied with simply modifying traditional images of the God-world relationship, they view the task of theology as identifying and elucidating new metaphors and models that will express Christian faith in ways appropriate for our day.

The first selection is from Roman Catholic theologian John F. Haught's book *God after Darwin: A Theology of Evolution*. Haught is identified with process theology, which views the world as an unfinished process and God as playing a dynamic role in this process. Eschewing the cosmic pessimism of the atheistic naturalists on the one hand, and the "religiously pallid" notions of God as "planner" of the universe promoted by the advocates of intelligent design on the other, Haught embraces a view of God as kenotic love and the power of the future. This sense of God as a self-emptying love that opens up a future of new possibilities for the world is based on the "Christ-event." Haught claims that this interpretation of a vulnerable and faithful God, whose creative power consists of a humble and loving "letting be" of the world, and who lures rather than coerces the world toward a redemptive future of promise is consonant with the randomness, struggle, and suffering in life's evolution. To those who find his view of God similar to the remote first cause of Deism, Haught replies that God's "self-distancing" and "self-limitation" are in fact the conditions of dialogical intimacy. Only a truly autonomous creation can enter into a relationship with God.

The next selection in this part is from Protestant theologian Sallie McFague's book *The Body of God: An Ecological Theology*. A panentheist, i.e., one who considers that the world does not exist apart from God but God is not identical with the world, McFague proposes combining the organic model of the world as God's body with the agential model of God as the spirit of the body to capture the immanence as well as the transcendence of God. She claims that God as the embodied spirit of the universe is a model that is compatible with interpretations of both Christian faith and contemporary science. She suggests, moreover, that by underscoring our bodiliness, our "concrete physical existence and experience that we share with all other creatures," this model promotes the well-being of our planet, for "it raises the issue of ethical regard toward *all* bodies as all are interrelated and interdependent."

Reflecting on how best to express the mode of creation, McFague again opts for combining two models, in this case joining a procreation model that sees the world as coming from or formed from God, with an emanationist model in which the life-giving energy of creation emanates from its divine source. The uniting of these models yields the image of a God who bodies forth the universe, which is enlivened and empowered by its source. McFague maintains that a procreative-emanationist model of divine creation is commensurate with the story of an evolving universe coming to us from postmodern science as well as with the account of continuing creation coming from Christianity. She finds it apt as a model "rich in suggestive power for expressing the profound dependence of all things on God, their basic bodily reality, and their changing, growing character." She also promotes this model as not supporting a dualistic hierarchy of mind and body. Finally, she considers the organic-agential, procreative-emanationist model able to unite the aesthetic and the ethical. As she says, this model presses us not only to "marvel at the wonders of the diverse, complex universe" but also to "identify with—and suffer with—bodies in pain."

The third selection in this part is theologian Ruth Page's essay "Panentheism and Pansyntheism: God in Relation," which was published in the book *In Whom We Live and Move and Have Our Being: Panentheistic Reflections on God's Presence in a Scientific World*, edited by Philip Clayton and Arthur Peacocke. Page faults panentheists who celebrate emerging complexity and the arrival of self-consciousness as reflections of divine purpose in evolution without adequately considering the costs, which she finds "disproportionate." In her view, extinction and disorder in the evolutionary process as well as the rise of pain, fear, and regret along with consciousness rule out any unambiguous perception of divine direction. Moreover, she maintains, a hierarchical view of evolution, which privileges human beings, reflects an anthropocentrism that creates theological problems concerning partiality in God.

As a corrective to the flaws that she identifies with panentheism, Page proposes an interpretation of the God-world relationship that she labels "pansyntheism." She suggests that God creates possibilities for creatures without designing any particular forms, including the human, toward which to aim. Creatures are thus free to evolve and act within this non-hierarchical framework of possibilities, with natural evil the result of conflicts between finite freedoms. Having granted freedom to creation, God acts by establishing and maintaining relationships, by "companioning" creation ("pansyntheism"). Page concludes that through a combination of presence and response, God the companion attracts rather than coerces and both rejoices and suffers with creation in the exercise of its possibility.

The last selection in this part is taken from theologian Gordon D. Kaufman's book *In the beginning ... Creativity*. Kaufman maintains that the traditional images of creator, lord, and father are no longer appropriate for thinking of God today. He argues that it is not possible to connect in an intelligible way contemporary scientific, cosmological, and evolutionary understandings of the universe and the emergence of life with a conception of God constructed in such anthropomorphic terms. He suggests instead that a more apt metaphor would be "serendipitous creativity."

Kaufman claims that thinking of God as serendipitous creativity preserves the notion of God as the ultimate mystery of things and connects God with the coming in to being in time of the new and novel. God as the creativity manifest in the ongoing evolution and development of the cosmos serves as the ultimate reference point of all action, consciousness, and reflection. In this context, whatever "creatively facilitates the forward movement of the evolutionary/historical trajectory of which we are a part" is to be considered good. Conversely, any human activity that is destructive of "the biohistorical constraints within which humankind must live and work" is evil. Kaufman thus maintains that a "de-anthropomorphized" God conceived as serendipitous creativity evokes a stance in the world that promotes ecological well-being. He concludes with reflections on ways in which his reconstruction of the concept of God diverges from traditional Christian understandings while still showing important continuities that "warrant considering this picture of God, the world, and the human as appropriate for Christian faith today."

Chapter 22

John F. Haught

EVOLUTION, TRAGEDY, AND COSMIC PURPOSE

AT THE END OF HIS IMPORTANT BOOK The First Three Minutes, physicist Steven Weinberg remarks grimly that the more comprehensible the universe has become to modern science the more "pointless" it all seems.[1] Many other scientists would agree. Alan Lightman has collected several of their reactions to Weinberg's oft-repeated claim. Astronomer Sandra Faber, for example, states that the universe is "completely pointless from a human perspective."[2] Physicist Marc Davis adds: "Philosophically I see no argument against [Weinberg's] attitude, that we certainly don't see a point. To answer in the alternative sense really requires you to invoke the principle of God, I think. At least, that's the way I would view it, and there's no evidence that He's around, or It's around."[3] And Margaret Geller, a Harvard astronomer responds: "Why should [the universe] have a point? What point? It's just a physical system, what point is there?"[4]

Although scientists do not deny the existence of design in the universe, science as such has no need to posit the existence of an intelligent designer. The complex patterning of life, as we now know, emerged only gradually in nature, by way of a long, drawn-out process of evolution that included a good deal of random, blind experimentation and a lot of what we humans would consider sheer waste. It is easy to look at the potholed pathway of life and conclude that the absence of direct and unambiguous design renders ours a purposeless universe, one incapable of fitting into any of our traditional theologies.

However, the question of whether there is a point or purpose to the universe is not answered simply by reference to evidence for or against a designer. Purpose is a much wider notion than design, and it can live much more comfortably with chance, disorder, and the abyss of cosmic time than can the all too simple notion of design. Thus, it is not fruitful for a theology after Darwin to counter the sense of nature's apparent absurdity simply by cataloging more and more apparent evidence of design. Evolutionists themselves are already quite aware of the order in nature. They are simply convinced that a purely naturalistic explanation of order is much more appropriate than the apparently superfluous appeal to an intelligent designer.

... [F]rom the point of view of Christian theology at least, canvassing nature for evidence of a divine "plan" distracts us from engaging in sufficiently substantive conversation with evolutionary science. Evolutionists have told a story about nature that is extremely difficult to square with the notion of a divine "plan." Nature's carefree discarding of the weak, its tolerating so much struggle and waste during several billion years of life's history on Earth, has made simplistic portraits of a divinely designed universe seem quite unbelievable.[5]

To admit this much, however, is not necessarily to conclude that there is no "point" or purpose to the universe. We must remember that science as such is not equipped, methodologically speaking, to tell us whether there is or is not any "point" to the universe. If scientists undertake nevertheless to hold forth on such matters, they must admit in all candor that their ruminations are not scientific declarations but at best declarations *about* science. Moreover, in hazarding such reflections, they will probably be influenced by any number of temperamental or ideological factors extraneous to science as such.

Thus, any respectable argument that evolution makes the universe pointless would have to be erected on grounds other than those that science itself can provide. And yet, even though science cannot decide by itself the question of whether religious hope is less realistic than cosmic pessimism, we must admit that any beliefs we may hold about the universe, whether pessimistic or otherwise, cannot expect to draw serious attention today unless we can at least display their consonance with evolutionary science. We must be able to show that the visions of hope at the heart of the Abrahamic religious traditions provide a coherent metaphysical backdrop for the important discoveries of modern science.

Inevitably, such a proposal will seem outlandish to the many intellectuals who intuitively consider evolutionary biology to be consistent only with a "tragic" interpretation of the universe. It is difficult for experts in the sciences to make out in the physical universe a solid basis for the steadfast hope that prophetic religions require. Alfred North Whitehead himself admitted that the ancient Aeschylean sense of tragedy has always been intertwined with modern science.[6] And even though a pessimistic interpretation of the cosmos is more the product of myth than of science, physicists and evolutionary biologists have generally displayed their ideas in such a way that tragedy seems to be their most natural setting. In particular, the Darwinian notion of impersonal natural selection, when combined with the second law of thermodynamics and the possible "heat death" of the universe, seems to require on our part nothing less than an honest pessimism about the future of the cosmos.

"Cosmic pessimism," the modern synthesis of science and tragic mythology, still poses the most serious cultural challenge to religions based on hope in a promising future. But the Abrahamic religions forbid our surrendering to the seductive lure of the seemingly more "realistic" stoicism around which so much of modern science has congealed. How then can we expect those whose minds have been steeped in this amalgam of science and pessimism to embrace the conviction that the cosmos and its evolution are fundamentally shaped by God's promises?

One prominent religious response to this question says that we should tolerate a sense of despair about the physical universe but look toward a state of immortal personal survival after death in a spiritual "heaven" detached from the material world. Although this solution is quite unbiblical and barely conceals the strain of cosmic despair that underlies it, more than a few believers have found considerable solace in its dualistic segregation of a supernaturally perfect realm "up above" from the imperfect and finally futile natural world "down here." The division of reality into the spheres of spirit and matter—and of humans into soul and body—provides a powerful answer to our personal longing for the eternal, and it apparently renders religiously innocuous the sober modern scientific conjectures about the destiny of nature, including the prospect that the material universe may be headed toward final catastrophe. Dualism, in other words, releases theology from the obligation of seeking a genuine consonance between religion and contemporary science.

However, any religious faith professing to abide within the framework of the biblical vision of hope for the future cannot be content with such a settlement; for the Bible clearly invites us to see all of reality, including the physical cosmos—and what we would now recognize as the entire sweep of its evolution—as profoundly stamped by the promises of God, participating along with humans in the quest for future fulfillment. If St. Paul's words about the whole of creation "groaning" for redemption mean anything at all, it is that from a religious perspective we can no longer consign nature to the realm of final futility.

However, if we are to envision a divine promise as so fundamental to the definition of the universe, doesn't this place theology in an even more intellectually tenuous position than ever? Modern science's long affair with tragic pessimism still persists, and we cannot expect that scientific culture will casually renounce so stable a union. The Darwinian discovery of life's epochs of struggle, waste, and suffering, along with contemporary physics' layout of a universe eventually dissolving into permanent deep freeze, is hardly suggestive of a world whose fundamental being is informed by divine concern for its future. How, by any stretch of the theological imagination, can we claim seriously that the natural world may be viewed more realistically within the framework of God's love and promise than within that of tragic pessimism?

Before we can deal with this question we must . . . state what we mean by the notions of God's love and promise. Curiously these two themes, though central to biblical faith, are often barely visible in formal discussions of science and theology. Too often, it seems to me, our conversations about science and God tend to drift along vaguely without much agreement on what kind of "God" we are talking about. Perhaps out of a spirit of openness to dialogue, theologians often allow scientific skeptics to define the terms of the debate, even though this generally means trimming off features that faith considers essential to its pictures of God. Moreover, in their efforts to find common ground with scientific skeptics, theologians sometimes tend to concede ideas about divine power and intelligence that may be quite out of keeping with actual religious experience. This accommodation has led many articles and books on science and religion into lengthy and uninteresting defenses of religiously pallid notions of God as a "designer" or "planner" of the universe, while the richer and more nuanced images of God given to religious experience hover helplessly in the background.

For example, in Christian theologians' dialogues with evolutionary scientists, it is easy to lose sight of faith's primordial experience of God as self-emptying love, and to focus instead on a much more abstract representation of the "deity," such as "intelligent designer." Unfortunately, the experience of God that occurred in connection with such events as the life and death of Jesus—an encounter with ultimacy that Hans Küng rightly calls a "revolution" in the whole human story of God-consciousness—is taken only minimally into theological engagements with science.[7] Especially in debates about the compatibility of religion with the randomness, struggle, and suffering in life's evolution, theologians typically find themselves guarding some bleary notion of divine "power" and "rationality" rather than bringing patently to the front faith's more troubling images of the compassionate mystery that pours itself out into the world in unrestrained and vulnerable love.

Moreover, . . . our treatises on God and evolution can easily become so sidetracked by obsession with the notions of order, plan, and design that we may ignore altogether another fundamental feature of biblical faith, namely, the experience of God as one who makes promises and who relates to the cosmos not by compelling it from the past but by opening it to an enlivening and unpredictable future.[8]

Evolution and divine kenosis

Steven Weinberg argues perceptively that it is useless to reconcile some vaguely construed and religiously uninformed concept of deity with modern science. Instead we must ask whether science is compatible with the idea of an "interested God," one who captures the hearts and souls of devout believers. After all, it is always possible to redefine the concept of "God," as Einstein himself did, in terms that will make it scientifically palatable. But if we are to be fully candid we must instead ask whether the sense of God *as operative in actual religious awareness* is consonant with contemporary scientific understanding. Weinberg claims that it is not. Contemporary physics and, especially, evolutionary science, he argues, point to an utterly impersonal and indifferent universe, one that rules out the "interested" God of religious faith.[9]

One does not have to accept Weinberg's conclusion in order to agree with him that we should connect our thinking about issues in science and religion to images and convictions about an "interested" God as these are found in actual religious experience rather than in philosophically watered down versions of theism. Of course, we cannot speak seriously about God's relationship to the scientifically understood universe without using philosophical or metaphysical language. But such discourse must remain tethered closely to the nuances of actual religious experience. For Christian theology, this would mean seeking to understand the natural world, and especially its evolutionary character, in terms of the outpouring of compassion and the corresponding sense of world renewal associated with the God of Jesus the crucified and risen Christ.

Christians have discerned in the "Christ-event" the decisive self-emptying or *kenosis* of God. And at the same time they have experienced in this event a God whose effectiveness takes the form of a power of renewal that opens the world to a fresh and unexpected future. As a Christian theologian, therefore, when I reflect on the relationship of evolutionary science to religion I am obliged to think of God as both *kenotic love* and *power of the future*. This sense of God as a self-humbling love that opens up a new future for the world took shape in Christian consciousness only in association with the "Christ-event"; and so, as we ponder the implications of such discoveries as those associated with evolution, it would be disingenuous of Christian theologians to suppress the specific features of their own faith community's experience of divine mystery. This means quite simply that in its quest to understand the scientific story of life, Christian theology must ask how evolution might make sense when situated in a universe shaped by God's kenotic compassion and an accompanying promise of new creation.

From science itself, of course, we have no right to expect any sweeping judgments about the meaning of evolution or cosmic process. Following its customary constraints, science must acknowledge that it is not equipped to discover the significance or value of anything. But from the perspective of a theological vision that takes seriously both biological science and what Christian faith understands as "revelatory" portraits of a vulnerable and faithful God, nature's evolutionary journey may exhibit levels of meaning that could never be illuminated apart from a prior commitment to such a revelatory framework.

Such an interpretative commitment, I would submit, is no more of an impediment to objectivity than is the equally a priori allegiance many scientists have to the myth of cosmic tragedy. It is now commonly agreed, after all, that some kind of commitment is a condition of, and not inevitably an obstacle to, knowledge. Even to begin scientific exploration, for example, a scientist must be committed already to such beliefs as "the universe is intelligible" or "truth is worth seeking." And these scientifically essential "faith" commitments, I believe, correspond much more approximately to religious visions such as the one I am presenting here than they do to the seemingly more "realistic" tragic modern envisagements of an ultimately pointless universe.

At the center of Christian faith lies the conviction (John 3:16) that "God so loved the world that He gave his only Son" to redeem and renew that world. Theologically translated, this text and many others like it imply that the very substance of the divine life is poured out into the creation, and that the world is now and forever open to an infinitely replenishing future. I am suggesting that those who envisage the universe as enfolded by such infinite love and promise will be able to appreciate aspects of "Darwinian" evolution that those committed to a more tragic spin on things might take as a reason for cosmic despair. St. Paul (Philippians 2:5–11) portrays Christ as one who "though in the form of God" did not "cling" to his divine status, but instead "emptied himself" (*ekenosen seauton*) and took the "form of a slave." It is to this image that Christian theology must always repair whenever it thinks about God's relationship to the world and its evolution.

Creation as "letting be"

. . . [W]hat has been especially troubling in Darwinian science is its picture of a world in which randomness mingles with the "impersonal" process of natural selection in such a way that evolution seems to have no direction or inherent meaning. A world that sponsors such a process may seem at first to be incompatible with the existence of a loving and effective God. But perhaps this is only because our philosophical notions of divine power are usually implicitly uprooted from any grounding in the actual religious intuition of God as self-emptying love. By ignoring the image of divine humility, it is easy for us to forget that intrinsic to the divine *kenosis* is its authorization of creation's striving for genuine independence vis-à-vis its creator. Love by its very nature cannot compel, and so any God whose very essence is love should not be expected to overwhelm the world either with a coercively directive "power" or an annihilating "presence." Indeed, an infinite love must in some sense "absent" or "restrain itself," precisely in order to give the world the "space" in which to become something distinct from the creative love that constitutes it as "other." We should anticipate, therefore, that any universe rooted in an unbounded love would have some features that appear to us as random or undirected.

. . . [E]ven in the original creation of the cosmos, the divine infinity may be thought of—in our imperfect human concepts—as "contracting" itself, foregoing any urge to direct the creation forcefully or to absorb it into the divine. An unrestrained display of infinite presence or "omnipotence" would leave no room for anything other than God, and so it would rule out any genuine evolutionary *self-transcendence* on the part of the cosmos. It is a humble "retreat" on God's part that allows the cosmos to stand forth on its own and then to evolve as a relatively autonomous reality distinct from its creative ground. In this sense, creation and its evolutionary unfolding would be less the consequence of an eternal divine "plan" than of God's humble and loving "letting be."[10] So if ultimate reality is essentially self-giving love, and if love in turn entails "letting the other be," then, theologically speaking, both the world's original coming into being and its indeterminate Darwinian transformation through time would be completely consonant with the Christian experience of God.

The world can have its own being and realize its own evolutionary potential, therefore, only if God's creative power and love consist of a kind of self-concealment. As I have noted, it is in its encounter with the crucified man Jesus—and not in philosophical reasoning alone—that Christian faith is given this key to God's relation to the world. The cross "reveals" to faith the self-absenting of a God out of whose limitless generosity the world is called, but never forced, into being and becoming. This kenotic image of God, even though inaccessible to philosophical and scientific rationality as such, nevertheless gives a surprising intelligibility to the cosmic whole in which Darwinian evolution turns out to have played so important a role.[11]

Not surprisingly, those scientific skeptics and theists whose ideas of God center primarily on the notion of "intelligent design" have found Darwinian ideas unacceptable. Skeptics have rejected a divine "planner" as incompatible with the undirected course of biotic evolution, whereas many theists have dismissed evolution contemptuously as incompatible with their notion of a designing deity.[12] A universe entertaining the degree of indeterminacy that Darwin's vision entails seems incompatible with a transcendent power and intelligence. God, the alleged "divine designer," is apparently not "in control" after all. Evolution appears to be a mindless lottery rather than the "mighty act" of an omnipotent God. And the enormous amount of time evolution takes seems to rule out the existence of God, since a truly intelligent designer would surely not have "fooled around" for so long (fifteen billion years or so) before bringing about human beings. The enormity of cosmic time simply adds to the suspicion that intelligence is something that emerged only recently, perhaps only in the evolution of the human species.

However, the God given to a faith shaped by the "Christ-event" is not first of all an infinite embodiment of what we humans narrowly understand as rationality, intelligence, or design, but an outrageously "irrational" and mysteriously humble love that comes to meet the world from out of the realm of an open and incalculable future. A theology attuned to this image of ultimacy suggests to us a way of rendering theologically meaningful the very same scientific data that have led a more "rationally" based theistic preoccupation with design to repudiate Darwinian theory, and that have led scientific skeptics to a tragic interpretation of nature.

The Creator's power (by which I mean the capacity to influence the world) is made manifest paradoxically in the vulnerable defenselessness of a crucified man. And such an expression of divine "power" is not only consonant with, but ultimately explanatory of, the curious world that evolutionary science now presents to us. The randomness, struggle, and seemingly aimless meandering that the evolutionary story of life discloses as the underside of its marvelous creativity is consistent with the idea that the universe is the consequence of an infinite love. The key to such an interpretation lies in faith's staggering discovery that a truly effective power takes the form of self-emptying compassion.

If God were "powerful" only in the restricted sense of possessing the capacity to manipulate things coercively, then the facts of evolution might be theologically problematic. But an infinite love, as the Roman Catholic theologian Karl Rahner has made clear, will not manipulate or dissolve the beloved—in this case, the cosmos. For in the act of seeking intimacy with the universe, God forever preserves the difference and otherness of that beloved world. God's creative love constitutes the world as something ontologically distinct from God, and not as a simple extension of the divine being. Consequently, the indeterminate natural occurrences that recent physics has uncovered at the most elementary levels of physical reality, the random events that biology finds at the level of life's evolution, and the freedom that emerges with human existence are all features proper to any world that is permitted and even encouraged to be distinct from the creative love that underlies it.

In order for the world to be independent of God, and therefore to undergo a genuine *self*-transcendence in its evolution, a God of love would concede to the world its own autonomous principles of operation—such as the "impersonal" laws of gravity, natural selection, and self-organization. This "self-distancing" of God, however, is in no sense apathy but, paradoxically, a most intimate form of involvement. In other words, God is nothing like the otiose and remote first cause of deism; for it is out of a longing to relate deeply to the world that God foregoes any annihilating "presence" to the world. This retracting of "presence," however, is the very condition of dialogical intimacy. God's will is that the world become more and more independent, and that during its evolution its own internal coherence intensify, not diminish.[13] But this "absent" God is "present" to and deeply united with the evolving world precisely by virtue of selflessly allowing it to achieve ever deeper autonomy—which occurs most obviously in the evolutionary emergence of human freedom. The God of self-giving compassion is in fact the only God that normative Christian faith can claim legitimately ever to have encountered, and yet this founding intuition about the nature of ultimate reality all too seldom enters into our thoughts about whether the universe has a "point" to it, or whether the evolution of life can be reconciled with religious hope.

God, cosmos, and the future

The God whom Christian faith identifies with infinite love is also one who—as a resurrection faith attests—opens up a new future for humans and for the whole of creation. Hope's intuition about the coming of an always new and creative future is no less central to Christian faith than is the paradoxical divine "power" that became manifest in the defenselessness of the Crucified. And so I have been suggesting that we connect our understanding of nature's evolution to the sense of God as the world's "future."

From the perspective of theology, in fact, it is the "coming of God" in the mode of a renewing future that *ultimately* explains the novelty in evolution. Even though cosmic pessimism would view the random or contingent events that allow for evolutionary novelty as utterly devoid of meaning, to a biblically informed faith these indeterminacies are essential features of any universe open to new creation. The fifteen billion years of cosmic evolution now appear, in the perspective of faith, to have always been seeded with promise. From its very beginning this extravagantly experimental universe has been bursting with potential for surprising future outcomes.[14] And the undeniable fact that life, mind, culture, and religion have emerged out of the barely rippled radiation of the primordial universe gives us every reason to suspect that the cosmos may still be situated no less realistically within the framework of promise than of tragedy. Even prospects of eventual cosmic doom are not enough to defeat the proposal that nature's present indeterminacies are the repository of promise. The so-called "heat death" that may be awaiting the universe is not inconsistent with the notion that each moment of the entire cosmic process is taken perpetually into, and preserved everlastingly in, the boundlessly redemptive future that faith names as God.[15]

To fit the whole of nature into the framework of a religious hope based on the sense of openness to surprising future outcomes is not nearly so great a stretch as it may once have seemed; for today we are beginning to notice just how much of nature's concrete complexity and indeterminate creativity the linear mathematical methods of modern science since Newton had left out. Scientific abstractions appealed greatly to the Cartesian ideal of complete and immediate clarity, and they gave us enormous power to analyze and manipulate our natural environment. But the full actuality of the natural world had meanwhile slipped out of the grasp of science.[16] And we have begun to realize only recently that the intellectual appeal of cosmic pessimism is supported not so much by nature itself as by abstract mathematical representations that inevitably overlook the elusive complexity and indeterminacy that open the cosmos to a genuinely novel future.

What modern science had passed over is now emerging palpably in the so-called sciences of "chaos" and "complexity." Nature, as we can now picture it (especially with the help of computer imaging), is composed of intricate adaptive systems that cannot be understood adequately simply by dissecting them into their constituent law-bound particulars. The makeup of the universe, from immense galactic clusters all the way down to infinitesimal quantum events, exhibits an unpredictably self-creative and self-organizing character to which the linear mathematics of mechanistic science is inadequate. Although materialist dreams are still around, significant doubts about the abstract ways of reading nature, which previously had fueled our fatalism, are now beginning to spread within the scientific community and are even spilling out into public awareness. The prospect of precise scientific prediction of final cosmic catastrophe is shakier than ever. If, as physicist John Houghton notes, science cannot even tell us where a billiard ball will end up a minute from now without taking into account the motion of electrons in outer space, it is hardly in a position to settle the question of cosmic destiny either.[17]

Although it may not be prudent for us to draw any theological conclusions directly from the new sciences of chaos and complexity, we cannot help but notice how severely they have challenged the quaint claims that impersonal laws of physics are running the universe to ruin and that we can make long-term predictions about the fate of the cosmos. It seems entirely plausible that the universe of contemporary science is more congenial to promise than pessimism.

Story and promise

Obviously neither science nor faith is in a position to predict the actual details of the cosmic future, but it is of great interest that science—especially since Darwin and, more recently, Einstein—now places the cosmos within a narrative setting in which the universe is a "story" open to an unpredictable future. The universe, as it turns out, is not eternal, nor is it just a set of abstract laws, nor a mere backdrop for human history. Rather, it is a creative project yet unfinished, and because it is unfinished it still has a future.

Currently most scientists agree that cosmic evolution began in a hot "big bang," after which the universe began to expand and cool, giving rise to atoms, stars, and galaxies. Eventually elements and compounds cooked up in some now burnt-out stellar ovens came together to form our own planet. After another billion years or so the Earth's surface cooled sufficiently to allow primitive forms of life to appear. Biological evolution on Earth, according to the most recent estimates, began about 3.8 billion years ago, but like most other episodes of cosmic process it was apparently not in a hurry. In its unfolding it was often hesitant, sometimes explosive, and almost always extravagant. After experimenting with less-complex forms of life, it eventually blossomed out into plants, reptiles, birds, and mammals. Not long ago, in our own species, evolution was endowed with self-consciousness.

The story has not been linearly progressive. For vast periods of time little happened, and much of the history of life's evolution can be captured in the image of a randomly branching bush. But all great stories have quiescent interludes, blind alleys, and unintelligible shoots; and a more sweeping view of cosmic evolution shows clearly, at least to those who care to notice, a narrative trend toward increasingly complex forms of natural order. Without too much difficulty, we can make out a kind of story line along which nature has traveled from trivial to more intricate and eventually sentient, conscious, and self-conscious states of being. Although neo-Darwinian biologists often highlight what they take to be the aimlessness of evolution, if we step back and survey the life-process within its larger cosmic context, it is hard even for the most entrenched pessimist to discount altogether the obvious "directionality" visible in the overall movement of the cosmos from simplicity to complexity. And to those of us who have been encouraged by faith to look for signs of promise in all things, it would seem egregiously arbitrary not to remark at how, at any past moment in its history, the cosmos has remained open to surprisingly beautiful future outcomes.

Astrophysics, for example, has instructed us recently that an incredible number of stunning physical coincidences had to have been present in the earliest micromoments of the universe in order for life eventually to appear and evolve. And although it may be unwise for theology to take the physics of the early universe as the basis for a new natural theology, the current scientific information is remarkably consistent with faith's conviction that the physical universe had always held at least the *promise* of emerging into life.[18] Though known to us only retrospectively, the early phases of the universe clearly contained the prospect of evolving toward such indeterminate outcomes as life, mind, and even spirituality. Cosmic pessimism, therefore, does not seem to provide a sufficiently comprehensive metaphysical format for organizing our current scientific understanding of the universe. Until not too many years ago, it may have been considered scientifically acceptable to think of the physical universe as inherently hostile to life, and to view life and evolution as absurdly improbable eventualities toward whose accidental appearance on our small planet nature was intrinsically "unfriendly." But today it is much more "scientific" to acknowledge that physical reality has always been positively disposed toward the emergence of life and consciousness, much more so than we had ever suspected prior to the emergence of contemporary scientific cosmology.[19]

Thus, if it is now evident that the ambiguous cosmic past held such enormous promise as the eventual emergence of life and mind, can we claim confidently that the *present* state of the cosmic story is not also pregnant with potential for blossoming into still more abundant new creation? Science by itself cannot answer the questions most important to faith. But in the panorama of cosmic evolution disclosed by science, faith is still permitted, perhaps even encouraged, to think of the cosmos as being called into yet newer ways of being.

A tragic perspective, of course, will simply assume that the world's future states are not really new but are instead the same old simplicity now just "masquerading as complexity." However, it is unthinkable that novel events could arise only out of the fixed past. Novelty must arise, of course, *in connection with* what is and what has been, for otherwise we would not grasp it as truly new. But it would not really be new if it were simply the algorithmic unfolding of a fully deterministic past. New possibilities can arise only out of the region of time that we refer to as the *future*. And since the future is such a boundless reservoir of novelty, we cannot assume that, simply because it is not fully present to us now, it is reducible to bare nonbeing (as both philosophy and science have often implied). Because of its faithful and inexhaustible resource-fulness, we must concede to the future some modality of *being*. Indeed, the biblical vision of reality's promise implies even that the future is the *most real* (though obviously not yet presently actualized) of all the dimensions of time. The future claims the status of being eminently real not only because it always shows up even after every present moment has slipped away into the past, but ultimately because it is the realm from which God comes to renew the world.[20]

However, as I have also emphasized, the future in its overflowing abun-dance is always hidden. By definition it cannot be fully captured in any fleeting present experience, or become fully spent in the fixity of the past. In its per-petual transcendence of the past and present, the future inevitably hides itself. Thus, I have envisaged God's self-concealment in an unavailable future as coinciding with the paradoxically intimate divine "absence" associated with the notion of *kenosis*. God's humble self-withdrawal, in other words, takes the form of God's being the inexhaustible "futurity" whose continuous arrival into the present is always restrained enough to allow the cosmos to achieve *its own* independent evolution. As biblical faith makes clear, God's "glory" is at present kenotically veiled, and where it does manifest itself, at least according to John's Gospel, it is, paradoxically, in the picture of the "lifted up" and crucified Christ.

From a biblical perspective, of course, the whole "point" of the universe is to manifest God's "glory"; but for the present, God's glory is revealed charac-teristically in a *kenosis* that endows the world with a surprising degree of auton-omy.[21] The self-emptying God refrains from overwhelming the universe with an annihilating divine presence but in the mode of futurity nonetheless nour-ishes the world constantly by offering to it a range of relevant new possi-bilities—such as those depicted by evolutionary science. At the same time, God's compassionate embrace enfolds redemptively and preserves everlastingly each moment of the cosmic evolutionary story.

Conclusion

Thus, in theology's conversations with contemporary science, it is more helpful to think of God as the infinitely generous ground of new possibilities for world-becoming than as a "designer" or "planner" who has mapped out the world in every detail from some indefinitely remote point in the past. The fundamental difficulty implied in the notion of such a "plan" for the world is that it closes the world off to any real future. Referring to some often over-looked ideas of Henri Bergson, Louise Young comments insightfully on the openness of evolution to the future:

As we view the groping, exploratory nature of the process—the many favorable mutations, the tragic deformities—it is apparent that we are not witnessing the detailed accomplishment of a preconceived plan. "Nature is more and better than a plan in course of realization," Henri Bergson observed. A plan is a term assigned to a labor: it closes the future whose form it indicates. Before the evolution of life, on the contrary, the portals of the future remain wide open.[22]

We might also say that God is more and better than a planner. A God whose very essence is to be the world's open future is not a planner or designer but an infinitely liberating source of new possibilities and new life. It seems to me that neo-Darwinian biology can live and thrive quite comfortably within the horizon of such a vision of ultimate reality.

Notes

1   Steven Weinberg, *The First Three Minutes* (New York: Basic Books, 1977), 144.

2   Alan Lightman and Roberta Brawer, *Origins: The Lives and Worlds of Modern Cosmologists* (Cambridge, Mass.: Harvard University Press, 1990), 340.

3   Ibid., 358.

4   Ibid., 377.

5   See Richard Dawkins, *River Out of Eden* (New York: Basic Books, 1995), 131.

6   Alfred North Whitehead, *Science and the Modern World* (New York: The Free Press, 1967), 10: "The pilgrim fathers of the scientific imagination as it exists today are the great tragedians of ancient Athens, Aeschylus, Sophocles, Euripides. Their vision of fate, remorseless and indifferent, urging a tragic incident to its inevitable issue, is the vision possessed by science. Fate in Greek Tragedy becomes the order of nature in modern thought."

7   Hans Küng, *Does God Exist?*, trans. by Edward Quinn (New York: Doubleday, 1980), 676.

8   For more systematic detail, see my book *Mystery and Promise: A Theology of Revelation* (Collegeville, Minn.: The Liturgical Press, 1993).

9   Steven Weinberg, *Dreams of a Final Theory* (New York: Pantheon Books, 1992), 244–245.

10 Examples of this kenotic view of creation can be found in Kabbalistic Judaism, in the writings of Simone Weil, and in Geddes MacGregor's *He Who Lets Us Be* (New York: Seabury Press, 1975), as well as in the writings of the Christian theologian Jürgen Moltmann. See, for example, Moltmann's *God in Creation*, trans. by Margaret Kohl (San Francisco: Harper & Row, 1985), 88. A contemporary Jewish restatement of the view that creation is grounded in God's self-withdrawal may be found in Michael Wyschogrod's *The Body of Faith* (New York: Harper & Row, 1983), 9–10.

11   This self-concealment, once again, is not a divine "abdication" in any deistic sense, but instead a deep form of intimacy of God with the world. That God is "absent" from the domain of coercive power still allows that God may be present in the form of an ultimate goodness.

12   See . . . for example, Phillip Johnson's book *Darwin on Trial* (Washington, D.C.: Regnery Gateway, 1991).

13   See Wolfhart Pannenberg, *Systematic Theology*, vol. 2, trans. by Geoffrey W. Bromiley (Grand Rapids, Mich.: Eerdmans, 1994), 127–136. "Theologically, we may view the expansion of the universe as the Creator's means to the bringing forth of independent forms of creaturely reality" (127). "Creaturely independence cannot exist without God or against him. It does not have to be won from God, for it is the goal of his creative work" (135). See also Elizabeth Johnson, "Does God Play Dice? Divine Providence and Chance," *Theological Studies* 57 (March 1996), 3–18.

14   The biologist Louise Young's book *The Unfinished Universe* (New York: Oxford University Press, 1986) is an excellent example of such a reading.

15   Process thought has been particularly effective in portraying how the experiences of the temporal cosmic past can be preserved plausibly and patterned meaningfully in the everlasting empathy of God. See Alfred North Whitehead, "Immortality," in *The Philosophy of Alfred North Whitehead*, ed. Paul A. Schillp (Evanston, Ill. and Chicago: Northwestern University Press, 1941), 682–700; and also *Process and Reality*, corrected edition, ed. David Ray Griffin and Donald W. Sherburne (New York: The Free Press, 1978), 340–341, 346–351; and Charles Hartshorne, *The Logic of Perfection* (Lasalle, Ill.: Open Court Publishing, 1962), 24–62, 250.

16   Whitehead argues that the seventeenth-century science was dominated by the "assumption of simple location," according to which we can understand things only by leaving out any consideration of the concrete and complex web of organic connections that tie them all together. This assumption in turn was the result of a logical error, the fallacy of misplaced concreteness, that mistook mathematical abstractions for concrete reality. See *Science and the Modern World*, 51–57, 58–59.

17   John T. Houghton, "A Note on Chaotic Dynamics," *Science and Christian Belief* 1 (1989), 50.

18   And since (relatively speaking) we may still not be too far removed from the cosmic dawn, who knows what other surprising and unpredictable outcomes lie enfolded in this promising creation?

19   Such a claim seems defensible independently of the scientific status of the so-called strong anthropic principle.

20   See Jürgen Moltmann, *The Coming of God: Christian Eschatology*, trans. by Margaret Kohl (Minneapolis: Fortress Press, 1996), 259–295.

21   Ibid., 323.

22   Young, *The Unfinished Universe*, 201–202.

Chapter 23

Sallie McFague

GOD AND THE WORLD

Major models of God and the world

THE FIRST VATICAN COUNCIL (1890) expressed a view of the relation of God and the world that is, with some variations, a common one in major creeds of various Christian churches since the Reformation:

"The Holy, Catholic, Apostolic, Roman Church believes and confesses that there is one true and living God, Creator and Lord of Heaven and earth, almighty, eternal, immense, incomprehensible, infinite in intelligence, in will, and in all perfection, who, as being one, sole, absolutely simple and immutable spiritual substance, is to be declared really and essentially distinct from the world, of supreme beatitude in and from himself, and ineffably exalted above all things beside himself which exist or are conceivable."[1]

What drives this statement is the passion to remove God from any real connection with the world—"really and essentially distinct from the world" sums it up. In fact, it is difficult to imagine how a God so described could have a genuine, significant relationship with anything outside the divine reality.[2] And yet the Christian tradition has insisted that God not only created the world but admired it and loved at least its human creatures sufficiently so that when they "fell," God became one of them, suffering and dying to redeem them from their sins. The two images of God—one as the distant, all-powerful, perfect, immutable Lord existing in lonely isolation, and the other as the One who enters human flesh as a baby to eventually assume the alienation and oppression of all peoples in the world—do not fit together. Jesus as the immanent, loving image of God is a surd, an enigma, against the background of the distant, exalted, incomprehensible deity. In its creedal statements on God and Jesus the tradition attempts to express this view of radical transcendence and radical immanence: the totally distant, "other" God, exalted and perfect, entered into human flesh in Jesus of Nazareth, so that this one man is fully divine and fully human. In the worldview current in first-century Mediterranean times and operable through the Middle Ages, that way of radicalizing and relating transcendence and immanence had some credibility; but it does not in our time. This view seems neither sufficiently radical (God is transcendent only over our world and especially human beings and immanent only in one human being) nor believable (it assumes a dualistic view of reality with God dwelling somewhere external to and exalted above the world and yet entering it at one particular point).

What other options are there for relating God and the world? The principal criteria guiding our analysis and critique of various options will be the radicalization of divine transcendence and immanence as well as . . . embodied experience, usefulness, and compatibility with Christian faith and the contemporary picture of reality. We will suggest that the model of God the spirit, the giver and renewer of her body, the universe, is one that is compatible with readings of both Christianity and postmodern science. A couple of brief comments about this proposal are necessary before setting it in the context of other traditional and contemporary models. First, it is a personal model of God, assuming that we will inevitably imagine God in our image, but to do so with the notion of spirit rather than self, soul, or mind suggests that divine agency is concerned not only with human beings but with all forms of life: God's spirit is the breath of life in all life-forms. Second, . . . the model of God as spirit of his body, the universe, implies that both terms, spirit and body, are . . . metaphors. Spirit is not really God, while body is a metaphor, nor is spirit closer to divine reality; rather, they are both forms of God's visible being, ways of expressing immanent transcendence and transcendent immanence suitable for creatures like us who are inspirited bodies. The depth and mystery of God are not available to us in this or any other model: the glory of God is only reflected in the world and then in a dim and distorted mirror. It is this dim, distorted mirror that we attempt to model.

We will have much more to say about our model, but with this sketch in mind let us look briefly at some alternatives in order to place the model within a broader context.[3] First, the deistic model, the simplest and least satisfying one, arose during the sixteenth-century scientific revolution. It imagines God as a clockmaker who winds up the clock of the world by creating its laws and then leaves it to run by itself. The model has the advantage of freeing science to investigate the world apart from divine control but essentially banishes God from the world. It is, sadly, the view of many contemporary scientists as well as Christians, with the qualification that some Christians allow periodic, personal interventions of God in times of crisis such as natural disasters, accidents, and death. The view encourages an irresponsible, idolatrous attitude in the scientific community, allowing it to claim for itself sole rights both to interpret and to dispose of the world. On the part of Christians it encourages an interventionist, God-of-the-gaps view of divine activity.

The second view of God and the world, the dialogic one, has deep roots in both Hebrew and Christian traditions: God speaks and we respond. It has been a central view within Protestantism and was highlighted in twentieth-century existentialism. In its contemporary form the relation between God and the world is narrowed to God and the individual: the I-Thou relation between God and a human being. As seen, for instance, in the writings of Søren Kierkegaard or Rudolf Bultmann, this position focuses on sin, guilt, and forgiveness and has the advantage of allowing for a continuous relationship with God, but does so at the expense of indifference to the natural and social worlds. The dialogic position assumes two tracks, religion versus culture (the latter including scientific knowledge and all social institutions such as government, the economy, the family), with each left to run its own affairs.[4] God and the human being meet, not in the world, whether of nature or culture, but only in the inner, internal joy and pain of human experiences. Liberation theologies have protested the focus on individual (usually white, male, Western, affluent) alienation and despair, insisting that God's relation to the world must include the political and social dimensions as well.

The monarchical model, the relation of God and the world in which the divine, all-powerful king controls his subjects and they in turn offer him loyal obedience, is the oldest and still the most prevalent one.[5] It is both a personal and a political model, correcting the impersonalism of the deistic model and the individualism of the dialogic. It also underscores the "godness" of God, for the monarchical imagery calls forth awe and reverence, as well as vocational meaningfulness, since membership in the kingdom entails service to the divine Lord. But since all power is controlled by the king, issues of human freedom and theodicy are highly problematic. Moreover, and most critical for our concerns, the king is both distant from the natural world and indifferent to it, for as a political model it is limited to human beings.[6] The continuing power of this model in liturgical use is curious, since contemporary members of royalty scarcely call up responses of awe, reverence, and obedience, but its nostalgic appeal, as evidenced in the gusto with which we all sing Christmas carols that are rife with this imagery, cannot be underestimated. Any model that would attempt to criticize or partially subvert it ought to look carefully at the main reason for its attraction: it is the only model that attempts to dramatize divine transcendence. Nonetheless, the model of God as king is domesticated transcendence, for a king rules only over human beings, a minute fraction of created reality. The king/realm model is neither genuinely transcendent (God is king over one species recently arrived on a minor planet in an ordinary galaxy) nor genuinely immanent (God as king is an external superperson, not the source, power, and goal of the entire universe).

A fourth model, the agential, also has strong backing in the Hebrew and Christian traditions. Here God is assumed to be an agent whose intentions and purposes are realized in history, especially human history. It has been revived during this century as a way of talking about divine purpose throughout the entire span of cosmic history.[7] The analogy that is often used in this model to explain divine action in the world is the human self realizing its purposes through its body: God is related to the world and realizes the divine intentions and purposes in the world, in a way similar to how we use our bodies to carry out our purposes.[8] This view of divine action has the advantage of internalizing divine action within cosmic processes; however, since these actions are one with the processes, it is difficult if not impossible to differentiate divine action from evolutionary history. Moreover, since the human being is the prototype for divine action, the human body emerges implicitly as the model for God's body, suggesting anthropomorphism: God is understood as a superperson with a high degree of control over the world in a way similar to our control over the actions of our bodies. Finally, at least in its contemporary form, the model has been advanced largely to satisfy intellectual puzzles: How might we imagine divine action in an internal rather than an external, supernatural fashion? The classic agential model, which is at heart personal (God as father, mother, lord, lover, king, friend), God as actor and doer, creating and redeeming the world, has profound ethical and liturgical dimensions, while the contemporary version does not. But if the model were God as spirit (breath, life) of the body (the world, universe) rather than the mind or self that directs and controls creation, the ethical and liturgical dimensions might reemerge.

The agential model should, I believe, be joined with the fifth and final major model, the organic, for either alone is lacking in light of our criteria but together they suggest a more adequate model. The organic model is the one on which this essay is focused: the world or universe as God's body. However, alone, that is, apart from the agential model, which suggests a center of being not exhausted by or completely identified with the world or universe, the organic model is pantheistic. The world is, becomes, divine. Christian thinking, with its ancient commitment to a transcendent deity who created a world distinct from himself has had, as we have seen, a highly ambivalent relationship to the organic model.

Two recent instances of serious reconsideration of it, both under pressure from the view of reality in postmodern science and both combining agency and organism, are process theology and the work of Teilhard de Chardin. Process thought moves toward a social view of agency (every entity or actual occasion is an agent, including God), while Teilhard suggests a more traditional view of God as the supreme agent guiding the evolutionary process toward more and more complex, unified agents.[9] The process version of organicism emphasizes the interdependence and reciprocity of all agents, with God as one among many, though the preeminent one, while Teilhard's version gives a greater role to divine purpose and direction. These are both exciting, provocative proposals with profound implications for an ecological sensibility. Process ontology, with its insistence on the agency or subjectivity of all entities, provides a basis for the intrinsic value of every created being, living and nonliving. Teilhard's view also underscores the value of each and every aspect of evolutionary reality, although in a more traditional sacramental mode. All things are being transformed through their processes of natural growth toward the divine source and goal of their existence.[10] Both of these variations on the organic model are panentheistic, not pantheistic; in both, divine transcendence and immanence are radicalized, with Teilhard expressing the radicalization mythologically and process theology conceptually. In differing degrees both are credible, persuasive readings of postmodern science and Christianity.

My essay is a continuation and development of these projects at the metaphorical level. While Teilhard certainly did work poetically and mythologically, as I have suggested, his images were rather esoteric (Omega Point, noogenesis), referring to parts of the process of evolutionary teleology. Process theologians, although conceptually oriented, have also suggested some powerful metaphors, notably A.N. Whitehead's notion of God as the Great Companion. They have also revived a limited use for the model of the world as God's body.[11] Both process theology and Teilhard are radical revisionings of the relation of God and the world; however, neither suggests an overall model for reimaging that relation.

Spirit and body

My essay undertakes such a task, although with a profound debt to the organic and agential models of Teilhard and process theology. The agential model preserves transcendence, while the organic model underscores immanence. Alone, the agential model overemphasizes the transcendent power and freedom of God at the expense of the world. Alone, the organic model tends to collapse God and the world, denying the freedom and individuality of both. But if the model were that God is related to the world as spirit is to body, perhaps the values of both the agential and organic models could be preserved.

Two related issues, however, face us immediately. The first is the suitability of *any* personal language for God as being compatible with contemporary science. The second, assuming that we can provide reasons for retaining agential language, is the *kind* of personal imagery that is most appropriate. The dilemma set by these issues is an acute one: the Hebrew and Christian traditions are profoundly and, I would argue, indelibly agential; yet postmodern science, as we have seen, does not appear to permit any purpose or agency apart from local causation. This dilemma has caused some theologians to retreat from personal language for God except in worship.[12] The implication is that personal language does not really refer to God but is necessary for liturgical purposes, while the proper way to speak of God in the context of postmodern science is impersonally. One unfortunate result of this position is a willingness to continue to use traditional metaphors for God such as God as lord and father (since they are "only" liturgical images), without working toward more appropriate ones.

This approach permits, I believe, too strong a control of science over theology. If it can be shown that *all* personal metaphors are incompatible with postmodern science, the case becomes stronger. But since little reconstructive work on such models has been attempted, the images in question are traditional ones, not necessarily all personal ones. I agree that the monarchical, triumphalistic, patriarchal imagery for God is impossible to square with an evolutionary, ecological, cosmological framework. Even some of the more intimate models—God as mother (and father), lover, and friend—need to be balanced by other, less anthropocentric ones.[13] But are all personal models worthless, discordant, incongruous from the perspective of contemporary science? Moreover, if we do discard them all and speak of God only or principally in impersonal terms, can we any longer pretend that we still belong within the Western religious paradigm? Finally, is not the refusal to imagine God in personal terms a gesture in the direction of disembodiment: we are embodied agents, and is it not therefore natural and appropriate, as the outermost contemporary evolutionary phylum, to imagine our creator "in our image"?

The major model we are investigating in depth is the combined agential-organic one of the universe (world) as God's body, a body enlivened and empowered by the divine spirit. We have dealt in some detail with the organic aspect of the model, the universe as God's body, but what of the agential or personal aspect, the spirit? To begin framing an answer to this question, we need to start with ourselves as the concrete, embodied beings we are. We are embodied personal agents, and if we are not to be surds or outcasts in the world, we need to imagine God's relationship to the world in a way that includes us, that makes us feel at home. Mechanistic, impersonal models exclude us; personal, organic ones include us. If the history of the universe and especially the evolutionary history of our planet makes it clear that we do, in fact, belong here and that evolution has resulted in self-conscious beings, then does it not make sense to imagine the relationship between God and the world in a manner that is continuous with that evolutionary history, especially if, as we shall suggest, there is a way of modeling personal agency that also touches one of the deepest traditions of Christian thought?

That tradition is of God as spirit—not Holy Ghost, which suggests the unearthly and the disembodied, nor initially the Holy Spirit, which has been focused largely on human beings and especially the followers of Christ, but the spirit of God, the divine wind that "swept over the face of the waters" prior to creation, the life-giving breath given to all creatures, and the dynamic movement that creates, recreates, and transcreates throughout the universe.[14] Spirit, as wind, breath, life is the most basic and most inclusive way to express centered embodiment. All living creatures, not just human ones, depend upon breath. Breath also knits together the life of animals and plants, for they are linked by the exchange of oxygen and carbon dioxide in each breath inhaled and exhaled. Breath is a more immediate and radically dependent way to speak of life than even food or water, for we literally live from breath to breath and can survive only a few minutes without breathing. Our lives are enclosed by two breaths—our first when we emerge from our mother's womb and our last when we "give up the ghost" (spirit).

Spirit is a wide-ranging, multidimensional term with many meanings built upon its physical base as the breath of life. We speak of a person's spirit, their vigor, courage, or strength; of team spirit, the collective energy of people at play; of the spirit of '76 or the spirit of Tiananmen Square, the vitality, grit, and resolution of a people banding together in a common cause to oppose oppression; of a spirited horse or the spirit of a sacred grove—animals, trees, and mountains can also have spirit.[15] All these connotations are possible because of the primary meaning of spirit as the breath of life: "Then the Lord God formed man [sic] from the dust of the ground and breathed into his nostrils the breath of life" (Gen. 2:7). Bracketing the sexism of the Genesis 2 creation story, it nonetheless suggests the prime analogy of this essay: the dust of the universe enlivened by the breath of God. Each of us, and each and every other part of the body as well, owes our existence, breath by breath as we inhale and exhale, to God. We "live and move and have our being" in God (Acts 17:28). Indeed we do. That is, perhaps, the most basic confession that can be made: I owe my existence at its most fundamental level—the gift of my next breath—to God. God is my creator and recreator, the One who gives and renews my life, moment by moment, at its most basic, physical level. And so does everything else in creation also live, moment by moment, by the breath of God, says our model.

We are suggesting, then, that we think of God metaphorically as the spirit that is the breath, the life, of the universe, a universe that comes from God and could be seen as the body of God. Both of these terms, spirit and body, are metaphors: both refer properly to ourselves and other creatures and entities in our experience of the world. Neither describes God. . . . Nonetheless, even with these qualifications, questions abound. Let us look at a few of them. Why choose spirit rather than other personal, agential terms such as self, mind, heart, will, soul, and the like? Does spirit language for God make sense in terms of post-modern science and the Christian tradition? Does contemporary science substantiate such language, or does it accommodate or allow it? Can Christians use the model of God as embodied spirit, and, more pointedly, in a transcendent sky-God tradition, is it pantheistic? Does it collapse God and the world?

One reason for suggesting spirit as the way to speak of divine agency is that it undercuts anthropocentrism and promotes cosmocentrism. Only a human being has a mind or self, whereas spirit, while able to include mind and self, has a much broader range. Most attempts to use the body metaphor in regard to God rely on the analogy of mind/body: God relates to the world as the mind (self) relates to the body. Not only does this form of the analogy involve difficult, often dualistic, arguments concerning the mind/body correlation, but, just as important for our considerations, it implies that divine activity in relation to the world is primarily intellectual and controlling: God is Mind or Will.[16] This is an old, deep tradition in the Hebrew and Christian traditions as manifest in Wisdom and Logos theologies: God creates the universe as its orderer, as the One who gives it direction, limits, and purpose. The emphasis is on the work of the mind, the work of intelligence and control. It is precisely this concern that surfaces in the ancient enterprise of natural theology: the need to answer the questions of why and how. But a spirit theology suggests another possibility: that God is not primarily the orderer and controller of the universe but its source and empowerment, the breath that enlivens and energizes it. The spirit perspective takes seriously the fecundity, diversity, range, and complexity of life and of life-supporting systems. It does not claim that the divine mind is the cause of what evolutionary theory tells us can have only local causes; rather, it suggests that we think of these local causes as enlivened and empowered by the breath of God. A spirit theology focuses attention not on how and why creation occurred either in the beginning or over the evolutionary aeons of time, but on the rich variety of living forms that have been and are now present on our planet. The breath of God enlivening each and every entity in the body of the universe turns our attention to a theology of nature, a theology concerned with the relationship of God and our living, breathing planet. The principal reason, then, for preferring spirit to alternative possibilities is that it underscores the connection between God and the world as not primarily the Mind that orders, controls, and directs the universe, but as the Breath that is the source of its life and vitality. The connection is one of relationship at the deepest possible level, the level of life, rather than control at the level of ordering and directing nature. And since, as we recall, our tendency is not only to model God in our image but to model ourselves on the models with which we imagine God, the metaphor of breath rather than mind might help us to support, rather than control, life in all its forms. Thus, in a spirit theology, we might see ourselves as united with all other living creatures through the breath that moves through all parts of the body, rather than as the demilords who order and control nature.

But is this model commensurate with twentieth-century science? If one understands the spirit of God as the source of the dynamic vitality of the universe and especially as the breath of all life-forms, then our focus is not on the purpose or direction of divine activity but on our dependence on God as the present and continuing creator. Our concern is not primarily intellectual but aesthetic and ethical: wonder and awe at the immensity, richness, and diversity of creation as well as gratitude and care for all its forms of life. Our response to this model is as grateful recipients of life rather than puzzlers over its mysteries. Contemporary science does not mandate or even imply such a model, but it is commensurate with an organic interpretation of its story. Since we and all other creatures and entities are in some sense inspirited bodies (even trees and oceans move with the winds), then if we were to think of God as in some sense continuous with this evolutionary history, one way to do so would be as the spirit of the entire body of the universe. This is not, of course, a scientific description nor is it a theological one; rather, it is a way of thinking about God and the world that makes sense in terms of postmodern science. It allows us to understand ourselves who have evolved into spiritual, embodied creatures as neither freaks nor surds in our world. It also allows us to think of God as the source of our being, the source of all being, not as the one who intervenes from the outside to initiate creation, patch it up, or direct it, but as the one who supplies us with the breath for all the incredible rich, teeming fecundity and variety of life.

It is a model of God and the world that focuses on "the wonderful life" that has emerged from evolutionary history, rather than on the divine ordering of the process. It does not attempt to enter into scientific discussions on the how and why of that history, but suggests that if one is *already* a person of faith (which cannot be arrived at or substantiated by postmodern science), then the picture of reality as an organic whole, a body, dependent on and sustained by the spirit of God, is one that fits with, is appropriate to, evolutionary history. This theology of nature is not a natural theology: it does not say that the scientific story gives evidence (even the tiniest bit) for belief in this or any other model of God and the world. All it says is that this way of conceiving of God and the world makes more sense in terms of the scientific picture than alternatives such as the deistic, dialogic, and monarchical models. But this is enough. A theology of nature does not ask for scientific proof, only for a picture to help us think and act holistically about God, ourselves, and our world.

Where does this model stand in regard to the Christian tradition? We can answer that question on one level simply and forthrightly by recalling the theme of the 1991 World Council of Churches assembly in Canberra, Australia: "Come, Holy Spirit—Renew the Whole Creation," or the affirmation from the Nicene[17] Creed: "I believe in the Holy Spirit, the Lord and Giver of Life." While the spirit of God, now the Holy Spirit, has often played a lackluster role in relation to the Father and the Son in Christian trinitarian thought, its credentials in both the Hebrew Scriptures and in the New Testament are more than solid.[18] The motif that runs throughout is the spirit as the source of life and the renewer of life: a theology of the spirit focuses on God as the creator and redeemer of life. The trajectory begins with the spirit of God hovering over the waters of chaos and breathing life into living beings; the spirit renews creation in the gift of baptism, the second birth; and fulfills it in the eschatological vision of all creation in harmonious union. One of the great assets of the model is precisely its amorphous character in contrast to the highly human, personal, and androcentric nature of Father and Son: spirit is not necessarily human, personal (though it is relational), or male. In fact, it often has been designated female; but it may be best that, for once in Christian reflection, we let God be "it."[19] "It" (the divine spirit) roams where it will, not focused on the like-minded (the fathers and the sons—or even the mothers and daughters), but permeating, suffusing, and energizing the innermost being of each and every entity in creation in ways unknown and unknowable in our human, personal categories.[20]

The joining of the spirit that gives life to every creature with the Holy Spirit that renews all creation suggests a connection between Christian theology and the two forms of evolution—biological and biocultural. Creation, the gift of the spirit, could be seen as the action of God in the aeons of evolutionary development, which has resulted in the wonderful life we see about us as well as in ourselves. (This is a retrospective reading of creation in evolutionary terms.) In the model of the universe as God's body, divine incarnation is not limited to redemption but is everywhere evident in the bodies that live through the breath of the spirit. Within this model of the universe as God's body, God's presence and action are evident as the breath of life that gives all bodies, all forms of matter, the energy or power to become themselves. This understanding of divine action in light of evolutionary development focuses on empowerment, not direction. It does not claim that God is guiding the process in general or in particular; rather, it suggests that all life, regardless of which individuals or species prosper, is dependent upon God. God's creative action is not intermittent or occasional; on the contrary, it is continuous and universal, for without the sustaining breath of God, all the wonderful life, including our own, would fade and die. The "purpose" of creation from this perspective, however, is not human beings (or any other species), but the fecundity, richness, and diversity of all that is bodied forth from God and sustained in life by the breath of God. Needless to say, creation in this picture involves enormous waste, suffering, and death for all kinds of bodies – to suggest anything less or different is sentimental and false to the contemporary scientific picture of reality.

In Christian theology, however, the spirit of God is also the Holy Spirit, the spirit shaped and made known in the Hebrew Scriptures as well as in the life, teachings, and death of Jesus of Nazareth and the community that formed around him. Moreover, evolution is not only biological; with self-conscious creatures it enters a historical, cultural phase. At this point divine purpose can be spoken of within the evolutionary process in a new and special way. It is not only empowerment of but also a direction for all that teeming life, a direction expressed by Christians in the stories, images, and ideas of the Hebrew people, its paradigmatic founder Jesus, and all the lives and understandings of disciples over the centuries. The guide for interpreting that direction is called the Holy Spirit, and it works through human beings: we become the mind and heart as well as the hands and feet of the body of God on our planet. Christians claim that God has been in the natural process as its creator and sustainer (the spirit of the body) since the beginning, but now that process has been given a particular direction (a "new creation") characterized by inclusive love, especially for the vulnerable and oppressed. For Christians, the spirit has been qualified or given shape and scope by the Holy Spirit and is a direction or purpose for life that depends on our cooperation as God's partners.

Hence, we can say that God's action as the spirit of the body is twofold. The spirit is the source of life, the breath of creation; at the same time, the Holy Spirit is the source of the renewal of life, the direction or purpose for all the bodies of the world – a goal characterized by inclusive love.

One central issue remains in regard to our model of God as the spirit of life bodied forth in the universe: Is it pantheistic? This is a complex issue in Christian theology with intricate historical dimensions we cannot settle here. Nonetheless, the criteria for models of God and the world operative in this essay – commensurability with postmodern science as well as our own embodied experience and the well-being of our planet – cause us to lean toward an interpretation of Christian faith that accommodates this model. Since the model is commensurate with contemporary science, mirrors our own experience as embodied spirits, and connects us at the basic level of life-giving breath with all other life-forms on our planet, we are encouraged to look to those traditions within Christianity that emphasize the spirit in similar ways. These traditions can be characterized as neither theist nor pantheist, but panentheist: "God is not exhausted by finite beings, not even all finite beings, yet God is in all finite creatures and apart from God there is nothing; nor is God 'apart' from anything."[21] This description of a panentheistic view of the relation of God and the world is compatible with our model of God as the spirit that is the source, the life, the breath of all reality. Everything that is is in God and God is in all things and yet God is not identical with the universe, for the universe is dependent on God in a way that God is not dependent on the universe. We joined the agential and organic models in order to express the asymmetrical and yet profoundly interrelational character of the panentheistic model of God and the world: while we, as members of the body, are radically dependent upon the life-giving breath from the spirit, God, as the spirit, is not so dependent upon the universe. Pantheism says that God is embodied, necessarily and totally; traditional theism claims that God is disembodied, necessarily and totally; panentheism suggests that God is embodied but not necessarily or totally. Rather, God is sacramentally embodied: God is mediated, expressed, in and through embodiment, but not necessarily or totally. . . .

Panentheism is, I would suggest, a strong motif in both Hebrew and Christian traditions that take seriously the mediation of God to the world.[22] These traditions deny, on the one hand, a picture of God as an external super-person (or Unmoved Mover) distant from and alien to the world and, on the other hand, a view of God as immediately available to the mind of human beings or as identified with natural processes. Rather, the panentheistic tradition is found in all those passages in the Hebrew Scriptures that mediate the divine presence through human words and acts as well as natural phenomena and in the New Testament in its central declaration that "the Word was made flesh" in Jesus of Nazareth. In all these instances, mediation and incarnation are central and, therefore, are open to, or ought to be open to, the embodiment of God, especially in its panentheistic form of the world (universe) as God's body and God as its spirit.

To sum up: we have suggested that God as the embodied spirit of the universe is a personal/organic model that is compatible with interpretations of both Christian faith and contemporary science, although not demanded by either. It is a way of speaking of God's relation to all matter, all creation, that "makes sense" in terms of an incarnational understanding of Christianity and an organic interpretation of postmodern science. It helps us to be *whole* people within our faith and within our contemporary world. Moreover, the model does not reduce God to the world nor relegate God to another world; on the contrary, it radicalizes both divine immanence (God is the breath of each and every creature) and divine transcendence (God is the energy empowering the entire universe). Finally, it underscores our bodiliness, our concrete physical existence and experience that we share with all other creatures: it is a model on the side of the well-being of the planet, for it raises the issue of ethical regard toward *all* bodies as all are interrelated and interdependent.

Creation: production, procreation, or procreation-emanation?

The Genesis creation story, however, does not suggest that the world is God's body; rather, the world and its creatures are products of God the Maker, the Craftsman, the Architect, the Sculptor. Whether one looks at Genesis 1 or 2, at the sweeping narrative of how God called into being the heavens and the earth, the seas and their teeming creatures, the land and its many animals and plants or at the more homey, domestic story of the molding of Adam and the other animals from the earth (and Eve from Adam's rib), the mode of creation is by word or by hand. In the first story, through the word ("Let there be . . .") God creates an aesthetic panorama ("it was very good"); in the second, God sculpts forms from "the dust of the ground." Creation is production and as such it is external to God; it is also totally dependent on God for its existence. Many Hebrew Scripture scholars seem united in the opinion, however, that it is not the externality, the production aspect of the Genesis account, that is critical, but the dependence of all forms of existence on God the creator.[23] If dependence, rather than externality, is the critical feature of the tradition's creation sensibility, then we might consider options other than the production model, which has several problems.[24]

The production model emphasizes the beginnings of creation rather than its continuing, ongoing character; it can speak of divine transcendence only in an external way, making it difficult to affirm the immanence of God; and it is intellectual or aesthetic, implying a dualistic hierarchy of mind and body. A procreation model of creation, on the other hand, says, simply, that the world comes from, is formed from, God rather than out of "nothing" or out of some material other than God. Lest the reader immediately recoil in horror at the thought of the universe as bodying forth from God, let us briefly consider the alternatives. "Out of nothing" (*ex nihilo*) is not in Genesis or even in the Bible (except for a cryptic mention in the book of Maccabees). Rather, it is an invention of the early church fathers to underscore the transcendence of God. But, we might ask, does it also allow for divine immanence, as an adequate model of God and the world should? "Out of some material other than God" suggests that there is another creator, the one who made this material, thus undercutting radical dependence of all of reality on God. "Out of God" claims that whatever is is in and from God, but it does not say that God is identified with or reduced to what is bodied forth. It claims that we live and move and have our being in God, but not vice versa. A metaphor to express this source of all life is not the Architect who constructs a world, but the Mother who encloses reality in her womb, bodying it forth, generating all life from her being.[25]

Before continuing, let us recall once again that we are dealing with models, not descriptions. Models are to be judged not by whether they correspond with God's being . . ., but by whether they are relatively adequate (in other words, more adequate than alternative models) from the perspective of postmodern science, an interpretation of Christian faith, our own embodied experience, and the well-being of our planet and all its life-forms. We only have models, and the Genesis story of the external Maker who produces an artifact is not, simply because of its age and status in the tradition, anything other than a model. What we must ask of all models is their relative adequacy on the basis of some agreed-upon criteria. I am suggesting that in light of the criteria operative in this essay, some version of the procreation model of creation is preferable to production models.

To make this suggestion more concrete, let us look at how the procreation model deals with the problems raised by the production model. On the issue of the beginnings of creation versus its continuation, a procreation (organic, growth) model has potential for expressing the ongoing character of creation in ways a production model does not. In the production model, creation is complete, finished, static; what is crafted is seen as an artifact that may be pleasing or beautiful, but it does not change. A procreation model, however, sees creation as emerging from God, as a body (in the case of the evolving universe, billions of bodies) that grows and changes. But our model, we recall, is not only or merely organic; it is also agential. Hence, it combines the pro-creation model with another in the tradition, the emanationist, in which the life-giving energy of creation emanates from its divine source.[26] The model, therefore, is not a pure procreation one in which the world is seen as God's child (reproduction) rather than as God's construction (production), but is a combination of the procreative and emanationist models: God bodies forth the universe, which is enlivened and empowered by its source. God is not the parent of the child, but the life of the body; our model does not highlight biological generation, but the dependence of all life on God. It borrows from the procreative model its physicality and from the emanationist model its continuing and profound connection with its source of life. Children grow up, move away, and can sever connections with those who gave them life, so the procreation model, while expressing powerfully the bodily base of creation, cannot capture its continuing dependence.[27] An emanationist model not only insists that all life derives from God, but that it continues to do so; thus, the dynamic, changing, evolving body that is all reality does not grow away from God, but in, through, and toward God.

Emanationist models of creation have a dialectical character: creation comes from God, attains partial separation, and returns to its source. Theologies influenced by these models, however, have often been idealistic, that is, centered in the mind, not the body, seeing the second phase, the partial separation, as a "fall" or a lesser state from the first or the third.[28] But if the emanationist model is combined with the procreative or the organic, this tendency is undercut, for the second phase is nothing less than God's own embodiment. It is not a lesser stage but, in fact, the only one we can know anything about. It is . . . wonderful beyond all imagining: it is the universe. Hence, we suggest that a procreative-emanationist model of divine creation is commensurate with the continuing creation of postmodern science, its story of the evolving history of the universe. It is a model rich in suggestive power for expressing the profound dependence of all things on God, their basic bodily reality, and their changing, growing character.

The model is also helpful when we turn to the issue of divine immanence as well as transcendence in relation to the world. The production model of the tradition has been heavily invested in protecting the transcendence of God, but has often done so by stressing divine control. In other words, transcendence was equated with sovereignty: it meant dominion over.[29] The result is to separate God and the world; God becomes the external Lord over the world. The monarchical and deistic models of God and the world both rely on this view of transcendence, and it has been one of the most problematic legacies of the Hebrew and Christian traditions in innumerable ways. Moreover, it does not help promote an ecological sensibility.

Divine transcendence need not mean God's external sovereignty over the world. A procreative-emanationist model of creation focuses our attention on a transcendent immanence, or an immanental transcendence. That is, it keeps our eyes on what we can see and touch and know: the universe as God's body with God's spirit as its enlivening breath is the place that we turn to learn of both divine transcendence and immanence. While transcendence can mean "to exist apart from the material universe," it can also mean "surpassing, excelling or extraordinary."[30] In the model of the universe as God's body, we look for divine transcendence not apart from the material universe, but in those aspects of the material universe that are "surpassing, excelling or extraordinary." This suggests that the universe could be a way to meditate on divine transcendence in a concrete, embodied way. In the model of the universe as God's body, we are invited to see the extraordinary in the ordinary, to see the surpassing wonder of divine transcendence in the smallest and largest dimensions of the history and present reality of the universe, especially our planet. Whereas in many models of divine transcendence, we must think in either concrete but shallow terms (the domesticated transcendence of the political models—God as king, lord, master over human beings) or radical but abstract terms (God as omnipotent, omniscient, eternal, infinite, and so on), in our model we can think concretely *and* radically. We are asked to contemplate the visible universe, God's body, as the place where the surpassing, extraordinary character of divine presence is to be found. The universe in its age, size, complexity, diversity, history, and beauty is the locus for our imagination to exercise its power in regard to what divine transcendence could, might, mean. It serves as a deep reflecting pool of divine magnificence and grandeur. To contemplate what we know of the universe, from the extraordinary ordinariness of a butterfly's wing to the ordinary extraordinariness of the Milky Way, is beyond all our capacities of imagination: the longer we reflect on either of these phenomena, the more filled with wonder we become. This mode of appreciating divine transcendence, the concrete, radical way, is what I have characterized as the mediating, incarnational way of the Hebrew and Christian traditions. Psalm 104 is an excellent example: "O Lord my God, you are very great. You are clothed with honor and majesty, wrapped in light as with a garment. You stretch out the heavens like a tent, you set the beams of your chambers on the waters, you make the clouds your chariot, you ride on the wings of the wind, you make the winds your messengers, fire and flame your ministers" (1–4). One looks to the world to discover the glory of God, for as Gerard Manley Hopkins put it, "The world is charged with the grandeur of God."[31] Only now, the world is the universe: the common creation story has given us a more magnificent, more awesome, way to speak of that grandeur. In this concrete picture we have a more radical metaphor of divine transcendence than either the domesticated or abstract models of transcendence can give us. The universe as God's body gives us a concrete way of meditating on divine transcendence; a meditation that knows no end, for we can never imagine such transcendence to its finish or limits. It will, the longer we contemplate its wonders, whether at the microscopic or the macroscopic levels (as well as the middle level of cows, pine cones, and caterpillars), call forth more and more depths to the meaning of divine transcendence.

To contemplate divine transcendence as radically and concretely embodied means, of course, that it is not one thing: divine transcendence, in this model, would be in the differences, in the concrete embodiments, that constitute the universe. It is not the oneness or unity that causes us to marvel at creation, but the age, size, diversity, complexity that the common creation story tells us about. If God in the procreative-emanationist model is not primarily the initiator of creation (the simplicity of the big bang), but the empowering, continuing breath of life throughout its billions of years of history and in each and every entity and life-form on every star and planet, then it is in the *differences* that we see the glory of God. God is many, not one, for the body of God is not one body (except as a universe), but the infinite number of bodies, some living and some not, that are the universe. To know God in this model is to contemplate, reflect on, the multitude of bodies in all their diversity that mediate, incarnate, the divine. . . . [T]here is no way to divine transcendence except immanently.

Finally, the procreative-emanationist model does not support a dualistic hierarchy of mind and body as does the production model. The latter depends upon an intellectual/aesthetic context: creation is of the mind, not the body. The production model obviously fits masculine and the procreation model feminine gender construction: " 'higher,' metaphysical or spiritual or *ex nihilo* creation and 'lower' or 'lesser' physical, natural or elemental creation."[32] In the first model, creation derives from a source that is itself disembodied (but presumably mental and agential), while in the second, creation is born of a physical source (but perhaps only physical). The procreative-emanationist model suggests that creation is from a physical source (it is God's body), but also from the life-giving center of the divine body (the spirit of God). This model is not dualistically hierarchical: there is no mind directing the body, but rather a body suffused with the breath and power of life. It also does not privilege the intellect over the body nor reduce creation to physicality alone. The model refuses the stereotypes of masculine versus feminine creation, one from the mind, the other from the body, claiming that neither alone is adequate even to our own human, creative experience, let alone as a metaphor of divine creation. What we see in evolutionary history is neither extreme, but a continuum of matter that gradually over billions of years becomes brain (mind) in varying ways and degrees. We have suggested that spirit is a way of expressing the enormous range of this development, at least from the inchoate gropings of an amoeba to the reflective self-consciousness of a human being (the term, of course, does less well with quarks and with God).

To review and summarize: . . . this organic-agential, procreative-emanationist, body-spirit model (for expressing the God-world relationship in our time) underscores creation as the continuing, dynamic, growing embodiment of God, a body given life and power for the evolution of billions of diverse entities and creatures. This body is . . . the visible, mediated form of God, one that we are invited to contemplate for intimations of divine transcendence. It is a concrete, radical, immanental embodiment of God's glory, magnificence, and power. We see this transcendent immanence, this immanental transcendence, in the intricate veins of a maple leaf supplied with the water of life, in the pictures from space of our blue-green marble of a planet, and in the eyes of a hungry child.

"And in the eyes of a hungry child": the model presses us not only to marvel at the wonders of the diverse, complex universe and especially our planet, but also to identify with—and suffer with—bodies in pain. If God is physical, if the universe is God's body, then the beauty and the vulnerability of bodies, the aesthetic and the ethical, unite. [. . .]

As we conclude this [essay], we must remind ourselves once again that we are dealing with models, not descriptions, and also that all models have limitations, including, of course, the one we have put forward. The organic-agential model, the world as the body of God, God as the spirit of the body, has several limitations: it focuses attention on bodily existence and needs; it pertains most appropriately to living creatures (and only by somewhat far-fetched, anthropomorphic analogies to other entities—certainly stars and rocks but also lichen and viruses, not to mention atoms and quarks); it says little about the point of all this breath and breathing—all the life that the spirit empowers. The question, however, is this: Does such a model help us to see some things we need to pay attention to both as Christians and as people of the twenty-first century? For instance, does the model of the world as God's body deepen the insight of the common creation story in a way that helps Christians to remythologize the relation of God and the world for our time? Does it help us to see what the immanence and transcendence of God might mean in an ecological context? Does it also help us to see all other bodies on our planet as incarnations of God, each one both beautiful and vulnerable? [Does] this theology—this way of speaking of God and the world—deepen the ecological context? . . .

Notes

1   Vincent McNabb, ed., *The Decrees of the Vatican Council* (London, 1907) as quoted by Grace Jantzen, *God's World, God's Body* (Philadelphia: Westminster Press, 1984), 102.

2   Process theologians have pressed this point repeatedly. Charles Hartshorne, for instance, describes such a God as "ECK," the supreme Eternal Consciousness, Knowing but not including the world. See his *Philosophers Speak of God* (Chicago: University of Chicago Press, 1953); also see John B. Cobb, Jr., and David R. Griffin, *Process Theology: An Introductory Exposition* (Philadelphia: Westminster Press, 1976), chap. 3.

3   For two treatments of the following models see chap. 8 of Ian G. Barbour, *Myths, Models and Paradigms: A Comparative Study in Science and Religion* (New York: Harper and Row, 1974) and the last chapter of Claude Y. Stewart, Jr., *Nature in Grace: A Study of the Theology of Nature* (Macon, Ga.: Mercer University Press, 1983).

4   See "Christ and Culture in Paradox" in H. Richard Niebuhr's classic study, *Christ and Culture* (New York: Harper and Bros., 1951).

5   Barbour writes as follows of this model: "The *monarchical model* of God as King was developed systematically, both in Jewish thought (God as Lord and King of the Universe), in medieval Christian thought (with its emphasis on divine omnipotence), and in the Reformation (especially Calvin's insistence on God's sovereignty). In the portrayal of God's relation to the world, the dominant western historical model has been that of the absolute monarch ruling over his kingdom" (*Myths, Models and Paradigms*, 156).

6   For a further elaboration of this model, see chap. 3 in *Models of God*.

7   For two treatments, see chap. 6 of Gordon Kaufman, *God the Problem* (Cambridge: Harvard University Press, 1972) and Barbour, *Myths, Models and Paradigms*, 158ff.

8   For a review of this point and literature, see Ian G. Barbour, *Religion in an Age of Science*, vol. 1 (New York: Harper and Row, 1990), 256–58.

9   For analyses of this point in Teilhard's work, see Barbour, *Myths, Models and Paradigms*, 160f.; also Ian G. Barbour, "Teilhard's Process Metaphysics," in *Process Theology: Basic Writings*, ed. Ewart H. Cousins (New York: Newman Press, 1971).

10   Teilhard speaks of this as the "economy of salvation," in which, through stages, the natural order is transformed first by its being taken up by humanity and then by Christ (see, for instance, the discussion in *The Divine Milieu: An Essay on the Interior Life* [New York: Harpers, 1960], 25).

11   A. N. Whitehead, *Process and Reality: An Essay in Cosmology* (New York: Macmillan, 1929), 16f. The classic process theology essay on the model of the world as God's body is by Charles Hartshorne, "The Theological Analogies and the Cosmic Organism," *Man's Vision of God and the Logic of Theism* (New York: Willett, Clark, and Co., 1941), 171–211. While Hartshorne uses the human body as the base of his organic model, he does so with a fine eye to sociality and diversity by focusing on the complex cellular constitution of the body.

12   See James M. Gustafson, *Ethics from a Theocentric Perspective*, vol. 1, *Theology and Ethics* (Chicago: University of Chicago Press, 1981), 179–89. See also Gordon Kaufman's critique of Gustafson's position ("How Is God to Be Understood in a Theocentric Ethics?" in *James M. Gustafson's Theocentric Ethics: Interpretation and Assessments*, ed. Harlan R. Beckley and Charles M. Swezey [Macon, Ga.: Mercer University Press, 1988]: 13–35), as well as Kaufman's own highly nuanced discussion of nonreified uses of personal metaphors for God (see especially chaps. 22 and 23, *In Face of Mystery: A Constructive Theology* [Cambridge: Harvard University Press, 1993]). Although the positions of Gustafson and Kaufman are substantially different, both are wary of agential personalism and neither suggests new personal metaphors in place of the traditional ones.

13   This present work is meant, in part, to balance the limitations of my use of these metaphors in *Models of God*. However, there is a basic compatability and complementarity between the model of spirit and those of mother, lover, and friend.

14   Even a very brief survey from an encyclopedia makes this point. In the Hebrew Scriptures, the Spirit of God is active in history, prophecy, and many other ways,

but especially as the source of life: "As the divine power is evident in a special way in the bringing forth and the maintenance of life, the Spirit of God is considered as the source of life (Gen. 1:2, 2:7, 6:3; Ps. 33:6, 104:29f, 146:4; Job 12:10, 27:3, 34:14f; Ezek. 37:7–10)" (article on the Holy Spirit, *Encyclopedia of Theology: The Concise "Sacramentum Mundi,"* ed. Karl Rahner [New York: Seabury Press, 1975], 643). In the New Testament, the redeemed community is constituted by the Holy Spirit. Christ is conceived through the Spirit, equipped with the Spirit at baptism, and driven into the desert by the Spirit: "The Spirit is the moving power behind every activity of Jesus. The opposition of men [sic] to the Spirit is called by Christ the unpardonable sin." Christ promised the Spirit in his absence and it was given at Pentecost: "The pentecostal outpouring of the Spirit is the beginning of the communication of the Spirit which continues through all time." In Paul one finds a wide field of Spirit theology too complex to define. The Spirit is active in everyday life, is the animating principle of the church, and is especially connected with baptism and the life of the baptized as well as the pledge of eschatological fulfillment (*Encyclopedia of Theology*, 643).

15   Steven G. Smith, in his study of the concept of spirit, notes that there are two central traditions: one, connected with Hegel, which posits spirit in history and mind; the other, from Martin Buber, which sees spirit in nature and especially in relationships. The first tradition focuses on spirit as mind, the second on spirit as breath or life. See *The Concept of the Spiritual: An Essay in First Philosophy* (Philadelphia: Temple University Press, 1988). It is obviously the second tradition that an ecological theology relies upon, as it allows not only for continuity across all forms of life, but also for relationship among the diverse forms. Jürgen Moltmann makes a related point when he notes that definitions of human death either unite or dissociate us from other forms: if death is defined as "brain death," the focus is on the head, but if breath is the criterion of life, then life is located in the whole living body (*God in Creation: A New Theology of Creation and the Spirit of God* [San Francisco: Harper and Row, 1985], 255).

16   The literature on this analogy for God's action in the world is large and complex. A classic essay on embodiment within a nondualistic mind/body framework is P. E. Strawson's "Persons," in *Individuals: An Essay in Descriptive Metaphysics* (Garden City: Doubleday-Anchor, 1963): 83–113. Theological positions range widely from Grace Jantzen's view of God's more or less total embodiment as a solution to both divine immanence and transcendence (*God's World, God's Body* [Philadelphia: Westminster Press, 1984]) to John Polkinghorne's rejection of divine embodiment as resulting in either God's tyranny over the world or capitulation to it (*Science and Providence: God's Interaction with the World* [Boston: New Science Library, 1989]). The tradition is full of examples of God's tyranny over the world, due to its refusal to consider any kind of embodiment, but God's absorption into the world is also a genuine problem if the classic organic model is operative. Thus, Thomas Tracy says that if we "construe our world as a single, functionally unified individual," then "to say that the world is God's body is to say that the processes unfolding in the universe are the processes of God's life, that God does not exist except in and through these processes" (*God's*

Action and Embodiment [Grand Rapids: Eerdmans, 1984], 112). Our embodiment model attempts to avoid that collapse, while it also tries to avoid tyranny. Some other recent treatments of God's action in the world that radicalize both divine immanence and transcendence are the following: 1) Jay McDaniel's process relational panentheism, in which the world has some degree of independence, even as our bodies have some independence from our psyches, a view that sees both God and the world as agents and patients (Of God and Pelicans: A Theology of Reverence for Life [Louisville, Ky.: Westminster/John Knox, 1989]); 2) Arthur R. Peacocke's unitive mind/brain/body view with top-down (transcendent) as well as bottom-up (immanent) action: "Just as our human personal subjectivity (the sense of being an 'I') is a unitive, unifying, centered influence on the conscious, willed activity of our bodies, and this is what characterizes personal agency, so God is here conceived as the unifying, unitive source and centred influence of the world's activity" (Theology for a Scientific Age: Being and Becoming – Natural and Divine [Oxford: Basil Blackwell, 1990], 161); 3) Catherine Keller's claim that the "politics of individualism" and a "theology of sheer transcendence" are connected – that a view of the self as separated from others and the world underlies a view of God as "pure structure of reflexive selfhood," curved in upon the divine self and essentially unrelated to the world (From a Broken Web: Separatism, Sexism and Self [Boston: Beacon Press, 1986], 37–43); 4) Gordon Kaufman's reconstruction of divine immanence and transcendence in terms of biological and cultural historical evolution, a view that, while not using the embodiment model, speaks of God as "the serendipitous cosmic process" in a way that at the same time preserves the mystery and transcendence of God, since God is beyond all our constructions as their "ultimate point of reference" (In Face of Mystery, chap. 19). What all of these attempts (including my own) to speak of divine action in the world have in common is the desire to avoid occasional or interventionist divine action while stressing the continuity and thoroughness – but noncontrolling and nondeterministic — character of the action. The sensibility behind this perspective was well expressed in 1889 by Aubrey Moore: "Those who oppose the notion of evolution in defence of a 'continued intervention' of God seem to have failed to notice that a theory of occasional intervention implies as its correlative a theory of ordinary absence" (as quoted by Arthur R. Peacocke in Religion and Public Policy, ed. Frank T. Birtel [New York: Crossroad, 1987], 32). See also Owen Thomas's helpful anthology of a variety of theological positions on divine action (God's Activity in the World, AAR Studies in Religion No. 31 (Atlanta, Ga.: Scholars Press, 1983), and Barbour's critique of various contemporary positions (Religion in an Age of Science, chap. 9, "God and Nature").

17   One of the richest and most moving treatments of the Holy Spirit is Korean theologian Chung Hyun-Kyung's address at the Canberra assembly. Here she invokes the Spirit through the spirits of all the oppressed, from the murdered "spirit of the Amazon rainforest" to the spirits of exploited women and indigenous peoples, victims of the Holocaust and of Hiroshima, as well as Hagar, Jephthah's daughter, Malcolm X, Oscar Romero and all other lifeforms, human and non-human, that like "the Liberator, our brother Jesus," have been tortured and killed for greed and

through hate. The closing words sum up this stunning hymn to the Spirit that moves through and empowers all life. "Dear sisters and brothers, with the energy of the Holy Spirit let us tear apart all walls of division and the culture of death which separate us. And let us participate in the Holy Spirit's political economy of life, fighting for our life on this earth in solidarity with all living beings and building communities for justice, peace, and the integrity of creation. Wild wind of the Holy Spirit blow to us. Let us welcome her, letting ourselves go in her wild rhythm of life. Come Holy Spirit, renew the whole creation. Amen!" ("Welcome the Spirt; hear her cries: The Holy Spirit, creation, and the Culture of Life" [*Christianity and Crisis*, 51 (July 15, 1991), 223]).

18   For an introductory overview of the Spirit tradition, especially as oriented in an ecological direction, see Krister Stendahl, *Energy for Life: Reflections on the Theme "Come, Holy Spirit – Renew the Whole Creation"* (Geneva: World Council of Churches, 1990). For an extensive, ecologically oriented theology of the Spirit, see Jürgen Moltmann's *The Spirit of Life: A Universal Affirmation* (London: SCM Press, 1992).

19   Stendahl supports this usage, as it frees us from the overpersonalism of the tradition: "The Spirit is the indispensable vehicle to take us towards an all-inclusive theology" (*Energy for Life*, 5).

20   Alice Walker makes this point in the following excerpt between Celie and Shug: "It? I ast. Yeah, It. God ain't a he or a she, but a It . . . It ain't something you can look at apart from anything else, including yourself. I believe God is everything, say Shug. Everything that is or ever was or ever will be" (from *The Color Purple*, in *Weaving the Visions: New Patterns in Feminist Spirituality*, ed. Carol P. Christ and Judith Plaskow [New York: Harpers, 1989], 103).

21   Raymond Keith Williamson, *Introduction to Hegel's Philosophy of Religion* (Albany, N. Y.: SUNY Press, 1984), 254.

22   Apart from process theology, two other notable panentheistic traditions are the Hegelian and the Tillichian. In spite of Hegel's focus on history to the detriment of nature, he insisted on both intimacy between God and the world and the mediation of God in the world: God "is not the world, nor is the world God, but the world is God's appearing, God's activity of self-manifestation, appearing which is completed in man. The world, and man in it, are real only to the extent that God is in them, and their true being is in God, which is another way of saying that the finite is the appearing of the infinite and has its being in the infinite" (quoted in Williamson, *Hegel's Philosophy of Religon*, 270). One of Tillich's central contributions was his insistence that Spirit is the most adequate term for God as it unites power (the depths of the divine) with meaning (the Logos) and together they account for "life" or the spirit: "The statement that God is Spirit means that life as spirit is the inclusive symbol for the divine life" (*Systematic Theology*, vol. 1 [Chicago: University of Chicago Press, 1951], 250). One of the values of Tillich's position is that life rather than mind is the primary designation of the divine spirit; hence, a foundation is laid for an inclusive theology. A contemporary follower of the Hegelian/Tillichian panentheistic tradition, Peter Hodgson, moves it yet further in that direction: "When I say 'world,' I mean the whole world – the cosmos as we know it, the

stars and planets, biological life, human consciousness, culture and history. This whole world is the figure, shape, or gestalt of God in the moment of difference; It is 'God's body.' 'God's got the whole world in his hands' " (*God in History: Shapes of Freedom* [Nashville: Abingdon Press, 1989], 106).

23   "The doctrine of creation . . . is preeminently an affirmation about the sovereignty of God and the absolute dependence of the creatures" (Bernard W. Anderson, "Creation in the Bible," in *Cry of the Environment: Rebuilding the Christian Creation*, ed. Philip N. Joranson and Ken Butigan [Santa Fe, N. M.: Bear and Co., 1984], 28). "In both testaments, the doctrine stresses the transcendence and freedom of God, the complete dependence of the whole creation upon the Creator, the reverence for all forms of life" (19). See also Richard J. Clifford, "Creation in the Hebrew Bible," in *Physics, Philosophy and Theology: A Common Quest for Understanding* (Vatican City State: Vatican Observatory, 1988).

24   The following analysis, especially of the procreative model, is indebted to Martha Weigle, *Creation and Procreation: Feminist Reflections on Mythologies of Cosmogony and Parturition* (Philadelphia: University of Pennsylvania Press, 1989).

25   This way of thinking has found favor in relatively establishment Christian circles. For instance, Arthur Peacocke claims that in the past, divine creation has been dominated by external, masculine images and a more internal one is needed, such as female birth: "Mammalian females . . . create within themselves and the growing embryo resides within the female body and this is a proper corrective to the masculine picture – it is an analogy of God creating the world within herself . . . God creates a world that is, in principle and in origin, other than him/herself but creates it, the world, within him/herself" (*Creation and the World of Science* [Oxford: Clarendon Press, 1979], 142). Grace Jantzen, in her book on the universe as God's body, writes: "God formed it [the world] quite literally 'out of himself' – that is, it is his self-formation – rather than out of nothing" (*God's World, God's Body*, 135). The strangeness of using the male pronoun here seems to have escaped Jantzen.

26   Hugh Montefiore gives a helpful analysis of three models of creation: making, organism, and emanation. In the emanation model, creation is empowered by the life-giving energy of the divine spirit and word (Gen. 1:2, 2:7; Ps. 104:30; Prov. 8:30). The Wisdom tradition picks up on the emanationist strand as does the Neoplatonic, in which all life comes from God and will return to God. See his "Report of a working group on environment in the Church of England," in his edited volume, *Man and Nature* (London: Collins, 1975).

27   The addition of the emanation component is not meant, however, to undercut in any way the foundation that the procreative model gives us in physical reality. Weigle points out that cosmogonies in which male creation predominates (creation by spirit, breath, dream, speech) are more highly valued by anthropologists than those with female procreation (creation by physical or natural means). "The former are too readily regarded as male and more highly valued, especially when they can be associated with the monotheism of a supreme (preferably masculine) deity; the latter are often considered female and less valuable for being related to nature and animism" (*Creation and Procreation*, 7). Gerda Lerner notes that because monotheism

arose within the context of patriarchy, images of creation were exclusively masculine and severed from procreation; thus, not only was divine creation understood
entirely in terms of mental production but so was human creation (*The Creation of
Patriarchy* [Oxford: Oxford University Press, 1986], 198). This division has meant a
dualism between creation (masculine, mind, "higher things") versus procreation
(feminine, body, "lower things"). The problem, however, is not monotheism but
patriarchy: the Source of life in the universe can be (and, we are suggesting, ought
to be) imaged as procreation rather than production.

28   In different ways, one sees this tendency in Augustine and Hegel, and also in Tillich,
whose treatment of the fall is, in significant ways, indistinguishable from creation
(see *Systematic Theology*, vol. 2).

29   Conrad Hyers describes the imagery of Genesis 1 as imperialistic and intellectual:
"The Priestly account . . . favors the image of the divine king who issues royal
commands, organizes territories, and rules over his dominion. In Genesis 1 the
imagery is lofty and transcendent, after the manner in which an imperial ruler is
elevated a considerable distance above his subjects" (*The Meaning of Creation: Genesis and
Modern Science* [Atlanta: John Knox, 1984], 98). The Genesis 2 tradition is more
homey and softer, with God as maker (potter and clay), but even here Hyers claims
that the biblical tradition steers clear of female birth imagery, seeing creation as "a
neuter category" of making – God as artist, architect, sculptor (135).

30   *Webster's New World Dictionary*, 2d ed., 1974.

31   Gerard Manley Hopkins, *Poems and Prose*, ed. W. H. Gardner (London: Penguin, 1953),
27.

32   Weigle, *Creation and Procreation*, 7.

Chapter 24

Ruth Page

PANENTHEISM AND
PANSYNTHEISM: GOD IN RELATION

PROCESS PHILOSOPHY and process theology have made a valuable contribution to theological thought, particularly in their description of the immanence of God as one pole of the divine being, thus emphasizing the proximity of God without surrendering ineffable transcendence. Further, in their view the whole sweep of creation is envisaged in the divine process, not simply the human chapter. The metaphysic of divine presence is expressed in panentheism, well defined in the *Oxford Dictionary of the Christian Church* as "The belief that the being of God includes and penetrates the whole universe, so that every part exists in Him [sic], but (as against pantheism) that His Being is more than, and is not exhausted by, the universe."[1]

Some problems in panentheism

Given that metaphysical background, however, there are various ways it may be applied to God's action in, and relation to, creation. Creation itself is a multiple conception and has to be considered as a whole project, as an evolving process, and as it affects every creature. Further, a description of what relationship involves will affect accounts of the Divine-creation relationship. Therefore, while accepting totally the definition of panentheism given above, I believe some more particular expositions of God in relation to creation have serious difficulties, which this [essay] will discuss. These difficulties may be overcome by a different model of relationship which I shall then proceed to describe in terms of *pansyntheism*: God with everything.

The first problem with some writing on panentheism is that it takes a wide overview of evolution, seeking to give it all a pattern. Thus, what are celebrated are emergent levels of *complexity* ("hierarchies of levels of complexity")[2] and the arrival of *self-consciousness*. This level of abstraction is, first, inadequate in itself as a description of evolution, the history of which is more ambiguous than that would suggest, and second, it leaves God with no more than a guiding hand through the process, an action which falls far short of any sense of relationship.

Certainly there has been an increase in complexity among life-forms. Humans are far more complex than an amoeba, more even than an orangutan, our near relative. But will complexity bear the weight attributed to it as one of the highest values in creation? The achievement is not a simple good. Increasing complexity in one direction decreases flexibility in another. Humans are small, slow creatures in comparison with other forms (which, if they could speak for themselves, might favor speed or size as the preferred value). Further, gains like complexity regularly have negative effects as well, as the cheetah's specialization in speed has sapped it of its fighting strength. A negative effect in the case of the human brain, which has enabled so much civilization and culture (though also so much devastation), is evident in the process of giving birth. The large head of a complex human baby has to descend a birth canal evolved for something smaller. The pains and dangers of childbirth are part of the price paid for complexity which cesarean operations do not adequately overcome.

Consciousness has been equally valued. "The contingency of human being is consistent with the working out of divine purpose in creation, that of eliciting the emergence of self-conscious persons."[3] Yet although consciousness has enabled humans to transcend their immediate situation and needs, it is not without its own ambiguity. To take one small example: it enables regret at the past and apprehension over the future in ways which do not contribute to present well-being. Apprehension is a state readily recognized after the destruction of the World Trade Center in New York. But unself-conscious creatures have no such foreboding. The Scottish poet Robert Burns wrote an apology to a mouse when he broke its nest with his plow. In that poem he expresses poignantly the human condition:

> Still thou art blest compared wi' me!
> The present only touches thee.
> But Och! I backward cast my e'e
> On prospects drear,

An' forward, though I canna see,
I guess and fear.[4]

Thus, in the first place, those features of evolution singled out as instances of God's guiding are themselves two-edged, ambiguous like everything in creation — a matter to which I shall return later.[5] Moreover, the celebration of advance ignores or belittles the cost incurred en route. Many panentheistic writers advert to the losses of creatures down the ages, allowing that the cost is prodigious, but not allowing themselves to be deflected from the pattern they are following. Philip Clayton, for instance, writes that "there are significant cases of *disorder* in the biological world, including the pointless death of thousands of species. Should not the case of disorder count against the hypothesis of a cosmic designer?" Nevertheless, he subsumes such unease under the process of *fides quaerens intellectum* (faith seeking understanding), for "*to the eyes of faith* it is impossible not to find signs of God's purpose and designs in the world."[6] I would not disagree with the belief that signs of God's purpose in the world are perceptible to faith, but whether the divine *design* is visible through "the pointless death of thousands of species" is a much more dubious proposition.

Extinction and disorder in the evolutionary process tell against any optimistic perception of divine purpose. When Moltmann gave his Gifford Lectures in Edinburgh, published as *God in Creation*, he expatiated on God's goodness in creating an open system, such that creation was not fixed from the beginning but was free to move and change.[7] Yet an open system is possible only when deaths and extinctions occur and vacant ecological niches are opened up. Thus, before *Homo sapiens sapiens* had even evolved, over 90 percent of species had become extinct. At the Moltmann lectures the dean of the veterinary school commented: "What God creates, God deletes," a view I find contrary to what I believe about God.

God may not be interpreted as directly creating (and hence deleting) living creatures. But if God is in any sense directing evolution toward complexity and consciousness, the losses are part of the process and the cost appears disproportionate. I came to my interest in faith and science issues through my work on ecotheology. In that connection Christians are being encouraged to help save endangered species, and the reason often given is that they are in some sense God's creatures. But it is a real question what Christian faith has to offer to the cause of preservation if before we had even evolved to add our own devastation, God was exercising an influence/effect which resulted in the extinction of over 90 percent of creation.

Finally on this point of emerging complexity and consciousness as the direction of God's movement through evolution, it is clear that the desire to invoke God's effects in this area is as fraught with difficulty as is the desire to see the divine hand in human history. Some time ago I argued that latter case: "By ignoring the total reticulation of events (C. H.) Dodd is making room for the action of God."[8] Indeed, historians have objected to all patterning of history as doing no justice to actual variety. Thus Pieter Geyl upbraids Toynbee for his *Study of History*: "To see a self-styled historian reducing the whole of the wonderful and mysterious movement of history to one single motif, rejecting whole centuries as uninteresting, forcing it all into a scheme of presumptuous construction, strikes [the historian] as going against all that history stands for."[9]

Mutatis mutandis, Geyl's remarks may be directed toward every over-simplification of evolutionary history. The study of evolution is not the same as the study of history. It does not, for instance, have the mind-set of other times to discern. But the strictures against making patterns in history, as blinding their proponents to counterevidence, playing up some aspects while leaving others as irrelevant, are the same as those against the selection of what is to count as important and what is to be dismissed as unimportant ("rejecting whole centuries [in this case aeons] as uninteresting [to God?]") in some versions of evolution within the panentheistic fold.

I am not arguing against the existence of emergence, or complexity, or the dawn of self-consciousness. These have clearly happened and have had many good results, as well as the less happy. I am arguing that the selection of these traits together with the ignoring of "unsuccessful" creatures which became extinct for any reason is to pattern evolution unjustifiably in the direction of human arrival. This is the fault of anthropocentrism, acknowledged now as an oppressive part of the Christian heritage in ecotheology, for it implicitly down-grades the nonhuman and decreases the importance of both human and divine care for the rest of creation. We believe God cares for each individual human, so why not each individual nonhuman? Jesus portrayed God as caring for each individual sparrow (Matt. 10:29), although there was a wider range to care about in humans. Such care, proper to each creature, should also appear in Christian accounts of evolution.

The downgrading of the nonhuman in the valuing of complexity sometimes becomes explicit, as in Charles Birch. "But why rate all life of equal value? If intrinsic value is 'measured' by richness of experience, it follows that creatures such as primates and whales have more intrinsic value than worms or mosquitoes."[10] (This raises another question for me. The post-World War II Britain of my childhood was a drab place compared to the richness of experience I have now. Did my intrinsic value increase, or has it been always the same by pure ontology without reference to context?) Daly and Cobb point out that Birch's hierarchy of richness of experience is different from the one of importance to the planet's survival, in which bacteria would have a much higher standing.[11] But that reinforces my point. Why choose a standard of value which is entirely ontological (a matter to which I shall return) as opposed to one of ecological fitness in interrelationship, which would suit the planet better, while believers must suppose God cares about the state of the planet? In that ecological scenario humans with their casual overuse of creation viewed only as a collection of resources would not rate highly. Gradings require a standard against which they take place. In many panentheistic accounts the acme is clearly an ontological account of chosen aspects of human being — anthropocentrism again — so that all other creatures are assigned a greater or lesser value in relation to human qualities.

This hierarchical view of evolution creates theological problems concerning partiality in God, if God also appears to value creatures more or less according to their richness of experience and proximity to the desired human traits. God surely values creatures for what they are and what they are doing in their own circumstances. (It is worth noting for comparison that I found no deficit in richness of experience during my childhood. It was what it was: whole in itself. It is presumably the same for nonhuman creatures.) Rather than working with hierarchies, theology could rejoice in the diversity of creatures and their interrelationship without prior gradings, and understand God to rejoice (or suffer) with creation as well. Considering how recently humans appeared in evolutionary time, God would have spent ages without real pleasure in creation if all that was happening was influence toward future qualities.

As my proposal that God rejoices in the diversity of creation implies, I am not arguing that the perception of ambiguity in evolution overturns all stances of faith. The philosopher Stephen Clark mounted a rigorous logical attack on the rationality of denying validity to any but "neutral" scientific facts.

> Scientists, they say, are only concerned with "facts" and moral (or metaphysical) preferences can never be grounded upon facts or rationally discovered. This does not seem to stop them from counting their own preferences more rational than those of zoophiles, while denying that any such preferences are rational at all. . . . The claim that only the laws of logic and empirical generalisations have any rational status has no rational status: for it is neither a law of logic nor an empirical discovery. . . . The objectivist identifies a right approach in the act of denying that there is a right approach.[12]

The matter of metaphysical or theological approaches to such matters as evolution is therefore right to be defended, but it should embrace the widest possible spectrum of information in order to avoid the criticism of partiality.

The sweeping, triumphalist overview of evolution would not be possible if attention were given to God with each creature and each species. Yet insofar as this happens within process thought, the nature of the relationship remains deficient. It is often held within process theology that God gives creatures an "initial aim" or "lure" to achieve the best they can in their circumstances.[13] The lure, as David Pailin describes it, is "to take just this, rather than any other concrete form — although (of course) it is open for the creature to use its creative freedom to actualise one of the other possibilities open to it."[14] This account raises a number of questions. Did God lure to "just this form" the innumerable instances of predator and prey, eat or be eaten, or is that a willful decline from the initial aim? Are all the extinct to be dismissed as not having responded adequately to the lure? What of external factors such as climate change (ice ages) and meteor strikes? On closer inspection, notions of "lure" in connection with evolutionary process have many practical problems. Issues of natural evil remain largely unaddressed and undermine Cobb and Griffin's account of the lure as creative love.[15]

Pailin certainly takes some notice of evil: "Natural evil may be the product of the non-compossibility of several values . . . or the outcome of random chance conjunctions or the result of unsuitable conditions."[16] That indeed seems to be a fair summary of the case. The issue then becomes whether these conditions are numerous enough and compelling enough to make beliefs about a divinely given initial aim impossible. For me there is particularly the colossal extent of extinction, both sudden extinctions like the one in which the dinosaurs perished and the steady background extinctions which go on all the time. Numbers are not everything, but the size of these numbers must give pause if God is said to be exerting a lure. (In all this discussion I take individual death to be a part of life, but the extinction of a life-form, a corner of creation, especially when caused by something as external as climate change, is a more serious theological matter.)

One solution: pansyntheism

There are four parts to this proposed solution to the foregoing problems. First I shall discuss what God may be said to have created, and then what the freedom of creation implies. After that come a description of the relationship which exists between God and every last creature, and finally an account of how God makes a difference to what goes on in the world.[17]

First, then, what did God create? I have learned much from process thought on God's creation of possibilities. Yet I find that the next step curtails the application of that notion. "But the sphere of possibility is purely abstract, lacking all agency to provide selectively for the need of new events. There must be an agency that mediates between these abstract forms or pure possibilities and the actual world."[18] But possibility is not a "sphere" in which actualities may be envisaged. Rather it is the condition within which things may or may not happen. Such an understanding moves toward action and relationship, away from the ontological slant within process construction, evident in the initial aim to a form of being, and the hierarchy of creatures with intrinsic value according to their being. Current theology is much more (and rightly) concerned with relationship, and although that may imply an ontology, it does not presuppose one. Thus the role of possibility may be seen as making beings-with-relationships possible rather than setting an ontological goal. Therefore I believe God to have created possibility as the possibility of possibilities without designing any particular forms, including the human, to be aimed at. That anything at all is now, has been, or will be possible is the gift of God in creation making possibility possible. It is a steadfast, loving gift as possibilities continue.

The obverse side of this account of divine creating is the freedom of the subsequent creation to evolve and act as it could within its possibilities. That freedom has produced the world's ambiguity, for it has resulted in, for instance, the earth's tectonic plates which later cause earthquakes, and the welcome production of a breathable atmosphere. Through that freedom of possibility life-forms have come about — often in competition with one another. But they have enjoyed their day and generation and (frequently) perished. This brief account of creaturely freedom extends freedom from the "free will defense" of Augustine concerning human moral evil to a defense of natural evil through the effects of multiple finite freedoms down through all time. In that case neither moral nor natural evil is to be attributed to any kind of scheme by, or influence from, God.

Yet that account on its own would distance God from the world and is little better than a modern form of Deism. For God could have created possibility but then abandoned creation to its own success and failure. But that is exactly where the value of panentheism lies, with its insistence that the world is in God. God cannot be distant from the world. Here also the current emphasis on relationship becomes important again, for God, who gave the freedom of possibility in the first place, is in relationship with every diverse creature which uses possibility to come into being — thereby responding to the Creator's gift. Yet this freedom is at the same time constrained by current circumstances, circumstances which have come about by the results of earlier use of possibilities.

If God may be said to be characterized by freedom and love in relation to creation, the very gift of freedom is loving. But that love also accompanies creation in its use of finite freedoms.[19] The whole of creation is companioned by God, not on the basis of hierarchy, but according to what is proper and necessary to the creature in its circumstances. As Jesus indicated, much is necessary for humans, but that "much" has to do with its widest range of possibilities. Humans form a species to which much has been given, and from which much is expected. As that suggests, the range of possible response from creation will differ according to each creature's possibilities.

Just as process theology has argued that God works by persuasion, so I believe relationship works by attraction. That emphasis on how relationship works does not make God passive as either a cosmic sponge or a pained onlooker. What God does is to establish and maintain relationships with all creation, and that is action as surely as anything more interventionist and directive. One need only think of the problems of relationship which occur in marriages to see that the connection requires attention and work so that lines of communication and support remain open, and that gives some glimpse of what it means to say God acts by making and maintaining relationships. At the same time, the divine must not be thought of as a glorified human establishing "personal" relationships. God relates to all according to their kind, being unlike humans in knowing what it is to be a tree frog or a jaguar, knowing indeed the particular situation of any jaguar better than the animal knows itself. I have used the word "relationship" for this connection, although it is a human term and may not be right for nonhuman creatures. But it is the only word we have for the kind of valuable connection I wish to indicate.

Humans are further limited in not being able to transcend the species barrier to discern what it is for a dung beetle, for instance, to respond to God. It will not respond in any way comparable to humans, but humans themselves need not think that theirs is the only manner of response. Yet one kind of response may be visible in the way nonhuman creatures resist death by fight or flight until their old age. Only humans commit suicide. Such tenacity is a form of response to the divine gift which made life possible. In a way, all divine-creaturely relationships will be one-sided, given that God understands the being, the relationships, the context of each creature perfectly — the actual as actual and the possible as possible — while creatures may respond only out of their own finite, more or less limited capacities. But that too God understands.

On the other hand, a relationship may not be equal, but it comes to fruition and has consequences when it is a known reality and is responded to and acted upon. The nature of the response, moreover, will naturally vary with each individual creature, but its primary component, apart from appreciation of life, may be described in human terms and then attributed with appropriate variation to other creatures. Since God is present but does not intervene, that primary component is creaturely attention, and no one has described what is involved in such attention better than Simone Weil. She illustrates it well through the story of the Good Samaritan. There the sufferer is "only a little piece of flesh, inert and bleeding beside a ditch; he is nameless, no one knows anything about him." In other words, there is no prior connection and nothing attractive to draw the attention. She continues: "Those who pass by this thing scarcely notice it, and a few minutes afterwards *do not even know that they have seen it*"; that is to say, something which is there is just not there for those with no attention. Further: "Only one stops and turns his attention towards it. The actions that follow are just the automatic effect of this moment of attention. The attention is creative. But at the moment it is engaged it is renunciation."[20]

One may go through life entirely taken up with one's own concerns, with the "estranged faces" Francis Thomson said missed "the many-splendoured thing."[21] In Weil's words, such people "do not even know that they have seen it." But to take one's eyes off oneself, to pay attention, is to catch the many-splendored thing, even if it is perceived through some inert and bleeding flesh. Weil may be optimistic in thinking that actions automatically follow from such perception: there may have to be more internal wrestling than that, and less clarity over what exactly to do. But she is right to say that attention is creative — it brings about a new perception of the situation leading to consequent action. It is in this joint way of presence and response that God the companion of all that is acts in the world with free creatures (pansyntheism), a powerful presence when attended to.

But Weil is also right to say that such attention is at the same time renunciation — the renunciation of the creature's self-absorption. Indeed, she interprets the act of creation as renunciation by God who freely allows finitude to come into being within infinity. For Weil the human participation of attention and response "is something sacred. It is what man grants to God. It is what God comes searching for as a beggar among men."[22] In a sense God is a beggar, for God will not remove creaturely freedom to have divine effects. But response opens up the possibilities of powerful divine relationship.

Thus the God who grants freedom to creation is not going to shape evolution toward complexity and self-consciousness, for the powerful presence has always been there, always seeking a response in the attention of all creatures and thus having effects in the world as the response is worked out. Yet again we do not know what counts as response and relationship in other creatures. But with the belief that God's love can never be a matter of more or less, nor given to some and withheld from others, comes the belief that response is always one of the possibilities for all creatures according to their kind.

There is one last important argument concerning relationship. Its proper preposition is "with" (hence pansyntheism) rather than "in" (extended panentheism) — or indeed "over." Thus any extension of panentheism to the proposition that God is "in" creatures, human or nonhuman, is questionable. A relationship is close, but not so close that one is overwhelmed by the other. Thus relationship is not fusion; rather it preserves some space between participants, a to-and-fro even in the coming together. It is the freedom, the attention, the sense of responsibility of each participant which make possible mutuality and joint action. God remains God while men and women (and indeed all creatures) remain themselves, capable of attention and response, but independent enough also to ignore God and wreak the havoc which selfishness can bring about.

A further argument against the notion of God "in" creatures is the ambiguity or the downright evil pervading creation. In a historic debate Reformed theologians argued against Lutherans that *finitum non capax infiniti* (the finite cannot contain/bear the infinite). Their concern was not so much how to fit the infinite into the finite, but rather with the sin of humans and the fallenness of all creation, such that it was held to be unfit to bear this good and holy God. The phrase, however, still has relevance, for even today, when there is no appeal to the fall, and much less absorption with sin, this remains a world of various competing or cooperating finite freedoms. It will be full of unforeseeable change, and always open to varieties of interpretation, and hence ambiguous. General patterns may have the result that what is good for some may simultaneously be bad for others, or that something which is good at one time may later become harmful. Particular instances of this principle could be multiplied. If God is "in" something, it should surely be good without qualification, and there is little that remains, or even appears, that way to everyone involved.

Another question would be what happens if a person or situation "in" which God is seen becomes worse. Has God left? Does God come and go? Or remain "in" even as matters deteriorate? "If God is 'in me,' internally directing my thought and action, what has happened to my freedom and responsibility? Or does God have to be held partly responsible for the ambiguities within my own best but humanly limited actions?"[23] It still seems possible to use "in" of someone or something so transparent to the relationship with God that the small distance of "with" is irrelevant. But in general use the notion of God with, God alongside, *always* present but not internal, obviates the difficulties of "in" and gives positive gain in the benefits of relationship.

It could be argued against this whole account of possibility and relationship that God, being God, would have foreseen that multiple finite freedoms, however they evolved, would jostle, constrain, and hurt one another. In that case, was the freedom worth it? I can only suggest that God, being freedom and love, desired the possibility of finite freedom and love, and took the attendant risk of constraint and evil, without which freedom and love are not possible in this world.

Notes

1   *Oxford Dictionary of the Christian Church* (Oxford: Oxford University Press, 1983), p. 1027.

2   Arthur Peacocke, *Theology for a Scientific Age* (London: SCM Press, 1990), p. 61. Peacocke is aware of the ambiguities, but still represents complexity and the development of consciousness as an upward trend.

3   Peacocke, p. 245.

4   Robert Burns, "To a Mouse," in *The Poetry of Scotland*, ed. Roderick Watson (Edinburgh: Edinburgh University Press, 1995), p. 372.

5   Tracing this ambiguity and discovering what it implies for theology was the subject of Ruth Page, *Ambiguity and the Presence of God* (London: SCM Press, 1985).

6   Philip Clayton, *God and Contemporary Science* (Edinburgh: Edinburgh University Press; Grand Rapids: Eerdmans, 1997), pp. 113–14.

7   Jürgen Moltmann, *God in Creation: An Ecological Doctrine of Creation* (London: SCM Press, 1985).

8   Ruth Page, "C. H. Dodd's Use of History Critically Examined," *Theology* 79 (November 1976): 330.

9   Pieter Geyl, *Debates with Historians* (London: Fontana/Collins, 1957), p. 203.

10   Charles Birch, *On Purpose* (Kensington, N.S.W., Australia: University of New South Wales Press, 1990), p. 133.

11   Herman E. Daly and John B. Cobb, Jr., *For the Common Good: Redirecting the Economy towards Community, the Environment, and a Sustainable Future* (Boston: Beacon Press, 1989), p. 378.

12   S. Clark, "Modern Error, Ancient Virtues," in *Ethics and Biotechnology*, ed. A. Dyson and J. Harris (London: Routledge, 1994), pp. 27–29.

13   Cf. John B. Cobb, Jr., and David Ray Griffin, *Process Theology: An Introductory Exposition* (Philadelphia: Westminster, 1976), p. 53. Peacocke explicitly distances himself from this view of God's action. See Peacocke, pp. 373–74.

14   David Pailin, *God and the Process of Reality: Foundations for a Credible Theism* (London: Routledge, 1989), p. 140.

15   Cobb and Griffin, p. 373.

16   Pailin, pp. 144–45.

17   This explanation is given at much greater length in Ruth Page, *God and the Web of Creation* (London: SCM Press, 1996).

18   Cobb and Griffin, p. 43.

19   Ruth Page, *The Incarnation of Freedom and Love* (London: SCM Press, 1991).

20   Simone Weil, *Waiting for God* (Fontana Books, 1959), p. 103, italics added.

21   Francis Thomson, "In No Strange Land," in *The Oxford Book of English Verse* (Oxford: Oxford University Press, 1949), p. 1049.

22   Simone Weil, "Are We Struggling for Justice?" in *Simone Weil: An Anthology*, ed. Sian Miles (London: Virago Press, 1986), p. 3.

23   Page, *Web of Creation*, p. 41.

Chapter 25

Gordon D. Kaufman

ON THINKING OF GOD AS SERENDIPITOUS CREATIVITY

. . . **I [HAVE EARLIER] PROPOSED** *serendipitous creativity* as a metaphor more appropriate for thinking of God today than such traditional image/concepts as creator, lord, and father.[1] [Here] I shall elaborate more fully and nuance more carefully that concept. It is no longer possible, I contend, to connect in an intelligible way today's scientific, cosmological and evolutionary understandings of the origins of the universe and the emergence of life (including human life and history) with a conception of God constructed in the traditional anthropomorphic terms. However, the metaphor of creativity—a descendant of the biblical concept of creation, and directly implied in the idea of evolution itself—has resources for constructing a religiously pertinent and meaningful modern/postmodern conception of God. In this [essay] the notion of creativity is explored with respect to the profoundly serendipitous mystery implied in it; its usefulness in orienting human life today, particularly in connection with contemporary ecological issues; and its implications for such traditional theological themes as the problem of evil and "God is love." The [essay] concludes with a brief characterization of what human life and faith would be like if ordered in relation to a God conceived as serendipitous creativity instead of a God defined in the more traditional anthropomorphic way.

Biblical texts . . . have been the most influential source of Christian and other Western thinking about God. When those texts were written, the earth and its immediate environment (the "heavens") were regarded as all that existed, the universe. And though this universe was doubtless immense to the humans living within it, it was minuscule by today's standards. In that historico-cultural situation it was not implausible to imagine some almighty personal being who existed before and apart from the universe and by all-powerful fiat brought it into being (as in Gen. 1). Moreover, one could imagine this superpersonal being taking up clay from the ground and forming creatures, including humans, out of it (see Gen. 2). Both of these types of creativity were well known at that time, and it is not surprising, therefore, that humans imagined the universe being brought into existence through acts of this sort. The biblical stories thus supplied an account of an ultimate origin of things and of an ultimate personal power behind all things—God—that still remains plausible to many.

In my view, however, we can no longer continue thinking of God along these lines. What could we possibly be imagining when we attempt to think of God as an all-powerful personal reality existing somehow before and independent of what we today call "the universe"? As far as we know, personal agential beings did not exist, and could not have existed, before billions of years of cosmic evolution of a very specific sort, and then further billions of years of biological evolution also of a very specific sort, had transpired. How then can we today think of a person-like creator-God as existing before and apart from any such evolutionary developments? What possible content can this more or less traditional idea of God have for those of us who think of the universe in our modern evolutionary way, according to which no life or consciousness can be imagined apart from the emergence of these very specific and quite extraordinary conditions?[2]

The idea of creativity, however (in contrast with the notion of a creator)—the idea of the coming into being through time of the previously nonexistent, the new, the novel—continues to have considerable plausibility today; indeed, it is bound up with the very belief that our cosmos is an evolutionary one in which new orders of reality come into being in the course of exceedingly complex temporal developments.[3] In my view, therefore, those interested in theological reflection and construction can and should continue to work with the idea of creativity, but they should no longer think of this creativity as lodged in a *creator-agent* (a concept no longer intelligible). There are a number of advantages to this move, though it also presents us with some serious ambiguities and problems.[4] In this [essay] I reflect on some of these, thus elaborating further and nuancing in certain respects what [I have earlier written[5]] about God as creativity.

I

First, let us consider briefly some features of the idea of creativity itself. It might be assumed that creativity is to be thought of as a sort of force at work in the cosmos, bringing the new into being. Some of the rhetoric in my writing and speaking (including within In Face of Mystery [Kaufman 1993a]) may suggest this. This sort of thinking in effect just substitutes the notion of force for God, implying that creativity is simply a kind of impersonal—instead of personal and agential—power. To make that sort of claim, however, presupposes that we know more about the emergence of truly new and novel realities than we actually do. But the notion of creativity itself carries a strong note of mystery. It differs from "mystery" in that it directs attention to the coming into being of the new, whereas "mystery" (when used in a theological context) refers to fundamental limits of all human knowledge (Kaufman 1993a, 54–69) and carries no such further meaning. But creativity is profoundly mysterious; as the ancient phrase creatio ex nihilo (creation out of nothing) emphasized, the coming into being of the truly new and novel is not something that we humans understand. We can see this most vividly, perhaps, when we consider the old unanswerable question, Why is there something, not nothing? As Nicholas Berdyaev put it, "Creation is the greatest mystery of life, the mystery of the appearance of something new that had never existed before and is not deduced from, or generated by, anything" (1937, 163). To regard creativity as a kind of "force" is to suggest that we have a sort of (vague) knowledge of an existing something-or-other when in fact we do not. All we really see or understand is that new and novel realities have begun to exist in time. There is a serendipitous feature in all creativity: more happens than one would have expected, given previously prevailing circumstances, indeed, more than might have seemed possible (Kaufman 1993a, 279).[6] In the case of evolving life we see that this occurs through chance variation and selective adaptation, but neither of these can properly be reified into "causes" or "forces" (in any ordinary sense of those words) that directly produce the new creation. Creativity happens: this is an absolutely amazing mystery—even though we may in certain cases, for example with the evolution of life, be able to specify some of the conditions without which it could not happen.[7]

Precisely because of this close connection with the idea of mystery, "creativity" is a good metaphor for thinking about God. If used properly, it preserves the notion of God as the ultimate mystery of things, a mystery that we have not been able to penetrate or dissolve—and likely never will succeed in penetrating or dissolving. This aspect of the notion of creativity draws us into a deeper sensitivity to God-as-mystery than some of our religious traditions do, with their talk of God as the Creator. For this latter concept seemed to imply that we knew the ultimate mystery (God) was really a person-like, agent-like being, one who "decided" to do things, who set purposes and then brought about the realization of those purposes—as a potter or sculptor creates artifacts (Gen. 2) or as a poet or king brings order and reality into being through uttering words (Gen. 1). Absent these models of creativity, the biblical writers might never have generated their radical notion of creation, eventually to be elaborated in terms of the formula of *creatio ex nihilo*. With Darwin, however, we have learned that significant creativity can be thought of in other ways as well. Indeed, according to evolutionary theory these human models of agential creativity themselves came into being ("were created") as cosmic processes in the course of long stretches of time brought into being certain very complex forms of life. The most foundational kind of creativity for us today, therefore, appears to be that exemplified in the evolution of the cosmos and of life, rather than that displayed in human purposive activity. Though we can describe the evolution-ary model with some precision, it in no way overcomes the most profound mystery at the root of all that is: Why is there something, not nothing? Why—and how—can the new actually come into being in the course of time? Nor does the Big Bang throw any light on these questions; it only succeeds in raising them over again in an extremely acute form.[8]

Thinking in terms of the ultimacy of the mystery of life and the world in this way is in keeping with the concern of the tradition of negative theology[9] . . . that we not reify God in any way, that we not think that we really know what or who God is (for example, an anthropomorphic agent who makes covenants with us, takes care of us in special ways, etc.). God is, in the last analysis, utterly unknowable. As the German hymn writer Gerhard Tersteegen (d. 1769) put it: "A God comprehended [that is, successfully captured in, and thus mastered by, our human concepts and images] is no God."[10] Pseudo-Dionysius, Maimonides, Thomas Aquinas, Eckhart, Luther, and others all understood this, though unfortunately they often compromised this insight by claims about special "experiences" of God or "revelations" from God (which, of course, gave humans a sense of profound knowledge, comfort, and cer-tainty). In the view I am presenting here, these compromises are no longer made: God is utter mystery, the mystery of creativity; speaking of God as creativity in no way diminishes the ultimacy of the mystery with which life confronts us.[11]

The metaphor of creativity, as I have been suggesting, is appropriate for naming God because (1) it preserves and indeed emphasizes the ultimacy of the mystery that God is, even while (2) it connects God directly with the coming into being—in time—of the new and the novel.[12] I highlight the significance of this second point by calling attention to the serendipitous aspect of creativity, a matter of special import when we attempt to think of God in this way. Humans, of course, are (so far as we know) the only beings that can or do take note of the creative processes and events in the world and who believe that apart from these processes we—and all else that makes up the world—would not exist at all. Only humans, therefore, are in a position to value the creativity in the world, and particularly to value its serendipitous character. If we value our own exist-ence, we can hardly fail to regard as serendipitous the continuous coming into being of the new that has led to the emergence of humankind through a highly beneficial (for us) though a quite surprising and chancy sequence of events. We would not exist had there not been a quite particular succession of happenings, summarized by astrophysicist Martin Rees as follows:

> For life like us to evolve, there must be time for early generations of stars to have evolved and died, to produce the chemical elements, and then time for the Sun to form and for evolution to take place on a planet around it. This takes several billion years. . . . The size of our universe shouldn't surprise us: its extravagant scale is necessary to allow *enough time* for life to evolve on even one planet around one star in one galaxy. This is an example of an "anthropic" argument, which entails realizing that the Copernican principle of cosmic modesty should not be taken too far. We are reluctant to assign ourselves a central position, but it may be equally unrealistic to deny that our situation in space and time is privileged in any sense. We are clearly not at a typical place in the universe: we are on a planet with special properties, orbiting around a stable star. Some-what less trivially, we are observing the universe not at a random time, but at a time when the requirements for complex evolution can be met.
>
> (1997, 229–230)[13]

It is thus quite appropriate to remind ourselves from time to time of the serendipitously creative character of the specific trajectory of the cosmic evo-lutionary process that produced us humans. Characterizing our trajectory in this way—and thinking of God in terms of the metaphor of serendipitous cre-ativity—are further examples of what (as Rees suggests) has come to be called *anthropic* thinking. That is, these examples call our attention to a feature of the universe that is of special importance to us humans, and they *name* this feature in a way that points out its significance not only for us humans but also for our understanding of the universe as a whole. These ideas are not merely of subject-ive human interest and import: they tell us something that is also objectively true of the cosmos within which we live. The symbol "God" has always func-tioned in this way to call attention to that reality believed to be of greatest importance for ongoing human life, and in this respect it is an anthropic idea (though it need not be an anthropomorphic idea . . .). The concept of serendipitous creativity can perform a similar anthropic function in relation to our modern/postmodern cosmological thinking, and for this reason I regard it as providing a useful way to bring the symbol "God" into significant connection with that thinking.[14]

II

In our use of the word "God," we humans are attempting to direct attention to what can be called the "ultimate point of reference" of all action, consciousness, and reflection. No regressive reflection seeking to push back to an ultimate starting point, no creative action moving toward an unstructured future, no appreciative feeling of worship or devotion expressing the orientation of the whole life of the self can intend some reality "beyond" God (Kaufman 1995, 14). But the idea of an ultimate point of reference is itself much more abstract than the concept of God. What more, then, should be said? In *In Face of Mystery* (Kaufman 1993a) and in this [essay] I have taken the position, following suggestions of theologian H. N. Wieman, that God should be thought of as creativity; creativity is the only proper object of worship, devotion, and faith today, the only proper ultimate point of reference for our valuing.[15] . . . Everything other than the ultimate mystery of creativity is a finite created reality that may indeed be valued and appreciated within certain limits, but which is itself always subject to distortion, corruption, and disintegration and thus must be relativized by the creativity manifest in the coming into being and the ultimate dissolution of all finite realities—that which alone may be characterized as "ultimate."

There is a problem here, however. Creativity understood as the coming into being of the new whenever and wherever this occurs—new evils (as we humans understand them) as well as new goods—raises some difficult questions. (On this issue I depart significantly from Wieman, for whom the "creative event" is always "the source of human good.") The biblical God, of course, was thought of as sometimes bringing into being what from our human perspective appear to be great evils, as well as goods: "Does evil befall a city, unless the Lord has done it?" asks the prophet Amos (3:6); "I make weal and create woe," says Yahweh through the mouth of Isaiah (45:7; see also Job, Jeremiah, and many other texts). In the New Testament, for the most part, God's fearful judgment and destructiveness remain despite the theme that "God is love" (as 1 John 4:8,16 put it). God is a frightening judge and destroyer as well as a forgiving father and redeemer; in this both Old Testament and New were consistently monotheistic. Thinking of God as serendipitous creativity—a mystery beyond our comprehension—is also consistently monotheistic.

However, if one takes this sort of position, can serendipitous creativity be regarded as always manifesting what is ultimately valuable for humans, a norm to be followed in all situations? Are we humans to emulate God's destructivity, God's bringing evils (as they seem to us) into being, as well as goods? These ideas may raise serious questions for Christians as well as others, although those who have regarded the warrior metaphor as apt for God (and Christ) have in the past been willing to draw these conclusions. For those who take a radically christomorphic faith-stance,[16] however, the creation of horrific evils can hardly be regarded as appropriate human activity. This concern has become particularly important today, when the human project can no longer tolerate the destructiveness of unrestricted warfare, for we now have the power to bring all human life (as well as much other life on planet Earth) to a halt. Clearly creativity without qualification—creation of historical trajectories going in almost any direction—cannot be regarded as a norm appropriate or helpful for the guidance of human life and activity: our human creativity, in accord with the normative christomorphic images, stories, and ideas in the New Testament, must be directed toward bringing goods into the world, not evils, toward healing, toward resolving disputes through compromise and mediation, toward overcoming the destructive momentums we humans have already brought into the ecological order on planet Earth and into the historical order of human affairs. The human creation of trajectories of massive destructiveness must be put out of bounds. But how can qualifications of this sort be reconciled with the claim that cosmic serendipitous creativity should be regarded as the ultimate point of reference in terms of which human existence is to be oriented, ordered, and normed?

This is not an insoluble issue. Problems arise here only if we think of serendipitous creativity in the abstract, as that creativity manifesting itself throughout the cosmos in trajectories of many different sorts, some of them in sharp tension with others.[17] However, when we consider that humans are neither responsible for nor can do much about most of what goes on in the universe, we can see (remembering the christomorphic principle) that the examples of creativity that are to be regarded as normative for us must be restricted to the *productive creativity* manifest on planet Earth and its immediate environment. Earth and its environment is really the only region of the cosmos that can be affected by our actions and projects (at least for the foreseeable future), and it is within this context that we must, therefore, seek to understand both our place in the created order and the activities appropriate for us to engage in; *productive creativity* alone is fitting, for clearly there is no reason to suppose that we humans have been in some way "authorized" (by an abstract cosmic creativity) to engage in extensive destruction of life and its ongoing momentums, which have taken thousands of millennia to emerge. Such a claim would manifest monstrous hubris and arrogance.

Thus, we must be quite constrictive in our thinking about our projects and our creativity: it is on a particular biohistorical trajectory that we humans have come into being,[18] and it is this trajectory that serves as the niche in Earth's ecological web where we must live and act. Doubtless this trajectory will end at some future time, but there is no basis for arguing that it is our proper human business to bring that about: our creativity, rather, should be exercised in searching out ways to live within our ecological niche on this planet, with a minimum of destructiveness of the other lines of life that also have their homes here. This is the moral implication of our growing ecological sensitivity and consciousness in recent decades: we no longer can live basically concerned with only the human project; our knowledges and sensitivities today enable us to understand that our project needs to fit much better into the broader ecology of planet Earth than often heretofore. It is our task today, therefore, to make whatever creative moves we can that will facilitate this. This does not mean that all destructive activity must be ruled out for humans; indeed, we need to destroy many of our own present patterns of action, ways of thinking, institutions, and so on, if we are to succeed in creating ecologically appropriate forms of human life on planet Earth. But destructiveness of this sort will be in the service of the further creative movement of the biohistorical trajectory that has brought us into being and continues to sustain us. Thus our creativity will be serving—rather than restricting or otherwise countering—the forward movement into the open future on planet Earth of the cosmic serendipitous creativity to which we seek to be ultimately responsible. In this way, the seeming paradox involved in regarding cosmic serendipitous creativity as the ultimate point of reference for our human devotion, thinking, and action dissolves away. Attempts to employ this ultimate mystery abstractly as a norm for making judgments about concrete cases here on Earth will always be obscure and dubious, as were attempts in the past to invoke "God's will" directly as justification for particular human decisions and actions.

These considerations bring us into a position from which we can take up briefly some further concerns that Christians might have respecting the proposal that we think of God as serendipitous creativity. Consider, for example, the Christian affirmation that "God is love" (1 John 4). In many respects this notion represents the epitome of Christian anthropomorphism/ anthropocentrism. Do the theological moves I am advocating rule out or make unintelligible this central Christian claim? The fundamental anthropomorphism of Israel's God-talk (as displayed in the Old Testament) helped prepare the way for using the metaphor "love" as the defining characterization of God in Christian thinking and practice. Because loving, caring attitudes and behaviors are of such importance in human life, thinking of God in terms of this metaphor had—and still has—great rhetorical power: God, the very creator of the universe, is seen here as standing in an intimate loving relationship with every person, God is "our father in heaven" who will meet every human need. "Even the hairs of your head are all numbered," as the words of Jesus put it (Matt. 10:30). Thus both the deep human longing for unlimited *agape-love* and an exceedingly powerful way of addressing that longing found significant realization in the conception of God as loving. The basic anthropomorphism of the early Christian conception of God made this thought seem both plausible and saving.

Does the move to a de-anthropomorphized God (as I am proposing) require us to jettison this whole way of thinking? No, it does not. What it does require is that we think through carefully the way this human need for love is to be understood in relation to serendipitous creativity. As we have been noting, it would certainly be a mistake to argue that cosmic creativity always manifests love for all the creatures involved: that would be unintelligible, indeed absurd, in face of all we know about nature "red in tooth and claw," to say nothing of the apparent origins of the universe in a Big Bang conceived in fundamentally physicalist terms. But there is every reason to maintain—in the theological position I am sketching—that the emergence of the love that has become of such central importance to human being and well-being must itself be seen as connected to the creativity that brought into being our humanity. In the processes through which our humanness was created, activity and attitudes and behaviors of the sort we call "loving" came into focus; love emerged with the human creatures who could respond to it. In our corner of the universe—that is, on the trajectory that has brought humans into being—capacities and needs for *agape*-love gradually became important and prized (at least in some quarters). So in and through our specifically human relation to God (as Christians have claimed), loving, caring attitudes and activities have become a significant feature, and love is both given and received—unlike the relations of creativity to many other spheres of the cosmic order, each of which has its own distinctive character.[19]

It would, of course, be improper to say simplistically and without qualification that "God is love," as Christians have sometimes done in the past; that would be to project on every feature and dimension of the universe what we find to be true and highly significant (only?) in our distinctively human sphere. But it is far from improper to say that not only in our relations with other humans, but also in our human relation to God (creativity) and in God's relation to us, *agape*-love has become an important feature. In that sense, we can still say, "God is love," although this is not the only way in which God should be characterized, nor is it the most fundamental or defining metaphor to use in thinking of God. That place must be reserved for the serendipitous creativity universally manifest. Of course Christians have always understood that a whole configuration of terms must be used in characterizing God ("power," "omnipresence," "eternity," "creativity," and so on), not "love" alone; indeed, to try to conceive God simply and completely in terms of the metaphor "love" would make both God and that metaphor unintelligible.

A brief word should, perhaps, be added here about the implications of all this for the concept of *evil*, a notion central in a number of religious traditions. I have argued elsewhere that this concept, and the correlative concept of salvation from evil, are generated largely by concerns about our own human well-being and fulfillment, on the one hand, and about human disaster or failure, on the other:

> The framework of valuation here is [as Spinoza argued] anthropocentric—at least initially. . . . The acts of generalization that occur as these complexes of terms are developed [in monotheisms], however, move toward transcendence of their anthropocentric origins. . . . And with the conception of God—though the name "God" initially designated, perhaps, that reality believed to be ultimately salvific of the human—there is clearly an attempt to indicate a point of reference in terms of which all else (including, of course, the human itself) can be assessed and judged. . . . [I]n radical monotheisms . . . the original awareness of evil as bound up with one's own pain and destruction [may become] completely concealed or even reversed (as in, for instance, the Calvinist triumphant willingness to be "damned for the glory of God").
> (Kaufman 1996, 87–89)[20]

Thus, though having its biological roots in the adverse response of living organisms to pain, the theological notion of evil in monotheistic traditions actually moved far beyond all anthropocentrism to the creation of a trans-human criterion for judging everything human: all human behavior, motivations, actions, institutions, and so on, were to be assessed in light of what God was thought to will and require (however good or bad that might seem to humans); living in faith came to be understood as involving the attempt to order all of life in terms of these divine requirements. Our human-centered judgments about right and wrong, good or bad, were overruled with the emergence of theocentric faith: what God is doing and what God wills for humanity became the ultimate criterion in terms of which all judgments of value and goodness, truth and meaning, were to be made; centering life on any other reality than God was idolatrous.

Obviously, these ideas can be connected fairly easily with the theological position sketched [here]. Indeed, conceiving God as serendipitous creativity—thus moving away from the anthropomorphic/anthropocentric tendencies in much traditional thinking—makes the theocentric feature of our God-talk more emphatic and austere than in most traditional views, and this is accomplished here (as just noted) without losing sight of God's loving relationship with humankind. The cosmic serendipitous creativity manifest throughout the universe is taken to be the ultimate criterion of all value and meaning, but the application of that criterion to our actual human living and dying cannot be made in these abstract terms but must be made, rather, in terms of the facticities of our human situatedness in the evolutionary/historical trajectory that has brought about and continues to sustain our human existence on Earth. Any human acts or practices, customs or institutions, that violate or are otherwise destructive of the biohistorical constraints within which humankind must live and work are to be characterized as "evil"; in contrast, whatever creatively facilitates the forward movement of the evolutionary/historical trajectory of which we are part—and is in relative harmony with the wider ecological order on Earth—is to be considered good, right, fitting.

Judgments made about values and meanings, about good and evil, continue here to have a direct bearing on and pertinence for human being and well-being, but they are no longer governed by essentially anthropocentric criteria. Because they are basically concerned with the ongoing sustainability of human existence within the web of life on planet Earth, they have a certain ecological objectivity—however difficult it may be, in specific cases, to ascertain in scientifically measurable terms just how this is to be conceived. "Evil" and "good," therefore, cannot be properly considered as merely a function of human desires and wishes.[21]

III

Let us step back now and take note again of the enormous difference in scale of today's vast universe as compared with the biblical one in which human God-talk began. The universe that we must take into account today—as we attempt to think about God and our obligations in the world—did not come into being just a short time before humanity was created. Nor does it consist largely in what is visible to the naked human eye; most of it appears to lie beyond the reach of even our most powerful telescopes and other instruments. Thus, both temporally and spatially this universe is of an entirely different order than anything imaginable by humans through most of history. Women and men have existed in this universe for only a minuscule fraction of its temporal development, and human activities and actions can have effects only quite locally on planet Earth and its immediate environment. Our place in God's universe and our responsibilities in God's world must thus be understood as much diminished from what our traditional stories and images suggest.

God also (and God's "eternity")—if God is to be thought of as the creativity manifest in the ongoing evolution and development of this entire vast cosmos (thus continuing a central theme of the monotheistic religious traditions)—will have to be conceived as much greater in scale and in mystery than anything suggested by the stories and images that informed and constituted most traditional thinking. The kind of personal intimacy with God fostered by many of these images—especially such anthropomorphic ones as "father," "lord," and "king"—no longer seems appropriate, or even imaginable or intelligible. So our human "relationships" with God will have to be conceived in much vaguer and less vivid terms than in the piety of the past—the characterization of God as serendipitous creativity straightforwardly suggests this—and our understanding of human existence as "under God" will be experienced as much more open, much looser, much less determinate and specific. Life no longer will be thought of or experienced as dependent on our unmediated direct relation to a divine being whose character and will, and whose requirements of the human, are fairly clear and distinct. Rather, we must come to understand that how we live out our lives and take responsibility for ourselves and our activities here on planet Earth are matters that we humans ourselves must work out as carefully and responsibly as we can[22]—normed of course (as we have noted) by the directions in which creativity appears to be moving in our part of the cosmos and by the christomorphic principle. Thus, our lives and our ethics—all of the matters bearing on how we live and think and act—will have to be oriented much more in terms of the overall context of human life here on Earth than traditional ways of thinking about God and our relation to God have suggested. Earth is our home, and it should no longer be said or thought that we are "strangers and foreigners on the earth ... [who] are seeking a homeland ... a better country, that is, a heavenly one" (Heb. 11:13, 14, 16).

Our modern/postmodern world-picture, taken together with the conception of God as serendipitous creativity, evokes a significantly different stance in the world than that associated with the Christian symbol-system as traditionally interpreted. The childlike trust and assurance and consolation, characteristic of the conviction that throughout our lives we are cared for lovingly by a heavenly father, are no longer available. In exchange, we humans become aware of ourselves as a unique species deeply embedded in the magnificent intricate web of life on planet Earth, with distinctive obligations and responsibilities to that web and the creativity (the coming into being of the new and the novel) manifest in it—creativity present and active throughout the cosmos and in all human cultural and religious traditions and activities. Thinking of God as creativity undercuts the arrogant stance of much traditional Christianity vis-à-vis the natural order as a whole, as well as with respect to other religious and secular traditions. Christians may no longer consider themselves to be authorized in what they say and do by God's special revelation.

Nevertheless, important continuities with traditional Christian understandings remain, continuities significant enough to warrant considering this picture of God, the world, and the human as appropriate for Christian faith today. . . . [U]nderstanding the ultimate mystery of things, God, in terms of the metaphor of serendipitous creativity manifesting itself in a variety of evolutionary and historical trajectories—instead of in terms of the anthropomorphic creator/lord/father metaphors that constituted the traditional picture of a God with largely anthropocentric purposes—facilitates (more effectively than did the traditional imagery) maintaining a decisive qualitative distinction (though not an ontological separation) between God and the created order. This distinction is the basis for regarding God (serendipitous creativity) as the *sole* appropriate focus for human devotion and worship, as that which alone can properly orient us in the world. All other realities, being created goods that come into being and pass away, become dangerous idols that can bring disaster into human affairs when worshiped and made the central focus of human orientation. To attempt to order one's life in terms of this important distinction between God (the ultimate mystery of things) and the idols, can only be, of course, a move of faith, of a deep trust in the mystery that has brought us into being and continues to sustain us. As biohistorical beings that have emerged on one of the countless creative trajectories moving through the cosmos, humans are indissolubly part of the created order and not in any way to be confused with the creativity manifest throughout the cosmos, in all its complexity, order, and beauty. We can exist only (as far as we are aware) within the boundaries and conditions of life found on the particular trajectory within the created order in which we have appeared.

Though strikingly different in important respect from some traditional Christian emphases, this understanding of God and of the human is clearly a form of *radical monotheism* (to use H. R. Niebuhr's term). As we have seen, it is a conception that can be developed into a Christian interpretation of human faith and life, if the creativity that is God is brought into significant connection with the poignancy and power of the stories and character of Jesus and the early church. The reconstructions of the conceptions of God and humanity suggested here thus provide a way for Christian faith to reconstitute itself in respects appropriate to our contemporary evolutionary/ecological sensibilities and knowledges.

Humans did not bring the world into being, and it is not we who sustain it. We did not create the evolutionary process, forever bringing into being new, unforeseeable forms of life. There is a powerful, awe-inspiring creativity manifest in our world—and indeed, in ourselves: the new, the novel, the unforeseeable, the previously unheard of, break forth roundabout us and in our midst; and human life continues to be sustained from beyond itself. This serendipitous creativity provides grounds for our hope for the future. Human life can go on and, we dare to hope, will go on. And we are called to participate ever more fully and effectively in the creative transformation of our existence that will enable this to happen.

Notes

1   [See Kaufman 2004, chapter 2.]

2   In many current discussions of religion and science issues by theologians, who otherwise seek to take modern evolutionary biology and cosmology seriously, there is a failure to come to terms directly with the problem stated here. See, for example, John Polkinghorne's subtle consideration of the idea of God's action in the world, in his otherwise excellent article "Chaos Theory and Divine Action": "The picture is . . . of an open future in which both human and divine agency play parts in its accomplishment. Christian theology has, at its best, striven to find a way between two unacceptably extreme pictures of God's relationship to the creation. One is that of the Cosmic Tyrant, who brings everything about by divine will alone. Such a God is the puppet master of the universe. . . . The detached God of deism, who simply watches it all happen, is another extreme, unacceptable to Christian thought. We seek a middle way in which God interacts with the creation without over-ruling it. . . . All that we are attempting to do in the present discussion is to show that one can take with all seriousness all that science tells us about the workings of the world, and still believe in a God who has not left the divine nature so impotent that providence cannot act continuously and consistently with cosmic history" (1996, 249). In this article Polkinghorne takes "with all seriousness all that science tells us about the workings of the world" with the exception of a *central* scientific understanding: that complex features found in our world, such as conscious intention, purposive action, deliberate creation of artifacts, loving attitudes and behaviors, and the like, can come into being only *after* billions of years of complex cosmic, biological, and historical development have provided the necessary conditions for their emergence to occur. But in the anthropomorphic model in terms of which Polkinghorne's God is conceived, these sorts of features are all taken for granted as present and active through all eternity. So Polkinghorne simply ignores an important scientific contention about complex realities, a rather

important exception to his claim to take "with all seriousness" what science tells us about these sorts of things. Further discussion of these matters will be found in [Kaufman 2004] chapter 3, especially sections I and III.

3   As brain scientist Terrence Deacon has observed: "Evolution is the one kind of process able to produce something out of nothing. . . . [A]n evolutionary process is an origination process. . . . Evolution is the author of its spontaneous creations" (1997, 458).

4   A full discussion of these pros and cons can be found in my book, Kaufman 1993a (see especially chapters 19 to 22).

5   [See Kaufman 2004, chapter 1.]

6   For elaboration, see the discussion of the "serendipity of history" in Kaufman 1993a, 273–80.

7   In recent theorizing about complexity, as it develops in highly intricate networks of life (and elsewhere), it is argued that changes may reach an unforeseeable "tipping point" where previous organizational patterns break down and new ones begin to emerge, thus bringing into being novel forms. For discussion of this sort of ongoing creativity in the world, see [Kaufman 2004] chapter 3, section III.

8   I do not discuss the Big Bang [here], but it is taken up in some detail in [Kaufman 2004] chapter 3. It is worth noting here, however, that it does not answer the question of why there is something, not nothing. We have no way of thinking of a purely spontaneous event because in all our experience events occur in a context in which they are preceded, surrounded, and followed by other events, so the very concept of "event" precludes the idea of any sort of absolute beginning. Augustine long ago was aware of these problems. Modern cosmologists are also aware of them, and are attempting to think of ways to contextualize the Big Bang. For discussions of these issues, see [Kaufman 2004] chapter 3, section I.

9   [See Kaufman 2004, prologue, section V.]

10   Quoted by R. Otto in The Idea of the Holy ([1917] 1950, 25).

11   This sort of move—enhancing the mystery-dimension of our God-talk by focusing on the metaphor of creativity, thus ceasing to reify person-agent metaphors—has the further advantage of facilitating conversation between Christian theologians and adherents to certain of the reflective dimensions of East Asian cultures. The Buddhist metaphor of sunyata (emptiness, nothingness), for example, seems to carry some motifs similar to the idea of creativity. Confucian thinking about "Heaven" and Taoist ideas of chaos also manifest similarities. Replacing the reifying notion of God as creator with creativity, in our theological reflection, may help prepare for more fruitful conversations with, and even collaborative thinking with, representatives of these East Asian traditions.

12   This linkage between God and the coming into being of the new in time was made long ago by Isaiah, who portrays Yahweh as saying: "I am about to do a new thing: now it springs forth, do you not perceive it? . . . From this time forward I make you hear new things, hidden things that you have not known. They are created now, not long ago; before today you have never heard of them, so that you could not say, 'I already

knew them' " (43:19; 48:6–8). For further discussion, see [Kaufman 2004] chapter 3.

13   For a summary of the details of the very close margins that have made these developments in cosmic evolution possible, see Rees 1997, chapter 14. See also William J. Broad, "Maybe We Are Alone in the Universe, After All" (2000). Some further discussion of these matters will be found in [Kaufman 2004] chapter 3, section III. If one takes claims such as these "with all seriousness" (as Polkinghorne puts it [see note 2]) how is it possible to continue to think of God as a human-like person/agent existing before and independent of any such complex developments?

14   It is important to recognize that the notion of serendipitous creativity accomplishes this objective without leading into or providing grounds for a teleological argument for the existence of (an agential) God. This is, thus, a modest or "weak" anthropism. See Rees 1997, chapter 15, for a thoughtful, brief discussion of various sorts of anthropic thinking. For an early full discussion of "the anthropic principle," see John D. Barrow and Frank J. Tipler's book, The Anthropic Cosmological Principle (1988).

15   [See Kaufman 2004, chapter 1.]

16   I characterize a faith-stance as "radically christomorphic" if it takes such New Testament emphases as (a) Jesus' radical teaching to "love your enemies" (Matt. 5:43–48), (b) the nonresistant posture of Jesus himself in facing his own enemies and acceding to his crucifixion, and (c) the Pauline admonition to have "the same mind be in you that was in Christ Jesus, [who having] emptied himself, taking the form of a slave, . . . humbled himself and became obedient to the point of death— even death on a cross" (Phil. 2:5, 7–8), to be paradigmatic for understanding what it means to regard God as "love" (1 John 4) and for defining the radical stance that is (should be) normative for Christian life and action. For elaboration, see Kaufman 1993a, chapters 25 and 26.

17   For further discussion of this issue, see my article "Is God Nonviolent?" (Kaufman 2003).

18   For fuller discussion of our human biohistorical reality, and the biohistorical trajectory that has brought us into being, see [Kaufman 2004] chapter 1, section II and especially chapter 3, sections II–IV; see also Kaufman 1993a, parts II and III.

19   A discussion of issues related to this will be found in [Kaufman 2004] chapter 3, section IV.

20   For further discussion of these issues, see Kaufman 1993a, especially chapter 24. See also Baruch Spinoza, Ethics, part IV (Spinoza [1677] 1989).

21   For further discussion of the problem of evil, see Kaufman 1993a, especially chapters 15 and 24.

22   This was also a note in traditional Christian thinking: "Work out your own salvation with fear and trembling; for it is God [i.e. creativity] who is at work in you, enabling you both to will and to work" (Phil. 2:12).

Bibliography

Barrow, John D., and Frank J. Tipler. 1988. *The Anthropic Cosmological Principle*. Oxford: Oxford Univ. Press.

Berdyaev, Nicholas J. 1937. *The Destiny of Man*. London: Geoffrey Bles.

Broad, William J. 2000. Maybe We Are Alone in the Universe, After All. *New York Times*, February 8.

Deacon, Terrence. 1997. *The Symbolic Species: The Co-evolution of Language and the Brain*. New York: Norton.

Kaufman, Gordon D. 1993a. *In Face of Mystery: A Constructive Theology*. Cambridge: Harvard Univ. Press.

——— . 1995. *An Essay on Theological Method*. 3rd ed. New York: Oxford Univ. Press. First edition 1975 by Scholars.

——— . 1996. *God—Mystery—Diversity: Christian Theology in a Pluralistic World*. Minneapolis: Fortress Press.

——— . 2003. Is God Nonviolent? *Conrad Grebel Review* 21 (1): 18–24.

[——— . 2004. *In the beginning . . . Creativity*. Minneapolis: Fortress Press.]

Niebuhr, H. Richard. 1960. *Radical Monotheism and Western Culture*. New York: Harper.

Otto, Rudolf. [1917] 1950. *The Idea of the Holy*. 2nd ed. London: Oxford Univ. Press.

Polkinghorne, John. 1996. Chaos Theory and Divine Action. In *Religion and Science: History, Method, Dialogue*, ed. W. Mark Richardson and Wesley J. Wildman, 243–52. New York: Routledge.

Rees, Martin. 1997. *Before the Beginning: Our Universe and Others*. Reading, Mass.: Addison-Wesley.

Spinoza, Baruch. [1677] 1989. *Ethics*. Trans. Andrew Boyle, revised by H. R. Parkinson. London: Dent.

Taylor, Mark C. 2001. *The Moment of Complexity: Emerging Network Culture*. Chicago: Univ. of Chicago Press.

Wieman, Henry Nelson. 1946. *The Source of Human Good*. Chicago: Univ. of Chicago Press.

Index

algorithm 75, 321; natural selection as 178–9, 197–200, 202–3, 205, 207–10, 212, 217–18, 238–9

anthropic principle 364–5, 375n14

anthropocentrism 309, 330, 332, 352–4, 367–70, 372

Aquinas, Thomas 60, 125, 188, 204, 225, 293–7, 363

argument from design: Aquinas's version 125, 188, 204; Paley's version 52, 62, 125–6, 129–37, 163, 173, 177–8, 182–4, 188, 229, 236–7; see also design; blind watchmaker; intelligent design

Aristotelian metaphysics 217, 247, 275, 282

Aristotle 15, 19–20, 204

Arkansas antievolution law 84, 93, 102, 110

Arkansas and Louisiana "balanced treatment" laws 84, 110–11, 128

atheism 5, 134, 179, 193, 219, 223, 224, 228, 236, 298, 307, 310; and Darwinism 85, 91, 178, 184; see also naturalism, atheistic

Atkins, Peter 187

Augustine 60, 229, 348n28, 355, 374n8

Ayala, Francisco J. 51–2, 83, 128, 224

Bacon, Francis 34, 97, 110

Barbour, Ian G. 5–6, 52, 291–2, 293, 343n5

Bartholomew, D. J. 256, 268n15

Bateson, William 64, 98

Beecher, Henry Ward 207

Behe, Michael J. 126–8, 159–73; *Darwin's Black Box* 126, 139–40, 142–4, 147, 150, 151, 155, 159, 167

beliefs, religious: compatibility (consonance, commensurability) with science 3, 223–6, 307–9, 311–12, 314, 316–17, 326, 330, 333–4, 336–7, 339; criteria for assessment 5, 34, 39–40, 45–7, 326, 335–6, 338, 342; incompatibility with science 3, 83–5, 125, 177–80, 317; see also metaphor; model; myth; paradigm; symbol

Berdyaev, Nicholas 362

Berggren, Douglas 20, 23

Bergson, Henri 322–3

Bethell, Tom 208

Bible, interpretation of: analogy of faith 13; authority 3, 7, 13; higher criticism 92–3; inerrancy 4, 7, 11–13, 91, 107, 108, 233; infallibility 3, 7–8, 10–11; inspiration 3–4, 7–12, 92; perspicuity 4, 7, 14; revelation 7–9; see also literalism, biblical; metaphor; myth; symbol

Big Bang 253, 273, 280, 289, 320, 341, 363, 368, 374n8

Birch, Charles 352

Black, Max 20–1

blind watchmaker 128, 178, 184–5, 208

Bonhoeffer, Dietrich 299

Bronowski, Jacob 18

Brunner, Emil 280

Bryan, William Jennings 93–7, 100–2

Buber, Martin 344n15

Bugge, T. H. 148, 150

Bultmann, Rudolf 327

Burke, Kenneth 17

Burrell, David 16, 25n3

causality 75, 132–4, 136, 247, 256, 262, 330, 332, 362; primary and secondary (*causa prima* and *causae secundae*) 205, 225, 281, 291, 294–8, 307, 318, 336; top-down vs. bottom-up 178, 198, 203–7, 237, 267n8, 345n16; whole-part constraint 224, 262; *see also* divine action; neo-Thomism; skyhooks, and cranes

Chan, Sunney 163–4

chance 264, 268n15, 273, 298–9, 311, 354, 362, 364; and law 206, 225, 255–8, 262, 287–93, 297–8, 300; *see also* contingency; determinism; indeterminism; randomness

chaos 178, 198; and order 203–5

chaos theory 288–9, 319

Christ-event 307, 314, 317; *see also* incarnation, divine; Jesus of Nazareth; kenosis, of Christ

Church, Alonzo 198

Clark, Harold W. 103

Clark, Stephen 353

Clarke, W. Norris 300

Clayton, Philip 308, 351

Cobb, John B., Jr. 352, 354

complexity 126, 134, 177, 181–2, 308, 332, 341–2, 374n7; increasing 259–63, 270n23, 289, 320–1, 329, 350–2, 357, 363, 373n2; organized 184–5, 291, 319–20; *see also* irreducible complexity

consciousness, emergence of 260–3, 265, 270n27, 289–91, 308, 309, 320–1, 350–1, 361; self-consciousness, emergence of 261–3, 265, 308, 320, 331, 335, 341, 350, 352, 357

consilience of inductions 52, 70

contingency 264, 269n17, 273, 297, 318, 350; *see also* chance; indeterminism; randomness

Copernican: principle of cosmic modesty 364; system 12; Revolution 194

Copernicus, Nicholas 194–6

cosmic pessimism, vs. religious hope 307, 311–15, 318–22

cosmic pyramid 178, 203–7, 208, 213

Cracraft, Joel 74

cranes *see* skyhooks, and cranes

creation: continuous (*creatio continua*) 253–4, 262, 282, 308, 333, 335, 337–9, 341; "out of nothing" (*creatio ex nihilo*) 280, 337, 341, 362, 363

creation science *see* creationism, scientific

creationism 3, 5, 84–5, 90–113, 125, 128, 177–80, 223; episodic 224, 227–30, 232–5, 237–44; progressive 84, 90–1, 92, 93, 101, 104, 107, 113; scientific 69, 84–5, 91, 97–100, 108, 109–11, 188, 193; special 90–3, 96, 105, 106, 108, 109, 112, 223–4; strict 83–4, 90–1, 99, 101, 103–4, 106–13, 244–5; young-earth 84, 102, 228–9; *see also* Darwinism, creationist opposition to; evolution education

creationist organizations: American Scientific Affiliation (ASA) 103–4, 106, 107, 108; Bible-Science Association 108, 109; Biblical Creation Society 113; Creation-Deluge Society 107; Creation Research Society (CRS) 107–8, 109; Creation-Science Research Center (CSRC) 109; Deluge Geology Society 103; Evolution Protest Movement 106, 113; Geoscience Research Institute 111; Institute for Creation Research 109, 110, 111, 113; Newton Scientific Association 113; Religion and Science Association 102, 103; Research Science Bureau 98; Victoria Institute 105

Crick, Francis 65, 208

Darrow, Clarence 101

Darwin, Charles 61–2; *The Descent of Man* 62; *On the Origin of Species* 51, 59, 61–3, 68, 70, 71, 73, 75, 83, 90, 138–9, 163, 184, 192, 197, 200, 201, 206, 217–18

Darwin, Erasmus 61

Darwin's dangerous idea 178–9, 193–6, 200, 212–13, 217, 239; *see also* algorithm, natural selection as; universal acid

Darwin's theory of evolution, overview of 51–3, 54–7, 58–60, 61–4; *see also* descent with modification; evolution, biological;

inheritance, blending; natural selection; neo-Darwinian synthesis; struggle for existence

Darwinism: and atheism 85, 91, 178, 184; creationist opposition to 5, 85, 92–5, 98–9, 102, 125, 233–4; friend of Christian theology 224, 251–2; intelligent design critique of 125–8, 142–4, 229, 234; and irreducible complexity 126–7, 139–42, 144–54; *see also* Darwin's dangerous idea; Darwin's theory of evolution

Davies, Paul 205–6, 289

Davis, Marc 310

Dawkins, Richard 128, 143, 148, 177–9, 208, 211–12, 219, 252, 255, 257, 270n27; *The Blind Watchmaker* 177; *Climbing Mount Improbable* 148; *River out of Eden* 177

Dawson, John William 90, 92, 93, 101, 102, 112

day-age theory *see* Genesis, interpretation of

de Beer, Gavin 208

deism 207, 248, 291, 307, 318, 326–7, 334, 339, 355, 373n2

de Maupertuis, Pierre-Louis Moreau 60

Dennett, Daniel C. 178–9, 188, 216–17, 219, 236–9, 252, 255, 267n8, 268n9; *Darwin's Dangerous Idea* 188, 267n8, 268n9

Descartes, René 17, 31–2, 73, 215

descent with modification 51, 55, 58–60, 61, 66, 68, 83, 125, 142, 201; *see also* Darwin's theory of evolution

design 177–8, 180, 184, 198, 213, 291; apparent 52, 177–9, 181, 184, 207–10, 236–8, 268n9, 311; and order 204–6, 311, 313; and purpose 126, 129–30, 132–5, 181–2, 184, 188–9, 204–10, 242, 310–11, 313; *see also* argument from design; cosmic pyramid; God as, designer; intelligent design

design argument, biochemical *see* intelligent design; irreducible complexity

Design Space 178, 209–10

determinism 262, 293, 297; *see also* chance, and law; indeterminism

deus ex machina 209; *see also* skyhooks, and cranes

de Vries, Hugo 64

Dewar, Douglas 105

Dewey, John 205, 207

divine action 291–3, 344n16, 373n2; interventionist 228, 238, 240–1, 248, 258, 262, 270n31, 282, 292, 327, 333, 345n16, 356; noninterventionist 246–9, 253–4, 262, 335; *see also* causality; God, models of; immanence, and transcendence of God; providence, divine; purpose, divine

DNA survival 178, 185, 189–91

Dobzhansky, Theodosius 58, 65, 195, 208, 219

Dodd, C. H. 352

Doolittle, Russell 148–51

dualism 308, 312, 326, 332, 337, 341, 344n16, 348n27

ecological theology 308–9, 329, 337, 339, 342, 344n15, 346n18, 351–3, 360, 366–7, 370–3

Einstein, Albert 108, 172, 225, 287, 314, 320

Eldredge, Niles 74, 268n8

Ellegård, Alvar 206

emergence, and continuity 252–4

empiricism 35, 36, 37

ethics 45–6, 47, 308, 309, 328, 333, 337, 342, 365–72

evangelical Christians 83, 90, 103–4, 105, 107, 112, 125, 223; *see also* fundamentalism, Christian

evil, problem of 178, 190–1, 265, 272n43, 309, 354–5, 358, 360, 365–6, 369–70; *see also* God as, suffering; pain; sin; suffering; theodicy

evolution, biological: fact of 5, 52–3, 66–7, 68–70, 83, 94, 193, 213; mechanisms 51–3, 58, 60, 67, 68–9, 73–6, 83, 128, 139, 142, 255–6, 267n8; phylogenies (paths) 52–3, 65–7, 68–9, 71–3, 83; propensities (trends in) 258–61, 269n18, 269n22, 270n27; *see also* Darwin's theory of evolution; neo-Darwinian synthesis; macroevolution; microevolution; purpose, in biological evolution

evolution, cultural and historical 335, 345n16, 372

evolution education: "balanced treatment" of creation and evolution 84, 91, 109–11, 128; legislation against 84, 91, 93, 100, 102, 110; intelligent design and 127–8; see also Arkansas antievolution law; Arkansas and Louisiana "balanced treatment" laws; Kitzmiller et al. v. Dover Area School District; Scopes trial

evolutionary psychology 179

evolutionary theism 179, 223; see also theistic evolution

existentialist theology 292, 327

Faber, Sandra 310

faith, and reason 5; see also beliefs, religious, criteria for assessment

Fales, Evan 128

Fiddes, Paul 265

Fisher, Ronald A. 64, 219

flood geology 99–101, 103, 106–8, 110, 113

formational economy of the universe 223–4, 227, 230–49; gaps vs. gapless 223–4, 233–5, 238–49, 254, 292; see also creationism; God of the gaps; naturalism

freedom (autonomy) 282, 290–1, 294, 297–300, 308, 309, 316–18, 322, 327, 330, 351, 354–5, 357–8; of God 275, 299, 329–30, 347n23, 358; see also indeterminism

free will defense of suffering 265, 355

functional economy of the universe 240–2, 245

fundamentalism, Christian 52, 68, 83, 92–109, 125, 249n1; see also Bible, interpretation of; creationism; evangelical Christians; literalism, biblical

Galileo Galilei 34, 194

gap theory see Genesis, interpretation of

Geller, Margaret 310

Genesis, interpretation of 3, 12–13, 83, 90–3, 95–6, 100, 101, 110, 125, 207, 229, 249n1, 265, 287, 331, 337–8, 348n29, 361, 363; day-age theory 84, 90–1, 92, 100, 101, 102; gap theory 84, 91–2, 100, 101

Gish, Duane T. 111

God as: composer 224, 254, 299; creativity vs. creator 309, 361–5, 371–2, 374n11; designer 126–7, 134–7, 144, 173, 185, 189, 236–7, 291, 300, 307, 311, 313, 316–17, 322–3, 326–7, 351; father 44, 265, 309, 328, 330, 360, 365, 368, 371; ground of new possibilities 283, 307, 309, 322–3, 354–5; handicrafter 60, 193, 237; love 226, 265, 280, 282, 298–300, 307, 313–18, 328, 330, 335, 343n13, 355, 358, 360, 365, 367–70, 375n16; Mind 204–5, 332–3; mother 328, 330, 338, 343n13; power of the future 283, 307, 314–15, 318, 321–3; risk-taking 225, 287–8, 297–300; serendipitous creativity 309, 345n16, 360, 362–73, 375n14; spirit 293, 300, 308, 326, 330–42, 343n14, 344n15, 346n18, 346n22, 347n26; suffering 225–6, 265–6, 276–8, 281, 282, 299–300, 307, 309, 353; see also God, models of

God of the gaps 128, 223, 327

God, models of 179, 223, 299–300, 307, 326–9, 365–6, 373n2; agential 292, 308, 328; emanationist 308, 338–9, 347n26; embodiment (procreation, world as God's body) 292, 308, 326, 328–42, 343n11, 344n16, 347n22, 347n24, 347n25, 347n27; monarchical (royal, king, lord) 224, 247, 291, 299, 309, 325–6, 327–8, 330, 334, 339–40, 343n5, 348n29, 360, 363, 371; non-agential vs. agential 361–3, 371–2, 374n11, 375n14; organic 308, 328–9, 343n11, 344n16; organic-agential 308, 329–37, 338, 341–2; patriarchal 330, 341, 348n27; procreative-emanationist 308, 338–9, 341, 347n27; production 337–41, 348n27, 348n29, 363; see also atheism; causality; deism; divine action;

evolutionary theism; immanence, and transcendence of God; kenosis, of God; neo-Thomism; panentheism; pansyntheism; pantheism; purpose, divine; theism; theistic evolution; Trinity

Gödel, Kurt 198

Goodman, Nelson 20, 22–3

Gould, Stephen Jay 74, 203, 252, 255, 261–2, 269n17

Gray, Asa 206–7

Greenspan, Neil S. 151

Griffin, David Ray 354

Guyot, Arnold 90, 92, 93, 101, 112

Habermas, Jürgen 273

Haldane, J. B. S. 64

Hamilton, William 76

Harold, Franklin 142–3

Hartshorne, Charles 342n2, 343n11

Haught, John F. 307–8

Hegel, Georg Wilhelm Friedrich 278, 281, 344n15, 346n22, 348n28

Heidegger, Martin 17, 283

Heisenberg uncertainty principle 256, 288

Heschel, Abraham 278

Hesse, Mary 17–18

Hick, John 26n21, 272n43

Ho, M.-W. 259

Hodge, Charles 3–4, 91

Hodgson, Peter 346n22

Hofstadter, Douglas 211

Holy Spirit 3–4, 13, 276, 331, 334–5, 344n14, 345n17; see also God as, spirit; spirit; Trinity

Houghton, John 319

Hume, David 184–5, 204, 205, 216; Dialogues Concerning Natural Religion 215

Huxley, Julian 65, 195

Huxley, Thomas H. 63, 202, 252

Hyun-Kyung, Chung 345n17

immanence, and transcendence of God 224, 228, 252, 254, 261, 265, 294, 296–7, 300, 308, 326, 328–30, 337–42, 344n16, 347n23, 349; see also divine action

incarnation, divine 334, 336, 340–2; in Jesus of Nazareth 275, 298, 326, 336; see also Christ-event; Jesus of Nazareth; kenosis, of Christ

indeterminism 144, 262, 271n31, 288–90, 292, 297, 299, 316–17, 319, 321, 345n16; see also chance; contingency; determinism; freedom; randomness

inerrancy of scripture see Bible, interpretation of

infallibility of scripture see Bible, interpretation of

inheritance: of acquired characteristics 61, 64; blending 63, 195; principle of 51, 54–6; see also Lamarkism; Mendelian genetics

instrumentalism: in religion 45; in science 38, 42

intelligent design (ID) 84, 125–8, 177, 180; Darwinism and 142–4; hypothesis 138–42; litigation over 127–8; scientific critique of 127–8, 165, 168–73, 185, 207–10; theological critique of 128, 223–4, 229, 232, 234–44, 307, 310–18; see also argument from design; design; God as, designer; irreducible complexity

irreducible complexity 126–7; counter-examples 144–54; scientific critique of 163–7; Darwinism and 139–42; definition 139; examples 139–41; see also complexity; intelligent design; mousetrap

Jantzen, Grace 344n16, 347n25

Jesus of Nazareth 219, 326, 335, 344n14, 345n17, 372, 375n16; crucified 265–6, 280, 316–17, 318, 322, 325; see also Christ-event; incarnation, divine; kenosis, of Christ

John Paul II, Pope 67, 286–7

Johnson, Elizabeth A. 225–6

Johnson, Phillip 242–3

Jonas, Hans 280–1

Kant, Immanuel 17, 216

Kauffman, Stuart 143–4, 267n8

Kaufman, Gordon D. 309, 343n12, 345n16

Keller, Catherine 345n16
Kierkegaard, Søren 281, 283, 327
Kimura, Motoo 65–6, 268n8
Kitzmiller et al. v. Dover Area School District
    128
kenosis (self-emptying) 273–4; of Christ
    225, 274–7, 279, 280, 307, 314–18,
    322, 375n16; of God 224–6, 278–83,
    292, 298–300, 307, 313–18, 322
Koestler, Arthur 19
Kuhn, Thomas 25n2, 36–8, 110
Kulp, J. Laurence 103–4, 106
Küng, Hans 313

Lamarck, Jean-Baptiste 61, 63
Lamarckism 61, 63, 73–4; neo-Lamarckism
    63–4
Lammerts, Walter E. 107
Lang, Walter 108
Laudan, Larry 84–5
laws of nature 92, 131–2, 138, 144, 217,
    225, 269n15, 290–2, 297–8, 318; see also
    causality; chance, and law; determinism
Leclerc (Buffon), Georges-Louis 60
Leibniz, Gottfried Wilhelm 207, 216,
    280
Lerner, Gerda 347n27
Lewis, C. S. 25n2, 27n27
Lewontin, R. C. 267n8
liberation theology 327, 345n17
linguistic analysis: in religion 45, 292; in
    science 38
Linnaeus, Carolus 61
literalism: biblical 3–4, 83, 90–1, 103–4,
    106, 125, 235, 241, 292; scientific 3; see
    also Bible, interpretation of; creationism;
    fundamentalism, Christian; metaphor,
    and literalism
Locke, John 203–6, 213, 216
Luria, Isaac 279–80
Luther, Martin 278–9, 363
Lyell, Charles 200, 251

macroevolution 229, 232, 234, 238; see also
    microevolution
Marsden, George 105

Marx, Karl 201, 204–5
materialism 96, 179, 219, 319; see also
    naturalism; reductionism
Maynard Smith, John 74, 210
Mayr, Ernst 65, 74, 195
McCoy, W. 269n23
McDaniel, Jay 345n16
McDonald, John 146, 152–4, 170
McFague, Sallie 4, 5, 308
McMullin, Ernan 43–4
Meléndez-Hevia, Enrique 164
memes 32
Mendel, Gregor 44, 63, 64, 195
Mendelian genetics 63–5, 73, 75, 195; see
    also inheritance; neo-Darwinian synthesis
metaphor: centrality of 3–5, 15–20, 22,
    24n2, 29; definition 4, 19–22, 24; and
    literalism 20, 22–4, 83; reference and
    truth of 4, 22–3; in religion 3–6, 15,
    20–1, 23–4, 224, 286–7, 299–300, 307,
    326, 329–30, 332, 338, 343n12; in
    science 3–6, 15–18, 23, 207; see also
    model; myth; symbol
microevolution 234; see also macroevolution
Midgley, Mary 4–5, 179
Mill, John Stuart 34
Miller, Kenneth R. 126–8, 143–4, 146–7,
    154; Finding Darwin's God 144
Mind 178, 198, 202, 204–5, 212–13; see also
    cosmic pyramid; God as, Mind
model: in religion 5–6, 21, 23–4, 39–40,
    44–5, 287, 307, 326, 335–6, 338, 342;
    in science 17–18, 23–4, 40–4; see also
    God, models of; metaphor; paradigm
Modern Synthesis see neo-Darwinian
    synthesis
molecular clock 65–6, 72, 74
Moltmann, Jürgen 224–5, 344n15,
    351
Monod, Jacques 30, 252, 256–7, 261
Montefiore, Hugh 347n26
Moody, Dwight L. 91
Moore, Aubrey 251, 345n16
More, Henry 280
Morris, Henry M. 106–13; The Genesis Flood
    106, 108, 113

mousetrap 127, 139, 141, 144–6, 151–4
Fig. 11.3, 161, 165, 170–1 Fig. 12.6; see
also irreducible complexity
Musser, Siegfried 163–4
myth 193, 312, 315, 329; centrality in
science and religion 3, 4–5, 28–9, 31–2;
remythologize 342; see also metaphor;
objectivity, of science; symbol

National Center for Science Education 146
natural selection 51–3, 54–7, 58, 60, 61–5,
67, 92, 138, 271n34; advantageous
properties 259, 261, 289; importance
debated 68, 69, 73–5, 77, 128, 143, 255,
267n8; and intelligent design 125–8,
139–42; and purpose 177–8, 184–5,
188, 196, 206–7, 242, 255–8, 261–3,
312, 315–16, 318; see also algorithm,
natural selection as; Darwin's theory of
evolution; evolution, biological
natural theology 92, 236, 321, 332, 334; see
also argument from design
naturalism: atheistic 5, 177–80, 219–20,
223–4, 228, 298, 307, 311; evolutionary
223, 228–32, 235–8, 241–6;
metaphysical 179, 196, 219, 242–3;
methodological (scientific) 143–4, 179,
219–20, 253, 255, 311, 315, 321; see also
atheism; cosmic pessimism; materialism;
reductionism
neo-Darwinian synthesis 29, 52, 58–9,
64–6, 73–7, 83, 195, 320, 323
neo-Thomism (dual agency) 225, 288, 291,
292–300; see also causality, primary and
secondary
Newton, Isaac 34, 36, 172, 280, 319
Newtonian: mechanics 36; world 287;
physics 288
Niebuhr, H. Richard 372
Nietzsche, Friedrich 25n2, 32, 201–2
Numbers, Ronald L. 84–5

objectivity, of science 5, 30–1, 35, 312,
315, 353; see also theory, scientific
On the Origin of Species see Darwin
Ong, Walter 20, 21

order see cosmic pyramid; design, and order
Orgel, Leslie 208
Owen, Richard 251

Page, Ruth 308–9
Pailin, David 354
pain 224, 260–1, 263–5, 270n26, 308,
342, 350, 369; see also suffering
Paley, William 52, 62, 126, 127, 128, 163,
173, 177–8, 182–4, 188, 229, 237;
Natural Theology 52, 62, 126, 163, 177,
182–4
panentheism 224, 308–9, 329, 336–7,
345n16, 346n22, 349–54, 355, 357; see
also immanence, and transcendence of
God
pansyntheism (God the companion) 308–9,
329, 350, 354–8
pantheism 224, 245, 267n5, 328–9, 332,
335–6, 349
paradigm: in religion 5, 39–40, 47, 298–9,
330; in science 5, 25n2, 36–7, 110; see also
beliefs, religious, criteria for assessing;
theory, scientific
paradigm shift 37, 39, 76
Patterson, Colin 69
Peacocke, Arthur 224, 345n16, 347n25
Pearson, Karl 64
perichoresis 276, 278; see also Trinity
perspicuity of scripture see Bible,
interpretation of
Plato 16, 125
plenary inspiration of scripture see Bible,
interpretation of
Polkinghorne, John 344n16, 373n2
Popper, Karl 35, 68, 110, 259, 269n22
positivism 22, 31
premillenialists 91–2, 96
Price, George McCready 98–108, 111–12;
The New Geology 100, 103, 106–7
process theology 282, 292–3, 299, 307,
329, 342n2, 343n11, 345n16, 346n22,
349, 354–6
providence, divine 225, 288, 291–3,
295–300, 373n2; see also purpose, divine
Provine, William 219, 242

punctuated equilibria 53, 74–5, 255
purpose 177–80, 186, 191, 330;
    appearance of 52, 186–9; in biological
    evolution 256, 315, 320; of creation 335;
    divine 135–6, 180, 189, 206–7, 258,
    261–2, 264–5, 271n31, 295–7,
    299–300, 308–9, 328–9, 332–3, 335,
    350–2, 354, 363; to the universe 246,
    252, 311, 318, 322; see also causality;
    design, and purpose; natural selection,
    and purpose; providence; teleology

Rahner, Karl 295, 317
randomness 75, 225, 255–8, 259, 260,
    269n15, 293, 297–300, 307, 310, 313,
    315–18, 320, 354; see also chance;
    contingency; determinism;
    indeterminism
realism, classical 37, 42
realism, critical: in religion 5, 44–5; in
    science 5, 38, 42–4
redemption 225, 274, 276, 281, 312, 319,
    322, 328, 334; see also salvation
reductionism 28, 179, 211–13, 217, 253,
    319, 321–2; see also materialism;
    naturalism
Rees, Martin 364
religious beliefs see beliefs, religious
remythologization see myth
reverse engineering 178, 188–9
revisionist theologians 223, 307
Richards, I. A. 20–1, 25n2
Ricoeur, Paul 17, 20–2, 26n12
Riley, William Bell 96–7, 98, 101
Rimmer, Harry 98–102, 106
Rizzotti, Martino 165
Rolston, Holmes 270n26
Rosenzweig, Franz 278
Ruse, Michael 52, 83, 126, 128, 150–1,
    179

salvation 45–6, 219, 225, 298, 369; see also
    redemption
Saunders, P. T. 259
Scholem, Gershom 280
scientific materialism see materialism

scientific method 3–6, 52, 63, 128, 287; see
    also naturalism, methodological;
    objectivity, of science; theory, scientific
scientific theory see theory, scientific
Scopes trial 84, 100–2, 106
scripture see Bible
Second Law of Thermodynamics 107, 233,
    267n4, 312, 313, 319
Segraves, Nell 109
selfish genes 190
Seventh-day Adventists 99, 102–3, 107,
    111, 113
Shekinah 225, 277–8, 281
Simon, H. A. 260, 263
Simpson, George G. 65, 258–9, 269n18,
    271n34
sin 276, 358; see also evil
skyhooks, and cranes 178–9, 207–12,
    237–9, 255, 258, 268n9
Sober, Elliot 268n8
social Darwinism 63, 193, 217
sociobiology 66, 75–6
Spencer, Herbert 63, 217
Spinoza, Baruch 17, 216
spirit 344n14, 344n15, 345n17, 346n18,
    346n19; see also God, as spirit; Holy Spirit
Stanley, Steven M. 74
Stebbins, George Ledyard 65
Stoeger, William 297
struggle for existence 51, 54–6, 62–3, 73,
    178, 308, 313, 317; see also Darwin's
    theory of evolution
suffering 180, 186, 190, 224, 260–1,
    263–6, 270n26, 272n43, 299, 307, 308,
    313, 335, 342; problem of 178, 190,
    265; see also evil; free will defense of
    suffering; God as, suffering; pain;
    theodicy
survival of the fittest 63
symbol 16, 26n12, 42, 83, 193, 283,
    364–5; centrality in science and religion
    3, 4–5, 28–9; see also metaphor, myth

Teilhard de Chardin, Pierre 329, 343n10
teleological argument see argument from
    design

teleology 201, 205–6, 290, 329, 375n14; *see also* purpose
theism 125, 257–8, 264, 314, 336; and evolutionary naturalism 229–32, 238, 243–5; *see also* evolutionary theism; panentheism; pansyntheism; pantheism; theistic evolution
theistic evolution 91, 93, 104, 105, 112, 242; *see also* evolutionary theism
theodicy 264, 272n43, 282, 327; *see also* evil; God as, suffering; suffering, problem of
theology of nature 273; vs. natural theology 332–4
theory of evolution *see* Darwin's theory of evolution; evolution, biological; neo-Darwinian synthesis
theory, scientific: criteria for assessment 5, 23, 37–8, 46–7, 126, 128, 168; and data 5, 34–8, 40, 110; as tentative 38, 43, 46, 52, 69–70, 234; *see also* model, in science; naturalism, methodological; objectivity, of science; paradigm, in science; scientific method
Thomas, Owen 292
Thomism *see* neo-Thomism
Tillich, Paul 346n22, 348n28
Tracy, Thomas 344n16
transcendence, of God *see* immanence, and transcendence of God
Trinity 225, 275–6, 334
Turbayne, Colin 23–4
Turing, Alan 198

universal acid 178–9, 201–3, 212–13;

critique of 179, 217; *see also* Darwin's dangerous idea
Urs von Balthasar, Hans 275
utility function 178, 188–90; God's 178, 189

Van Till, Howard J. 223–4

Waddington, Conrad H. 30, 267n8
Wallace, Alfred Russel 63, 206
watchmaker argument 52, 62, 126, 129–35, 177, 182–5, 237; *see also* argument from design; blind watchmaker
Watson, James 65
Weil, Simone 356–7
Weinberg, Steven 212, 310, 314
Weismann, August 64
Whewell, William 70
Whitcomb, John C., Jr. 106–7, 109, 112; *The Genesis Flood* 106–8, 113
White, Ellen G. 99
Whitehead, Alfred North 16, 311, 324n15, 324n16, 329
Wilberforce, Samuel 202
Williams, George C. 211
Wilson, Edward O. 74
Wittgenstein, Ludwig 16
World's Christian Fundamentals Association 96, 98
Wright, George Frederick 93, 101
Wright, Sewall 64

zimzum 225, 279–80